Paul Valéry

Consciousness & Nature

Paul Valéry

Consciousness & Nature

CHRISTINE M. CROW
Lecturer in French, University of St Andrews

CAMBRIDGE
AT THE UNIVERSITY PRESS 1972

Published by the Syndics of the Cambridge University Press
Bentley House, 200 Euston Road, London NW1 2DB
American Branch: 32 East 57th Street, New York, N.Y. 10022

Library of Congress Catalogue Card Number: 71-160088

ISBN: 0 521 08257 9

Printed in Great Britain
at the University Printing House, Cambridge
(Brooke Crutchley, University Printer)

To Alison

Contents

Acknowledgements

I should like to record my gratitude to Professor L. J. Austin for the help and encouragement I received during the original preparation of this work as a Ph.D. thesis submitted to the University of Cambridge, and to thank my examiners, Professor C. A. Hackett and Professor W. N. Ince, for their useful comments. I should also like to thank Dr Alison Fairlie for first arousing my interest in Valéry while I was an undergraduate at Girton College. During my three years as a research student I was supported by a State Studentship from the Ministry of Education (1962–1965), and I also held an Old Girtonian Studentship (1962, 1963) and a French Government Scholarship for work in Paris (1964). I am pleased to acknowledge the debt owed to these awards. My thanks go to Madame Agathe Rouart-Valéry for permission to publish extracts from Valéry's *Cahiers* and prefaces, and to Messrs. Gallimard for permission to quote from the Pléiade edition of Valéry's collected works. Finally, I should like to thank the Syndics and staff of the Cambridge University Press for undertaking to publish this book, in particular the chief editor and the sub-editor, who gave me the benefit of their great patience and skill.

Abbreviations

A.J.F.S.	*Australian Journal of French Studies*
AUMLA	*Journal of the Australasian Universities Language and Literature Association*
C.A.I.E.F.	*Cahiers de l'Association Internationale des Études Françaises*
F.M.L.S.	*Forum for Modern Language Studies*
F.S.	*French Studies*
M.L.R.	*Modern Languages Review*
PMLA	*Publications of the Modern Language Association of America*
R.H.L.F.	*Revue d'Histoire Littéraire de la France*

* * * * * *

Throughout this book lower-case roman numerals followed by arabic refer respectively to volume and page of Valéry's *Cahiers* (facsimile version in 29 volumes (Paris, C.N.R.S., 1957–1961)). The letter 'P' preceding a reference signifies the Pléiade edition of Valéry's collected works (*Paul Valéry: Œuvres*, ed. J. Hytier, volumes I and II (Paris, Gallimard, 1957 and 1960)).

Square brackets within quoted matter indicate either ellipsis by the author of inessential words or phrases, or enclose explanatory or other interpolations by the author.

Preface

This study is the revised version of the Ph.D. thesis I submitted to the University of Cambridge in 1968. It is an attempt to explore something of the complex and varied expression given by Valéry throughout his life to a simple, ever-present theme: human consciousness and its relation to the natural world. 'Nature' is, of course, a notoriously vague term, as Valéry was the first to recognise. By opposing the terms 'Consciousness' and 'Nature', I do not intend to suggest that consciousness for him was some kind of epiphenomenon distinct from the natural universe, but simply that my main concern is his many-levelled expression of the potential interplay between human awareness and forms and processes distinct from itself. Is it true, for example, as many critics have tended to suggest, that constant emphasis on the theme of self-awareness, in particular the power of consciousness to become aware of its own existence, precluded sufficient responsiveness to the resources of the natural world to make Valéry a great nature poet, or that insistence on the primacy of conscious control prevented him from achieving a fully integrated vision of the rôle of emotion and unconscious development in intellectual life?

The subject falls into three parts roughly corresponding to the distinction Valéry made himself between three closely interrelated systems: 'Corps', 'Esprit' and 'Monde', each of which he considered to play its part in the complex network of relationships comprising human 'reality': the reality on which consciousness depends for its existence and which it helps modify in return as a 'natural' agent of differentiation, evaluation and choice. The first part, *Consciousness and the self*, describes Valéry's attempt to isolate, in the most general language possible, the finite mental conditions necessary to self-awareness, and to express its dynamic presence in the intricate balance of individual human experience as a whole. The view is taken that Valéry is concerned not so much with defining a pre-existent entity, 'mind', in terms of the physical laws governing mental operations, as with discovering a descriptive *method* which enables him to make the maximum creative use of the transformational principle he felt to be the potential of individual experience and which, in his own case, he felt the practice of poetic composition particularly strongly to activate and reveal. This view is supported by the important distinction Valéry is shown to make between 'knowing' and 'understanding': between the 'knowledge' of life which is 'open' to man through the biological and physical sciences, for example, and the 'understanding' of life which is 'closed' to man in any total sense, since he remains involved in the mysterious fact of his own perception, emotion and desire to summarise: a living organism whose boundaries are necessary to the preservation of the organisational capacity of the mind itself. The theme of love is put forward at this point as forming the apex of Valéry's exploration of the potential exchange between individual consciousness and the physical, emotional and intellectual resources of the self once the boundaries of human life are fully recognised and tested to the extreme.

The second part, *Consciousness and external nature*, concentrates on the type of imagination at work in Valéry's response to the forms and processes revealed in the natural world as a further source of exchange between nature and individual possibility – forms and processes which appear at the same time as a direct source of symbol and image in some of his finest poetry. Interest in the organisational principles that appear to operate in human intelligence is but one aspect of a far wider interest on Valéry's part in natural morphology and morphogenesis: the processes of conservation and transformation revealed to the 'eye' of the creative imagination by individual organisms other than man.

Finally, the third part, *Intellectual creativity and natural growth*, attempts to draw together and interpret in the light of his own creative practice the comparisons and contrasts Valéry so often makes between the natural product and the human artifact. It is thus possible to discuss his own views on the nature of analogy, before examining the analogies he makes himself between principles of natural development and principles of intellectual creativity. A discussion of the rôle allowed to 'organic' forms and processes in poetic composition and in intellectual development in general is presented as the logical conclusion to a work whose central subject can now be seen to involve what Valéry calls 'Poétique': in its widest sense, the realisation, within the closed system of the natural universe, of individual human possibility.

The mutually illuminating nature of Valéry's theory and practice of 'Poétique' has made it possible to examine, side by side with his explicit statements on the relation between consciousness and nature, the expression of the theme in his poetry and dialogues, and in the principles of intellectual creativity embodied in his thought as it developed throughout his long writing life. In order to try to present the many 'levels' of his work in a way which does justice to his own sharp awareness of the 'projective' relationship between language and experience, I have drawn on the material in his notebooks as much as on the works written for publication, attempting to correlate the two sources as much as possible and concentrating, where secondary sources are concerned, on those works of criticism published since the *Cahiers* have opened the way to greater understanding of the unusual range and unity of Valéry's thought. It is to be hoped that any inconsistencies in the use of terms such as 'consciousness', 'intellect', 'emotion' and so on, will be justified in the context in which they are used, above all by the consideration that Valéry introduced such terms himself simply as abstract tags in the system of intricate inner relationships which he felt that only constant experiment with language and awareness of the nature of language, perhaps ultimately only the poem, born from such awareness, could creatively explore.

St Andrews C.M.C.
March 1971

Part One:

Consciousness & the self

1 Consciousness

Valéry was interested all his life in the nature of consciousness, particularly in its highly developed form of individual self-awareness. 'Mais chaque vie si particulière possède toutefois, à la profondeur d'un trésor, la permanence d'une conscience que rien ne supporte', he wrote in 1919 in the *Note et Digression* added years later to one of his first major essays, *Introduction à la Méthode de Léonard de Vinci:* '[...] cette profonde *note* de l'existence domine, dès qu'on l'écoute, toute la complication des conditions et des variétés de l'existence' (P I, 1228). Personal notes confirm the constancy with which he turned his attention to the changing degrees of self-awareness that appear to accompany so much of our mental activity, and above all his desire to give some form of expression to the complex unity he felt to underlie the fluctuations of our intellectual life.

'La *conscience* nous montre la pensée en tant que pensée. Donc, elle dégage à chaque instant celui qui pense de chaque pensée particulière' (ii, 40); 'la conscience embrasse d'un coup plus de choses que l'intellect n'en peut travailler' (ii, 733): in jottings like these Valéry is content simply to refer to an area of experience by means of the general term 'conscience'. Yet his alertness to the the nature of language itself – the language in which we express and even partly create our experience – leads him to ascribe to such terms a purely limited function. The position is playfully stylised in *Lettre d'un Ami*, part of the cycle of writings devoted to Monsieur Teste, the earliest of the symbolic heroes in the drama of language and experience which so many of Valéry's writings seem designed to explore. 'J'en suis venu hélas,', confesses the imaginary author of the letter, 'à comparer ces paroles par lesquelles on traverse si lestement l'espace d'une pensée, à des planches légères jetées sur un abîme, qui souffrent le passage et point la station. L'homme en vif mouvement les emprunte et se sauve; mais qu'il insiste le moins du monde, ce peu de temps les rompt et tout s'en va dans les profondeurs' (P II, 53). It might be said that two characteristic linguistic expeditions branch out in Valéry's writings from the useful platform provided by his own rapid use of abstract terms. On the one hand there is an attempt to set aside the complex *content* of consciousness in order that its *form* may be revealed. On the other, there is an attempt to restore by poetic means the irreducibility of individual experience itself. It seems possible to suggest that many of his dramatic protagonists, Narcisse, the 'Jeune Parque', the speaker in *Le Cimetière Marin* and so on, are the products of a need to synthesise the two forms of expression. Only in poetry could Valéry combine the insights of formalism with the quality of subjective experience.

Since the main part of this study will be concerned with his expression of the part played by consciousness in the complex balance of a human being's experience as a whole, it seems necessary to establish briefly in advance what particular phenomenon he understood by 'la conscience' in relatively 'objective' terms. A sheet-anchor in the intricacies of Valéry's thought (and undoubtedly a sheet-anchor for him in the handling of his own experience) is the fact that even the most complex psychological themes are necessarily related at some stage to description in straightforward bodily or functional terms.

Investigation of the *Cahiers* has already shown that Valéry approaches consciousness (and likewise the whole mind, 'l'esprit', the total set of mental relationships of which consciousness is part) as a highly advanced organisational activity on the part of the nervous system, and that he sees this activity in turn as the product of the complex interaction between an individual human organism and its environment. 'La "conscience" est un fonctionnement ou liée à un fonctionnement – Ce fonctionnement est celui même du syst[ème] nerveux central' (viii, 573).[1]

Consciousness for Valéry is both intermittent and transitory, part of a changing relationship between self and world finally overcome by death. Such a vision obviously encourages unification of the most diverse points of view from which it is possible to approach mental activity: not only psychological and physiological, but also conscious and unconscious, intellectual and affective, purposive and random. It is therefore not surprising that a blending of traditional opposites should emerge as one of the most striking features of Valéry's thought.

[1] Quoted by Judith Robinson in *L'Analyse de l'Esprit dans les Cahiers de Valéry* (Paris, Corti, 1963), 107.

However deeply interested in the idea of a possible structural analogy between consciousness and other organisational *activities* in the natural world, Valéry certainly does not confine his interest to this aspect. What obviously concerns him above all is the distinctive nature of the power of consciousness in terms of subjective *capacity*: the capacity to discern or differentiate. He considers consciousness to be able to differentiate not only the self from the outside world and the past from the present, but also the self from its own perceptions, even from its own awareness. As a result is born 'la conscience de la conscience' and the feeling of an impersonal, unchanging self ('moi no. 1' or simply 'moi') from which the personal self 'moi no. 2') with all its changing thoughts, sensations and emotions can seem totally distinct.

'[...] et comme l'oreille retrouve et reperd, à travers les vicissitudes de la symphonie, un ton grave et continu qui ne cesse jamais d'y résider, mais qui cesse à chaque instant d'être saisi, le *moi* pur, élément unique et monotone de l'être même dans le monde, retrouvé, reperdu par lui-même, habite éternellement notre sens; cette profonde *note* de l'existence domine, dès qu'on l'écoute [...]' (P I, 1228): Valéry's intellectual biography shows his own unusual 'listening' power. The formation of the power dates, he constantly points out, from 1892 (the time of his famous intellectual crisis):[1] '*Je suis* un système terriblement *simple*, trouvé ou formé en 1892 – par irritation insupportable, qui a excité un *moi* no. 2 à détacher de soi un *moi* premier [. . .] comme *une masse nébuleuse en rotation*' (XVI, 45). '1892' becomes a convenient peg on which to hang a series of attitudes, the cypher growing in importance as Valéry grows away from the experience in time, or rather, grows *towards* it in that its implications have the possibility of taking root in his mind. Since one of the aims of a later chapter[2] is to discover if any changes take place in his attitude to '1892', or if, as has been suggested, he maintained an 'obstinate fidelity to the adolescent choice which lay at the root of [his] *aventure intellectuelle*'[3] (the choice of his conscious rather than 'secondary' self), it seems important to consider the nature of the 'choice' involved. Perhaps only attention to the 'point of view' from which Valéry is approaching experience can provide a means of resolving the apparent contradiction between his unusually powerful grasp of mental unity and the dualistic imagery he

[1] See also chapter 3, 54. Valéry related this crisis of self-awareness to an experience of unrequited love. The discovery of the poetry of Rimbaud and Mallarmé seems to have emphasised a similar feeling of discrepancy between inner and outer power.

[2] Chapter 9: *Genius and growth*.

[3] J. M. Cocking, 'Duchesne-Guillemin on Valéry', *Modern Language Review*, LXII (1967), 59.

frequently adopts – when referring, for example, to a sensation of division between 'being' and 'knowing' ('être' and 'connaître') or to a 'pure' and 'impure' self.

Valéry admits that at the time in question he had become aware of a particular kind of suffering caused by the uncontrollable recurrence of ideas or images already painful in themselves: 'J'ai été amené à regarder les phénomènes mentaux rigoureusement comme tels à la suite de grands maux et d'idées douloureuses', he writes when the habit of keeping notebooks begins to develop: 'Ce qui les rendait si pénibles était leur obsession et leur insupportable retour' (i, 198). Partly through awareness of his own reactions during an experience of love, he can be found building up a view of mind as a form of system where, whatever the content of experience, the 'phase-changes' follow a cyclic pattern. It is a vision which he will express time and time again, often through imagery borrowed from the laws of transformation and equilibrium used to describe thermodynamic systems,[1] and often through sustained poetic means. The rôle attributed to consciousness in such experience is a major one. It is *because* the conscious self feels itself to be the only free centre of identity in a closed system of affective life that an experience of tension and anxiety is created when that centre is threatened by other phases of the system, and a painful sensation of oscillation is set up between 'être' and 'connaître', incompleteness and plenitude. Throughout Valéry's life the themes of 'conscience' and 'douleur' remain inseparably linked.

The experience of 1892 has another aspect, however. 'Je finis par détacher leur répétition de leur signification' (i, 198), Valéry had continued in his account of the obsessional ideas and images through which he had first arrived at his notion of consciousness, and, referring later to an experience of uncontrollable emotion as far back as early adolescence, he writes: 'Je me refroidis aussitôt, et observai, avec une jouissance exquise et neuve, le mécanisme des accès. [. . .] Plus je voyais distinctement ce développement d'une dissipation d'énergie, plus je m'éloignais vers je ne sais quel extrême opposé de la sensibilité [. . .] et plus je me sentais prendre une vérité à sa source, acquérir à l'égard des valeurs débordantes, une défense définitive' (xxi, 769). Such notes obviously refer to the vital intellectual power to substitute, for the paralysing sensation of being trapped in a circle of unbearable involuntary associations, the excitement of

[1] The wider relevance of this choice is discussed by N. Bastet in 'Faust et le Cycle', *Entretiens sur Paul Valéry* (sous la direction d'Émilie Noulet-Carner), Décades du Centre Culturel International de Cérisy-la-Salle, nouvelle série 7 (Paris, Mouton, 1968), 115.

detecting their pattern of development in time. Valéry is discovering what he calls 'le recours à soi seul' (i, 25). Perhaps this is not far from the kind of 'attitude centrale' (P I, 1201) described in the essay on the creative imagination of Leonardo da Vinci as being the mainspring of both science and art. Even in the early stages of his thought, consciousness seems to have been for Valéry an activity which introduces into the unity of the rest of the natural world the very sense of division or anxiety from which a new, human unity can be constantly formed (e.g. P II, 66).

To recapitulate and expand, four main points of use in later discussion can perhaps be suggested about Valéry's approach to experience. First, the universality of his subject-matter. 'Mon objet est de faire penser – et de me faire penser moi-même, –', he writes, 'à des choses auxquelles on ne pensait pas à cause de leur présence ou trop proche ou perpétuelle' (xxiv, 876). The power of detachment is no intellectual monstrosity born suddenly in a thunderstorm (that of the 'nuit de Gênes' of 1892), but a common human potential which the mental events of that time served but to throw into relief. This universality seems vital if Valéry's thought is to be fruitfully linked with a common human experience and one which a whole tradition of artists express in some form: Montaigne, Constant, Stendhal, Proust, Malraux, Sartre and Nathalie Sarraute to name but a few.

Very few writers, however – and this is the second main point to consider – have concentrated on presenting experience from so exclusive a standpoint. Indeed, in 1943 near the end of his life, Valéry wrote in a letter to Émile Rideau, rather as Mallarmé was drawn to clarify his 'Grand Œuvre' in writing to friends:

> Je ne me suis jamais référé qu'à mon MOI PUR, par quoi j'entends l'absolu de la conscience, qui est l'opération unique et uniforme de se dégager automatiquement de *tout*, et dans ce tout, figure notre personne même, avec son histoire, ses singularités, ses puissances diverses et ses complaisances propres. Je compare volontiers ce MOI PUR à ce précieux Zéro de l'écriture mathématique, auquel toute expression algébrique s'égale . . . Cette manière de voir m'est, en quelque sorte, consubstantielle. Elle s'impose à ma pensée depuis un demi-siècle [. . .] (P II, 1505)

The reason for the at times infuriating persistency of this 'manière de voir' – reflected in Valéry's approach to history, philosophy, literary biography and so on – is undoubtedly the particularly active nature of his own self-awareness, coupled with his need creatively to exorcise the anxiety it caused him by intellectual analysis of that very experience. 'Mon Caligulisme [. . .] volonté d'épuiser mon principe de vie,', he wrote near the end of his life, 'de former, produire attendre un moment après lequel tout autre soit incomplet, imparfait, indiscernable, etc. Je fus ou suis l'idée de ce moment qui foudroie tous les autres possibles ou connus. Moment. César [. . .] Pas de redites: construire pour se détruire' (xxviii, 822).[1]

It follows from the particularly close connection between method and object of analysis in Valéry's *Cahiers* that an element of great selectivity is often at work – almost as if he is identifying with the rarest of human potentialities in order to increase their chance of survival. Of this he himself is well aware. 'L'*esprit* est excessif de nature; mais il faut que la *personne* le tempère', he writes, for example, 'Toute une morale tient dans la seconde proposition, et ma religion consiste peut-être dans la première',[2] or, extending the same kind of argument less self-critically to the question of artistic expression:

> On me fait quelquefois la remarque et le reproche de mon insensibilité. Je ne m'en défends pas. Je dis: je sépare instinctivement l'écrivain de l'individu. [. . .] Un être me semble d'autant moins 'sensible' qu'il exhibe et *utilise* le plus son sentiment. Il me répugne de toucher certaines cordes [. . .]. Peut-être ai-je grand tort et me privé-je par là des effets les plus puissants et les plus généraux. Mais il ne faut conclure du silence à l'absence. (xiv, 741)

'Suivons donc un peu plus avant la pente et la tentation de l'esprit',[3] the *Note et Digression* continues accordingly, and invites the reader to envisage the potential journey of consciousness to the extreme limits of its domain where 'Cet orgueil conducteur l'abandonne étonnée, nue, infiniment simple sur le pôle de ses trésors' (P I, 1230).

Valéry's thought has, then, a marked tendency to try to unfold the possibilities of a single instant – often an instant of extreme conscious existence – rather than to concern itself with tracing the development of experience along a horizontal axis. This should obviously be taken into account in any critical assessment. Judith Robinson remarks that after Valéry's rich analysis of intellectual activity, his thought on the rôle of

[1] Quoted by J. Duchesne-Guillemin in 'Les *N* Dimensions de Paul Valéry', *Entretiens sur Paul Valéry*, 24 ('Possession de soi–Dégagement').

[2] *Lettres à Quelques-Uns* (Paris, Gallimard, 1952), 192.

[3] See M. Raymond's study *Paul Valéry et la Tentation de l'Esprit* (Neuchâtel, La Baconnière, 1946).

emotion may strike the reader as inadequate – in fact that his opinion of its negative function almost inevitably falsifies his view of the mind.[1] This consequence seems to me to be based on what is not necessarily the best approach in the first place. A 'negative' view of emotion applies only to one 'level'. It is part of the tension caused by the constantly renewed search for 'emotions' in which consciousness is fully and harmoniously involved, as the following chapters will attempt to show.[2] But above all, is it so certain that the mind can be approached in any other way than through the type of highly personal observation that Valéry brings to it, offering as he does an insight into the birth of generality through his own experience as 'la mesure des choses' (P I, 1358)? 'The curious, variable relationship between perceived dynamic patterns and the perceiver's self plays a rôle in a number of insufficiently explored mental states, such as pity, [. . .] identification, self-control, self-estrangement', suggests a psychologist, 'Here are tasks that will be noticed and approached when "emotions" and "feelings" have ceased to obstruct the view'.[3] Many of Valéry's writings in the *Cahiers* surely gain in interest when the idea of a predetermined distinction between intellect and emotion is set aside, together with the idea of what necessarily constitutes a 'subjective' and 'objective' view of the mind. His writings seem to me to yield most fruit when seen as an attempt to explore his own consciousness at the point where the range of its potentials in depth seems at its most dynamic and intricate and where it therefore reveals the greatest contact with 'universal' patterns of experience such as the urge to organise, create and understand.

The third point of importance for the ensuing study, then, is the unashamedly 'emotive' source of Valéry's 'intellectual' method, '*accroissement de conscience*' (xviii, 225), as he once called it. The habit of approaching experience from the point of view of its maximum generality was born as a defence rather than as a substitute for feeling, 'défense profonde, raison majeure, raison d'État' (xxi, 880). 'Théorie du Moi pur [. . .] cette thèse si abstraite me paraît et me vient naturelle, à ce moment de trouble et de nerfs' (xv, 291), Valéry observes, or, formulating a closely related paradox in more general terms: 'toute connaissance est compensation à une perturbation qui se nomme *sensibilité*' (viii, 3). Obviously taking his particularly acute sensitivity as model, he is drawn throughout his life to regard any categoric distinction between 'intelligence' and

[1] Robinson, *L'Analyse de l'Esprit*, 156.

[2] E.g. chapter 3.

[3] R. Arnheim, *Towards a Psychology of Art* (London, Faber and Faber, 1966), 318.

'sensibilité' as purely academic,[1] and to pursue by every linguistic means possible the idea of a type of mental structure based on what he once called 'le point mystérieux d'union intérieure des puissances de la vie et de celles de l'esprit'.[2] That the phrase should have occurred in a letter of homage to Ronsard is obviously significant with regard to Valéry's own poetic achievement. In fact he adds that this vision is his own means of representing 'l'âme d'un poème'. I shall suggest that the theme of a tension in the conscious mind between 'être' and 'connaître' may be seen as the guarantee rather than the refutation of the vision of mental unity on which Valéry's art of poetic modulation is very largely based.

The final point of relevance here is the relationship of consciousness to time and change and consequently to the notion of 'le Moi pur', which is obviously intertwined with Valéry's notion of consciousness. Are consciousness and 'le Moi pur' synonymous? It is apparent by now that Valéry is not concerned with a permanent aspect of mind when he writes of 'la conscience'. His notes constantly draw attention to the fact that not only does the major part of the mind's activity take place below the threshold of conscious awareness, but even the activity of consciousness itself is of an intermittent nature dependent on certain mental conditions. 'Si l'homme perd la conscience avec la vie', he notes, for example, '– Mais il la perd déjà pendant la vie même et pour des altérations de soi moindres que la mort' (vii, 473).[3] Although Valéry views consciousness itself as a ceaseless movement of differentiation from everything perceived, 'un refus indéfini d'être quoi que ce soit' (P I, 1225), he never forgets that this very movement is at any moment likely to be disrupted by the different rhythmic patterns of illness, emotion, accident or sleep, or that the 'liberty' on which depends so great a range of individual experience is very largely dispensable to the strict maintenance of life (P I, 926).

What of 'le Moi pur' in such a system? Obviously Valéry's notion of a pure, impersonal self no more implies an absolute essence than does his notion of consciousness in general. As an aspect of mind it is equally dependent on the physical conditions of the nervous system. To speak of a quest for 'le Moi pur' and its inevitable failure may therefore tend to be misleading.[4] Yet whereas Valéry writes of consciousness as an impermanent, though potentially recurrent aspect of mind, he writes of the notion of self in terms of an invariant: 'Le Moi comme je le définis est ce qui se déduit d'une invariance par rapport à la variété des expériences possibles'

[1] *Lettres à Quelques-Uns*, 234. [2] Ibid., 219.
[3] Quoted by Judith Robinson, *L'Analyse de l'Esprit*, 86, n. 3.
[4] See, for example, M. Raymond, *De Baudelaire au Surréalisme* (Paris, Corti, 1940).

(vii, 148). 'Le Moi pur', Judith Robinson states, is seen by Valéry in mathematically inspired terms as 'l'invariant suprême du groupe de transformations le plus général possible',[1] and she goes on to suggest that although in some of his published works, notably the *Note et Digression*, Valéry seems to treat the terms 'le Moi pur' and 'conscience' almost as synonymous, by the time of the notebooks of his maturity he can be found making a distinction between the two.[2] How can such a suggestion be reconciled with Valéry's definition of 'le Moi pur' near the end of his life, in the letter to Émile Rideau already quoted, as 'l'absolu de la conscience, qui est l'opération unique et uniforme de se dégager automatiquement de *tout* [. . .]' (P II, 1505)?

First, what does Valéry mean by taking as his definition of self an invariant in a group of transformations? It seems possible to illustrate his thought on the subject by referring to the phenomenon of sleeping and dreaming, on which he reflects time and time again as a kind of testing-ground for his major interests: an experience in which self persists although full self-awareness does not. The most abstract of Valéry's writings suggest that he defined the state of being asleep by the formal symbolism of a phase where the elements are far less intricately co-ordinated than is possible when the mind is awake.[3] Accordingly, he thought of the state of wakefulness as being distinguished from the sleeping state by a smaller number of possible transformations of one phase into another and therefore by a greater number of possible invariants owing to the greater organisational restrictiveness involved. By describing 'le Moi' as an invariant in the most general group of transformations possible, Valéry implies, then, that 'self' is simply a set of formal relationships of which consciousness cannot always be one of the variables. It seems characteristic of his defensive wariness of using concepts until he has examined their 'conditions d'existence' (xxiii, 553), that he should approach consciousness by attempting to track its roots in a soil where only its powers of re-emergence exist, and furthermore that he should describe it as a sensation of the arbitrary nature of the self, the self that makes it possible: '*Avoir conscience de soi, n'est-ce pas sentir que l'on pourrait être tout autre?* Sentir que le même corps peut servir à cette quantité de personnages que les circonstances demandent; et le même MOI s'opposer à une infinité de combinaisons, parmi lesquelles toutes celles que forme automatiquement le kaléidoscope du rêve?' (P II, 1508–9).

[1] Robinson, *L'Analyse de l'Esprit*, 73. [2] Ibid.

[3] See Judith Robinson's chapter on 'Le rêve et l'analyse de la conscience', *L'Analyse de l'Esprit*, 104–33.

To return, then, to the question of a possible divergence between 'le Moi pur' and consciousness, it is possible to agree with Judith Robinson that Valéry's notion of self – 'le Moi' – is indeed one which precludes identification with consciousness. But at the same time it is far from clear that Valéry associates the term 'le Moi pur' with anything other than the highest level of consciousness or detachment from the personality. The force of the associative distinction is rendered by the word 'pur' which he tends to reserve for the products of a highly organised selective process on the part of consciousness itself: 'Parmi l'ensemble touffu des sensations nous choisissons, en sortant de la domaine de la signification, qui reproduit le désordre même de la vie, pour entrer dans la voie de l'ordre, de quoi mettre à part des éléments purs'.[1] In the line from *La Jeune Parque* 'Mystérieuse MOI, pourtant, tu vis encore!' (P I, 105) Valéry seems to be referring to the preservation of self through an intermittence on the part of consciousness, yet it is only when the fully selective power of self-awareness returns that such a relationship with the world regains any subjective significance. It is this mysterious action of mutual illumination between self and consciousness which seems to be suggested by Valéry's description of 'le *moi* pur' as an 'élément unique et monotone de l'être même dans le monde, retrouvé, reperdu par lui-même' (P I, 1228). Just such 'rediscovery' of her own 'unité' de présence (IX, 644) characterises the Parque's experience.

The resonance of this theme of solitary self-identity throughout Valéry's writings makes it possible to suggest that there is after all no real contradiction between, on the one hand, the notion of 'le Moi pur' put forward in the *Note et Digression* in a way which suggests inseparability from consciousness, and on the other, the notion of 'le Moi' as a purely formal relationship possible when the mental conditions determining the presence of consciousness are unavailable. When Valéry writes in 1943 'Je ne me suis jamais référé qu'à mon MOI PUR, par quoi j'entends l'absolu de la conscience, qui est l'opération unique et uniforme de se dégager automatiquement de *tout* [. . .]' (P II, 1505), he is referring to the self as a formal equilibrium no more dependent on consciousness than on sleeping and dreaming, but one which nonetheless only gains its specifically human significance when it reaches the threshold of individual awareness. In Valéry's case this 'self' was raised to still further levels by the introspective discipline he deliberately adopted and allowed to develop through the processes of poetry and analysis. 'Le

[1] *Cours de Poétique*, leçon 3 (Vendredi 17 décembre 1937), *Yggdrasill*, 2 ème année (25 janvier 1938), 154.

Valérysme apparaît quand la force qui monte au cerveau est assez grande, non seulement pour engendrer la pensée, mais aussi *la pensée de la pensée* [. . .]', as M. Bémol suggests.[1]

This discussion has served to suggest that Valéry's notes on consciousness are often simply an abstract form of reference to a complex experience which he attempts to express by different methods in other parts of his work. This being so, it is necessary to give some idea now of the experience of consciousness in some of Valéry's dramatic protagonists or 'vivants de synthèse' (xxviii, 159), as he refers to them. By exposing the inner structure of experience in this way he can give the feeling of the dynamic interaction of different stages of experience and thus explore a whole range of different possible reactions to the basic relationship between consciousness and life already described as part of his formal analysis: 'L'inconscience c'est le jeu même de la connaissance son fonctionnement *incessant* et son entraînement – La conscience est une tentative pour juger ce jeu – le diriger et l'appliquer. Ces deux choses ne s'opposent pas' (ii, 278).

Narcisse

The first major example of these 'synthetic' beings is Narcisse. It was through his work as a poet that Valéry gradually became aware of the suitability of the Narcissus myth, or, more specifically, of the image of the man watching himself in the fountain or mirror, as a symbol of consciousness or self-awareness. The first poem, *Narcisse parle* of 1891, he saw as 'le chant d'un malheureux trop beau',[2] the excuse for a brief elegy on the theme of beauty and unassuaged desire. The image obviously has its roots deep in the poetry of Symbolism. But of the second poem, *Fragments du Narcisse*, written between 1919 and 1921[3] and published later in *Charmes*, he wrote:

> Bien des années plus tard, je repris ce thème si pur, et m'en fis un exercice. Ce travail me conduisit à examiner mon sujet sous divers aspects, c.-à.-d. à rechercher ce que l'on peut trouver d'essentiel dans la rencontre d'un être avec son image. Ce n'est plus la beauté de son visage et de son corps qui apparaît alors au Narcisse. C'est le contraste entre l'Unique et

[1] *Paul Valéry* (Paris, Société d'Édition 'les Belles Lettres', 1949), 418.
[2] Quoted by P.-O. Walzer in *La Poésie de Valéry* (Genève, Cailler, 1953), 273.
[3] See J. R. Lawler, *Lecture de Valéry* (Paris, P.U.F., 1963), 100.

> l'Universel qu'il se sent être, et cette personne finie et particulière qu'il se voit dans le miroir d'eau.[1]

The usual connotations of the myth – love of the self and of personal beauty – have been replaced by the more general and specifically Valéryan theme of contrast between 'impersonal' consciousness on the one hand, and finite personality on the other, or between universality and particularity, the two perfectly brought together in the image of the darkening pool, where Narcisse watches incredulously the fading reflection of his own frail, mysterious and individual self. Similarly Valéry makes an important distinction between what he considers to be Narcissism of the Gidean type in which 'la passion de l'être' is involved, and his own more dispassionate kind born from 'la merveille que le reflet d'un *Moi pur* soit *un Monsieur*; un âge, un sexe, un passé, des probabilités et des certitudes' (xv, 274). (This 'manière de voir' nevertheless has its own capacity to exalt a certain kind of being, as the following chapters will attempt to show.) He cannot emphasise enough that the 'real' subject of the Narcissus myth is 'la confrontation du Moi et de la personnalité' (iv, 181).

'Mais ceci n'a pas figuré dans mon poème', Valéry added to his remark on *Fragments du Narcisse*, and he writes in the *Cahiers*, where the theme is extensively explored outside the poem:[2] 'La proximité est chose extraordinaire. Je n'ai pas su le dire dans le Narcisse, dont c'était le vrai sujet et non la beauté revenant sur elle-même. Substitution essayé d'un être autre et indépendent à la partie spontanée du moi' (vii, 627). Whether successful or not in Valéry's eyes in giving a feeling of the yearning of the 'universal' self to absorb the 'unique' personality, the poem certainly throws more light on the quality of the response of consciousness to the existence of the self in the world than do the abstract statements concerning 'le Moi pur' so far examined. 'Il n'y a pas de nom pour désigner le sentiment que nous avons d'une substance de notre présence' (P I, 927): the poem seems to create in the reader the 'nameless' 'rayonnement' (vii, 32) of just such an inner 'présence'. No longer does consciousness appear as a kind of series of empty mirrors, but 'une troisième dimension par où la connexité du monde gagne et s'enrichit' (ii, 901).

In the course of a brief evocation obviously designed for just such a dramatic scenario as his *Cantate de Narcisse* (P I, 403), the last part of the Narcissus trilogy, Valéry writes – perhaps half involving an audience in the creation of his subject-matter? – 'Actions subtiles. Attentions qui se concentrent peu à peu sur les points les plus précis, abandonnant le reste

[1] Quoted by P.-O. Walzer, *La Poésie de Valéry*, 273.

[2] E.g. iv, 135; viii, 234; xviii, 707.

obscur du monde, et au centre de la sphère éclairée, cherchant, perdant, trouvant' (xii, 580). The 'regard' of consciousness is essentially selective. The details of the real world shift in precision according to the degree of 'attention'[1] accorded to them. With a little less concentration on his own image in the pool, Narcisse would be more aware of the world around him; with a little more concentration, he would cease like Teste ('Ce que je vois m'aveugle' (P II, 38)) to see his external image at all. In other words, the preservation of his own image depends on the maintenance by Narcisse of a certain type of perception, while at the same time the coming of evening will inevitably obliterate the very aspect of himself he is drawn to try to preserve. The monologue of *Fragments du Narcisse* remains accordingly in the key of a sensuous yet semi-tragic lyricism. Valéry is expressing one of the purest, yet at the same time most vulnerable relationships between consciousness and the self. The fading image in the pool is obviously symbolic of any 'inevitable' aspect of experience: bodily limitation, the sensation of an irretrievable past, the separate identity of another person, the idea of death, and so on. Time and time again Valéry seems to be concerned with that elusive margin of freedom centred on man's reaction to the inevitable, the freedom to adapt or to resist, up to a certain point, and thus to bring to bear on nature the 'daimôn d'action' or '*présence-puissance*' of human possibility (xix, 918).

Monsieur Teste

Someone who stretches this margin of freedom to its limits but without ever quite losing 'la plasticité humaine' (P II, 18), the power to adapt or redirect his attention when necessary, is Monsieur Teste, the second main figure in Valéry's intellectual gallery. Valéry looks back on the creation of Teste in his preface of 1925, written twenty-nine years after the publication of *La Soirée avec Monsieur Teste* (the first of a series of writings stretched over the main part of his life). Teste was born, he recalls, 'pendant une ère d'ivresse de ma volonté et parmi d'étranges excès de conscience de soi' (P II, 11). It is not difficult to see that he represents the same defensive reaction to anxiety[2] that Valéry himself had begun to cultivate a few years before in 1892. '[. . .] rapide ou rien. – Inquiet, explorateur effréné' (P II, 38), Teste possesses almost to the point of

[1] 'Attention' is a very important phenomenon for Valéry and seems to imply the directive element introduced into memory, perception and so on by a certain form of self-awareness.

[2] Cf. C. Mauron, *Des Métaphores Obsédantes au Mythe Personnel* (Paris, Corti, 1964), 190.

pastiche all those characteristics of impatience[1] and self-engendered anxiety which Valéry so often attributes to himself, sensations caused by a sense of 'étrangeté intérieure' (P II, 1509) rather than by external stimulus. He has obviously drawn extensively on his own 'Log-Book' of 1896 for many of the thoughts to be given to Teste.

This element of self-identification should obviously not obscure the purely partial nature of the comparison and the deliberate exaggeration involved in the creation of the literary figure. 'M. Teste est mon croque-mitaine. Quand je ne suis pas sage, je pense à lui' (i, 248), Valéry once wrote, emphasising the element of extremism involved in the idea of Teste. A work like *La Soirée avec Monsieur Teste* yields most fruit when studied as a piece of complex dramatic writing through which, playing on the element of 'vertigo' induced in all Teste's *entourage* and skilfully transmitted to the reader,[2] Valéry can humorously play off the mysterious power and intransigence of Teste's intellect against the simple, private life and anonymity of Edmond Teste, the external man. Because it deals with a living symbol of consciousness, consciousness in the form of a man with physical needs and inconsistencies, the Teste Cycle can provide an ironic variation on the interplay of consciousness, intelligence and communication in *time* which so deeply concerned Valéry in all its forms.

'Conscious – Teste, Testis' (P II, 64) is one of the entries in *Pour un Portrait de Monsieur Teste*. Many of the comments given to Teste himself such as 'Je suis étant, et me voyant; me voyant me voir, et ainsi de suite ...' (P II, 25) are obviously based on the same feeling of 'dédoublement' (viii, 633) that Valéry attributes to consciousness itself, his own in particular – for example: 'Mon sentiment très marqué d'une différence profonde *entre moi-même et moi*' (P II, 1509). In Valéry's case a whole life gives rise in part to a feeling of detachment; in the case of Teste the process is almost reversed: a whole life is the result of this attitude. This being so, the reader is placed in an ambivalent position from which he can both feel concern for the rigidly limited nature of Teste's life, reflected in the barrenness of its externals, and yet at the same time wonder at the intense degree of vitality and purpose which seems to spring from that very limitation. 'Il arrive que la Tour d'ivoire émette des ondes puissantes, d'elle-même inconnues' (P I, 1149), as Valéry once wrote.

1 See W. N. Ince, 'Impatience, Immediacy and the Pleasure Principle in Valéry', *F.M.L.S.*, II (1966), 180–91 and Christine M. Crow, 'Valéry, Poet of "patiente impatience"', *F.M.L.S.*, III (1967), 370–87.

2 See W. N. Ince, 'Composition in Valéry's writings on M. Teste', *L'Esprit Créateur*, IV (1964), 19.

The difference between consciousness as a natural reflex and consciousness as the basis of a whole life-style is an interesting one, and by creating a figure who exists for the sole purpose of extending the duration of his rarest capacities, Valéry suggests some important paradoxes. 'Supposé un observateur "éternel" dont le rôle se borne à répéter et remonter le système dont le *Moi* est cette partie instantanée qui se croit le Tout', the definition of 'Conscious – Teste' continues, 'Le Moi ne se pourrait jamais engager s'il ne croyait – être tout' (P II, 64). The act of analysis counters 'delusion'. Teste *knows* that the most cherished belief or opinion is subject to the same kind of randomness and chance as his own personality, and – more important still – that even his own power of consciousness may therefore be something relative despite its necessary illusion of centrality. By pushing consciousness to the point at which it induces a characteristic scorn ('mépris') towards *any* fixed attitude or totem, itself included, Valéry is uncovering a vital form of lucidity superior to consciousness as a 'natural' activity and thus the redirection of the 'transcendental' drive of consciousness into practical intellectual power.

'*Pouvoir*', Valéry once wrote, 'En toute matière "intellectuelle" la notion capitale est celle de Pouvoir, Possible ou impossible' (xiii, 528). The most fundamental aspect of Teste's intellectual discipline is indeed the strict differentiation he makes between the possible and impossible. To the central question 'Que peut un homme?', symptomatic of Valéry's own thinking, he tells himself 'Je combats tout, – hors la souffrance de mon corps, au delà d'une certaine grandeur' (P II, 25). The greatest of Teste's aims is not, then, one of an impossible violation of the conditions of life such as an avoidance of change, as it seemed to be for Narcisse. Instead he tries to accept and foresee his own reactions to the basic data his intelligence tells him he cannot circumvent – what Valéry calls in his notes 'l'impuissant effort de sa volonté de témoin contre l'infernale puissance des Corps^{C} et du Monde^{M}, et surtout des réactions intestines de l'Esprit^{E}' (xxiii, 302). The point at issue is not whether Teste will be able to avoid pain or fear, then, but whether he will be able to avoid the pain of pain, the fear of fear and so on. Valéry's technique deliberately leaves the innermost feelings of Teste a mystery, choosing to express only his own ideal of himself and its effect on those around him, equating him almost with the impersonality of a completed work of art. Does his external self amount after all to what he 'really' is?

Seen in this basically existentialist light, Teste is no longer the monster of detachment, but the intellectual hero, converting his awareness of limitations into fresh ambitions, redirecting the energies he has derived from life towards the modification of life according to his own mental needs. 'Il travaillait constamment, mais finalement sans s'en apercevoir, à substituer *sa* profondeur à toutes choses (que l'on peut toutes regarder comme superficielles) et à rendre toute profondeur superficielle' (xxv, 351), Valéry notes. The name given by Teste himself to this goal of a deliberate re-distribution of his energies in time is '*Maturare!*...' (P II, 18). The theme will be central to this study as a whole.

If any conclusion can be drawn from this brief survey of the relationship between consciousness and nature in the Teste Cycle, it is perhaps a feeling of the 'open-endedness' of consciousness; its ceaseless tendency to move beyond anything that seems detrimental to its own maximum use. At the same time, a paradox is exposed. The more Teste experiences the power of conscious detachment, the more he needs the consolidating process of an intellectual discipline to keep that power intact, and the more he builds up a reserve of energy which the type of existence he has chosen cannot really satisfy. 'Si un homme qui a travaillé son esprit en largeur et en profondeur, ne s'engage pas enfin dans le siècle où il se serve de cet esprit organisé', Valéry wrote in 1942, 'il risque de voir retourner à la dissolution naturelle et quotidienne sa structure acquise, car ce n'est que la vie extérieure qui peut désormais l'empêcher de revenir à l'état spontanément *informe* de la nature de l'esprit' (xxv, 635).[1] It is left to Valery's Faust to symbolise this consolidatory involvement in life, the power to '*réaliser* son gain' as the same passage continues. Teste represents the *discovery* of the potentiality of consciousness in its simplest, most extreme form. Yet just as Faust will need to incorporate the initial attitudes of Teste to preserve him from the new dangers to consciousness inherent in involvement, so in Teste himself can be felt a hint of what is to come in Faust. In his attitude to the unsatisfactory nature of language,[2] in his indifference to the kind of 'unequal' love offered by Madame Teste, in his scorn for the communal 'bêtise'[3] of society, the reader can feel the latent power of the artist, the lover, the political leader that Teste *could* be if he chose to be. For Teste actually to realise his powers in this way would be to forfeit his unique rôle as 'le démon même de la possibilité'

1 Quoted by P. Roulin in *Paul Valéry: Témoin et Juge du Monde Moderne* (Neuchâtel, La Baconnière, 1964), 185 ('Valéry et l'engagement').

2 See Christine M. Crow, '"Teste parle": the question of a potential artist in Valéry's M. Teste', *Yale French Studies*, no. 44 (1970).

3 C. A. Hackett suggests that 'bêtise' implies 'life in its undifferentiated, biological form; and it includes everything that tends to submerge us in the flow of life, instead of enabling us to resist, and to swim against the current' ('Teste and "La Soirée avec Monsieur Teste"', *F.S.*, xxi (1967), 115).

(P II, 14). Yet in the very barrenness of Teste's perfectly controlled existence, and in the energy with which he cultivates every act of self-discipline designed to preserve his consciousness from oblivion, Valéry seems to be playing with the paradox that Teste is as much endangered by immobility as was Narcisse by the dark. Might not the reason why he is presented in the preface as a monster who cannot exist more than a few hours in real life (P II, 13) be that consciousness itself may be incapable of existing fully for long without enlisting in its own support the apparently alien activities of communication, creation and involvement? '– Bien (dit M. Teste), l'essentiel est contre la vie' (P II, 73): seen in the context of the Cycle as a whole, the meaning of this statement is not as negative or clear-cut as it might at first appear. It hovers ceaselessly, as does the whole persona of Teste, between the impoverishment of consciousness without nature and the impoverishment of nature in turn without the special combinatory activity of man.

La Jeune Parque

In the Teste Cycle the 'dialogue' between consciousness and the self is largely presented through Teste's relationships to other people. In the poem *La Jeune Parque*, on the other hand, the mind of the protagonist herself – 'la Personne qui parle' (xxix, 92) – is the only point of reference. Valéry must find a language capable of following both the fluctuations of the heroine's consciousness as she wakes from sleep, questions herself, returns to sleep and reawakens, and the constant preoccupation of that same consciousness with itself. He must express from within 'un moi insaisissable et pourtant doué de permanence'.[1] Valéry responded to the challenge by creating a system of 'modulations' by which various themes and tones can be subtly interwoven in depth at the same time as the central thread of the work unfolds progressively. The following remarks are intended to deal not with the genesis or total exegesis of the poem,[2] but with the aspect of its thematic structure of greatest relevance to the present discussion, what Émilie Noulet calls 'le chemin *vers* la conscience et vers la lucidité, ou, si l'on veut, la prise de conscience de la conscience'.[3]

'[. . .] la peinture d'une suite de substitutions psychologiques et en somme le changement d'une conscience pendant la durée d'une nuit',

[1] L. Perche, *Valéry, les Limites de l'Humain* (Paris, Édns. Centurion, 1966), 10.

[2] Studies by A. R. Chisholm, J. Duchesne-Guillemin, G. W. Ireland, J. R. Lawler, O. Nadal, H. Sørensen and P.-O. Walzer are listed in the bibliography. See also L. J. Austin, 'Modulation and Movement in Valéry's Verse' in *Yale French Studies*, 44 (1970), 19–38.

[3] *Entretiens sur Paul Valéry*, 105.

is Valéry's description of the 'sujet véritable' of the poem (P I, 1613), or, carrying further his diffidence about the importance or even the possibility of defining the 'subject' of a poem, he suggests that 'La J. P. qui n'a, à proprement parler, de sujet, dérive de l'intention de définir ou désigner une connaissance de l'être vivant, qu'il ne suffit pas de reconnaître mais qu'il faut apprendre' (xxiv, 117).

Writing of the notion of 'substitutions psychologiques' and 'le changement d'une conscience' so important to Valéry both as poet and analyst, J. Duchesne-Guillemin states: 'Mais ce principe fut mis en péril dès que Valéry reconnut l'impossibilité de traiter en elle-même cette suite psychologique, sans le secours ou le détour de toute la vie sensible, physiologique, dont elle s'accompagne'.[1] This thematic widening is, of course, more than a formal exigency, as the same critic goes on to point out: 'Tout un aspect du moi, l'aspect charnel, sensuel, fait irruption dans la conscience, et c'est cette irruption qui met en branle le drame [. . .]'.[2] Although the sexual aspect of the poem, the magnificent invocation to the tossing trees of Spring in particular, was, as Valéry says, 'surajouté' (P I, 1621), there seems to be no justification for seeing such elements as in any way subsidiary to the central drama of the poem once complete. As so often, the formal challenge becomes for Valéry a means of extending the genesis of the poem over a longer period of time and thus working round to the natural equilibrium of a subject, 'la *forme* complète d'une phase entière humaine' (iv, 11). Consequently, it seems that *La Jeune Parque* yields most fruit when all possible 'levels' of interpretation (the erotic, the 'affectif', the generally representative and so on) are seen not as separate or parallel metaphors but as the substance from which the elusive central experience of 'le changement d'une conscience' is actually built up. In fact it is the very flow of these experiences, ceaselessly 'modulating' into each other in a manner Valéry claims to be inspired by the music of Glück and of Wagner, which gives the feeling of the implacable pulsation of a human consciousness finding its way through its own reactions until it gains a temporary harmony of its own.

It is frequently said that *La Jeune Parque* reflects many of the abstract discoveries about the mind which Valéry had made during the famous 'silence' in which he published no poetry, the period from 1892 to 1912. The idea of a constant creation of order from contact with disorder in the manner mentioned above would be one of them. It is equally true, however, that he is making full use of the emotive power of poetic lan-

[1] *Études Pour un Paul Valéry* (Neuchâtel, La Baconnière, 1964), 44.

[2] Ibid., 55.

guage, a use which he had up to a point deliberately 'postponed' in order to pursue more abstract research.[1] A sensation of 'postponement' and 'catching-up' is in a sense present in the structure of the Parque's experience too. From the opening cry of separation from an alien self: 'Qui pleure là [. . .]?' (P I, 96), to the final reconciliation with herself, the young woman is seen to unite in the same single thread of consciousness the vastly different 'speeds' or 'time-scales' of intellectual and emotive reaction.[2] It has already been suggested that 'conscience' and 'douleur' are closely related in Valéry's work. That a sensation of mental suffering coincides with the coming of consciousness is suggested in the Parque's waking experience: 'J'interroge mon cœur quelle douleur l'éveille,/Quel crime par moi-même ou sur moi consommé? . . .' (P I, 97). However, the very same pain is deeply linked with the experience of intellectual integration with life towards which she is moving, and this is brought out in the poem equally strongly. With her 'soif de désastres' (P I, 96) – rather similar to M. Teste's need to 'Créer une sorte d'angoisse pour la résoudre' (P II, 68) – the Parque is drawn again and again to her own distress, clinging to it as if it were more authentic than any other experience she has ('Mais je tremblais de perdre une douleur divine!' (P I, 99)). The total movement of the poem from unconscious happiness, through painful duality, to the reluctant beginnings of conscious harmony is underscored by the motif 'conscience/douleur' which brings about that very movement.

It is true that consciousness, and with it the desire for knowledge (symbolised in the poem by the serpent's sting), introduces into the experience of the Parque a tragic duality.[3] Yet this statement must not be allowed to obscure a contrapuntal pattern of self-therapy: only when it is signalled to the intellect in the form of an anguish introduced by consciousness can the deep disturbance or 'crime' felt by the Parque on an unconscious level begin to be resolved.[4] 'Si le moi pouvait parler' (vii, 227, cf. P II, 41), Valéry once reflected. By using language in its most deliberately ambivalent form and expressing more than one 'tonality' simultaneously as in the above example, he is obviously attempting to render the complexity of mood experienced by an inner self made articulate.

Other aspects of the verbal organisation of the poem can be seen to re-inforce the effect of a unifying consciousness transcending the duality which torments the Parque. The 'anisotropic' nature of her experience

[1] See below, 239–40.
[2] See chapters 8 and 9.
[3] Cf. Robinson, *L'Analyse de l'Esprit*, 167.
[4] Cf. Mauron, *Des Métaphores Obsédantes*, 192.

('être' and 'connaître') is expressed by metaphors of coldness and intransigence on the one hand (the temple, altar, bleak sky and so on) and by metaphors of rich sensuality on the other (trees, fruit, the breast and so on). Yet these two systems of metaphor and the tensions of life and death, detachment and involvement which they represent, are still intricately related by the single monologue in which the Parque narrates her experience, *the act of conscious ordering becoming in itself a vital agent in the movement towards plenitude.* This is true even at the most extreme point of the equation referred to by J. Duchesne-Guillemin as 'esprit/sterilité',[1] the point at which a sensation of intense separation from life produces the illusion that consciousness could extract itself from temporal development without any change to itself and that it must therefore re-create time in order to live.[2] In the very verb tenses with which the Parque describes 'ennui', for instance, the dimension of her own intelligence recapitulating the past and foreseeing future change is introduced:

> J'étais à demi morte; et peut-être, à demi
> Imortelle, rêvant que le futur lui-même
> Ne fut qu'un diamant fermant le diadème
> Où s'échange le froid des malheurs qui naîtront
> Parmi tant d'autres feux absolus de mon front.
>
> (P I, 101)

Indeed, the outcome of the poem is implicit throughout the monologue in the combination of tenderness and lucidity with which even the most bitter dilemmas of the intellect are expressed.

What, then, is the real tone of the Parque's acceptance of 'life' at the end of the poem? '. . . Alors, n'ai-je formé, vains adieux si je vis,/Que songes?', she asks herself, as the principle of change already inevitably at work is finally and self-critically assessed:

> [. . .] Si je viens, en vêtements ravis,
> Sur ce bord, sans horreur, humer la haute écume,
> Boire des yeux l'immense et riante amertume,
> L'être contre le vent, dans le plus vif de l'air,
> Recevant au visage un appel de la mer;
> Si l'âme intense souffle, et renfle furibonde
> L'onde abrupte sur l'onde abattue [. . .] . . .

[1] *Études pour un Paul Valéry*, 54.
[2] Cf. G. Poulet, *Études sur le Temps Humain*, I (Paris, Plon, 1965), 355

concluding:

> Alors, malgré moi-même, il le faut, Ô Soleil,
> Que j'adore mon cœur où tu te viens connaître,
> Doux et puissant retour du délice de naître,
> Feu vers qui se soulève une vierge de sang
> Sous les espèces d'or d'un sein reconnaissant!
>
> (P I, 110)

To stress only the glorious, 'sun-lit' quality of this re-birth would surely be as erroneous as to suggest that the Parque has been forced to adopt some kind of cheap compromise where lucidity is concerned.[1] It is, after all, despite herself ('malgré moi-même') that she turns to 'life', or rather to a fuller relationship with herself than was possible when only the desire to maintain a constant level of self-awareness held sway. Yet the potential warmth and triumph to be the reward of that difficult acceptance are already present in the image of the rising sun beginning to penetrate her being, a sun which will go on rising to a fuller contact with life at a later stage. The Parque has survived her contact with the dark, and, consequently, the light of conscious detachment, which Valéry compares in the *Note et Digression* to a solitary lamp reflected infinitely by a series of mirrors (P I, 1216), appears by the end of the poem less persuasive than the light of the waking mind as a whole.

'Ce que je pensais, mes images demeurant les mêmes ne sont plus regardées de moi, mais me regardent, me changent [...]', Valéry wrote on the back of one of the manuscripts of *La Jeune Parque*.[2] When the Parque begins to exist like the anonymous viewer in Robbe-Grillet's *La Jalousie*, as a window on an inner world, the reader seems free to be able to carry further into a new stage of awareness the process in which the Parque is engaged without option. At the end of the poem she herself is at a stage past the sluggish, unreflective happiness symbolised by Eve in *Ébauche d'un Serpent*; past the discovery of a potentially tragic separation symbolised by Narcisse, and past the violent struggle against involuntary experience symbolised by La Pythie.[3] In fact the Parque seems to exist

[1] See, for example, Walzer, *La Poésie de Valéry*, 220.

[2] Quoted by G. W. Ireland in 'La Jeune Parque – Genèse et Exégèse', *Entretiens sur Paul Valéry*, 101.

[3] See below, 51-3. For a suggestive comparison between *La Jeune Parque* and *La Pythie* see Monique Maka-de Schepper, *Le Thème de la Pythie chez Paul Valéry*, Bibliothèque de la Faculté de Philosophie et Lettres de l'Université de Liège, CLXXXIV (Société d'édition 'Les Belles Lettres', 1969), 26, 179–94.

as a companion figure to M. Teste, with the difference that the power made available to her by the survival of a crisis allows her at least to contemplate willingly acceptance of the kind of involvement he scorns or even fears.[1]

The ending of *La Jeune Parque* naturally invites comparison with that of *Le Cimetière Marin*, the protagonist of which forms another major figure in Valéry's expression of the drama of consciousness and nature. Where in the first poem, published in 1917, the sun is seen rising, in the later poem, a work of Valéry's maturity published in 1920, the sun is already at its zenith and the mind of the speaker at a later stage of development. Where the Parque's experience is knife-edged in places, the 'amateur d'abstractions' of *Le Cimetière Marin* represents the achievement of a finer balance of his different mental exigencies. It is as if the minds of Teste and Madame Teste are temporarily combined. There is a difference from the tone of the Narcisse myth, too. Although the same theme of a confrontation between universality and individuality is evoked, the tone in *Le Cimetière Marin* is closer to wonder than to tragedy, almost as if Valéry's comment 'Quelle merveille qu'un instant universel s'édifie au moyen d'un homme [. . .]!' (P I, 351) were being contrasted with 'le malheur de l'homme d'être un peu plus universel qu'il ne faut' (viii, 204). The experience crystallised round the speaker here in a network of light and shade, calm and movement, is as deep as that attributed by the Parque to a preconscious existence, yet transferred to the fully conscious mind and expressed accordingly in the present tense.

The images through which this experience is created will be examined later in this study: the melting fruit, the tiny flecks of foam about to break out into movement, the relatively unchanging sky compared with the changing human consciousness, and so on. By the end of the poem they have each played a part in the triumphant upsurge of living energy with which, in the form of the vigour of wind and waves tearing him from his book, the narrator – he is still the narrator even now – is able to accept change, and to accept it without any fear of detriment to the total self of which thought and detachment will later again be part. It is this daring which seems to be reflected in the transfer of the verb 'oser' to the waves as they are suddenly shattered into a vertical shower of powdery drops, persuasive despite the hesitant 'tenter de vivre' of the intellect:

[1] The theme of a possible fear of movement on the part of Teste is suggested by Norma Rinsler in 'Stillness and Movement in Valéry's Poetry', *Essays in French Literature*, VI (1969), 43.

Consciousness

La vague en poudre ose jaillir des rocs!
Envolez-vous, pages tout éblouies!
Rompez, vagues! Rompez d'eaux réjouies
Ce toit tranquille où picoraient des focs!

(P II, 151)

Le Cimetière Marin remains one of Valéry's most satisfying expressions of the potentially dynamic interchange between the natural world and human consciousness in its most universal form.

Faust

There is finally the 'voice' of the figure at the end of Valéry's life to consider, the voice of Faust. For many years Valéry held in mind the writing of what he sometimes thought of as a 'Troisième Faust'.[1] The result was the play *Mon Faust*, published 'unfinished' in 1941 in two parts: *Lust* (in three acts) and *Le Solitaire* (in two), together with many notes from which can be pieced together parts of a projected fourth act to *Lust* ('Lust IV') and a few hints on the possibility of a third act to *Le Solitaire*.[2] In terms of the drama of natural light through which Valéry so often symbolises the changing potentials of human consciousness, Faust stands at the evening of his life, 'le Crépuscule du Possible' ([F. III] xxiv, 823). His mind is not concentrated on the future, as was that of Teste or of the Parque, but rather on the present, and to a present known to be fleeting and limited, Faust can paradoxically bring the intellectual resources of all Valéry's other protagonists. Where Teste has only one voice, Faust combines many. Since some of the main themes of *Mon Faust* (mental rejuvenation, the integration of intellect and emotion through love, and so on) will be discussed later,[3] it is necessary simply to compare here the different 'tones' of a relationship between consciousness and nature brought to life in the Faust of *Lust* and the Faust of *Le Solitaire*.

In a recent study called 'Valéry's *Mon Faust* as an "Unfinished" Play', Judith Robinson points out that critics have overlooked, when stressing the serenity, peace and fulfilment of the famous garden scene at evening in the middle of Act II, that 'Faust's moment of inner poise is very transient' and marked by an undercurrent of growing emotional tension

[1] P.-O. Walzer dates the project from at least 1935 ('Valéry entre dans la Pléiade', *Journal de Genève*, 28–9 jan. 1961).

[2] Details of the notes made before and after publication are given by J. Duchesne-Guillemin, *Études Pour un Paul Valéry*, 195–212.

[3] See chapters 2 and 9.

between himself and Lust.[1] The context of the scene in the rich parody presented by the play as a whole must not be left out of account. It is nonetheless this very element of transience and parody which emphasises the point most relevant to the present discussion, namely that Faust's capacity for a moment of perfect harmony with himself, with the natural world and with another human being, is achieved not through the abeyance of powers of lucidity, irony and detachment such as were symbolised by Teste, but by virtue of those very same Testian characteristics. 'VOIR suffit, et savoir que l'on voit. . .'. (P II, 322), Faust says in the monologue that forms the apex of the play, and, 'Voilà mon œuvre: vivre. N'est-ce pas tout? Mais il faut le savoir [. . .]' (P II, 322). The 'mais' is important. It forms a kind of double pivot, suggesting both the vital necessity of consciousness as part of the only meaningful differentiation between human experience and physical oblivion, and at the same time the power of consciousness itself to destroy enjoyment – a theme which will break out in *Le Solitaire*.

Faust's calm and tender relationship with Lust, 'Mlle Natura',[2] a relationship symbolised by the garden scene, is indeed, then, one of 'promesses': 'Promesses pures, rien de plus. Car rien ne passe en délice la promesse . . . Surtout, rien de plus. . .' (P II, 319).[3] But it is the quality of this same preference for promise or potentiality which nourishes the 'moment privilégié' of the present. 'L'état d'exaltation féconde est celui des échanges les plus *libres*' (viii, 5), Valéry once wrote. It is in just such freedom of exchange between intellect and emotion – a freedom symbolised in this case by exchange with another human being, Lust – that the harmony of Faust's mind is realised. The result is tenderness: 'l'échange inouï, muet, de ce que je ne sais pas en moi, ni de moi, contre ce que je ne sais pas en toi, ni de toi' (P II, 1412).[4] Valéry develops the theme of tenderness in his notes for the projected fourth act of *Lust*. Accordingly there can be no doubt, as Judith Robinson suggests,[5] that the swing of the pendulum so marked in the first three acts from coldness to warm involvement and back to coldness again, would have emphasised still further at the end of the play the moment of positive affirmation of the reciprocity of life and consciousness to which – as in *Le Cimetière Marin* – the structure of the work repeatedly points. And even here, in the conditional perfect with which Faust speaks of the consummation of his love for Lust

[1] *A.J.F.S.*, VI (1969), 430.
[2] Duchesne-Guillemin, *Études pour un Paul Valéry*, 207.
[3] See Robinson, *A.J.F.S.*, VI (1969), 434.
[4] See also below, 60.
[5] *A.J.F.S.*, VI (1969), 437.

('Oh, Lust, c'est toi que j'aurais choisie' (P II, 1413)), the stress is subtly laid on the equivalence between the perfection of the present moment and the intellectual capacity to maintain a balance between detachment and desire. The extreme contact with life at the end of *Le Cimetière Marin* was expressed after all in terms of a Dionysian rupture of equilibrium. Is Faust paradoxically more positive by postponing this contact?

The Faust of *Lust achieves* tenderness where Teste was tender only through enervation. Where Teste stores intellectual energy for a use that is always future, Faust receives back from life the energy of his own mature mind and is capable of radiating it to others in the form of love and art. His is the fruition of the 'lucide tendresse' and 'maternité muette de pensées' evoked by Valéry in the early poem *Profusion du Soir* (P I, 86), the title of which finds itself embedded in the dialogue of the garden scene so many years later (P II, 320).

Le Solitaire

It is important when assessing the view of consciousness and nature evoked in *Le Solitaire*, the second part of the Faust drama, to be clear about its relationship to the first fragment, *Lust*. The two parts are obviously intended to be complementary, and nothing would be further from Valéry's 'method' than to make *Le Solitaire* his last word on the subject.[1] 'Valéry a cherché la satisfaction, esthétique et logique à la fois', suggests L. J. Austin of this 'method', 'd'adopter à tour de rôle des points de vue différents ou même contradictoires, et de les pousser jusqu'à leurs conséquences les plus extrêmes. Et cependant, même alors, un courant sous-jacent d'ironie souriante ou insidieuse ne laisse jamais perdre de vue l'existence du point de vue opposé'.[2] Even as the ambiguous, provisionary quality of *Lust* suggests Faust's hesitancy before the potential trap created by his own affirmations, so a certain paradoxical tension in *Le Solitaire* suggests the value hidden in negation itself.

Where *Lust, la demoiselle de cristal* is presented as a 'comédie', *Le Solitaire, ou Les Malédictions d'Univers* is a 'féerie dramatique'. Its symbolic setting is a very high place. 'Faust monte aux terrasses de son esprit', points out Lucienne J. Cain.[3] But where Teste for want of anything better had still believed in the idol of his own intellect, Le

[1] F. Pire writes of the probable 'dernier mot de Valéry', *La Tentation du Sensible chez Paul Valéry* (Paris, La Renaissance du Livre, 1964), 94.

[2] 'Paul Valéry: "Teste" ou "Faust"?', *C.A.I.E.F.*, XVII (1965), 246.

[3] *Trois Essais sur Paul Valéry* (Paris, Gallimard, 1958), 126.

Solitaire is past such trifles. He has shed them one stage lower down the mountain and continues up into the almost impossibly rare heights of total solitude, perhaps the 'netteté désespérée' of the *Note et Digression* (P I, 1225). 'L'intelligence n'est qu'un théâtre de solitaire' (ii, 821), Valéry once wrote, though naturally seeing the theatre image as naïve in isolation,[1] and Le Solitaire asks Faust rather similarly: 'Et la pensée n'est-elle pas la solitude même et son écho?' (P II, 384). He then proceeds to give an account of his own total rejection of man's capacity for thinking: 'Moi aussi, j'ai cru longtemps que l'esprit, cela était au-dessus de tout. Mais j'ai observé que le mien me servait à fort peu de chose, il n'avait presque point d'emploi dans ma vie même' (P II, 386). To Le Solitaire everything important in life is in inverse proportion to consciousness; consciousness corrupts pleasure, aggravates pain and infects life to the core.

Lured by the apparent strength and truth of this argument, Faust reaches similar extremes of desperate negation, for it is, of course, a potential of his own mind which he finds echoed in the solitary voice. Imprudent enough to eavesdrop on a would-be solitary monologue (an example of comic irony in the play), Faust is thrown down a precipice for punishment, and, having been called to life again by the 'fées', rejects all the possibilities of mental rejuvenation they offer,[2] only to conclude with true 'Faustian' world-weariness:

Le souci ne m'est point de quelque autre aventure,
Moi qui sus l'ange vaincre et le démon trahir,
J'en sais trop pour aimer, j'en sais trop pour haïr,
Et je suis excédé d'être une créature.

(P II, 402)

It has not often been pointed out that if the theme of *Le Solitaire* is total negation, its effect is curiously different. In fact it brings alive some of the most intriguing paradoxes concerning the interplay of self-preservation and negation inherent in Valéry's thought. In the first place, by his conscious negation of 'l'esprit' and assumption of bestiality (a kind of 'être bête et le savoir'), Le Solitaire calls into play an intelligence of a particularly forceful kind.[3] The intellectual exhilaration he derives from total negation is apparent in the very syllables of his invocation to chaos:

[1] Hackett, *F.S.*, XXI (1967), 120.

[2] Cf. the 'coup de tête' which makes Faust see all things anew (xxvii, 73) and the remark attributed to Méphistophélès: 'Je te rajeunirai encore une fois!' (xi, 814).

[3] Duchesne-Guillemin, *Études pour un Paul Valéry*, 207.

Oh . . . Passez en moi, Vents superbes!
Couchez en moi toutes les herbes,
Rompez les ronces du savoir,
Foulez les fleurs de ma pensée,
Broyez les roses de mon cœur,
Et tout ce qui n'est pas digne de ne pas être!

(P II, 391)

True, Faust is not Le Solitaire. Le Solitaire is an echo of an extreme temptation that he himself dare not completely follow. Yet where even Faust is more negative than Le Solitaire is in his refusal of this energy, an energy which, like the guile of the serpent in *Ébauche d'un Serpent*, can ironically inject into man the kind of consciousness which leads to the human activities of artistic creation, thought and love. 'Cette puissance extrême de négation qui m'est parfois donnée, par-ci, par-là', Valéry wrote under the rubric 'Ego.F.III', 'et qui n'est que ce qui m'impose une observation des choses et de moi, m'a conduit en quelques occasions à un effort pour la surmonter en l'appliquant à elle-même, quand j'ai cru trouver ce qui fût plus fort qu'elle, une valeur positive à connaître', and he adds 'Ceci est le secret de mes deux ou trois grands désastres' (xxix, 833). It seems that the Faust of *Le Solitaire* may represent something of this same tendency towards 'la négation de la négation'.[1] In his effort to deny even Le Solitaire, who represents the natural power of negation without which no mind is complete, Faust is exercising in extreme form the kind of self-affirming consciousness which led to the Testian precept 'l'essentiel est contre la vie' (P II, 73).

Through all his 'vivants de synthèse' Valéry can be seen to trace the rhythms of psychological life which underlie the most diverse experiences. It is characteristic that this interest in the inner structure of experience should lead at the same time to the desire to express the complex range of reactions possible within those limits.[2] Valéry is interested above all in the juncture of the self-determining aspects of consciousness with the natural rhythms of life. The following chapters will attempt to suggest the dynamic rôle of consciousness in specific realms of experience such as scientific thinking, love and art.

[1] Duchesne-Guillemin, ibid., 207.

[2] 'Ainsi l'esprit peut en quelque sorte ajouter à un certain moment ses parties, c.à.d. les organiser et les faire entrer dans une présence [. . .] Rien de nouveau dans les donneés; mais une grande nouveauté par la réaction que leur action combineé provoque' (ix, 644).

2 *Knowing & understanding*

'*Knowing*' *life: the biological sciences*

One of Valéry's strongest intellectual needs seems to have been to gain total understanding of the mind as a biological phenomenon – '*En somme pouvoir penser l'être pensant*' (viii, 514) – and thus perhaps to counter a feeling of the uncontrollable nature of experience itself. This does not mean that he considered such understanding possible, however, or that he equated it entirely with scientific knowledge of life. The first part of this chapter will examine his attitude to biological science in general, that is, to the philosophical question of the study of living things by the living. It is an attitude which will be seen largely to determine the 'method' he seems most likely to adopt himself when turning to 'l'étude de l'être vivant' (P I, 832),[1] the study of the plant as a representative living organism, for example, and above all the study of the mind itself.

Valéry's remarks on the subject form a complex amalgam of questions, criticisms, rapid synthetic sketches and so on, often with no clear dividing lines.[2] On the whole they seem to fall into three main groups, however. In the first, often under the heading 'Bios' – the phenomenon of life in a relatively objective sense[3] – he attempts to sketch out problems: the little

[1] The phrase is used by Valéry to describe Descartes' main interest. He is known to have kept a file which reveals, particularly in the notes taken during the second World War, how much Descartes came to mean as a symbol of the relation between science and philosophy (see Judith Robinson, 'New Light on Valéry', *F.S.*, XXII (1968), 47–8).

[2] Compare with the suggestion made by P. Laurette in *Le Thème de l'Arbre chez Paul Valéry* (Paris, Librairie C. Klincksieck, 1967), 123.

[3] E.g. xix, 696; xxi, 855; xxiv, 769; xxv, 754; xxvii, 42, 50; xxix, 262. Use of the term 'Bios' in this sense is mentioned by R. Schubert-Soldern in *Mechanism and Vitalism* (London, Burns and Oates, 1962), xi–xii.

that is known about 'life' or what still remains to be known. In the second, he describes more radical difficulties, difficulties connected with epistemology and the nature of 'knowing' itself. In the third group, in the form of rapid collections of ideas largely drawn together by the notion of structure, he suggests his own approach to living organisms. It is mainly the first two of these groups that are relevant to the present stage of discussion, though it will be possible to suggest in the course of examining them why the third group introduces a tone of enthusiasm and excitement that the first two rarely possess.

Valéry's interest in contemporary developments in physics and mathematics is well-known.[1] Yet despite reasonably wide reading (on the subject of evolutionary theory, for example),[2] relatively very little enthusiasm seems to have been directed towards developments in biology. Why should this be?

One significant reason is probably that the science of biology itself was not nearly so advanced in Valéry's day as that of physics and other related disciplines. '[. . .] notre connaissance de la vie est insignifiante auprès de celle que nous avons du monde inorganique', Valéry wrote in 1937, characteristically using as his criterion of 'connaissance' the power to reproduce or predict certain results by the simplification of a phenomenon 'en opérations imaginaires et volontaires' (P I, 899). It is only relatively recently, for example, mainly in the field of genetics, that biology has entered a corresponding analytic or molecular stage in which emphasis is laid on structure rather than on content of information,[3] and only more recently still that an attempt has been made to replace the *deus ex machina* of the gene in a more dynamic context. Such movements have been characterised by a methodological awareness relatively absent in the early stages of biology. A brief, general survey of the main trends in biological opinion concerning the distinguishing features of life will suggest where Valéry's own thought might stand in relation to such semi-philosophical developments.[4]

It seems true to say that in the first third of the century both mechanists and vitalists sought the distinguishing features of life in terms of characteristic operations: the taking in of physico-chemical molecules from the

[1] See, for example, F. E. Sutcliffe, *La Pensée de Paul Valéry* (Paris, Nizet, 1955); Robinson, *L'Analyse de l'Esprit*; Laurette, *Le Thème de l'Arbre*.

[2] Details are given by Judith Robinson, *L'Analyse de l'Esprit*, 55.

[3] See J. C. Kendrew, *The Scientific American* (March 1967), 141.

[4] The main lines of the following survey are based on C. H. Waddington's contribution to *Towards a Theoretical Biology*, I Prolegomena, IUBS Symposium, ed. C. H. Waddington (Edinburgh U.P., 1968), 1–31.

environment and their synthesis into a more complex structure. It will become obvious later[1] that Valéry was deeply in tune with this vision of the distinguishing features of life as a local increase in order by means of specific synthesis. It will be obvious at the same time, however, that his general wariness of any apparently definitive formula leads him to make certain reservations even here. What of the living organism's power to adapt to change and to reproduce, for example? Under the heading 'Les sciences de la "Vie" et le plus grand effort de compréhension', he lists the main problems in 1922 as 'espèces', 'reproduction', 'instincts', 'mimétisme', 'mémoire', 'hérédité', 'variation', and concludes 'Nous ne comprenons rien à la vie' (ix, 36).

Now it was precisely these kinds of problem that led geneticists in the last part of Valéry's career to question the 'living matter' definition of life and to describe its distinguishing features instead in terms of the power to reproduce at the same time as to take part in a form of long-term evolution, and, of course, many advances in understanding the 'coding' of chemical information have since taken place. Whereas this approach had the advantage of making it possible to envisage the development of life from inorganic materials, however, it is considered by some biologists to have moved too far away from the notion inherent in the earlier physiological approach, of a unique complexity of organisation. After all, is it certain that machines for the transmission of mutable hereditary material would necessarily be recognised as having the characteristics of living things? It has recently been suggested that, although not unique in the way that the early vitalists thought it to be, life may still be distinguished from other physico-chemical organisations by a form of activity made possible by a particularly marked difference between the time constants involved. The model for such an organisation would be a dynamical system of far greater sophistication than the earlier mechanistic views allowed.

Without unduly overstating the case, it seems possible to suggest that Valéry came surprisingly close to the kind of synthetic approach to living organisms implicit in this last view of life, as his constant stress on the relation of forms to time as well as to space will prove. Such a vision is the natural corollary of his preference for models combining the maximum specific structure with the maximum instability or range of oscillatory power. In fact it is interesting to speculate that his notion of the mind as a kind of resonating system passing cyclically through a set of changing states or phases corresponds structurally to the organisational activity

[1] See in particular chapter 6, *Growth and decay*.

that is now sometimes considered to take place on many different 'levels' of life including that of the cell. Seen in this light, Valéry's conscious analogies between mental and physiological activities are doubly illuminating. Not only do they have coherence in terms of his own creative universe, but they are the proof that his particularly 'open' approach to scientific problems was a means of establishing links with those aspects of the scientific thinking of his day which have turned out to have a capacity for growth and the greatest exploratory power. The attitude behind this approach can now be studied in detail.

Much of Valéry's distrust of the 'life' sciences of his day stems from his suspicion of the vagueness of the word 'Vie'.[1] After the comment 'Tout est insuffisant – sélection etc – évolution', he adds, for example: 'Et ce nom ou notion même de *Vie*' (ix, 36), or even, with reference to the past attempts of scientists to define life: '[. . .] le succès de leur effort fut toujours assez vain: la vie n'en est pas moins' (P I, 1310). This kind of drastic overlap, between description of a method of enquiry on the one hand and of the object of enquiry on the other, provides a clue to the nature of the pessimism behind Valéry's comments. The notion of 'vie' has become associated with the inevitable frustration of the intellectual need to summarise and define '*une fois pour toutes*' (xiv, 574).[2] When he scathingly associates biology itself with 'similitudes' (xi, 175), Valéry is therefore revealing an important ambivalence. On the one hand he seems to be criticising the whole scientific attempt to summarise the complexity of life by formulae which need constant modification in the light of changing evidence. On the other hand he seems to be championing the vital restlessness and ambition of the intellect itself in its encounters with the irreducibility of life. '[. . .] rien de plus ennemi de la nature, que de *voir les choses comme elles sont*', says Éryximaque in *L'Âme et la Danse*, referring to the pure and absolute boredom generated by 'la vie toute nue, quand elle se regarde clairement' (P II, 167). Already Valéry's mistrust of biology can be seen to be based on the suspicion that it may never catch up with the vigour and variety introduced into life by the mind making the discovery. Life is continuous and changing; the formula fragments and arrests – in fact Valéry explicitly associates the 'method' by which man constructs with the inorganic world, concluding 'et c'est pourquoi la physique est plus avancée que la biologie' (xx, 784; cf. i, 328).

There are, then, far more fundamental reasons behind Valéry's

[1] E.g. xxiii, 509; xviii, 138.

[2] Cf. Laurette, *Le Thème de l'Arbre*, 135 and N. Bastet, 'Faust et le Cycle', *Entretiens sur Paul Valéry*, 117.

pessimistic attitude to the biology of his day than its relative methodological immaturity compared with other disciplines. The most general reason of all is the condition he refers to as 'l'asymptotisme de l'être et du connaître' (ix, 807).[1] Because of the very nature of its necessary abstract divisionism or interruption of the 'wholeness' of life, the activity of 'connaître' cannot for Valéry grasp the unity of nature – 'le Tout'[2] – of which it is already itself but a single effect. Even less, as an aspect of mind, can consciousness comprehend the mind itself: 'Pour comprendre ce que peut être la conscience, il faudrait une autre conscience de degré supérieur' (vii, 24). In the curiously powerful 'intermediate' language of a work like *Réflexions simples sur le corps* where Valéry's imagination as biologist-humanist-philosopher comes into its own, he writes of precisely this problem: 'C'est sur ce fond de difficultés fatiguées que vint se dessiner mon idée absurde et lumineuse: "J'appelle *Quatrième Corps*, me dis-je, l'inconnaissable objet *dont la connaissance résoudrait d'un seul coup tous ces problèmes, car ils l'impliquent*"' (P I, 931). This idea of a 'Quatrième Corps' provides a clue to the direction in which Valéry's own biological thinking is moving: towards a science which takes awareness of its own difficulties as the cornerstone of a new, relative power.

It was at precisely the point of the failure of 'objective' knowledge to grasp life in its entirety that many of Valéry's contemporaries such as Bergson tended to turn away from science altogether. Valéry's response is different. He retains a belief – obviously encouraged by his mathematical and architectural interests – in the power of science to progress by a constant revision of its methodology and to use its grasp of relationships as a means of 'handling', though not of 'understanding' life. Just such an alternative to the 'impasse' of 'objective' biological enquiry is stylised in the probing and humorous dialogue *L'Idée Fixe*. 'Après tout il n'y a pas de raison pour qu'un être vivant puisse parvenir à se représenter la vie . . .' (P II, 243), remarks the doctor to his companion, or 'Il est étrange que de toutes choses, *ce sont les choses vivantes qui déconcertent le plus l'être vivant* . . .' (P II, 265). The dialogue technique enables some of the attitudes present in the dense synthetic jottings of the *Cahiers* to be separately explored. The doctor here, for example, less concerned than his companion about the impossibility for science ever to comprehend life in terms of some total formula, seems to represent, rather like Camus' Dr Rieux in *La Peste*, the rewards of 'hope' when redirected into the

[1] Quoted by P. Laurette, *Le Thème de l'Arbre*, 135.

[2] Cf. Teste's definition of the conscious self as 'cette partie instantanée qui se croit le Tout' (P II, 64).

relative conquest of life by practical action, in this case by medical intervention. Indeed, the notion of the doctor or surgeon[1] appears in Valéry's writings as the symbol of a kind of '*Antiphysis*' (xxvi, 299), capable like the human intellect itself of transforming nature by a system of acts abstractly organised, and thus converting into the power to modify existence its own failure to understand life in an absolute sense. '[...] la *Vie* considérée comme une matière modelable, quelle "nouveauté"!' (xxvi, 52), he notes. From this point of view at least, it is not entirely true to say that Valéry does not consider man capable of creating his destiny in the existentialist sense.[2]

This disbelief in any absolute progress in biology may seem to be nowhere more pronounced than in Valéry's remarks on the theory of evolution, so widely debated in the first part of his career and so central to the notions of chance, order and determinism with which his interest in living organisms involves him in detailed concrete form. 'La "théorie de l'évolution", je n'ai jamais pu la prendre pour autre chose qu'une imagerie [...]' (xxix, 442), he writes, or, '[...] je ne suis pas évolutionniste [...]' (iv, 650). Judith Robinson suggests accordingly that 'il n'a jamais considéré l'évolution comme un fait scientifique établi'.[3]

Superficially this attitude on Valéry's part might seem to be related to his reluctance to conceive of the power of life to break out of the 'cycle' or closed system of nature to which he considered it to belong, except – and in a strictly limited sense – through the modifications introduced by human consciousness. Closer inspection of this apparent scepticism about evolution reveals, however, that it is the confusion between 'fact' and hypothesis which is mainly the butt of his criticism. 'Pas de *vrai* sans vérification – Mais de l'utilisable et de l'excitant' (xxix, 442), he notes after apparently dismissing the theory of evolution as 'une imagerie', or, in 1941, 'En biologie, le Principe de l'Évolution a déjà perdu de sa première autorité'.[4] In taking it upon himself to attack the most popular topic of contemporary biology, evolutionism, Valéry was simply waging war against the aura of dogma and mysticism that was beginning to surround

[1] See the *Discours aux Chirurgiens* (P I, 907–23). Valéry's interest in medicine is described in P. Chardon's *Paul Valéry et la Médecine* (Armand Fleury, 1930). He showed particular interest in neurophysiology and neuropathology (see Robinson, *L'Analyse de l'Esprit*, 56), echoes of which can be found in *L'Idée Fixe* (P II, 195–275), for example.

[2] A rather different suggestion is made by Judith Robinson, however (*L'Analyse de l'Esprit*, 179).

[3] *L'Analyse de l'Esprit*, 55.

[4] 'Vues personnelles sur la Science', *Vues* (Paris, La Table Ronde, 1948), 51.

evolutionary theory as much as it had the old spiritualist theories of matter and mind.[1] Like so many of his remarks which appear unjustified when removed from their context, these jibes against evolutionary theory become meaningful in the context of a wider interest in the psychology of thought and in the relation of all ordering processes to points of view in time. '[. . .] si l'on fait abstraction des connaissances qui n'expriment qu'un pouvoir certain d'action extérieure', Valéry suggests, 'le savoir restant n'est évalué que par une sorte de jugement "esthétique", qui lui donne vie et vigueur en chacun, et définit pour chacun sa vérité. Même la condition de non-contradiction, de conformité aux lois logiques, n'est en dernière analyse qu'une condition esthétique'.[2]

Valéry's constant stress on problems of methodology did in a sense draw him away from the more specific 'objective' problems of science, problems which in the case of Descartes he calls 'des problèmes qu'il n'eût pas inventés' (P I, 838). Yet it is certainly not true that the scientist who attempts to analyse the basic assumptions behind his method has no contribution to make to science, any more than that the poet who is aware of the processes of poetic composition is failing to be a poet. By criticising Darwin's evolutionary theory for what amounts to failure to distinguish the incompleteness of an analogy (that between the type of development of a single organism and of the whole organic world),[3] Valéry once more shows his ability to grasp those aspects of scientific thinking with the most 'universal' growing power. According to recent opinion in biology, evolution may indeed be most fruitfully treated as 'une méthode particulière de développement' (i, 398): it may refer to only one of the time constants already mentioned in connection with the living organism.[4] 'Il y a toujours en moi *de quoi ne pas* préférer une solution', Valéry notes himself of such an almost instinctive 'method'; 'C'est une forme singulière de fécondité que cette fécondité à conséquences négatives' (P II, 1525).

Apart from guaranteeing a general flexibility of thought, Valéry's 'method' comes fully into its own in one main area, then, an area he himself refers to indirectly in his essays on Descartes as 'le développement de la conscience pour les fins de la connaissance' (P I, 839). 'Considérer

1 See Laurette, *Le Thème de l'Arbre*, 144.

2 'Réponse de M. Paul Valéry' (to the question 'Les Sciences de l'esprit sont-elles essentiellement différentes des Sciences de la Nature?'), *La Revue de Synthèse* (oct. 1931), 9–11.

3 For a similar view of Darwin's theory see Agnes Arber, *The Mind and the Eye* (C.U.P., 1954), 42–3.

4 See C. H. Waddington, *Towards a Theoretical Biology*, 18. See also chapter 6, 135, n2.

toute chose – quoi que ce soit à l'aide d'un être humain explicite [Moi] au lieu de la regarder sans songer à cette contrepartie nécessaire' (iv, 79), he suggests. This conscious 'égotisme' is considered to have two vital consequences. On the one hand it nourishes the self with a pressing sense of its own generality, the inescapable need to 'exploiter son trésor de désir et de vigueur intellectuelle' (P I, 840); on the other, it offers a 'système de référence du monde, foyer des réformes créatrices qu'il oppose à l'incohérence, à la multiplicité, à la complexité de ce monde aussi bien qu'à l'insuffisance des idées reçues' (P I, 840).

'La seule vérité réelle est celle instantanée, imposée par les circonstances du moment à la diversité qu'on appelle un Homme' (P II, 1479), Valéry writes in accordance with this notion of subjective empiricism. It is partly in the light of the value of instantaneous subjective experience that he had expressed impatience with evolutionary theory: 'Je n'ai pas les siècles psychologiques qu'il faut pour ces mutations. Je n'ai que quelques minutes et en quelques minutes, même de pensée, il est impossible de donner un sens à ces propositions transformistes' (iv, 650). But it is also in the light of this notion that he outlines his belief in the need for sustained study of instantaneous perception itself: 'Il faut, avant tout, se faire une notion précise du changement. Non le définir, sans doute, ni monter au ton métaphysique. Il s'agit de caractériser ses propriétés. Elles résultent de l'expérience' (P II, 1458).

In the course of such definitions of his own 'method' of approaching 'les phénomènes, l'univers physique, les êtres vivants' (P I, 841), Valéry might be said to have steered clear of two charges: that of 'subjectivism' on the one hand and of 'intellectualism' on the other. To the first charge he virtually replies that his form of intuition is to be an 'intuition *savante*' (viii, 657) based on the great importance he attached 'aux notions, lois, principes des sciences qui font que le temps spatialisé n'est plus tant un flux qu'un système d'éléments coordonnés'.[1] To the second charge, made specifically this time, by Bergson, he replies that he is rather 'un *formel* – et que le fait de procéder par les *formes* à partir des formes vers la "matière" des œuvres ou des idées donne l'impression de l'intellectualisme par analogie avec la logique. Mais que ces formes sont *intuitives* dans l'origine [. . .]' (xiv, 103).[2] Valéry's particular form of 'rigueur imaginative' (i, 25) will be seen at work in his approach to the plant or tree.[3] It remains to ask now what rôle he accords to this part deductive, part

[1] Laurette, *Le Thème de l'Arbre*, 130.

[2] Quoted by P. Laurette, *Le Thème de l'Arbre*, 145. See also chapter 9, 228–9.

[3] See chapter 6.

inductive approach in the kind of scientific observation concerned with a 'level' too remote for the immediate perceptions of an observer to come into play (P I, 836).

The scientist to consider at this point is Heisenberg, whose uncertainty principle was formulated in 1927, bringing to a head the notion suggested by experiments in quantum physics throughout the 1920s that in investigations at the atomic scale there is an inevitable degree of interaction or complementarity between instrument of perception and data under observation, for example the disturbance of an electron by the photons used to detect its location and speed. As a consequence the description of the electron's behaviour would have to remain undetermined or imperfectly specified. Either its location or its speed could be determined precisely, but never both at once.[1]

The impression given by Valéry's thought as a whole is that he naturally recognised the importance of this principle. Not only does he frequently show himself to be conversant with it (bringing the idea into a *Discours sur l'Esthétique*, for example, where he talks of pleasure and pain as introducing into an intellectual construction a notion of incommensurability similar to 'cette dépendance réciproque de l'observateur et de la chose observée, qui est en train de faire le désespoir de la physique théorique' (P I, 1298)), but also, as the same example indicates, he is conscious of the relevance of the principle to his own particular interest in the problem of understanding mental processes in which the observer himself is involved. Many of his remarks on the necessity of attempting to incorporate into all considerations the 'contrepartie nécessaire' (iv, 79) of the observing self seem, superficially at least, to be directly comparable with statements by Heisenberg concerning the need to allow for the interference of informing processes with elementary particles.[2]

Why, then, when it comes to specific mention of Heisenberg, does Valéry, as Pierre Laurette briefly points out, refer to 'la prétendue indétermination de l'électron' (xiv, 112), express scepticism concerning the idea of complementarity (xxiii, 488) and in short show almost as much disapproval of 'les relations d'incertitude' as he does of notions of [finalistic] determinism and causality at the other end of the scale?[3]

A quick answer might be the non-originality of the principle on a general philosophical level, for it is obvious that, as in the case of evolu-

[1] See, for example, L. von Bertalanffy, *Problems of Life* (London, Watts & Co., 1952), 177.

[2] E.g. W. Heisenberg, *La Nature dans la Physique Contemporaine* (Paris, Gallimard, 1962), 18–19.

[3] *Le Thème de l'Arbre*, 138.

tionary theory, Valéry is choosing to attack popular philosophical interpretation rather than the precise implications of the uncertainty principle in a particular context for immediate practical ends. 'Indétermination – On en fait une grande affaire – Heisenberg', he writes, for instance, 'Or, rien de plus commun que de ne pouvoir observer une propriété d'une *chose* sans se priver de considérer une autre' (xxv, 355). The universality of the idea of complementarity, at least on a general level, is supported by a statement in the *Cours de Poétique*: 'Je retrouve la notion de complémentaire dans tous les domaines de la sensibilité et même dans le monde mathématique. Elle est aussi dans la poésie et en tous les points: par exemple dans la très obscure question du rythme, par exemple dans la question très difficile des "figures", images, etc . . ., notion pourtant fondamentale'.[1]

It is when Valéry's remarks are approached in terms of his attempt at linguistic criticism, however, that the deepest reasons for his scepticism are revealed. The meaning of 'indétermination' is not clear, for instance. Does it refer to method of perception of object perceived? It seems to be the ambivalence surrounding Heisenberg's principle which most disturbs Valéry, an ambivalence which allowed as one of the philosophical consequences of predictional uncertainty the possible indeterminacy of the universe itself,[2] as opposed to a principle of chance organisation – a principle to which he would be much more likely to subscribe.

It is already apparent that Valéry is fully conversant with the shift in scientific thinking from a 'continuous' to a 'discontinuous' interpretation of the relation of the observer to the physical world. The same shift in emphasis is apparent in his own definitions of scientific observation, as F. E. Sutcliffe has attempted to show.[3] At the time of writing the *Introduction à la Méthode de Léonard de Vinci*, for example, Valéry assumes that by the creative discovery of relationships between things, the intellect turns the apparent discontinuity of the world into an order which can be objectively verified; from approximately 1920 onwards, however, in the essay *Au sujet d'Eurêka* (P I, 854–67), for example, he can be seen to incorporate more and more the suggestions of modern physics that the properties of matter cannot be seen independently of the point of view of an observer, in other words that there is no way of verifying that the

[1] *Cours de Poétique*, leçon 4 (Samedi 18 décembre 1937), *Yggdrasill*, 2 ème anneé (25 janvier 1938), 155. For the sense in which Valéry uses the term 'complémentarité' see chapter 4, pp. 82, 83n.

[2] See *La Philosophie Contemporaine*, II, ed. R. Klibansky (Firenze, La Nuova Italia Editrice, 1968), 295.

[3] *La Pensée de Paul Valéry* (Paris, Nizet, 1955).

order created by the intellect is separate from itself.[1] The point of interest here is surely that this shift in knowledge can scarcely be said to alter the fundamental emphasis in Valéry's thought concerning the relationship between consciousness and nature. Indeed, a movement away from an ideal of objective verification in an absolute sense might even be said to strengthen the element of creative independence already present in the idea of scientific observation as an 'act of faith' on the part of the intellect, to use the phrase of Einstein which Valéry frequently admires (e.g. P II, 263). 'La découverte des fameuses relations d'incertitude, loin de signifier pour son esprit une abdication de son pouvoir en face de la Nature, marque l'avènement d'une indépendance nouvelle.'[2]

Thus Heisenberg's idea of an interaction between the observer and what is observed is certainly not alien to Valéry's thought. It is an idea to which his experience of the interdependence of intellectual and affective processes in the psychological field had predisposed him all along. The main reason for his hesitancy in associating himself with Heisenberg must lie elsewhere. Now Heisenberg's observations were made with specific relation to the atomic scale of reference, to 'la physique par relais'. Valéry's vision of nature relates, on the other hand, to the macroscopic scale of reference, to the area of experience where, because of a concentrated band of human perception, classical notions of form, harmony and structure still hold sway. This by no means implies that Valéry was unaware of the relativity of such notions to the macroscopic scale. Indeed, it is the point of interchange between the two visions which seems most to interest him: 'J'échange continuellement un monde qui se pourrait assez facilement rapporter au monde que fait soupçonner la physique et la science des vivants, contre un monde original, toujours d'aplomb, toujours âgé de quarante ans, toujours éveillé, lucide, toujours susceptible d'être entièrement exprimé par un langage [. . .]' (iv, 15). Might it be the tendency of Heisenberg's principle to lend itself to an interpretation of the universe in which such a distinction between relative frames of reference is disregarded to which Valéry indirectly objects? 'Nous devons nous rendre compte que nous ne sommes pas spectateurs mais acteurs dans le spectacle de la vie', writes Heisenberg.[3] However aware of the involvement of the mind in nature, Valéry never doubts the existence of a vital distinction between the perceiving self and the rest of the universe. This is surely why he prefers the mathematically harmonious vision of nature

[1] See Sutcliffe, ibid., 111, 127.
[2] M. Jaffard, *Le Monde* (16 fév. 1955).
[3] *La Nature dans la Physique Contemporaine*, 19.

postulated by Einstein[1] to the ambiguous non-human universe he believed Heisenberg's principle to imply, were its frame of reference not precisely specified. '*La distance* [. . .] *entre la théorie et l'expérience est telle*', says the imagined Einstein of *L'Idée Fixe*, '*– qu'il faut bien trouver des points de vue d'architecture*' (P II, 264), and to the charge of mysticism brought against his artist/scientist hero, Einstein's admirer replies 'Mais il s'agit ici d'un mysticisme à *terme* . . . Celui-ci est surveillé, limité; utilisé comme tel . . . la nature de l'esprit fournit ce que refuse la nature des choses' (P II, 265).

It seems possible that despite his growing lack of interest in the principle of 'objective' verification, and despite his lack of enthusiasm for the biology of his day, Valéry was nonetheless optimistic about the power of the scientist one day to 'know' life at least in the sense of being able to represent its properties to his own satisfaction.[2] 'La biologie comme le reste, va de surprise en surprise;', he writes, for example, 'car elle va, comme le reste, de moyen nouveau à moyen nouveau d'investigation. Il nous apparaît que nous ne pouvons songer à nous arrêter un moment sur cette pente fatale de découvertes, pour nous faire, tel jour, à telle heure, une idée bien établie de l'être vivant' (P I, 804).[3] Even here, there is no notion of transcendence, however. The words 'nous ne pouvons songer à nous arrêter', 'la pente fatale' and so on, suggest that Valéry is viewing such progress as but a further example of the inescapable classificatory activity of 'connaître': 'une *éducation fatale* [. . .] un ordre qui persiste et qui se réalise par tous les moyens' (iv, 98).

'*Understanding*' *life*

At the same time as Valéry removes the idea of mystery from the scientific study of life, then, he puts it back into the experience of existence itself, 'le mystère que quelque chose soit' (viii, 50). Life may be totally 'known', but it cannot be 'understood'. 'Comment conduire son esprit pour qu'il puisse connaître et comprendre la vie, puisqu'il y a antinomie entre ces deux réalités?', writes M. Bémol, introducing the two terms whose distinction is so important in Valéry's thought.[4]

What does the term 'comprendre' imply for Valéry? '*Comprendre*,

[1] Cf. Laurette, *Le Thème de l'Arbre*, 139. In Einstein's work Valéry found his intuitions into the nature of 'points de vue' strikingly confirmed (see Robinson, *L'Analyse de l'Esprit*, 41).

[2] Cf. F. E. Sutcliffe, 'Hegel et Valéry', *F.S.*, VI (1952) 55, n. 11 ('Valéry ne désespère pas de voir un jour expliquer scientifiquement le phénomène de la vie').

[3] Cf. P I, 357, 799, 910; P II, 218.

[4] 'La Méthode dans les Sciences selon Paul Valéry', *Biologica* (jan. 1951), 79.

c'est consumer [. . .]' (xxviii, 701), he notes, or, 'J'ai essayé, j'essaie, j'essaierai, j'aurai essayé de . . . comprendre – comprendre, trouver ce qui annule, ce qui Nous annule' (x, 436).[1] When compared with 'connaître', which may mean the slow piecing together, over a life-time, of knowledge which it may have taken the life-times of other individuals to prepare and which is still for ever changing and incomplete, 'comprendre' signifies in Valéry's personally re-experienced etymology the concentration into a single moment of the total capacity of the thinking and feeling self. To think and to feel is to be part of a ceaseless movement from disorder to order and back (see e.g. P I, 1172); to 'understand' would mean, therefore, to escape from such a cycle by the mental annulment of the self that remained to engender further movement. '[. . .] s'il en fût une *suprême en soi* et *par soi*', says Teste of such a total 'thought', 'nous pourrions la trouver par réflexion ou par hasard; et étant trouvée, devrions mourir. Ce serait pouvoir mourir d'une certaine pensée, seulement parce qu'elle n'a point de suivante' (P II, 37).

Like Teste, who has already been seen to embody the notion, Valéry values highly the power of the mind to distinguish between the 'possible' and 'impossible', even when that 'impossible' includes the notions to which its own attempted reorganisation of life gives rise. He distinguishes in this case, then, between on the one hand the experience of impatience or 'Caligulisme' (xxviii, 822), and on the other the impossibility of fulfilling the desire for total comprehension to which such impatience gives rise. Fulfilment of such a desire would destroy the conditions of life on which the total self depends for its experience in the first place, as M. Teste well knew. In this sense it seems true to suggest that a deep bond exists in Valéry's thought between the notion of 'incomprehensibility' and the preservation of life itself on the level of 'sensibilité'.[2] Not very long before his death in 1945 he wrote in his notes 'Plus fort que le vouloir vivre et que le pouvoir comprendre est donc ce sacré C[œur]' (xxix, 909). In this last extreme distinction between on the one hand the mysterious fact of physiological existence represented by the heart and on the other the differently orientated desires of the mind, Valéry movingly confirms the idea of a separation between the aims of nature and the aims of consciousness present throughout his thought. Even as he writes, it is his consciousness which still serves lucidly to detect the distinction and to convert it into constructive form, the basis of science and art.

This survey has given only an abstract outline of the interweaving of the themes of 'connaître' and 'le *ne pas comprendre*'. Just how important

[1] Quoted by N. Bastet, *Entretiens sur Paul Valéry*, 118. [2] See below, 61–2.

it was to Valéry is suggested by the fact that he has chosen to embody it poetically in the prose-poem *L'Ange*, of which he once noted with something of his usual 'affectation de formalisme'[1] that there was no preconceived subject, but only 'l'idée du seul cheminement, une manière de s'avancer étant le *but* vrai' (xxii, 716). Again, an early draft in the *Cahiers* (viii, 370–1) proves that the work is not a swansong without reference to Valéry's past intellectual quest, as has sometimes been supposed.[2] He wrote it in 1922 and retouched it near the end of his life. Using the image of the man and the fountain already familiar in the Narcisse poems, and grafting it on to another central image of his thought, that of the Angel,[3] Valéry evokes in bare impressionistic terms 'une manière d'ange', a man, a consciousness, 'une tristesse en forme d'homme', faced with his own mysterious humanity and incomprehensibly moved to tears:

> 'O mon étonnement, *disait-il*, Tête charmante et triste, il y a donc autre chose que la lumière?'
>
> *Et il s'interrogeait dans l'univers de sa substance spirituelle merveilleusement pure, où toutes les idées vivaient également distantes entre elles et de lui-même* [. . .]
>
> *Et pendant une éternité, il ne cessa de connaître et de ne pas comprendre.*
>
> (P I, 206)

'Dans [. . .] *l'Ange*', suggests M. Raymond, 'Valéry avoue que s'il croit se "connaître", il ne peut se "comprendre". L'unité globale, l'identité foncière du *moi* sont de l'ordre du mythe; elles sont toujours au-delà de toute pensée.'[4]

A deep emotion, sometimes expressed in tears, is undeniably at the centre of the relationship between consciousness and life for Valéry, then. 'Et c'est là, au sein même des ténèbres dans lesquelles se fondent et se confondent ce qui est de notre espèce', says Tityre in the *Dialogue de l'Arbre*, where the presence of this mystery is evoked with admiration and awe, '[. . .] que se trouve ce que j'ai nommé la *source des larmes*: L'INEFFABLE. Car, nos larmes, à mon avis, sont l'expression de notre impuissance à *exprimer*, c'est à dire à nous défaire par la parole de l'oppression de ce que nous sommes . . .' (P II, 183). In *L'Ange*, such tears are connected

1 J. Duchesne-Guillemin, 'Valéry au Miroir', *F.S.*, XX (1966), 350.

2 See, for example, N. Suckling, *Paul Valéry and the Civilized Mind* (O.U.P., 1954), 123, 198.

3 See below, 59.

4 *Paul Valéry et la Tentation de l'Esprit* (Neuchâtel, La Baconnière, 1964 (1946)), 75.

with a form of anguished solitude.[1] This is not always the case, however. Not only anguish, but surprise and the gradual transmutation of surprise into relief and peacefulness are all present in the passage of *La Jeune Parque* devoted to the slow progress of the tear:[2]

> Je n'implorerai plus que tes faibles clartés,
> Longtemps sur mon visage envieuse de fondre,
> Très imminente larme, et seule à me répondre,
> [. . . . .]
> Tu me portes du cœur cette goutte contrainte,
> Cette distraction de mon suc précieux
> Qui vient sacrifier mes ombres sur mes yeux,
> Tendre libation de l'arrière-pensée!
> [. . . . .]
> Dans le temps que je vis, les lenteurs que tu fais
> M'étouffent . . . Je me tais, buvant ta marche sûre . . .
> – Qui t'appelle au secours de ma jeune blessure?
>
> (P I, 104)

The tear introduces into an intellectual dilemma the vital experience of 'lenteur', and the conflict between 'être' and 'connaître' is temporarily resolved.

One of the essential characteristics of Valéry's art is its power to orchestrate the many different tonal reactions that can be produced by a single experience. Hidden in the complex reactions of the Parque can be detected the germ of a reaction to 'non-comprehension' quite different from the anguish symbolised in *L'Ange*.[3] It is a reaction which Valéry symbolises separately in the figures of Madame Teste and of Lust. 'Il y a une belle partie de l'âme qui peut jouir sans comprendre' (P II, 26), says

[1] Even here, there is an implicit link with aesthetic experience and the notion of joy. In words very similar to those of *L'Ange* ('*une Tristesse en forme d'Homme qui ne se trouvait pas sa cause dans le ciel clair*' (P II, 205)), Valéry refers to a work of art, such as the music of Bach, as soliciting 'les larmes et la joie les plus difficiles, celles qui se cherchent *une cause et qui ne la trouvent point dans l'expérience de la vie . . .*' (P I, 676). Cf. '*Larmes de divers ordres*' (P II, 339).

[2] Cf. 'Une larme qui vient de ton sang au moment de ta peine [. . .] étonne l'esprit qui ne peut concevoir la cause et la génération de cette transmutation . . ./Car le propre de l'esprit est d'ignorer de la vie tout ce qui lui semble inutile à son opération' (P I, 332). See also O. Nadal, 'Les "Larmes de l'esprit" dans la Jeune Parque', *Mercure de France* (oct. 1957).

[3] Valéry notes Degas' description of him as 'Ange' (xviii, 860). The theme of 'Ange/Bête' will be discussed later. See below, 58–9.

Madame Teste as she tries to summarise her relationship with Teste (who is perhaps her equivalent of the mysteries the true thinker finds in himself), and Lust says to Faust rather similarly: 'Mais je n'ai pas besoin de comprendre. [. . .] Mais c'est votre voix qui se fait suivre, comme une musique. Elle me porte . . . tout auprès des larmes . . .' (P II, 321).

Madame Teste and Lust obviously represent pure spontaneous feeling, and as such they offer to Teste and to Faust an alternative reality to that of reflective consciousness. The reactions of Teste and Faust to this alternative are very different, however. To Teste, the alternative is a temptation, if not to be entirely overcome by an act of will, then at least to be minimised. Madame Teste is accordingly relegated to the status of a piece of property, the conventional wife to be used when called upon. To Faust, the alternative presented by Lust is a positive challenge. Where Teste had used the unknown as a mere platform for building up total self-knowledge ('Maintenant je me sais par cœur. Le cœur aussi' (P II, 24); 'Mon mouvement va de ma faiblesse à ma force' (P II, 40)), Faust with all his riches of knowledge and experience allows himself to be moved in the form of tenderness by what is still unknown ('ce qu'il y a de plus précieux dans la vie [. . .] c'est précisément ce qui [. . .] se trouve ou se retrouve dans la présence et la correspondance, ou dans l'échange inouï, muet, de ce que je ne sais pas en moi, ni de moi, contre ce que je ne sais pas en toi, ni de toi' (P II, 1412); 'Quoi de plus fort que cette faiblesse qui nous dérobe à toutes forces [. . .]' (P II, 1412)). In Faust's relationship with Lust, the very 'comprendre' previously seen to mean only an impossible ambition with self-destructive implications, is given a positive though still elusive existence in the words of Faust: 'Qui me comprendra si tu ne me comprends pas!' (P II, 1412).[1] That such an experience can be given even relative formulation can be seen, in terms of the deep poetic logic of the play, as Faust's reward for fully accepting the 'incomprehensibility' of life in the previous sense.

'Prends garde! Celui qui parle dans ton cœur n'en sait pas plus que toi' (P I, 332), says the inner voice which Valéry expresses in *Avec Soi Seul*, a fragment included in *Mélange*. In the context of his thought as a whole, this need not be interpreted as the voice of experience rejecting the kind of values achieved by Faust in his relationship with Lust. By making Lust herself, not Faust, symbolise the experience of 'ne pas comprendre', Valéry is surely implying that it is the conscious recognition of this experience by Faust that is of value, not the experience in itself. This is supported by many abstract comments elsewhere such as

[1] See chapter 3, 59, 61.

'Se sentir ne pas comprendre [. . .] est précieux [. . .]' (xviii, 908), 'Du Non comprendre – grand sujet' (xvii, 524) or 'Le *ne pas comprendre*, bien reconnu, comme re-dessiné, doit engendrer une activité et une lucidité, exactement *comme une trouvaille*' (P II, 1527); 'Si tu ne comprends pas quelque chose, arrête-toi et regarde toi ne pas comprendre' (xxix, 247).

This does not mean that Valéry attempts to preserve or express only those aspects of the raw material of experience which have been filtered by the conscious mind into a mould of its own. On the contrary. One of the most characteristic of his ambitions as an artist seems to have been to express those elements of experience where the mind is surprised by its own powers of perception, teased by the overpowering sense of the richness and complexity of a reality always changing and always beyond its grasp. It is to this area of expression that some of his finest prose-poems belong, poems where the quality of some fleeting sensation is paradoxically proposed to the intellect as holding the main source of its wealth. There is the fragment *A la Vie* of the selection *Poésie Brute*, for example:

Amère comme tu sais l'être – Ô Vie
Amère et douce comme tu sais l'être!
Amère et douce et lourde comme tu sais l'être, Ô Vie
Amère et douce et lourde et leste et longue et brève
comme tu sais l'être, Ô Vie.
Comme il n'y a que des larmes qui
Sachent juger, équivaloir, payer tels instants beaux,
Il n'y a qu'un rire qui puisse à tes maux bien répondre.

(P I, 354)

Such apostrophes[1] make use of the word 'Vie' in quite a different sense than do the scathing aphorisms in which Valéry rails against some blind process outside the filtering mechanisms of human reaction.[2]

To conclude, it seems possible to suggest that one of the finest paradoxes to emerge from Valéry's writings, and the one which his particular techniques will be seen the most effectively to explore, is that the intellect may be nourished by experiences wider than itself. 'Penser *biotiquement*'

[1] Cf. 'Ô Vie,/Plus je pense à toi, VIE,/Moins tu te rends à la pensée . . .' (P I, 201); 'Ô vie, Ô mal te voici' (xxiv, 823); 'Ô vie, chose partagée entre ces milliards de participants' (xviii, 27). The same form occurs in the prose-poem 'Accueil du Jour', *La Revue de France* (1 jan. 1932).

[2] E.g. ' "Vie" – vomissement' (xvi, 383); P. Laurette cites the ironic proposal to replace the word '*Vie*' by 'un terme analogue à *Moisissure*' (xxviii, 155) (*Le Thème de l'Arbre*, 134).

(xxvi, 693) was one of Valéry's main aims, notes P. Laurette.[1] Retaining all his life the conviction that the intellect cannot 'know' the processes of its own mental life to the point of controlling them – a conviction seen to be reflected in his constant stress on the purely partial nature of scientific knowledge, however admirable – Valéry's exploration of the complex interrelation of 'être' and 'connaître' suggests nonetheless his belief in a kind of vital awareness capable of noting the rhythms of its own existence and of assuring some form of human continuity in the chaos of affective life. It is because of the powerful nature of this form of awareness and not because of any failure to sustain the intellectual values at the heart of his thought that Valéry can write so often of mystery and surprise as being amongst the most precious and necessary qualities of human life.[2] Through them the mind may be said to introduce an opening of its own in the closed universe of the natural world. 'C'est ce que je porte d'inconnu à moi-même qui me fait moi [...]', says Teste himself, 'Les lacunes sont ma base de départ' (P II, 40).

1 *Le Thème de l'Arbre*, 136.

2 E.g. 'Quoi de plus fécond que l'imprévu pour la pensée' (P II, 1523); 'Surprise – Fait capital' (xxiv, 867); 'Le plaisir intellectuel consiste *réellement* à se surpasser, à s'étonner soi-même' (v, 652); 'J'attends de moi d'heureuses surprises. *Veni Creator Spiritus*. O moi, étonne, émerveille, comble moi!' (xxiv, 283); 'Mystère, mystère/Qu'es-tu devenu?' (xxiii, 260).

3 Consciousness, emotion & the nature of love

Emotion

The previous chapter on the distinction in Valéry's thought between 'knowing' life in the scientific sense and 'understanding' it in an absolute sense has served to introduce his treatment of the theme of uncontrollable feeling ('affectivité') and emotion in individual experience. Here too the question arises, how far Valéry was prepared to see consciousness as a modificatory agent in nature. Is it really true as J. Hytier comments, that he 'ne semble pas s'être posé le problème d'une rectification des sentiments',[1] or even, as Judith Robinson suggests, that Valéry seems to have left aside in favour of his rich expression of the different aspects of consciousness,[2] 'toute la gamme des sentiments complexes, délicats, pleins de nuances qui se mêlent au fonctionnement le plus élevé de l'intellect, et qui en sont même inséparables'?[3]

'Quant à moi, *jusqu'au bout* fut mon désir', Valéry wrote looking back on his life, '1° en fait d'intellect [. . .] 2° en fait d'affectivité: sensibilités (a) sensorielles. (b) Amour [. . .]' (xxix, 765). That the theme of 'affectivité' should have been as central to his thinking as that of the intellect should present no paradox. Valéry tried, as he so often admitted, to study the workings of the mind in its totality, to make for himself 'une idée plus simple et aussi utilisable que possible de l'être vivant'.[4] Indeed, his imaginative preference for modes of expression offering the maximum power of synthesis led him to conceive of 'le fonctionnement d'ensemble'[5]

[1] *La Poétique de Valéry* (Paris, Armand Colin, 1953), 43.

[2] *L'Analyse de l'Esprit dans les Cahiers de Valéry* (Paris, Corti, 1963), 156.

[3] Ibid., 163.

[4] Quoted by W. N. Ince, *The Poetic Theory of Paul Valéry* (Leicester U.P., 1961), 46 (see also P. Chardon, *Paul Valéry et la Médecine* (Paris, Édns. Armand Fleury, 1930), 23–4).

[5] Ibid., 35.

of a human being in terms of what might be called a series of relational affinities. 'Ce que je voudrais me représenter', he continues,

> c'est le mécanisme à notre échelle, et en particulier les actions réciproques du système nerveux, du système musculaire, des glandes et de leurs sécrétions, dans leurs rapports immédiats avec les variations qui se produisent dans le système nerveux. C'est le *mot-à-mot* de la vie, la génération des instants successifs, en quelque sorte, le domaine dans lequel nos passions, nos émotions, toutes les transformations de notre vie perçue, se passent.[1]

When Valéry writes of his interest in the order of the intellect on one hand and in that of 'affectivité: sensibilités' on the other, he is referring, then, not so much to a simple division between two different faculties, as to a division of interest between on the one hand the organisational activities of the intellect, and on the other the network of 'affective' or involuntary experience to which the intellect itself belongs. 'Sensibilité', as W. N. Ince points out, is Valéry's term for 'the composite internal state of mind and body'.[2] It is in accordance with this kind of definition that he can write without exaggeration 'Je suis celui qui n'oppose jamais, qui ne sait pas opposer, l'intelligence à la sensibilité' (P I, 1403) or 'Opposer "l'intelligence" à la "sensibilité" est réellement comique' (v, 584).

Valéry's description of the '1892' crisis and all it came to stand for has already suggested that he felt there were strong rhythms or cycles at work in experience, rhythms which consciousness might perceive but be powerless to avoid.[3] Indeed he was seen to refer to Teste as representing that part of the mind which 'assiste [. . .] avec une douleur toute contraire à son essence, à l'impuissant effort de sa volonté de témoin contre l'infernale puissance des Corps^{C} et du Monde^{M}, et surtout des réactions intestines de l'Esprit^{E}' (xxiii, 302). Even the briefest view of Valéry's references to strong uncontrollable experiences such as sickness, anger, fear or indeed any violent emotion[4] seem to show a scorn, anguish or resentment proportionate to the degree of awareness involved. '[. . .] plus l'esprit est

[1] Ibid., 46. [2] Ibid., 38. [3] See above, 5–6.

[4] E.g. 'Se sentir rougir, s'entendre rugir, se trouver fauché par une image ou porté à l'extrême de l'agitation, quels tableaux insoutenables à la conscience!' (P I, 344); 'Considérer ses émotions comme sottises [. . .]', says Teste, '. . . Quelque chose en nous, ou en moi, se révolte contre la puissance inventive de l'âme sur l'esprit' (P II, 70). 'Cough, mépris' (vii, 770), Valéry writes (often using a foreign word when something he feels humiliating is involved. Cf. 'my heart' (xxix, 909)). Teste is made to cough just before he asks 'Que peut un homme?' (P II, 23).

complexe, moins il accepte que son homme soit ému [. . .]' (P I, 344), he writes. From this vision of a basic resistance on the part of consciousness itself to emotive or physiological disturbance, there is still an extremely long way to go, however, before Valéry could be said not to have considered the possibility of 'une rectification des sentiments' in the sense of an alignment with the inevitable on the part of the intelligence.[1] Because of the particular 'focus' involved in Valéry's comments on the most disruptive effects of 'affectivité' (a focus on the actual sensation of consciousness itself, 'un refus indéfini d'être quoi que ce soit' (P I, 1225)),[2] some of the most important qualities present in his view of intellectual experience are deliberately played down (the power to predict or remember, for example, or the power to make allowance for changeability).[3]

Criticism is partly based, in the case of Judith Robinson's comments, on the suggestion that a personal approach to emotion in terms of a purely negative disturbance prejudices Valéry's view of the mind as a whole.[4] It is true that he draws frequent analogies between emotive disturbance and the increase of entropy or disorder in a machine.[5] Yet do these thermodynamic analogies point to a purely negative note where his whole view of emotion is concerned? It is perhaps necessary to enquire what rôle he accorded to disturbance itself, not simply from a functional point of view but from the point of view of the mind's total creative capacity.[6] Might it not be the case that, far from reinforcing the traditional opposition between reason and emotion,[7] Valéry's vision of the power of emotion to reverberate throughout the whole sensibility into consciousness itself, is the guarantee of a unity of mental experience which enables consciousness to reverberate in the reverse sense, and to lead to a whole

1 J. Hytier continues his comment: 'Il semble bien que le rôle de l'intelligence dans la vie affective doive consister dans un effort pour incliner les sentiments dans un sens acceptable aux yeux de la raison et non dans une vaine tentative de mutilation ou d'extirpation' (*La Poétique de Valéry*, 43).

2 See above, 7, 10.

3 Cf. 'Mais n'est-ce point là la recherche de M. Teste: se retirer du moi – du moi ordinaire en s'essayant constamment à diminuer, à combattre, à compenser l'inégalité, l'anisotropie de la conscience?' (P II, 66).

4 *L'Analyse de l'Esprit*, 156.

5 Quoted by Judith Robinson, ibid., 156.

6 Valéry compares the vital disorder or 'inégalité' introduced by 'sensibilité' to the 'différence thermique' or non-equilibrium required by a machine (e.g. P II, 222; XV, 569).

7 Judith Robinson, for example, suggests that 'On est surpris et déçu de voir cet ennemi déclaré des catégories traditionnelles maintenir en la renforçant une des plus vieilles de toutes les oppositions: l'opposition entre l'émotion et la raison' (*L'Analyse de l'Esprit*, 156).

range of subtle feelings in which intellect and emotion are inextricably linked? 'Il y a un réflexe intense de vomissement de sa condition d'homme', Valéry once wrote of this same creative tendency of consciousness to react intensely and passionately[1] against the passivity otherwise imposed by uncontrollable feelings, 'Chose merveilleuse, l'instinct dit de conservation (de la vie) est une des manifestations de cette puissance car il répond à la menace de la mort, il repousse ainsi cette condition de la vie – qui est la mort. "Je ne veux pas être *homme*"' (xviii, 191).[2] Use of 'humain' in a disparaging sense is simply one of the elements in Valéry's attempt to isolate the 'inhumain' or 'surhumain' of which man is capable (P I, 1485), in other words man's *specifically* human, individual capacities such as language, art, science and perhaps the kind of emotion Valéry refers to as belonging to 'l'ordre de l'esprit' rather than to 'l'ordre du "cœur"'.[3] 'Il ne faut pas confondre produits de l'esprit avec la production des œuvres de l'esprit',[4] he characteristically suggests.

The theme of continuity between emotive disturbance and intellectual creativity is perhaps nowhere more pronounced than in *La Pythie*. Unlike the protagonist in *Le Cimetière Marin* who speaks from a moment of perfect mental equilibrium from which the 'morne moitié' or inevitable shadow inseparable from the light of consciousness can be seen as purely potential, the Pythia's inner monologue is reported during the actual rupture of that equilibrium by violent emotion, at the very moment when 'l'ouragan des songes entre/Au même ciel qui fut si beau!' (P I, 133). Particularly in the first part of the poem where she undergoes the illusion that her consciousness has been invaded by a force alien to her whole being, Valéry's images are at their most stark and violent. Emotive, sexual and general psycho-physiological implications proliferate simultaneously around the simple structure of the myth of possession by the god.

1 Cf. 'Le plus fort de mes sentiments est la haine même de mes sentiments' (iv, 450); 'Au fond, je suis en proie au mépris de mes sentiments, qui sont malheureusement très vifs et très cruels en moi' (viii, 654). It is this critical self-awareness that enables Valéry to make genuine comments on human nature on the basis of personal experience.

2 Cf. 'L'*homo* me fait vomir' (*Correspondance A. Gide–P. Valéry* (Paris, Gallimard, 1955), 515). The phrase 'l'humain trop humain' sometimes used by Valéry is obviously an echo of Nietzsche's 'menschlich allzu menschlich'. Parallels and contrasts can be found in E. Gaède's *Nietzsche et Valéry* (Essai sur la comédie de l'esprit) (Paris, Gallimard, 1962).

3 Lettre/Préface to M. C. Ghyka's *Le Nombre d'Or*, I (Paris, Édn. de la N.R.F., 1931).

4 *Cours de Poétique*, leçon 4 (Samedi 18 déc. 1937), *Yggdrasill*, 2 ème année (25 jan. 1938), 155.

Although the Pythia appears locked in on herself like the 'ouroboros' or snake biting its own tail,[1] even this experience contains the seeds of the vital movement of memory and reflection already seen at work in the experience of the Parque at a different stage. 'La Pythie tout entière se voit reptile', suggests Monique Maka-de Shepper, 'mais sa pensée la sauve de sa propre "morsure". Grâce à la même image différemment orchestrée, "morsure" et "fumée" d'un côté, "vipère" et "mémoire" de l'autre, le poète fait apparaître la Pythie luttant contre le dieu d'abord, ensuite se souvenant de cette "forme préférée" qui fut la sienne avant le cruel "don des écumes".'[2] By means of the inner monologue technique this important movement towards self-awareness leads to the point where the Pythia feels the imminent unification of her 'deux natures' and begins to resolve her conflict in language. The triumphant but still ironically separate proclamation at the end of the poem seems to confirm the obscurely creative nature of the instincts unleashed by emotional disturbance and finally ordered into 'transcendental' form:

> Honneur des Hommes, Saint LANGAGE,
> Discours prophétique et paré,
> Belles chaînes en qui s'engage
> Le dieu dans la chair égaré,
> Illumination, largesse!
> Voici parler une Sagesse
> Et sonner cette auguste Voix
> Qui se connaît quand elle sonne
> N'être plus la voix de personne
> Tant que des ondes et des bois!
>
> (P I, 136)

This strangely disturbing, yet exhilarating poem confirms more than any abstract statement that the 'Apollonian' orientation of Valéry's thought is never mere rationalism. Like the existence of Dionysus in Greek thought, it might be said to symbolise the fact that he is 'deeply and imaginatively aware of the power, the wonder, and the peril of the Irrational'.[3]

[1] Valéry often used this image or the image of two snakes interlaced with each other as the symbol of 'sensibilité'. A study of Valéry's 'gnostic' interests has been made by J. M. Cocking, 'Towards *Ébauche d'un Serpent:* Valéry and Ouroboros', *A.J.F.S.*, VI (1969), 187–215.

[2] *Le Thème de la Pythie chez Paul Valéry* (Paris, Soc. d'Édn. 'Les Belles Lettres', 1969), 90.

[3] E. R. Dodds, *The Greeks and the Irrational* (University of California Press, 1963), 254.

'Mais amour n'est rien; ni *rien n'est rien* sans la résonance et toute-puissance "irrationnelle" du système caché de la vie neuro-viscéralé' (xvi, 506), Valéry even wrote. With its insight into the deep unity of emotive and intellectual experience, *La Pythie* forcefully contributes to his exploration of the essentially ambiguous, mobile relationship between consciousness and the 'natural' self.[1] It is a relationship which can now be traced through the theme of love from the crudest levels of 'affective' experience up to the highest levels of emotion, for it is simply not true to say that Valéry leaves out of account the range of complex feelings inseparable from the intellect itself.[2]

Love

One of the greatest contributions to literature hidden in the *Cahiers*[3] could certainly be called 'de l'Amour'. Brief prose-poems,[4] epigrams,[5] analytical fragments, the 'Dramatis personae' of a 'drame de l'amour' (xxix, 774):[6] all these indicate that the theme haunted Valéry throughout his life. Growing in intensity according to fluctuations of personal experience, it seems nonetheless to have been constantly present in some form. The reason is clearly that love relates to the elusive continuity between sensory, affective and intellectual experience that Valéry's mind needed so urgently to capture and express. It is an experience which he considered to offer the bridge between 'la vie nécessaire (ou animal simple) et la vie intellectuelle ou inutile' (xxix, 92); 'le retour ou le rattachement à une condition d'être-vivant, – le rappel du prix de cette condition – le consentement au réel, au trouble, à l'énergie donnée par une

1 Cf. 'Amour, peut-être, ou de moi-même haine?' (*Le Cimetière Marin* [P I, 151]) and 'inépuisable Moi! . . .' (*Fragments du Narcisse* [P I, 126]).

2 See p. 48, n. 3.

3 Suggestions on the unity of the *Cahiers* can be found in J. Duchesne-Guillemin's 'Valéry au Miroir', *F.S.*, xx (1966), 348 and Judith Robinson's 'L'Ordre Interne des Cahiers de Valéry', *Entretiens sur Paul Valéry*, 255–81.

4 E.g. i, 30 (see below, 79).

5 E.g. 'L'Amour est une éducation vicieuse du syst[ème] nerveux' (xiv, 540); 'Il n'y a pas d'amour durable à deux têtes [. . .]' (xxiv, 364); 'Amour n'est rien sans l'esprit. Ici commencent les difficultés' (xii, 718).

6 E.g. the dialogue of Stratonice, Antiochus and Érasistrate (xv, 373; xvi, 165, 202; xvii, 906; xx, 714). See the suggestion made by Lucienne J. Cain, *Trois Essais sur Paul Valéry* (Paris, Gallimard, 1958), 191, and developed by P.-O. Walzer in 'Valéry: Deux Essais sur l'Amour: Béatrice et Stratonice', *R.H.L.F.*, LXVIII (1968), 66–86. E.g. also the projected 'drame' of Orpheus and Eurydice (viii, 460, 464). See the details given by W. Stewart in 'Le Thème d'Orphée chez Valéry', *Entretiens sur Paul Valéry*, 169.

source extérieure' (xiv, 268), or even 'la clef qui ouvre pour moi le moi' (x, 336). Valéry's own question 'Quelle place donner à l'amour dans l'esprit?' (x, 89) is therefore of great relevance to this study as a whole.

'Le combat de l'amour avec une Intelligence est un "sujet" merveilleux' (xvi, 194): the first time that the theme of love enters the *Cahiers* it is in the form of 'l'amour passion',[1] which Valéry undoubtedly saw at the time as a combat between the intellect and the rest of the 'sensibilité', even between consciousness and the 'secondary' self. It was from this experience that he considers to have grown the whole 'method' of defensive self-awareness already discussed: 'Toute ma "philosophie" est née des efforts et réactions extrêmes qu'excitèrent en moi de 92 à 94, comme défenses désespérées, l'amour insensé pour cette dame de R[2] que je n'ai jamais connue que des yeux' (xxii, 842). Passion represents the involuntary, emphasising the purely observational power of consciousness as a result. Yet this 'negative' experience of love threw into relief Valéry's belief that consciousness is part of a finite system open to understanding through awareness. It is in the light of this same discovery that he begins to express the possibilities opened to the intelligence by the work of art.

One of the first 'levels' on which to approach Valéry's writings on the subject could once more be that of linguistic criticism. The word 'Amour' introduces a vague concept dangerously 'creative' in its own right. It tends to whip up experience through a second-hand view of the world. Valéry's notes are full of comments such as: 'La passion de l'amour est la plus absurde. C'est une fabrication littéraire et ridicule' (ii, 559); 'L'Amour exactement institution d'une "religion"' (vii, 858); or, 'Le mot "Amour", il m'est tout simplement odieux [. . .] *il rend semblables*. Je n'ai jamais pu supporter l'impression de répéter un refrain que tous ont fredonné' (P II, 433). Not only the abstract concept is the butt of these criticisms. Many of them are imperceptibly linked with a kind of Testian scorn for the fact that, however unique it feels itself, the 'Moi' must inevitably discover in the experience what it shares with the rest of humanity.

1 Some of the fluctuations of his attitude are traced by J. Duchesne-Guillemin, *F.S.*, XX (1966), 360–1. See also P.-O. Walzer, 'Introduction à l'Érotique Valéryenne', *C.A.I.E.F.*, XVII (1965), 217–29.

2 Cf. 'B', 'Bice' or 'Béatrice'; and 'N.R.' or 'Néère'. For links between these signs and biography see Duchesne-Guillemin, *Études pour un Paul Valéry*, 30–3, 205 and 'Paul Valéry et l'Italie', *M.L.R.*, LXII (1967), 49. Apart from the sign 'Mme de R' or 'Rov' which dates from the 1890s, the second sign appears after 1921 and the last nearer the end of Valéry's life.

'*Aimer* c'est *imiter*' (xvii, 296; P I, 315); 'AMOUR! éternel sculpteur du même groupe' (P I, 317).

When he attacks the 'literary' treatment of love, Valéry is obviously choosing to overlook that Flaubert, Constant, Stendhal and others have stylised in literature itself the very same discrepancy between general concept and individual experience which he is at pains to preserve for different treatment. At the same time, the terms of his attack serve to suggest the form that this different treatment might take. 'L'amour peut être étudié plus profondément [. . .]' (i, 445), he suggests, or, 'Peindre l'amour. On le peut, soit par tableaux, soit par les sentiments; et c'est ce qu'ont fait les auteurs./Mais au lieu de le peindre il serait plus profond d'essayer de fixer ce qui en fait la *magie*, l'apparence "infinie" et qui ne consiste pas du tout dans la volupté quoi qu'elle y joue [. . .] un rôle essentiel [. . .]' (xiv, 393). I shall suggest that Valéry's particular contribution to the 'literature' of love lies in the region of what he calls 'l'intellect [la conscience] de l'amour' (i, 310), his expression of the attempted fusion of 'Érôs et Psyché – ou Noûs' (xix, 668).

'Mon sens naturel de la physique humaine' (v, 806), he once noted, and, 'Ce paradoxe vivant, le mien, de subir une espèce de poète en somme, en moi, et de posséder à un degré singulier le sentiment du fonctionnement' (v, 131). From countless jottings in the *Cahiers* it is clear that the physical aspect of the love theme provides a source of constant meditation: meditation on the sexual act as a complex cycle of energy; meditation on the interconnections of sensory and psychological experience in general; meditation on the rôle of consciousness in behaviour where it is not only an autonomous perceiver but also the centre of a dynamic state. Thus the rubric 'Érôs' may head such perceptions as 'Cependant l'acte même est à mes yeux le type plus digne d'observation, peut-être l'acte le plus complet qui soit, le modèle qui comprend, assemble, exige la co-ordination la plus générale et réalise un cycle de O à O bien net – avec psychie, sens, muscles, glandes, seuils, disruption – rôle et *localisation* de la conscience' (xx, 707);[1] 'devenir demande au lieu de demeurer réponse, et devenir tel pour avoir franchi le seuil qui sépare la vie mentale de la vie organique' (ix, 133), or 'Étrangeté de l'acte' (xxiv, 239) (an echo of the same sense of strangeness that the Narcisse of the poem in *Charmes* is made to feel before the contorted movements of pairs of lovers separate

[1] Cf. 'C'est pourquoi l'action d'Erôs est si utile à méditer. Elle est le type le plus complet de fonctionnement vital total [. . .] L'invention de l'âme est une conséquence de la méconnaissance du corps [. . .]' (xxviii, 28). See also xx, 707; xxii, 318; xxiv, 186, 192, 352. The 'Érôs énergumène' of Faust (P II, 282) appears in the *Cahiers*, xxiv, 185.

from himself (P I, 127)). Above all, Valéry seems to have been intrigued by the possible confirmation offered by the idea of sexual activity that the capacity of the self for detached awareness may depend on a set of conditions not always present in experience: '– et l'esprit (E) s'effaçant sous la charge et la foudre du MOI qui cesse, un instant, de s'opposer et de refuser, mais qui se confond dans un éclair de temps à je ne sais quoi d'extrême' (xxii, 696).

One of the most interesting features of these meditations on 'l'acte d'Erôs', then, is the frequency with which Valéry associates it analogically with the same patterns of extremism and limitation, mobility and equilibrium, intermittence and renewal that make up his idea of a 'cycle fermé' in 'l'esprit'. 'Sexualité', he notes, for instance, '[. . .] je pense aussitôt, par divagation qui m'est propre et familière, à transposer. Je songe à l'esprit' (xviii, 545), or he may suggest in an inverse sense: '[. . .] ne trouvez-vous pas que l'acte lui-même est à la fois simple et bien complexe? C'est à lui que je n'aurais jamais dû cesser de penser, dans mon cours du Collège sur la poétique'.[1]

One of the most fruitful consequences of this 'divagation par analogie' is the range of 'correspondances' by which it allows Valéry to deepen his poetic evocation of a theme without needing to have recourse to abstract comparison: in *La Pythie*, where the surface theme is consciousness, for example, or in *Les Pas* where it is love. In *L'Âme et la Danse* the flame-like energy of the dancer, 'l'acte pur des métamorphoses' (P II, 165), seems to symbolise simultaneously, because it has found their common denominator, the patterns in time of consciousness, art and physical desire.[2] It is by analogy with the dance that Valéry sometimes refers back in turn to 'l'acte d'Erôs', 'une danse – sacrée, certes, – qui tend à exhausser *quelque chose vers* un certain *point* – analogue à un *cri* [. . .] rupture au seuil' (xxix, 456). Thus it is no mere coincidence that Madame Teste describes her husband's sexuality (after the humorous passage where she admits to feeling like the prey of an eagle) in much the same imagery that denotes the semi-mystical side of his intellectual quest: 'Ce n'était pas trop de toute l'énergie de tout un grand corps pour soutenir devant l'esprit l'instant de diamant qui est à la fois l'idée, la Chose, et le

1 Reported in *Propos Familiers* (Paris, Grasset, 1957), 120. Cf. 'une sorte de partition avec ses portées et simultanéités. Une portée sensorielle, une physique, une actionnelle, une énergétique, une chimique. Et tenir compte du temps vivant' (xxii, 696). This is the same kind of analysis Valéry thought it necessary to apply to 'l'esprit'.

2 Cf. 'Amour – ballet' (xvi, 444); 'Athikté – mêlée à un rite phallique' (xix, 668). 'Elle était donc l'être même de l'amour', says Phèdre of Athikté (P II, 164).

seuil et la fin' (P II, 30). Consciousness, like the act of love, is evoked as a ceaseless movement towards the limits of its own threshold with the natural world.

It is not only through analogies born on the level of functional comparison that Valéry links 'Érôs' and 'Psyché'. 'L'amour dans la perfection de son acte est le drame de l'accomplissement de la connaissance' (XXIX, 575), he once wrote.[1] One of the richest areas of his analysis of love can be approached through the theme of what he calls 'l'amour comme moyen': love as the means of uniting the whole of one's intellectual, emotive and sensory resources in direct experience:

> Le grand dessein est de donner un sens nouveau à ce qui est Amour, ou œuvre. Alors l'amour est une œuvre. L'œuvre est acte d'amour.
>
> Ceci entendu au *sens le plus précis*. Je m'entends. L'Amour devenant une œuvre. Ceci veut dire que ce qui est généralement le but, la cime, la victoire sur la volonté, d'une part; sur le seuil des sensibilités, de l'autre part – n'est alors qu'un moyen – devient signes, indication – comme une forme dont le sens dérobé au vulgaire, n'est soupçonné que des plus rares – ceux qui acquièrent *le droit de ne vivre qu'une fois*.
>
> (XXVII, 416–17)

'*Pousser l'amour* où il n'a jamais été' (XXIX, 804), Valéry wrote near the end of his life:

> Je puis dire et prononcer ceci sur moi-même que j'ai fait ce que j'ai pu pour que le thème monotone de *l'amour* reparaisse à *l'octave supérieure*. C'est le même thème et ce n'est pas du tout le même et j'ai fait ce que j'ai pu pour que l'autre thème, le thème de l'intellect se dégageât de ses emplois 'utiles' et se mariât avec le premier. Tout ceci avec toutes les faiblesses, erreurs, fautes et lacunes que l'on voudra. Mais, depuis 50 ans, je *tombe* vers le moi-même, *mon poids*. Vers mon plus haut,
>
> (XXVII, 41–7)

and:

> Cependant c'est une grande pensée que d'avoir voulu inventer un amour de degré supérieur, un amour se dégageant de l'amour

[1] Cf. 'Il faudrait dans *Lust* un accès dans F[aust] qui opérât la transformation [. . .] de l'état Érôs à l'état Noûs [. . .]' (XXIV, 16). See Duchesne-Guillemin, *Études pour un Paul Valéry*, 211. For a possible illustration of this process see above, 54.

ordinaire comme celui-ci s'est dégagé de la fonction de reproduction. Ainsi la pensée et ses œuvres inutiles se sont dégagées de la pensée et des actions appliquées, etc.

(xxiv, 375)

Comments like these suggest that 'l'amour à l'octave supérieure' was Valéry's way of referring to a yet further extension in the conscious mind of the kind of bifurcation of the purely 'human' away from purely 'natural' ends which already fascinated him on the physical level: 'Rien plus riche [. . .] à méditer que le processus à double voie: Amour/ Reproduction' (xxiii, 19).[1] It was as if he envisaged the complex relationship between the 'sensibilités' of two human beings as being potentially capable of creating a degree of conscious awareness even higher than that of one.[2]

In whatever terms conceived – whether in terms of sensory awareness as opposed to purely reproductive activity or in terms of the complex experience of love as a whole – it is important to see that Valéry's notion of a bifurcation of the purely 'human' away from the purely 'natural' (a notion at the heart of his meditations on aesthetic experience as well as on love) in no way involves the 'mystical' consequences its vocabulary sometimes seems to imply.[3] On the contrary, its sole components are to be re-organisations of physical and emotional experience in the fully conscious mind. 'Une voie "sublime" – sans issue. . .?', he notes under 'Lust IV', of the mind's desire to procreate in its own way, 'Au lieu du *faire un enfant* – cela veut faire . . . ce qui n'a jamais été, – un état de choix, qui s'oppose au cycle vital, et qui soit le chant, l'hymne de la sensibilité célébrant, accomplissant le thème "*une fois pour toutes*" – "*au dessus de tout!*"' (xxvi, 153).[4] 'Les amants devaient être des êtres assez faits l'un pour l'autre pour pouvoir s'abandonner ensemble à la fonction qui éloigne un instant le caractère impur d'être humain, fait du vivant une bête et un dieu, sensation plus extase, non plus

1 'Quelle certitude, quel seuil, quelle fin (et non quel plaisir –) cherche le – plaisir? – Plus avant que la volupté, plus follement que délicieusement, plus durement que suavement, plus comme essai, plus comme offrande au désespoir que comme œuvre de jouissance, se manifeste à l'intellect l'acte d'amour' (x, 437).

2 E.g. vii, 830; xi, 551.

3 E.g. xxi, 773; xv, 852 (see below, 234, 255).

4 Compare with the prose-poem *L'Unique*: 'Mais tandis que le moment même de l'esprit aspire à ce qui lui semble sans exemple, et que j'espère en des états exceptionnels, chaque battement de mon cœur redit [. . .] *que la chose la plus importante est celle qui se répète le plus*' (*Petits Poèmes Abstraits, Revue de France* [1 jan. 1932]).

pensée' (vii, 868), Valéry once wrote. The idea of a potential fusion of 'Érôs' and 'Psyché' is one of the most rewarding Valéryan twists to the Pascalian theme 'ni Ange ni Bête' (P I, 199) which runs throughout his work. 'Mais les Anges eux-mêmes, les Archanges fidèles', says Lust to Méphistophélès,

> tous ces fils de lumière et ces puissances de ferveur ne peuvent pas comprendre . . . Ils sont purs, ils sont durs, ils sont forts. Mais la tendresse! . . . Que voulez-vous que des êtres éternels puissent sentir le prix d'un regard, d'un instant, tout le don de faiblesse . . . le don d'un bien qu'il faut saisir entre le naître et le mourir. Ils ne sont que lumière et tu n'es que ténèbres . . . Mais moi, mais nous, nous portons nos clartés et nous portons nos ombres . . .
>
> (P II, 349)[1]

'Je suis mon seul modèle', Valéry wrote of *Mon Faust*, 'car Lust et Faust sont *moi* – et rien que moi. L'expérience m'a montré que ce que j'ai le plus désiré ne se trouve pas dans l'autrui – et ne peut trouver *l'autre* capable de tenter sans réserve l'essai à aller jusqu'au bout dans la volonté de . . . *pousser l'amour où il n'a jamais été* . . . cet amour a contre lui la médiocrité humaine' (xxix, 804). It is sometimes assumed from such a statement that Valéry approached art as a means of supplementing the inadequacy of direct experience. Such an interpretation seems to neglect the force of the word 'model', however. Valéry surely implies that he is expressing in the form of a symbolic encounter between two separate human beings, Lust and Faust, the quality of an experience already located within the self. Lust is not the fully integrated intelligence required as a partner if 'l'amour à l'octave supérieure' is to exist in the sense that Valéry has defined it. She seems to represent what he refers to in a prose-poem called *La Rentrée* as 'Ce féminin de l'être [. . .] ce don de refuge que nous prêtons à ce que nous aimons le plus profondément, à la femme d'entre les femmes. Celle aussi qui ne comprend pas.'[2] Analysis of the symbolism of the play has already suggested that Lust does not understand Faust's intellect and is therefore but one potential of what in him is a single sensibility, 'être' and 'connaître'. 'Où est la femme à deux têtes?/Pour le monstre que l'on serait/SI L'ON SE VOYAIT', Valéry

[1] Cf. 'Rien de plus délicieux que le mélange de l'esprit à la vie [. . .]. L'on est toujours tenté de les dissocier et opposer. Mais un repas excellent tout animé de mots et d'idées, nous fait semblables à des dieux (et peut-être supérieurs à eux). Ainsi du mélange d'amour et d'esprit' (P I, 317).

[2] 'Poésie Perdue', no. 390–1 (1966), 158.

once wrote.[1] The fantasy of the bicephalous partner is obviously his way of referring to the impossibility for 'le Moi pur' to absorb itself in another, and therefore indirectly to the necessity for love to seek something other than 'un autre Même' in the Narcissean sense.

It can be seen, then, that the relationship between Faust and Lust creates a paradox. Although love exists between them, the play still suggests, through the symbol of the ambiguity of their union, that the meeting of Faust with a mind as fully integrated as his own is still not a reality. But at the same time as the desire for 'un autre Même' hovers unfulfilled throughout the play, it is the quality of this solitary ideal which enriches Faust's *real* relationship with Lust. 'L'étrange aventure en profondeur guidé rien que par l'instinct de trouver le Même dans l'Autre', says Faust in the project for 'Lust IV',

> de chercher à tâtons, au travers de la beauté ou de l'intellect, au moyen et au-delà des caresses et des luxes nerveux ou des prestiges de l'esprit (qui sont des moyens) je ne sais quel joyau de vie, un talisman sans prix dont la possession permet de passer (sans s'engager dans la sottise des hommes ou dans le désordre des événements) le temps qu'il faut qu'on passe au service de la Bête de chair et de sang qui porte notre nom – Cela est tout ou rien selon les êtres. Si j'employais les mots de tous, je dirais que c'est là le devoir.
>
> (P II, 1413)

Thus where Teste allows the desire for 'un autre Même' (P II, 1413) basic to consciousness itself to prevent him from approaching Madame Teste otherwise than as a kind of object with no hold over him, Faust uses that desire, now as relative to him as consciousness, in order to venture into a tenderness for Lust partly based on the understanding on his part that she like him is still unique and alone. In *Mon Faust* Valéry has still not shown the reciprocation of this understanding of uniqueness on the part of *both* partners, however. Lust is contained within Faust like a child in the womb,[2] although she in turn gives him as part of his total relationship with her the power to be her child as well (P II, 1414), when he wishes to be. 'Ce que je sens pouvoir être par toi m'attire' (xxviii, 691), Faust says. Fortified by the 'talisman' of tenderness, Faust is ready in turn to be contained and observed by the integrated intelligence

[1] Quoted by J. R. Lawler, 'Light in Valéry', *A.J.F.S.*, VI (1969), 375.

[2] Cf. the idea suggested in a different context by Norma Rinsler, 'Stillness and Movement in Valéry's poetry', *Essays in French Literature*, VI (1969), 53.

equal to his own which is for ever absent in the play, just as Valéry felt it to be absent from his own life:

> J'aurais pu apporter à l'Amour si le destin l'eût voulu, une contribution: Une cruauté envers moi-même, et une conscience rigoureuse, qui jointes à mon sens naturel de la physique humaine et à ce mysticisme sans objet, qui est en moi, eussent peut-être, si quelque femme s'était rencontrée ayant du corps et de l'esprit un sens analogue, une fureur intelligente et expérimentale, un pressentiment de la volupté comme *moyen* – c'est là le neuf, – eussent, dis-je [. . .] peut-être pu faire de l'Amour quelque chose [. . .]
>
> (v, 806)

The quotation is from a relatively early notebook, but it is partly echoed in the description of the subject of 'Lust IV' at the end of his life as 'amour comme je le conçois – et l'ai vu périr deux fois' (xxix, 706).

It is important to see that it is not Valéry's ideal of love which he views as chimeric in reality, irrespective of whether or not he felt himself to have experienced it personally, but the possibility of transcending the sensation of solitary uniqueness at the heart of consciousness: 'Il ne peut y avoir qu'une seule tentative [. . .] une seule tentation comparable à la tentative d'aller sur un autre astre – c'est de poursuivre la chimère d'une connaissance immédiate de la transformation de *Moi* en *Toi*' (viii, 373). For this very reason, the one notion which remains permanent in his notes as a basis for the masterpiece of intellectual love of which he dreamed so often, is that of understanding: the shared comprehension of the irremediable power and uniqueness of individual solitude, the power which can attempt to destroy and consume the 'self' of another person as much as its own: 'le même obstacle que dans soi, le même *rien* réel, le même *tout* latent qu'en soi' (xiv, 268). '[. . .] avoir compris ensemble' (ix, 525), Valéry writes, or '*Seul et seule font un/être seul à deux/Laure – Béatrice – Comprendre*' (viii, 373); 'Solitude du moi *à deux*!' (x, 89). Extreme love is 'un effort qui de la différence des sexes s'élève à la différence des êtres contre celle-ci – à la puissance d'un acte de connaissance contre l'impénétrabilité des *uniques*' (xviii, 14).

Valéry's comments very often suggest that he viewed the experience of friendship as being the closest approximation in his own life to this ideal.[1] The notion of the distorting effects of 'l'amour passion' makes

[1] E.g. P I, 1750; P II, 45; vi, 478; xxi, 894; xxvi, 761. See also the preface by R. Mallet to *A. Gide–P. Valéry, Correspondance 1890–1942*, 35.

him constantly hesitate as to whether love *can* achieve the same perfection: 'AIMER passionnément quelqu'un, c'est avoir cédé à son image puissance de toxique [. . .]' (P I, 349).[1] However, it is equally clear that his ideal of 'l'amour à l'octave supérieure' approximated itself to a form of total friendship. Writing of what he once called 'l'impuissance de la sensibilité à franchir autre chose qu'un seuil', he added: 'Mais ceux qui comprennent ceci lui donnent une valeur supérieure' (xxix, 805).[2] This ideal – the shared comprehension of limitation – grew stronger as Valéry grew older, as the rich expression of the theme in the last notebooks proves. In this sense it provides a moving variation on the theme of the 'non-comprehensibility' of existence discussed in the previous chapter. The activity of analysis which is constant throughout Valéry's life gradually crosses over to the point at which it becomes by its own inner logic the central feature of an ideal of shared awareness, a means of reinstating the emotional and physical resources of the self on the highest possible level of communicated existence. By virtue of awareness of awareness, 'le Moi pur' itself has become the centre of an experience of intellectual plenitude.

Love and aesthetic emotion

'Il y a une sorte d'amour distincte à la fois de la passion et du divertissement; qui les compose', Valéry writes in *Autres Rhumbs*, 'et qui, de l'énergie de l'une et de la liberté de l'autre, peut, à force d'esprit, de tendresse et de tact, faire une manière d'œuvre, et même de chef-d'œuvre . . . entre deux miroirs' (P II, 699). This beautiful passage, one of many where a constructive effort of synthesis on the part of the intelligence is evoked, invites the comparison between love and aesthetic experience. The comparison is suggested by Valéry himself. He writes, for example, 'Aimer au degré suprême, est attacher à un être une puissance d'émotion absolue – comme cette émotion que donne certaine musique – mais celle-là comme *véritable* – et non reconstituée par l'art' (xvi, 553), or, '*présence d'absence*. Sensation bien connue, souvent excitée par musique' (xviii,

[1] Valéry is fascinated by the 'transformation d'un être quelconque en *Objet Aimé*' (xxiv, 698); he prefers the image of 'intoxication' to the Stendhalien one of 'cristallisation' (ix, 640; cf. vii, 830), resenting the instability of such love (e.g. xiv, 394; vii, 819). 'L'amour "profond"' implies growth and is defined as a love 'qui a atteint et franchi le seuil du compréhensible' (xxvi, 770) (see below, 232).

[2] Cf. the passage from vii, 728 quoted by W. Stewart in 'Le Thème d'Orphée chez Valéry', *Entretiens sur Paul Valéry*, 167, where Valéry mentions trying to follow 'la dynamique difficile d'un système double, de deux mondes impénétrables . . . l'un et l'autre avec illusion qu'ils se pénètrent'.

358). There is a point of human existence, he believes, where 'musique, poésie, passion, corps [. . .] sont comme une seule goutte d'énergie de la plus haute valeur [. . .]' (ix, 525).

The first point that might be made in the course of such a comparison could be that love and art both grow up for Valéry from what is an essentially negative view of 'nature' without human intelligence, the kind of view epitomised in *Le Solitaire*. 'Ce qu'il y a de plus précieux dans la vie', says Faust in the notes to 'Lust IV', 'et qui seul peut la faire aimer, garder, regretter, c'est précisément ce qui la refuse, la domine, l'apaise et la consomme' (P II, 1412). Tenderness is described in the *Cahiers* as just such a 'refus de la vie' (vii, 748), 'une sorte de jugement porté par le fond de l'âme sur toutes choses humaines [. . .] cet amolissement, cet adieu universel, ce retirement avec larmes naissantes, cet abandon, cette démission, ce penchement, ce refus' (vii, 837), and from many of Valéry's notes it is apparent that he views art too as springing from a feeling of human solitude. 'Sur la tristesse fondamentale de la vie – (et qui fait l'éclat de la rare joie!) [. . .] chantons un beau chant', he notes, expressing the simplest elements of this feeling, '– chante, mon âme, un beau chant qui proteste que tu n'as rien compris à toute cette vie' (vii, 533), or 'J'ai appris du moins, la continuité de cette chaîne de tourments [. . .] le *chant*' (viii, 41).

This is not to say that art, any more than love, is for Valéry a purely spontaneous production of the 'sensibilité créatrice' (xviii, 86); 'Le chant n'est pas de l'esprit [. . .] Mais esprit peut transporter les transports dans un domaine extraordinaire' (xvi, 506), he once wrote, and similarly, of physical love,

> La sensation suprême d'Erôs est un élément brut et commun – de la route de vie, qui vaut infiniment pour la plupart; mais non pour l'esprit qui y pense.
>
> Mais qui prend une valeur bien plus qu'infinie pour cet esprit, quand, comme un diamant taillé et monté magnifiquement, il s'insère dans une composition de toute la sensibilité de l'être et des richesses généralisées de ses combinaisons imaginaires et abstraites – au milieu du champ de ses énergies;
>
> (xxi, 827)

or 'L'Amour est idiot, mais c'est le seul moyen de se sentir l'intelligence de la vie' (xviii, 10). Common to both art and love is the possibility that the intelligence may co-ordinate and reorganise for human ends some of the richest natural energies of life valueless in themselves.

It follows that one of the most striking features of Valéry's analysis of the two themes is the notion of vital energy. Where 'passion' in its most destructive form represents the degradation of energy or the increase of entropy throughout the human system,[1] 'L'Amour heureux nous rend présente toute notre force. Il crée la surabondance, qui est le bien des biens, et la nécessité des plus belles œuvres [. . .]. L'amant heureux est riche. C'est un milliardaire physiologique et psychologique' (viii, 40); 'La valeur vraie (c'est à dire utilisable) de l'amour est dans l'accroissement de vitalité générale qu'il peut donner à quelqu'un' (vii, 137). Similarly art represented for Valéry 'le rayonnement d'énergie libre dans *tout l'être*' (xviii, 417), a 'voice' with a more than usual degree of organisation (xv, 900) which would augment the 'sensation de vivre' of (in the case of poetry) poet and reader alike. That the creative energies of both art and love could come to be fused together in the mature mind, art engendering love and love art, is confirmed by Valéry's own admission of 1938: 'Il est étrange que les vers que je puis faire maintenant ne soient plus que dédiés à l'Erôs – Soleil couchant. Bien plus étrange que jamais l'idée de versifier *par amour*, *sur l'amour* ne me souvienne entre 15 et 30 ans. Elle m'eût choqué – n'admettant pas de relation directe entre Art et le moi d'amour' (xxi, 909).[2]

'Aimer grandement quelqu'un c'est le rendre inépuisable' (xxviii, 524), Valéry once wrote, and 'the other' is referred to in *Mélange* as 'une manière d'infini nerveux *sous forme finie d'objet*, un trésor sensible inépuisable, etc' (P I, 316). There can be no doubt about the closeness of this phrasing to the notion of 'infini esthétique' central to Valéry's view of art.[3] '*Tu es*', the passage continues:

> Voilà qui est une merveille inconcevable. *Tu es*, et ceci étonne tout ce que je suis, transforme toutes valeurs, change les pierres en or autour de toi, colore les choses mortes et nulles, annule les pas qui vont vers toi et les fatigues, mesure les temps qui sont près de toi et les temps qui sont loin de toi avec des mesures bien différentes.
>
> (P I, 316)

'Un amour d'un certain genre doit se nommer enchantement, charme' (xv, 423), he writes. It is no coincidence that the collection of his mature

[1] See above, 50. Cf. '*Amour*, *Esprit* – les deux formes de lutte désespérée contre *la Loi de perte*' (xxvi, 715; cf. xii, 800).

[2] The poems of *Charmes* which have love as an explicit theme are *Les Pas*, *L'Abeille*, *La Fausse Morte*, *L'Insinuant*, *La Dormeuse*.

[3] See Ince, *The Poetic Theory of Paul Valéry*, 50.

poems, *Charmes*, has the same 'magic' title. The 'magic' of art, like the 'magic' of love, was something Valéry tried all his life both to understand and to create, the emphasis of the two activities varying in intensity until, in the latter part of his life in particular, neither the one nor the other can be said to predominate. As far as the nature of the 'magic' is concerned, it undoubtedly lay for him in the capacity of the human mind to create like Orpheus[1] out of the finite patterns of natural life an 'infinite' object ('la *magie*, l'apparence "infinie"' (xiv, 393)), one whose infinity he defined in turn as the capacity for ever-renewed reception and emission of creative energy on the part of the artist or lover himself. 'L'art proprement dit est production de choses qui créent le besoin qu'elles satisfont [. . .]. C'est par là que l'art a du rapport avec l'amour' (x, 3). Above all it is his attempt to express the restless movement of consciousness away from as well as towards its 'magic' creations[2] which distinguishes Valéry's expression of the themes of art and love.

[1] E.g. 'Car je vous *invente* – Moi *l'inventeur de ce qui est*, Orphée!' (viii, 362) (quoted by W. Stewart, *Entretiens sur Paul Valéry*, 168).

[2] 'Je ne danserai pas devant ton arche, autrui, autre que moi – je ne te ferai pas croire de merveilles . . . Que m'importe cette comédie. C'est moi-même qu'il me faut séduire, apprivoiser, capter, éprendre. [. . .] Cet exigeant être ne se paye que du plus réel. Il est prose étant lui et seul . . . étant la signification dernière – le vers étant intermédiare . . . tout le sublime, le beau n'est que voile [. . .] Musique très belle, je sais que tu me mens' (iv, 354) (quoted by J. Duchesne-Guillemin, *F.S.*, xx (1966), 364).

Part Two:

Consciousness & external nature

4 Nature & imagination

'Anti Nature'

'[. . .] – contrairement à ma petite légende, – j'adore ce qu'on appelle Nature, à condition de ne la jamais nommer', Valéry wrote to Vielé-Griffin in 1898.[1] Before turning to the sensitive response to the natural world which is undoubtedly expressed in his work, it would seem useful to examine the 'anti Nature' legend which he recognised as having grown up around him even at an early stage in his life. On what was it founded?

Insistence on the clause 'à condition de ne la jamais nommer' suggests that Valéry's criticism of 'Nature' may have much the same basis as his criticism of 'Vie', examined in the previous chapter. 'Le hasard est nom d'impuissance. Nature de même' (i, 185): the attitude is indeed familiar: distrust of 'des choses vagues' (P II, 1040), of another of those 'vases fissurés' (viii, 591) with which it is impossible to reason, or, to use the humorous phrase in *L'Idée Fixe*, of another of those verbal 'perroquets' 'qui ne supportent pas le regard' (P II, 238). Wittgenstein and his followers considered such words to lead to a form of 'mental cramp'[2] growing out of problems of purely linguistic origin, and Valéry's attitude appears to be very similar (though with the important difference that he never seems to be prepared to suggest a systematic transfer of the study of the structure and limits of language to the study of the structure and limits of thought). Although he was willing to admit to a kind of intoxicated pleasure at the magic reverberation of 'Le seul nom de NATURE' (P II, 1040), he is quick to distinguish such pleasure from the constructive or combinatory aim of the intellect. Hence such comments as: 'Quel est notre degré de parenté avec la "Nature"? Mais d'abord, celle-ci existe-t-

[1] *Lettres à Quelques-Uns* (Paris, Gallimard, 1952), 61.
[2] M. White, *The Age of Analysis* (Mentor, 1955), 102.

elle?' (vii, 149); 'Quant à la "Nature", ce mythe...,' (P II, 1311). There is a fine irony in that the 'anti nature' legend round Valéry needs for its existence what he himself would consider a linguistic myth in the minds of his critics. The attitude reaches a head in his attack on Rousseau, or rather on popular reaction to Rousseau, for 'inventing' an ideal of 'Nature' to be rediscovered every hundred years or so: 'Je ne puis penser que la "Nature" était inconnue avant Rousseau' (P II, 603).[1]

Is it all simply a question of the disinterested delineation of areas of linguistic muddle by the self-styled analytical philosopher? Something in the persistent scorn and repetitiveness of Valéry's remarks suggests that it is not. 'Il suffit pour me comprendre', he once wrote, 'de joindre à un jugement et sentiment de dépréciation de la vie (qui est à la base de toutes les mystiques) un jugement non moins dépréciateur des définitions [. . .]' (xxix, 805). Analysis of the set of associations which Valéry frequently implies by his own usage of the word 'Nature' suggests that his dislike is based on what he once called 'la vision d'une éruption verte, vague et continue, d'un grand travail élémentaire s'opposant à l'humain, d'une quantité monotone qui va nous recouvrir' (P I, 1167). In choosing to attack 'Nature' Valéry is really expressing mistrust of philosophies of human nature which value the inverse characteristics of conscious intelligence. 'Je me sens *ange* [. . .] et *contre-ange*', he once wrote to Gide, 'L'entre-deux me donne le mal de mer. L'Homme est *redite*, et je suis *constance*; l'homme est *surprises* et je suis . . . *ratures* . . . *Comprends* si tu peux.'[2] 'Nature' could equally well be used for 'Homme' in this context. Detailed aspects of the actual natural world aroused Valéry's admiration and interest in proportion to the transformational capacity they activate in the beholding mind.

'Le retour des saisons [. . .] donne l'idée de la sottise de la nature et de la vie, laquelle ne sait que se répéter pour subsister' (P I, 208), he writes, singling out the attribute of nature most alien to consciousness: 'Pas d'Etc. dans la Nature, énumération totale. La partie pour le tout n'existe pas dans la nature – L'esprit ne supporte pas la répétition' (x, 105). Nature seems alien not only to the general ability of the intellect to take short cuts by a system of abstract relationships, but also to Valéry's own self-avowed intellectual 'impatience'.[3] Thus he can be found writing: 'Je ne connais rien aux moissons, aux vendanges. Rien pour moi dans les Géorgiques' (P II, 667), and, in the preface to his own translation of

[1] Cf. P I, 1287; P II, 603.

[2] *A. Gide–P. Valéry, Correspondance 1890–1942* (Paris, Gallimard, 1955), 515.

[3] See below, 183: 'le génie considéré comme un raccourci' (ix, 895).

Virgil's *Bucolics*: 'La vie pastorale m'est etrangère et me semble ennuyeuse. L'industrie agricole exige exactement toutes les vertus que je n'ai pas. La vue des sillons m'attriste [. . .]' (P I, 208). This is a theme close to the half-metaphorical jotting in the *Cahiers*: 'comment peut-on cultiver la terre [. . .], gratter tant d'hectares?' (xviii, 916). 'The idyllic life of the shepherds and the most personal experiences of the poet himself, which are blended in this poetic *salade russe*, wakened in Valéry no answering chord.'[1]

This 'anti natural' attitude obviously has its own literary echoes. It can be related in certain respects to 'Decadent' Symbolism, the arena in which Valéry made his literary début as a young man. 'Hélas! je ne suis pas l'homme de Dieu ni de la campagne. L'extase et l'herbe ne me surexcitent que pour une demi-journée', he wrote half boastfully to Gide in 1896.[2] The statement is close to Baudelaire's 'Je suis incapable de m'attendrir sur les végétaux',[3] and Valéry's admission to Duhamel: 'Mon cher, j'ai beau voyager, on me montre toujours le même paysage',[4] finds its echo in Huysman's *A Rebours* in the phrase 'la dégoutante uniformité des paysages'.[5] 'Un dieu seul peut aimer sérieusement une fleur vraie, sachant la pousser' (iii, 821), Valéry remarks in an early note-book in words worthy of a Des Esseintes, or he may write of 'une production simple, bête comme tout ce qui est sincère et nature' (P I, 398). 'Nature, I do think, if she had her own way, would grow nothing but turnips', wrote Oscar Wilde in an aphorism similarly directed against blind monotony, and Whistler 'how dutifully the casual in Nature is accepted as sublime, may be gathered from the unlimited admiration daily produced by a very foolish sunset'.[6]

Although he comes close to the notion of will-power valued by the 'decadent' Symbolists, Valéry rarely dwells on their associated urge towards the deliberately over-sophisticated and hyper-civilised.[7] Apart from the vocabulary of jewels and precious stones in his earliest poetry, often used to counteract some violent movement,[8] there are few such

1 L. A. Bisson, 'Valéry and Virgil', *M.L.R.*, LIII (1958), 501.

2 *A. G.–P. V. Correspondance*, 255.

3 *Correspondance Générale* (Conard, 1947), 321. (Letter to F. Desnoyers, 1855.)

4 Quoted by P.-O. Walzer in *La Poésie de Valéry* (Genève, Cailler, 1953), 390.

5 Quoted by H. Mondor in 'Paul Valéry et "A Rebours" ', *Revue de Paris* (mars 1947), 4–18.

6 Quoted by Enid Starkie in *From Gautier to Eliot* (London, 1960), 44.

7 Distinction suggested by Alison Fairlie in *Baudelaire: Les Fleurs du Mal*, Studies in French Lit., no. 6 (Edward Arnold, 1960), 17.

8 See examples given by Norma Rinsler, 'Stillness and Movement in Valéry's Poetry', *Essays in French Literature*, VI (1969), 36.

ornaments in his verse. Indeed, it is only when *boutades* such as 'on me montre partout le même paysage' are taken out of their context that they appear to have any connection with true 'Decadence'. In another context, particularly later on in his life, Valéry could just as well have written, like Hugo: 'ces grands aspects (*soleils couchants*, etc.) ne sont jamais "la même chose", et je ne me crois pas dispensé de regarder le ciel aujourd'hui parce que je l'ai vu hier'.[1] 'Toujours le même enthousiasme, mais pas la même "nature"' (ix, 134), he writes, this time transferring the idea of repetition in nature to the sameness of human response.

A similar set of critical associations is based for Valéry on the notion of surfeit and uniformity in nature. '*Naturel* un peu partout' (i, 80) is one of many ironic understatements on the subject. This attitude is present in his distaste for the luxuriant, aimless abundance of vegetable life 'en masse' as opposed to the single tree or the pure landscape of sea, sky and rock. It is a dislike carried over into his reading habits. He writes in the preface to a translation of Guatemalan legends, for example: 'Quel *mélange* [my italics] de nature torride, de botanique aberrante, de magie indigène. [. . .] J'ai cru avoir absorbé le suc des plantes incroyable, [. . .] rien ne me paraît plus étrange, – je veux dire de plus étranger à mon esprit.'[2] The 'nausea' of Sartre's Roquentin in the face of the chestnut tree and its surroundings is not far off ('J'aurais souhaité qui'ils existassent moins fort, d'une façon plus sèche, plus abstraite, avec plus de retenue'),[3] though this reaction has only to be compared with that of La Jeune Parque towards the 'passionate' trees of Spring for it to be clear that it is conflict, not disgust, that is involved on this level of Valéry's critique. 'Nature', like human 'sensibilité', is governed by the demon 'Brouilliamini' (P II, 908) or 'mélange' from which consciousness differentiates itself:

> Un esprit n'est que ce mélange
> Duquel à chaque instant, se démêle le Moi.
>
> (P I, 286)

That he is attacking a scale of values closely connected with a 'literary' view of the world is emphasised by the close link between Valéry's hatred of 'paysage' and his dislike of certain types of painting and literature concerned with descriptive technique. 'Le mot de *description* lui était hostile, comme une tendance vers *l'indistinct*', writes Madame

1 Quoted by J.-B. Barrère in *La Fantaisie de Victor Hugo*, III (Paris, Corti, 1950), 3.
2 Preface to M. A. Asturias' *Légendes du Guatemala* (Marseilles, Les Cahiers du Sud, 1932).
3 *La Nausée* (Paris, Gallimard, 1938), 180.

Lucienne J. Cain, going on to point out that the phrase '*Composition d'un Port*' was infinitely more attractive to Valéry than '*Description d'un Port*'.[1] The link in his mind between 'paysage' and the already unpleasant idea of description (e.g. xv, 416) is quite clearly explained in *Degas Danse Dessin* where he suggests that 'le développement du paysage semble bien coïncider avec une diminution singulièrement marquée de la partie intellectuelle de l'art' and that 'l'invasion de la Littérature par la *description* fut parallèle à celle de la Peinture par le paysage' (P II, 1219; cf. ix, 68). 'La vue des sillons m'attriste, jusques à ceux que trace ma plume' (P I, 208), Valéry had written, while the remark 'comment peut-on cultiver la terre?' (xviii, 916) is a symbolic quip against the type of literary creation which postulates a reader of whom nothing more active is demanded than the ability to get through a very long work. It is as if the furrows of a ploughed field and the laborious descriptions in a novel ('la Marquise sortit à cinq heures') are one in Valéry's mind. 'Les romanciers donnent la vie, – et je ne cherche, dans un certain sens – qu'à l'éliminer' he once remarked.[2] This is not the place to discuss the inadequacies of Valéry's definition of the novel, nor to suggest the remarkable similarities with the 'Nouveau Roman' which his attitude reveals once it is taken instead simply as an attack on certain traditional kinds of narrative techniques.[3] Proust and the novel, Rousseau and Nature: like Molière and the drama,[4] these names are simply Valéry's personal shorthand method of referring to what he fears and despises within his own terms of reference: the blind, undiscriminating prodigality of nature without the individual counter-effort of the human mind.

'La première affaire d'un artiste est de substituer l'homme à la nature et de protester contre elle', Baudelaire had written.[5] Valéry makes many similar remarks, for instance: 'L'existence de l'Humanité ne se justifie que par quelques résultats anti-naturels qu'elle a atteints' (P II, 901). But whereas in Baudelaire's case imagery was rarely taken directly from the natural world, Valéry's 'protest' is made through poetry in constant contact with the themes and images of nature. Nature may be 'méchante'

1 *Trois Essais sur Paul Valéry* (Paris, Gallimard, 1958), 60–1.

2 Preface to M. Courtois-Suffit's *Le Promeneur Sympathique* (Paris, Plon, 1925).

3 Particularly the attitudes in Robbe-Grillet's *Pour un Nouveau Roman* (Paris, Édns. du Minuit, 1963).

4 Compare with W. N. Ince, 'Valéry on Molière: an Intellectual out of Humour', *M.L.R.*, LX (1965), 41–7.

5 *Œuvres Complètes* (Paris, Gallimard, 1961), 930. See the discussion of this attitude in L. J. Austin's *L'Univers Poétique de Baudelaire* (Mercure de France, 1956), 88 (see also F. W. Leakey's *Baudelaire and Nature* (Manchester U.P., 1970) for an interesting view of the subject as a whole).

(P II, 891), 'Diable' (P I, 618) or 'poison' (P II, 331), but it is also 'hasard' (xxiii, 86), 'tout et n'importe quoi' (P II, 1311), the mixture of orderly and disorderly material out of whose 'inégalité' (P I, 837) the human imagination can create order of its own. This is how Valéry summarises the situation in general terms:

> La Nature, par elle-même est informe. Elle ne connaît point d'ensembles, point de figures, ni même d'instants. La terre est ici, la mer est là; mais il n'y a point de relations entre ces choses, autres que les relations locales de leurs atomes de proche en proche. Mais l'homme est introduit dans ce chaos. Le chaos se fait paysage [. . .] l'œil s'établit dans son empire . . . c'est alors que l'esprit se montre, et recherche dans cette création admirable que vient de faire la vue, le programme et le prétexte des actes qui vont extraire de la nature ce qu'elle ne savait pas qu'elle contenait.[1]

'Je vois la nature à ma façon', Valéry writes:

> 'Je pense à ceci en regardant une grande chèvre dans les oliviers. Elle mordille, bondit. *Virgile*, pensai-je. Jamais l'idée de peindre ou chanter cette chèvre ne me fût venue. Virgile prouve que l'on peut en faire quelque chose. Je la regarde donc. Elle cesse aussitôt d'être chèvre – Et l'olivier cesse d'être olivier. Ici commence *moi* – c'est-à-dire un regard que je voudrais bien définir.' (P I, 312–13)

One of the self-attributed consequences of this form of extreme self-awareness is a kind of 'Testian' mental blindness in the face of visual reality: 'Une fois de plus, je constate qu'en présence des choses mêmes je suis absent' (P I, 54); 'Moi le Serpent, Avaleur de toutes les couleurs de la vie' (viii, 138). 'Comment fait-on pour detruire l'habitude qui empêche de voir une chose?' (i, 201), Valéry asks, however. Is it so certain that the animal and the tree always 'cease to be themselves' in his work? I shall discuss here the relationship between sensation and abstraction as it appears in the detailed context of Valéry's own evocation of the natural world, for it seems that the kind of consciousness previously mentioned as a power of detachment becomes itself an instrument of voluptuous power and involvement when activated to the full in the presence of things. 'Je cesse de voir pour penser à ce que j'ai vu', Valéry

[1] Introduction to *Le Golfe de Salerne*, a collection of engravings by Belobodoroff, Collezione dell'Obelisco (Rome, Bestetti, 1952).

writes, but also, 'Je cesse de penser pour voir' (v, 263). 'Not a nature poet', writes L. A. Bisson, 'yet we know that certain natural phenomena [. . .] penetrated his being and moved him deeply, exciting the whole range of his intellectual and creative powers'.[1]

Valéry expresses the same paradox symbolically through his own poem *Ébauche d'un Serpent* where certain extreme consequences of a tendency towards the negation of the real world are ironically entertained through the serpent:

> Soleil, soleil! . . . Faute éclatante!
> Toi qui masques la mort, Soleil,
> Sous l'azur et l'or d'une tente
> Où les fleurs tiennent leur conseil;
> [. . . . .]
> Tu gardes les cœurs de connaître
> Que l'univers n'est qu'un défaut
> Dans la pureté du Non-être!
>
> (P I, 138–9)

Not only is the serpent himself moved by the beauty of Eve's body in the garden, lit up by the very sun he has mockingly apostrophised as a snare for the intellect, but, as A. R. Chisholm points out, the whole poem builds up, through the resplendent image of the growing tree, the superiority of man's conscious (that is, thinking and feeling) contact with life, a contact in which even the negative elements of the intellect symbolised by the serpent are, like the poison strychnine in certain medicines, a necessary tonic part.[2]

'*Imagination abstraite*'[3]

'Mon écriture me révèle le changement volontaire qui s'est fait en moi, d'intuitif concret en intuitif abstrait' (P I, 20), Valéry is reported to have written in 1893, when the foundations of his conscious response to nature[4] and perception were being laid. Teste and the in many ways parallel creation of Leonardo, at least the Leonardo of the early essay of 1894, obviously represent elements of his own attitude in magnified form. For example, Teste, however scornful of 'le "talent" de vos arbres' (P II, 22), manifests a far from indifferent attitude to the physical world when he

[1] 'A Study in "le faire Valéryen" ', *F.S.*, x (1956), 310.

[2] 'Valéry's "Ébauche d'un Serpent" ', *AUMLA*, xv (1961), 19–29.

[3] See P I, 626 (Valéry attributes the quality to Mallarmé).

[4] See above, 5.

says: 'Je veux n'emprunter au monde (visible) que des forces – non des formes, mais de quoi faire des formes. [. . .]. Point de décors. Mais le sentiment de la matière même, roc, air, eaux, matière végétale – et leurs vertus élémentaires' (P II, 69). And to Leonardo, Valéry's 'cerveau ideal' (xxiii, 74), is attributed a love of the mental exercise '*qui lui rendra la plus intense sensation de sa force*' (P I, 1261). Leonardo is praised for his sensitivity to 'la volupté de l'*individualité* des objets' (P I, 1170) (shapes of falling rock, curling wisps of smoke, the merging of foliage and air, patterns of migrating birds in flight, forms of distant trees and so on); for precisely the kind of imagination which augments 'la jouissance sensuelle par les artifices et les calculs de l'intelligence' (P I, 1258).

Leonardo is the artist: Monsieur Teste, the potential artist. However it is clear that in both minds there is a close parallel between actual perception of nature and awareness of the possibility, realised or non-realised, of using art to augment the patterns of consciously deepened response. Just as Teste rejected a passive 'public' relationship with nature only to delight privately in one in which his mind is activated to the full, so he rejects 'littérature' only to retain a belief in '*Ars*' (P II, 67).[1] Valéry's attitude to the closely related themes of art and nature follows much the same pattern. With the tendency to suffer if his whole mind were not engaged in an experience ('Et que j'ai souffert, tout le temps, de n'avoir pas tout le temps la sensation de ma présence entière' (v, 52)), he is drawn, like Teste and Leonardo, to approach perception of the natural world – as he approached the experience of poetic composition – in the way that gives the strongest sensation of conscious existence. 'Comment transformé-je ceci!', he writes under the rubric *Organa* in the first note-book, after having conjured up the elemental substances in a landscape: 'je vois le feuillage, par exemple je le *suis*, j'imagine l'opération soit de le suivre dans son cours vers le haut et ses chutes – soit de le figurer avec pinceau ou autre moyen' (i, 678).[2] Throughout even the most abstract parts of the *Cahiers* brilliant 'aquarelles' or fragmentary descriptions with the intensity of prose-poems[3] reflect the urgency of this desire to record the quality of immediate perception; to make of natural textures and their

[1] See Christine M. Crow, '"Teste parle": the question of a potential artist in Valéry's M. Teste', *Yale French Studies*, no. 44 (1970), 160.

[2] Cf. Valéry's description of the subject-matter of his notes as 'ce qui me semble de nature à accroître *mon* pouvoir de transformation, – à modifier par combinaison – mon *implexe*. Ceci suppose une sorte de croyance à je ne sais quelle *édification*, par additions et corrections successives. Croyance qui vaut ce que vaut une croyance' (P II, 1525).

[3] E.g. 'le vers de Soleil' (XII, 838).

relationships the talismans of future intellectual strength. Valéry rejected only passive perception, not that which seemingly 'disturbs the natural order of things'.[1]

It is clear by now that lack of interest in 'décor' in the passive sense is compensated on Valéry's part by other forms of response. 'J'avoue être beaucoup plus touché moi-même, en fait d'impressions du monde extérieur, par la dite substance des choses que par le décor',[2] he writes, or, in words very similar to those given to Teste, he describes the satisfaction of 'l'imagination de la *matière* des choses: eau, roche, pulpe des feuilles, le sable tres fin, la chair' (P II, 1507).[3] Dismissing the changing perspectives of a landscape as accidental – and, presumably, non transformable – he adds, 'Mais au contraire, la *substance* des objets qui sont sous mes yeux, la roche, l'eau, la matière de l'écorce ou de la feuille, et la figure des êtres organisés me retiennent' (P I, 1468). And as if conscious of the powerlessness of the human imagination to transform these substances in any 'objective' sense, he confesses that: '[. . .] le grain d'une roche, la dureté d'un tronc, la vie froide de feuilles saisies à pleine main, l'inertie de l'eau – m'arrêtent, m'immobilisent et m'accablent bien plus que les espaces "infinis" qui effrayaient l'Adversaire' (XVI, 504) (not the first difference from Pascal). Indeed, it is around sensitivity to natural substances in their irreducible individuality that Valéry's own 'mysticisme de la réalité pure'[4] mostly revolves. Unconcerned with any philosophical denial à la Berkeley of the existence of the material world ('Je n'aurais jamais inventé de discuter de la *réalité du monde sensible*' (P II, 1525)), his vision of life is partly based on a sense of mystery before the apparent immobility of matter, when matter itself is known to be comprised of internal motion on a different scale ('ordre de grandeur').

The *Cahiers* and published works are full of instances of this 'puissance de transformation', the imagination, at work on its own scale of perception: for example, in the way in which separate substances are played off one against the other: stone columns silhouetted against the sky in *Cantiques des Colonnes*; foliage across water in *Le Cimetière Marin*; the branches of a tree tossing in the air in *Au Platane*. 'La séparation parfaite de ces substances [sand and water] m'enchante', Valéry writes in a note introducing his own preferred type of 'Paysage':

1 Rinsler, *Essays in French Literature*, 42.
2 'Gabriela Mistral', *Revue de Paris* (fév. 1946), 3–7.
3 Cf. 'Je ressens de même les paysages, qui, après tout, sont des *accidents* . . . naturels, j'ai la sensation de l'arbitraire de leurs formes' (P II, 1507).
4 See Robinson, *L'Analyse de l'Esprit*, 214–15 and W. N. Ince, 'Être, Connaître et Mysticisme du Réel selon Valéry', *Entretiens sur Paul Valéry*, 205.

> Un vaste végétal se tord et se redresse sur le sable, élève enfin à la face même du soleil une forte et régulière union de palmes énormes, infiniment déliées. Cette netteté est celle de la plus belle journée de la Création. J'attends sur ce bord les artistes de la première Egypte, Thalès lui-même, et un autre personnage tranquille, pour manger le gros poisson bouilli et mettre ensemble tout ce que nous savons.
>
> (iv, 98)

Unlike the confused, 'impure' vision of the world associated with the term 'nature', this kind of visual clarity or purity is equated with mental well-being and generosity (shown in the sharing of food and knowledge). The poem *Palme* is not far away with its similar 'annunciation' theme: the angel bringing food and drink as a symbol of the inter-fertilisation of consciousness and the world. There too the combination of sand, foliage, clear air and water (or sap) is involved.

'Une plante extrêmement fine et délicate se risque et se découpe avec bonheur et netteté sur l'œil, se dessine sur le vague', he writes similarly in another notebook, '[...] Ces interstices donnent l'impression d'une transparence, d'un regard à travers une matière fluide et inconstante' (v, 839). It is interesting to see that Valéry equates this kind of transparency or clarity[1] with a state of mental harmony in which the different exigencies of the mind can be involved. The theme of clarity of composition unites, he says, 'mes faces de Janus' (xvi, 514). For Lust, too, 'la demoiselle de cristal', as she is called in *Mon Faust* (P II, 278), 'Le jour du bonheur est transparent' (xxix, 29).

Thus it is through this experience of visual perception (just as the angel 'speaks' with his eye to the vision of the beholder in *Palme* (P I, 153) that Valéry is able to express not only the most desperate but also the most balanced and enriching relationship of consciousness with life; the vindication of 'l'esprit créateur'.

'La comparaison entre sensations [...] est initiale, germe de pensée' (xxi, 744), Valéry writes. The idea can be linked with the well-known passage in *Inspirations Méditerranéennes* describing the moment when, before the elaboration of image or hypothesis, the mind is still in contact

[1] Cf. 'Lucidité est séparation, est PURETÉ, non confusion' (xv, 849); '[...] la connaissance limite – la netteté des formes et des corps' (P I, 542); 'Rien ne prouve que cette netteté n'est pas chose toute humaine' (v, 279). The experience of 'enchantement' is described in crystalline terms (P II, 601) and so is that of enchantment mingled with fear (P I, 309). Cf. the poems *Féerie* and *Même Féerie* (P I, 77–9). Some of the wider aspects of the crystalline theme are discussed by J. R. Lawler in 'The Serpent, the Tree and the Crystal', *L'Esprit Créateur*, IV (1964), 34–40.

with its united intellectual, physical and emotional wealth: 'Là, les ingrédients sensibles, les éléments (ou les aliments) de l'état d'âme au sein duquel va germer la pensée la plus générale, la question la plus compréhensive, sont réunis: de la lumière et de l'étendue, du loisir et du rythme, des transparences et de la profondeur...' (P I, 1093). Awareness of the co-ordinatory nature of perception leads Valéry to a characteristic interest in consciously co-ordinating things. 'Le goût et désir de combiner' (i, 109), the faculty, basic to the imagination, of perceiving relationships,[1] leads him, for example, to speculate in an early notebook on what he calls 'l'accouplement des matières' or 'accords par matériaux', the coupling of natural substances such as 'feu et feuilles', 'feuilles rouges et eau', 'chair et terre', 'fruit ouvert et terre' (i, 391). In the following chapter I shall look in detail at two of these combinations: foliage and water, and foliage and fire, and it will become clear how close is the imagined juxtaposing of textures to fully-fledged analogy in the poetic sense. Here I shall look simply at examples of the last combination, flesh, fruit and earth.

Valéry seems particularly fond of evoking the texture of skin and the substances of earth or rock. The two come together metaphorically in a phrase like: 'O terre brune/douce terre humée, chair tendre, herbe où la brise habite' (i, 329). Sometimes a sexual theme is involved, as in the following fragment which seems in some ways like a much more sensuous version of the heavily stylised poem *La Fausse Morte* in *Charmes*:

> Tordue est la chose dure, douce et chaude (la fille)
> Polie et mouvante, lance l'air qui brûle
> Terre entière qui se lève, et me porte
> Étendue fraîche, étendue tiède, forme qui devient
> nouvelle sous la force,
> Voyage immobile, tendre au bras, du sommet aigu
> Pierre exquise, pour boire

Flesh as a stone recalls the image of *Poésie* where the Poet complains to his Mother, Intelligence: 'Et la chair s'est faite pierre/Qui fut tendre sous mon corps' (P I, 120), an example of how the near-allegorical never loses touch with the physical in Valéry's poetry. There is often even a curious tension between the two (in this case the images of breast and milk/intelligence and inspiration reinforcing each other but never coinciding completely). Similarly, in the famous line of *Le Cimetière Marin*: 'L'argile rouge a bu la blanche espèce', potentially stark associations are held back not only through the incantatory sound patterns, but by the gentle

[1] Cf. Baudelaire's 'reine des facultés', *Œuvres Complètes* (Paris, Gallimard, 1961), 1037.

physical blending of 'chair et terre'. It is in *La Jeune Parque* that what Lucienne J. Cain has called a 'drame tellurique'[1] is most pronounced. Here the body of the young woman is evoked in terms of its surroundings of sea and rock or sunlit isles, natural shapes and textures altering in hardness and softness according to the degree of mental conflict involved.[2] The relationship between inner and outer worlds established by this device enables Valéry to suggest that the experience of conscious detachment at its most extreme can recreate an intimate continuity with the natural world. It is interesting to note, too, that a line which has just been seen to suggest the flesh of a woman as it appears to her lover ('Terre entière qui se lève, et me porte') is echoed in the cry of the Parque for unity with her surroundings and thus with herself:

> Terre trouble...et mêlée à l'algue, porte-moi,
> Porte doucement moi...
>
> (P I, 105)[3]

The theme of fruit will be seen to play an even larger part in Valéry's work: 'Je réfléchis à perte de vue sur l'arbre, sur le fruit [...]' (xi, 343).[4] 'Reconstruire la saveur de fruits' (i, 809):[5] the mental exercise postulated in the first notebook foreshadows the words of Faust at the end of his life: 'Un certain goût de fraises ou, plutôt, le souvenir de ce goût, plus puissant encore' (P II, 289). Valéry writes similarly of 'le plaisir de palper les fruits';[6] or of 'La douceur de la chose effleurée' (xvii, 508). There are constant indications here of a kind of imagination which, like that of Leonardo, accentuates 'la jouissance sensuelle par les artifices et les calculs de l'intelligence' (P I, 1258). From the point of view of the attraction provided by a combination of textures, he may be drawn to note the visual effect of fruit on leaves (i, 50), of fruit on water (P I, 1090) (the coloured fruit floating in the harbour at Sète), or of fruit in the dust ('Qu'un peuple à présent s'écroule, [...]/Dans la poudre qu'il se roule' (P I, 155) at the end of *Palme*).[7] In *Les Grenades* it is the physical shape and texture of the pomegranates – the curvature of their taut but some-

[1] *Trois Essais*, 76.

[2] Cf. H. Sørensen, *La Poésie de Paul Valéry* (Copenhagen, 1944), 315.

[3] There are many lines in the first notebook with obvious relevance to *La Jeune Parque*, e.g. i, 214, 253, 257, 415.

[4] See below, 170–5.

[5] Cf. 'On devrait classer les fruits comme les lettres de l'alphabet. Il y en a de palatals ou palataux, il y en a qui font mal aux dents, les *d* et les *t*. Les dattes sont liquides et labiales' (*A. Gide–P. Valéry, Correspondance*, 402).

[6] Preface to Berthe Morisot, *Seize Aquarelles* (Édns. des Quatre Chemins, 1946).

[7] Cf. the portrait by Ligier-Richer of a skeleton holding fruit, that Valéry had in his room in the Rue Gay-Lussac as a young man (P I, 21).

what bumpy skins stretched over the seeds within – which give rise to the analogy with human foreheads, as much as do more important themes of process or temporal development to be discussed later. 'Ce fruit *est*. Il a un poids et une résistance à la pensée' (viii, 408): Valéry *is* alert to external texture and substance, through the mental sensation they evoke. The idea of the 'resistence' to thought offered by physical substance might even be said to accentuate the sense of a compensatory flexibility of relationship and comparison.

This aspect of Valéry's 'imagination abstraite' can be illustrated further by the example of his sharp awareness of a discrepancy between what we know of nature and what we see. 'Pour l'œil l'arbre ne respire pas' (iv, 792), he writes, or: 'Si des variations sont trop lentes, elles nous échappent, [...]. Telle la croissance d'un arbre' (iv, 118). To Monsieur Teste, knowledge of such a limitation on the part of the senses offers no reward but itself: further knowledge ('Les sens ne sont pas assez subtils pour voir que des changements ont eu lieu. Je sais bien que ce n'est le même jour, mais je ne fais que le savoir' (P II, 42)). But Valéry proves that to the *whole* mind an object such as the tree can be more visually rewarding on the macroscale precisely because of what the intellect knows it fails to see on the microscale.

The mechanism of the eye is not complex enough to perceive the growth of a tree: the imaginative process here is almost the opposite of that involved when Valéry speculates in his first notebook (anticipating a now familiar experience in the cinema) on what it would be like to visualise the speeding up of natural growth: 'Voir en une seconde un arbre sortir de terre, s'éployer et cent fois dans cette seconde, fleurir, jaunir, se dépouiller, refleurir, les feuilles et fleurs tombées cent fois, cent fois avoir pourri' (i, 68). In the first case the imagination savours the limits of its power by giving way to the object; in the second, it rewards itself with an impatience directed towards the violation in the mind's eye of the object itself. A little later Valéry writes:

> Je puis concevoir un arbre fleurir, verdir, rougir, se dépouiller, refleurir etc. avec une vitesse seulement bornée par la condition de pouvoir distinguer ces transformations [...] Mais je ne puis ainsi considérer l'ensemble des choses sans rien omettre. Si je substitue *ma* vitesse à celle des phénomènes...
>
> (iv, 129)

Again freedom of imagination is used as a means of emphasising a biological observation (the difference between natural and conscious time-scales) rather than as a means of exploring the imaginary at the expense of the real. There is nothing contradictory in that a strong relativistic vision should have as its object a precise view of the natural world. Robbe-Grillet's *La Jalousie* richly expresses the same paradox.

These last examples illustrated the power of the imagination to derive strength from knowledge of perceptual limitation. 'Mon mouvement va de ma faiblesse à ma force', Monsieur Teste had said (P II, 40). Equally many examples occur in Valéry's notes and poetry of the opposite kind of imagination: imagination in which the power of the perceiving mind is made the basis of the observation or image despite its inescapable limitations: '[...] je suis comme enfermé dans ma propriété de percevoir. Toute la diversité de mes vues se compose dans l'unité de ma conscience motrice' (P I, 864). 'Collines lisses – qui ont l'air de coulées de cendre fine [...]. Je m'étonne des distances jugées de l'œil par petitesse des hommes' (xviii, 910), Valéry notes for example. Knowledge of the complementarity between eye and object adds particular emotion to the act of perception, something like the 'lucide tendresse' he expresses in *Profusion Du Soir* before the vast formations of clouds at sunset:

> Une crête écumeuse, énorme et colorée
> Barre, puissamment pure, et plisse le parvis.
> Roule jusqu'à mon cœur la distance dorée,
> Vague!... Croulants soleils aux horizons ravis,
> Tu n'iras pas plus loin que la ligne ignorée
> Qui divise les dieux des ombres où je vis.
>
> (P I, 88)

Similarly, with the shutting of the eyes (a capacity Sartre denies his characters in *Huis Clos*) can come the power to deny the whole visible world (xxix, 873).[1]

It is perhaps in the contemplation and evocation of two remote natural phenomena, the sea and the stars, that this strong sense on Valéry's part of the reciprocity or complementarity between perception and its object can most easily be observed. First the sea. 'Une écume s'allume, *de temps à autre*, sur le champ de la mer, et ces *temps* sont créés par le hasard' (P I, 290), he writes, suggesting the imprint of chance and time on individual sensitivity. The image of 'un éclat d'écume sur la mer' is used elsewhere to describe the germination of an idea from a random impression: would the impression not have left as little trace as a flash of sunlit foam on the

[1] See L. J. Austin, 'Paul Valéry: "Teste" ou "Faust"?', *C.A.I.E.F.*, XVII (1965), 248.

sea 'si (ce jour-là) l'esprit n'était comme "sensibilisé" à tel ou tel ordre de développements possibles?' (P I, 314). Behind such remarks is the implication that it is the rich connexity of human 'sensibilité'[1] which cannot fail to link the random configurations it perceives into a form of pattern. The theme is made explicit in a remark where, expressing the imaginative empathy or projection into the scene of the whole being of a beholder, Valéry writes:

> Je suis l'écume qui monte sur la roche et en
> rejaillit et redescend, à un mille d'ici.
> Mon 'âme' est 'là-bas'. Là-bas est un foyer
> Où se concentrent, se composent, se reconnaissent
> Les puissances de figure et de mouvement que les
> Images de cette écume viennent exciter 'en moi'.
> Je donne la distance, le relief, l'assaut, le
> rythme, la durée... *là-bas*, où je suis, et
> ne suis...
>
> (P I, 353)

Such a passage could provide the framework or 'field' for the 'regard marin' of the protagonist in *Le Cimetière Marin*, likewise fascinated by 'maint diamant d'imperceptible écume' (P I, 148). The verbal resources of the poem allow Valéry to suggest the counterbalancing elements of the observer's response: mingled pride and tenderness at the fragile but intense power of the beholding mind over the scene it helps to compose. Into the meaningless ideal of an 'absolute' existence man introduces the vital missing elements of creative detachment, boundary and doubt:

> Tu n'as que moi pour contenir tes craintes!
> Mes repentirs, mes doutes, mes contraintes
> Sont le défaut de ton grand diamant...
>
> (P I, 150)

A similar sensitivity to the mental organisation of a scene governs much of Valéry's contemplation of the stars. 'Nous ne pouvons voir de constellation au ciel que nous ne fournissons aussitôt les tracements qui en joignent les astres' (P I, 1314), he notes, or '[...] quand nous parlons de constellations, nous savons bien qu'il n'y a aucune relation, sauf dans notre sensibilité, entre les étoiles qui les composent selon les lignes

[1] Valéry sometimes describes 'sensibilité' in terms of a 'gêne' or complementarity between mind and object (e.g. *Cours de Poétique*, leçon 4 (samedi 18 déc. 1937), *Yggdrasill*, 2 ème année (25 jan. 1938), 155). See above, 39.

virtuelles créés par nous'.[1] Interest in Poincaré's *La Valeur de la Science*[2] may have heightened Valéry's awareness of two kinds of relationships or 'lignes virtuelles', both equally dependent on the observer: the relatively objective relationships or 'rapports' that can be determined between the stars astronomically, and their relationship with human sensitivity (xxix, 27–8). Both visions for Valéry are equally valid. It is the spirit at the root of both art and science which he evokes as artist in *Ode Secrète*:

> O quel Taureau, quel Chien, quelle Ourse,
> Quels objets de victoire énorme,
> Quand elle entre aux temps sans ressource
> L'âme impose à l'espace informe!
>
> (P I, 152)

The mood of this poem is not crudely jubilant. Through images of disintegration ('Vainqueur lentement désuni') as well as of concentration ('L'âme impose à l'espace informe'), it seems to express something of the loneliness and inevitability present in the human imagination as it weaves from the stars patterns which it cannot help but make, and which it knows to be solely its own. As in *Le Cimetière Marin*, where the same theme is presented, the real triumph involved is one of the power of consciousness – the 'consciousness' created in the reader – to remain distinct from its own ordering capacity: 'type de l'acte ordre [...] acte qui joint' (xix, 906).

Valéry has already been seen to disclaim any fear of 'les espaces infinis qui effrayaient l'Adversaire' (xvi, 504). In his essay on Pascal (*Variation sur une Pensée*) he proposes that the mind is capable of creating its own defences against such fear, since human 'solitude' is a more complex phenomenon: 'un sentiment éperdu d'être soi, d'être unique, – et cependant d'être seul. Je suis tout et incomplet. Je suis tout et partie' (P I, 469). The *feeling* of human centrality, the intellectual capacity to dislodge the notion, and the acquisition of a new creative confidence because of it: 'Il faut donc que notre esprit s'excite soi-même à se défaire de sa stupeur et à se reprendre de cette solennelle et immobile surprise que lui causent le sentiment d'être tout et l'évidence de n'être rien' (P I, 470): this triple theme has already been seen as the basis of the mental ethic of Teste.[3] Valéry's imagination never loses touch with this form of natural 'existentialism'. It remains one of the strongest features of his evocation of the natural world.

[1] *Cours de Poétique*, leçon 12 (Samedi 29 jan. 1938), *Yggdrasill* (25 mai 1938), 26.
[2] R. S. Jones, 'Poincaré and Valéry: a note on the "Symbol" in Science and Art', *M.L.R.*, XLII (1947), 487.
[3] See above, 17.

'Sensibilité intellectuelle'

This particularly active and outgoing type of imagination is not Valéry's only response to external nature. Almost equally often he expresses moments when natural objects appear to impose a deep imprint on the 'sensibilité', calling forth in turn a delicate intellectual response. Still characterised by the basic distance between consciousness and nature at the heart of Valéry's writings, things like the sea, the stars or a falling leaf are available as symbols of human reaction because of the sharpness with which they make the observer aware of a corresponding emotion in himself. This can be illustrated, for example, from Valéry's particular sensitivity to things in nature as fragile and changing as the self, yet from which the mind remains perpetually distinct even at the moment of its most intimate response: the twirling of a single leaf, the piercing of a single star, or the cycle of the sun from dawn to twilight. In *Confiteor de l'artiste*, Baudelaire writes that a tiny sail shimmering on the horizon 'par sa petitesse et son isolement imite mon irrémédiable existence'.[1] Valéry expresses a similar emotion ('voir [. . .] et savoir que l'on voit' (P II, 322)) in relationship to small distinct objects. A ship in *Profusion du Soir* seems to carry with it as it disappears into the night ('Et l'espace a humé la barque minuscule' (P I, 88)) the irretrievable key to the richness of the mind which perceives it, while a mysterious girdle in *La Ceinture* becomes the last frail link between the beholder and the fading visible world. Of the sight of a circling bird Valéry writes: 'Le moindre incident égale infini' (vi, 200). The tiniest object, 'la moindre chose réelle' (P I, 1165), has the power to set up infinite repercussions in 'la sensibilité intellectuelle' (P I, 1095), the kind of 'resonance' which so many of Valéry's poems explore and prolong.

Take the theme of the leaf, for example. It is not only the great tossing dramas of the wind in a tree which stimulate Valéry's imagination, but 'l'unique bruit d'une feuille' (v, 839) or the twirling of the individual leaf: 'L'arbre calmé, je cherche et trouve encore une petite feuille qui oscille' (P II, 659). A note in the *Cahiers* – 'Cette feuille qui tremble touche à toute ma (chair et à toute mon histoire)' (iii, 617) – is obviously closely linked to the line in the poem *Équinoxe*: 'Une feuille qui tombe a divisé l'année/De son événement léger' (P I, 161). A further passage serves to throw light on the sensitivity involved:

> Une rose (feuille) qui tombe a divisé le jour (l'année). Pour une conscience, ce corps qui tombe, ce bruit d'une goutte

[1] *Œuvres Complètes* (Paris, Gallimard, 1961), 232.

> divise toutes choses en deux époques. Il y a deux mondes, l'avant et l'après. Mais cet autre corps là ou ailleurs n'a pas éprouvé de changement. Il est *encore* dans le passé. La maison n'a pas entendu l'heure. L'horloge n'a pas senti son aiguille tourner. La sensibilité est la première division universelle.
>
> (vii, 10)

Again a strong sense of the relativity of the event to human sensitivity is concerned. Unlike the human being, the animal, 'si sensible soit-il au moindre froissement/De la feuille de l'arbre' (P I, 201), does not bring to its reaction the experience of consciousness in time.

'Poursuivre dans ta profondeur cette chute pensive de l'âme comme une feuille morte à travers l'immensité vague de la mémoire' (P I, 476), Valéry writes, fusing the theme of falling leaf and human sensitivity still further, and to La Jeune Parque her own heart is: 'Un frémissement fin de feuille, ma présence' (P I, 107). It is this kind of sensitivity which makes for the perfect reciprocity between the Narcisse of *Charmes* and his surroundings, his whole presence inseparable from the hushed, vibrant presence of nature interwoven into his monologue, and his whole destiny inextricably bound up with the slow fall of leaves and even of heavy objects – objects seemingly slowed down by his own sensitivity?[1] – into the pool below:

> O présence pensive, eau calme qui recueilles
> Tout un sombre trésor de fables et de feuilles,
> L'oiseau mort, le fruit mûr, lentement descendus,
> Et les rares lueurs des clairs anneaux perdus.
> Tu consommes en toi leur perte solennelle;
>
> (P I, 126)[2]

Under the rubric 'Narcisse philosophe', Valéry had written in the *Cahiers*: 'Ce feuillage si délié, qui embrouille mes regards, qui s'enchevêtre et s'imite et diffère comme à l'infini, défiant ma pensée, visible et non imaginable, il n'est pas de moi. *Tu m'étonnes*, *donc tu es*' (vii, 31). Thus he suggests a kind of relative mental certainty in the existence of the self and of external nature based on the 'cogito' of surprise, the passage continuing: 'Je suis *sûr* que ces choses existent [...] j'en suis *sûr*, mais cette certitude, je sais qu'elle a même puissance que celle de ma propre existence, et *pas plus*. Les choses *sont* en tant et pour autant que je *suis*.

[1] See Rinsler, *Essays in French Literature*, 37.
[2] Cf. 'Si la feuille éperdue effleure la nappée/Elle suffit à rompre un univers dormant ...' (P I, 122).

Pas plus! (vii, 31). The difference between this and an axiomatic statement lies in the insistence that such a feeling is in itself a changing one, as must be any proposition depending on 'sensibilité' – the rôle of which Valéry once defined as being to disrupt any 'static' equilibrium of mental powers inhibitory to the exploratory self-preservation of man (P I, 470).

This kind of delicate link between consciousness and nature is present in Valéry's evocation of the reciprocity between natural movement and human change, for example: 'l'extrémité des arbres me remue toujours, m'emporte et me tord dans NOTRE profondeur' (iii, 98), or 'Sens debout le vent neuf instantanément frais durcir. Il fait mouvoir l'ombre et les feuilles noires. Et jusque dans mon cœur il presse des forêts. Et je change' (ii, 915). Nor is the sensitivity to human change concerned a 'tied' associative reaction. The immobility of the leaves on a tree can have the same effect as their mobility, emphasising the human by contrast: 'Je change – Qui me fuit? Ses feuilles immobiles/Accablent l'arbre que je vois' (*Équinoxe*, P I, 159). To the protagonist of *Le Cimetière Marin*, the seemingly motionless sky intensifies both human variability and the relative constancy of human consciousness, as he calls on nature to witness his changing yet perceived experience: 'Beau ciel, vrai ciel, regarde-moi qui change!' (P I, 148).

Another natural object on which a particular 'sensibilité intellectuelle' may centre in Valéry's notes and poetry is the star, the single star as opposed to the constellations previously mentioned. Indeed, Valéry's preferences in nature often seem to lie, as his critique of 'Nature' has already hinted, not with the great uniform landscape or forest, but with the scene composed of single objects: 'non pas un paysage, mais un arbre, et dans cet arbre le dessin d'une branche; non pas un ciel mais le contour d'un nuage, et dans ce contour, une couleur, un ton'.[1] La Jeune Parque, when 'seule avec diamants extrêmes', is reduced to anguished tears of loneliness (tears quite different from the tears of relief she was seen to shed at a stage of greater acceptance of her affective self). The loneliness is reflected in the rhetorical power of the verse, through which, with biblical resonance, the almost impersonal voice of Language throughout the ages seems to speak to her through her own mind:

> Tout-puissants étrangers, inévitables astres
> Qui daignez faire luire au lointain temporel
> Je ne sais quoi de pur et de surnaturel;
> Vous qui dans les mortels plongez jusques aux larmes

[1] Lucienne J. Cain, *Trois Essais*, 158–9.

Ces souverains éclats, ces invincibles armes,
Et les élancements de votre éternité,
Je suis seule avec vous [. . .]

(P I, 96)[1]

Two quotations concerning the single star will suggest, unlike the piercing of these many stars, a much more gentle emotion. Valéry notes, for example: 'A quatre heures je regardais le palmier orné d'une étoile. Ce calme infiniment doux, source immobile de la journée, était infiniment voisin de la source des larmes' (viii, 588), and:

Étoile. Au ciel uni mat bleu
Sombre – à corps noir – quelque chose
  infiniment douce, vive et élevée
perce, accompagnée d'éclat, de distance
  de pureté, pénétration, finesse
isolement – *présences.*

(ii, 186)[2]

The tears in the first quotation are of a far less desolate kind than those of the Parque at the opening of the poem. This is but one further indication that the 'nature' symbols in Valéry's poetry will also shift according to the human response they evoke and express in turn.

In the preceding examples Valéry shows a power of appreciating and expressing how the slightest movement or event in nature can reverberate through the whole human sensitivity. 'La reprise monotone du roulement de la douce houle use et polit indéfiniment la bizarrerie de ton âme' (P I, 313), he writes, mingling outer and inner world in a manner reminiscent of Baudelaire, or 'Roule jusqu'à mon cœur la distance dorée,/ Vague!' (P I, 88). Sea, stars, foliage, wind, all are made, without losing their individual identity, to express something of the relationship of consciousness and nature of interest here. This sensitivity shows itself equally strongly in Valéry's treatment of natural light or the cycle of the sun, the last theme to be examined in this chapter. Here perhaps more than anywhere can be seen his ability as an artist to avoid any suspicion of pathetic fallacy while at the same time making shifting natural light effects instruments for measuring human mood in all its subtle fluctuations

1 Cf. A. R. Chisholm: 'not a paucity of stars, but on the contrary [. . .] a great clustering mass of them' (*An Approach to 'La Jeune Parque'* (Melbourne U.P., 1938), 11).

2 Cf. 'le phénomène optique qui fait l'homme voir soi à peu près comme les astres le voient' (vii, 32) (also P I, 469).

('la self-variance'). 'Dominée dès l'aube par une contemplation – puis active, élégante, musculeuse jusqu'aux réflexions du couchant et à la prière de la nuit' (ii, 901): the particular 'pensée' of dawn, midday and twilight is evoked time and time again in Valéry's notes and poetry. Only a very few examples can be selected here.[1]

First dawn. It is well-known that this was for Valéry a privileged moment, closely associated with the writing of the *Cahiers* themselves, and therefore with a particular lucidity and solitude. Some of his most beautiful prose fragments attempt to express the parallel themes of the day's initial freshness and plenitude on the one hand, and, on the other, the complexity of the waking consciousness before the unfolding of more developed thoughts. The two levels become inextricably linked. For example:

> Aube. Ce n'est pas l'aube. Mais le déclin de la lune, perle rongée, glace fondante, et une lueur mourante à qui le jour naissant se substitue peu à peu – J'aime ce moment si pur, final, initial. Mélange de calme, de renoncement, de négation [. . .]. C'est le coucher et l'assoupissement du moi le plus seul.
>
> (P I, 311–12; vii, 732)

In the poem *A L'Aurore. . .* Valéry evokes the paradoxical shock suffered by the sensibility on discovering that the light of early morning holds a tenderness and beauty which seems to belie its own deep vigilant suffering throughout the night. A wound seems to be inflicted on suffering itself:

> A l'aurore, avant la chaleur,
> La tendresse de la couleur
> A peine éparse sur le monde,
> Étonne et blesse la douleur
>
> (P I, 159)[2]

In the poem *Neige* however, consciousness wakes to wonder at the transformation of appearances undergone during its own absence in sleep:

> Oh! combien de flocons, pendant ma douce absence,
> Durent les sombres cieux perdre toute la nuit![3]

'Quand tu penses, ne sens-tu pas que tu déranges secrètement quelque chose; et quand tu t'endors, ne sens-tu pas que tu la laisses s'arranger

[1] See also J. R. Lawler, 'Light in Valéry', *A.J.F.S.*, VI (1969), 348–75.
[2] See Lawler, ibid., 35.
[3] Quoted by J. R. Lawler, ibid., 353 and 357.

comme elle peut?' (P II, 123), asks Socrates in *Eupalinos*. It seems that Valéry's dawn poems go to the heart of phenomenological reality and the dynamic balance between consciousness, the self and the outer world. It is this same experience of dawn which provides the central drama of *La Jeune Parque*, where, after her symbolic struggles with the dreams and shadows of the night, the Parque wakes to rediscover herself through the very same process by which light shapes the pale ambiguous landscape into recognisable form. Dawn is a moment of isolation and transition, discovery and acceptance so complex in terms of human sensitivity that Valéry makes the birth of the day dependent on the bodily and mental presence of the Parque herself:

> Je te revois, mon bras, . . . Tu portes l'aube . . .
>
> (P I, 105)[1]

Mid-day is likewise an emblem of human sensitivity, the full sun calling forth a primitive sensuality ('nu au soleil sur mon lit tout illuminé/ nu, seul, fou, Moi!' (P I, 354)), or in the case of Sémiramis, seeming to reflect the violent self-destructive power of consciousness itself at its most voluptuous and intense (P I, 195–6). In *Le Cimetière Marin* the mid-day sun meets its measure in the eye (or consciousness) of its beholder:

> L'âme exposée aux torches du solstice,
> Je te soutiens, admirable justice
> De la lumière aux armes sans pitié!
>
> (P I, 148)

The sun here provides a perfect example of Valéry's symbols at work. There is no *abstract* link between pure light and human lucidity. The sun is made equivalent to an absolute through human experience, and in the changing of the sunlight and the changing of experience, Valéry has the perfect means of suggesting the contingency of the idea of an absolute on human desire.

'Tout se passe comme dans certains êtres si sensibles que la seule approche de la nuit leur fait venir aux yeux des larmes inexplicables' Valéry wrote in his homage to the poet Léon-Paul Fargue.[2] This kind of sensitivity is obviously close to his own. Evening, like dawn, is a moment of transition; the transition of day into night and similarly, as is

[1] Cf. Rinsler, *Essays in French Literature*, 52.

[2] 'Notules sur Léon-Paul Fargue' in 'Hommage à Léon-Paul Fargue', *Les Feuilles Libres*, XLV–XLVI (1927).

suggested by the poems *Profusion du Soir* and *La Ceinture*, the transition of consciousness into sleep with its wider associations of extinction in death. In *La Jeune Parque* the evening is linked with the mental reward of memory and tenderness ('Ressusciter un soir favori des colombes' (P I, 101)) as opposed to the relentless mental responsibility of a new day ('l'aube me dévoilait tout le jour ennemi' (P I, 101)). Notes on the theme of evening suggest a premonition of the diffusion of conscious concentration in sleep; a vast, relaxed lucidity akin to the experience of memory, in which consciousness and 'self' are no longer opposed: 'L'indifférence tend vers l'enchantement, sur la fin de l'après-midi. A demi marbre, à demi fumée. Souvenir sans bords, sans balustrade, sans véritables souvenirs, même – la *forme* seule de la mémoire l'aspiration d'une perspective' (iv, 69). In *Mon Faust* the soft evening light corresponds to the peaceful yet alert quality of Faust's mature consciousness. 'Votre visage, à cette heure', says Lust, 'est le plus beau de vos visages. Il propose à la riche lumière du couchant ce qu'elle peut éclairer de plus spirituel et de plus noble' (P II, 319). Unlike the distinct light of dawn, the rich colours of sunset produce no wound of surprise in the sensibility of the beholder, but rather the confirmation of its own inner wealth, a wealth which in the case of Faust is connected with the intellectual achievement of accepting an end to the potential endlessness of consciousness[1] – and for the external world to coincide with the rhythms of consciousness is one of the strongest human needs expressed by Valéry's work.

'. . . C'est une chose étrange que le Jour', he writes in *Mauvaises Pensées*, in a passage of great relevance to this discussion of the rôle of the cycle of the sun in his work,

> Étrange, c'est dire *étrangère*. Étrangère à la pensée, qui semble raisonner, créer, spécifier, vivre à sa guise son désordre et son ordre de pensée, sans égard à cette énorme horloge de lumière qui mesure ce qu'elle manifeste et manifeste ce qu'elle mesure . . .
>
> Mais la marche du Jour, si elle est insensible dans l'exercice de l'esprit, toutefois secrètement lui impose une variation de ses forces, – c'est-à-dire une coloration, un relief, une énergie, une évaluation diurnes de ses idées.
>
> Le Jour et le Corps, deux grandes puissances . . .
>
> (P II, 810)

[1] Cf. N. Bastet, 'Faust et le Cycle', *Entretiens sur Paul Valéry*, 115–28. Cf. 'Le but de perfectionnement d'une vie [. . .] *pourrait être* de comprendre en profondeur la *mort* comme *condition de la vie* [. . .] comme *besoin*' (xxvi, 315).

The question posed at the beginning of this chapter was whether a strong sense of abstraction and detachment such as Valéry's might combine with an appreciation of sensuous detail and a sensitivity to the penetrating influences of the natural world. It should be apparent by now that no contradiction is involved in the co-existence in his work of detachment and involvement, movement and immobility, precision and fluidity. For Valéry, it is because of, not despite, the power of detachment that consciousness can return 'auxivresses de l'instinct particulier et à l'émotion que donne la moindre chose réelle' (P I, 1165) and that the objects of the natural world are 'les objets que l'on laisse et l'on retrouve – doués de vertu substantive . . .' (XXI, 861).[1] He has after all the powers of a 'nature poet' of the finest order. The following chapters will attempt to follow this particular imagination further in its detailed confrontation with individual living phenomena such as the tree, and finally with the major themes of natural growth and development which run throughout his poetry and thought.

[1] Cf. 'Qui ne les a pas traversés [states of intense introspection] ne connaît pas le prix de la lumière naturelle et du milieu le plus banal' (P I, 1221).

5 *Living things*

'Et ce qui n'est pas moins caractéristique de cet attrait que le problème de la vie exerce sur son esprit', writes M. Bémol,

> Ce sont toutes ces notes où [Valéry] exprime les sentiments, les impressions, les idées qui naissent en lui lorsqu'il soumet à sa méthode de contemplation directe la vie animale ou végétale, qu'il s'agisse de l'oiseau, du chien, de la mouche, du tigre, de l'huître, de l'arbuste ou de l'arbre. Et, comme il est naturel, cette méditation sur la vie trouve parfois chez Valéry son achèvement sous forme de poésie [. . .].[1]

From this list I have selected three themes to examine in detail: the insect, the bird and the tree. The first two are minor themes, not usually treated at length, while the last is a major theme already treated from several points of view.

Reflections on animals are less common, possibly because Valéry was not so likely to observe actual examples as he wrote, for a 'mélange' of actual incidents obviously sparks off much of his thought, however 'pure'. There are, of course, a few examples to note: the serpent of *Ébauche d'un Serpent* which, although it belongs to more archetypal imagery, Valéry nonetheless evokes sensuously with its 'triangle d'émeraude' and 'langue à double fil' (P I, 138); the magnificent tiger evoked in *Mélange* (P I, 293–5); the oyster, again in *Mélange*, which opens like 'la *pudica mimosa*' (P I, 318); or the racehorse, 'cheval de course', a focal point for many immediate observations on speed and muscular economy (for example, in the little known prose-poems *Aux Courses* and *Amazone*),[2]

[1] *Paul Valéry* (Paris, Société d'Édition 'Les Belles Lettres', 1949), 256–7.
[2] *Petits Textes* (Commentaires de Gravures), *N.R.F.* (1er jan. 1928), 55–65.

as well as for an ideal of mental discipline referred to by Valéry as 'Gladiator' (the name of a famous racehorse).[1] There are also a considerable number of references to the animal in general, as might be expected from a writer so frequently drawn to speculate on life in all its forms. The dog and sometimes the cow are mentioned in order to highlight some contrast with human behaviour, for example, in their indifferent reaction to the stars, or to time (P II, 230; P II, 126).

Meditations on the insect or the bird can perhaps be grouped into three sections: its intrusion into a would-be autonomous train of thought; its own physical attributes; and lastly, the particular response it causes in human consciousness as the proof of the existence of organised life apart from itself. Jottings throughout the *Cahiers*, sometimes accompanied by fleeting sketches, provide most of the material needed to compile this picture, though sometimes a theme can be followed through into an image used in a poem or other piece of formal writing.

The theme of the intrusion of external nature into thought is not, of course, confined to the living creature. A similar set of associations centres, for example, on the theme of scent. '*Odoratus impedit cogitationem*' is a phrase of St Bernard appropriated by Valéry, as can be seen from *Mélange* (P I, 308), from several instances in the *Cahiers* (e.g. VI, 14, 113) and from the lecture in *Variété* where he goes as far as to suggest that the power to incorporate contradiction and contingency into rational processes is the mark of the true thinker (P I, 1352). A scent may sometimes be linked with an involuntary memory as a privileged centre of experience (P II, 858). It may also be seen as a potentially disruptive agent in thought, a temptation to the intellect: 'Je me perds dans ce parfum et les ébauches trop vivantes qu'il ordonne' (P I, 308; cf. P II, 432). 'Le diable est l'esprit subtil, sensible seulement au parfum des roses ou à la confusion des feuillages, sensible seulement à la vie d'alentour', writes F. Pire.[2] This 'vie d'alentour' is, of course, another way of referring to the affective self, the self that is active when La Jeune Parque is drawn to the scent of orange blossom ('la narine jointe au vent de l'oranger' (P I, 100)) or when La Pythie is intoxicated by the aroma of burning herbs ('ivre d'empyreumes' (P I, 133)). The question becomes: what reaction does Valéry express to the invasion of thought by involuntary processes with roots deep in the affective self? 'Un parfum annule la

[1] See Judith Robinson, 'Valéry's conception of training the mind', *F.S.*, XVIII (1964), 227–35.

[2] *La Tentation du Sensible chez Paul Valéry* (Bruxelles, La Renaissance du Livre, 1964), 71.

méditation', the same critic continues, 'mais au lieu de répandre la confusion et la débauche dans l'esprit qu'il suscite, ce parfum porte Faust "au comble de son art".'[1] Like Teste, Faust has known the vital power of 'le ne pas s'adapter – ne pas épouser ce qui arrive' (iv, 16); but, unlike Teste, he is willing to go further in the complementary power of intellectual adaptation, 'le s'ajouter ce que l'on a trouvé' (ix, 730) (an art that Teste is sowing, but of which he is not seen to reap the fruits). In this way, the enticing scent of fresh roses is made to seem Faust's intellectual triumph, rather than his intellectual defeat.

A similar pattern of rejection and acceptance can, I think, be discerned in the case of the interruption of a train of thought by the sight of an insect or by the sight or sound of a bird.

The insect

It is not surprising to find the theme of the insect, particularly the fly, in the works of other writers concerned with a high degree of reflective consciousness. Montaigne notes that his mind is 'assassinated' by 'le moindre bourdonnement de mouche',[2] and Pascal writes: 'elles gagnent les batailles, empêchent notre âme d'agir'.[3] The last remark with its suggestion of resentment at the intrusion of the outside world into the would-be sufficient domain of the mystic is close to comments in the *Cahiers* such as: 'Une mouche brise les fils d'une composition d'idées' (xvi, 885), or, in the negative words of Le Solitaire: 'A quoi, à quoi ne se livre-t-il pas, l'esprit? La moindre mouche le débauche' (P ii, 388). 'Voici un philosophe qui spécule sur le monde, sur la connaissance; il dispose de l'espace et du temps;', Valéry writes in *Analecta*, 'pense dans la plus grande généralité; se distingue de son mieux de l'instant . . . mais sa pensée est au milieu d'objets et de petits incidents – de bruits, et des brusques reflets d'une fenêtre crevant de soleil qu'on ouvre en face de la sienne' (P ii, 718), or 'l'intellect le plus soi; la plus propre, la plus fine pensée sont à la merci du moindre incident du réel' (v, 399).

Monsieur Teste's reaction would probably be attempted indifference and semi-withdrawal. Indeed, the image of the fly is humorously used to describe Madame Teste, who represents a minor challenge to his mental autonomy: 'Je suis une mouche qui s'agite et vivote dans l'univers d'un regard inébranlable; et tantôt vue, tantôt non vue, mais jamais hors de vue' (P ii, 32), she says.[4] That she should present an element of intrusion

[1] Ibid., 72.
[2] *Essais*, iii, 13 (ed. M. J. V. Leclerc) (Paris, Garnier Frères, 1925), iv, 241.
[3] *Les Pensées*, no. 83 (éd. Strowski, 1931), 69.
[4] Cf. iv, 451.

at all suggests a certain tension on Teste's part, the maintenance of abstraction by constant acts of elimination. Yet Valéry's own comments on how the interruption might appear to the thinker (for example: 'il se perd et se retrouve, et se retrouve un peu différent, tantôt ne se comprenant plus; tantôt plus éveillé' (P II, 719)), suggests a willingness to recognise its possible value, the vital rupture of potentially circular processes. 'Une tache d'encre', he writes under the rubric, *Accident:*

> De cet accident je fais une figure avec un dessin dans les environs. La tache prend un rôle et une fonction dans ce contexte. Et ceci est analogue à la pensée de Pascal: 'J'avais une pensée. Je l'ai oubliée: J'écris, au lieu, que je l'ai oubliée'.
> L'accident est *rattrapé*, *rédimé*.
>
> (P II, 710)

There are many indications, in practice as much as in theory, that the ability to transform an 'interruption' plays a large part in Valéry's poetics (e.g. v, 193), and that he is as capable of 'divergent' as of 'convergent' thought. In terms of self-discovery, reaction to the fly is equally positive whether mental tension is relaxed or increased, a paradox Valéry summarises in the lilting epigraph to *Mélange*:

> Esclave d'une mouche ou maître d'une loi,
> Un esprit n'est que ce mélange
> Duquel à chaque instant, se démêle le MOI.
>
> (P I, 286)[1]

'Une mouche sur le papier à pas menus/Parcourt mes lignes inégales' wrote Apollinaire.[2] When it comes to meditations on the insect, Valéry shows himself equally responsive to the element of delicacy involved. It might even be said, as in the example of his reactions to a single leaf in the previous chapter, that the smaller the creature or incident, the stronger is the reaction, since more personal concentration is involved. In *Histoires Brisées* he speculates on 'un personnage que l'on representerait [. . .] dans son fauteuil, fumant, et le regard se fixant assez vite, de soi-même [. . .] sur un objet assez petit' (P II, 457). The 'regard' expressed in his own work is as capable of noting the details of that object as of abstracting it to infinity as does Teste. For example, 'Une très petite

[1] Cf. P II, 206 (where the discontinuous or unstable motion of the fly is compared with the mind in a state of 'non-attention') and P I, 311 (where the mobility of a 'Regard' is evoked in terms of the same imagery).

[2] 'A la Santé', *Œuvres Complètes* (Paris, Gallimard, 1956), 143.

bête se déplace sur le parquet' (xxiv, 788): interest is aroused by the movement of the insect or by its power of combining symmetry and motion, 'la symétrie des animaux mobiles est commandée par leur mouvement. [. . .] Un insecte est stationnaire, travaille de ses palpes et pattes sur place – puis brusquement jaillit vers ailleurs' (xi, 345). The same power of detailed observation is behind the image used in *L'Âme et la Danse* where the dancer's movements are compared with 'la puissance de l'insecte, dont l'innombrable vibration de ses ailes soutient indéfiniment la fanfare, le poids et le courage!' (P II, 161). Valéry constantly speculates on the imitation of a natural phenomenon by the conscious mind.[1] He writes here: 'Il faudrait à mon esprit cette force et ce mouvement concentré, qui suspendent l'insecte au-dessus de la multitude de fleurs' (P II, 165). To complete the analogy, thought itself would be a dance, 'Un état qui ne serait que d'action [. . .] comparable à la vibrante station d'un bourdon ou d'un sphinx devant le calice de fleurs qu'il explore, et qui demeure, chargé de puissance motrice, à peu près immobile, et soutenu par le battement incroyablement rapide de ses ailes' (P I, 1396). In this way the insect is the natural representative of Valéry's comments on energy, action and duration – the notion of 'équilibre mobile' (xii, 642) which culminates in his eulogy of the dance. It is obviously something of the aesthetic emotion connected with the idea of the dance and indirectly with human consciousness which can then be transferred back to contemplation of the insects dancing an intricate ballet round a 'piège à mouches' (xv, 796).

Alertness to insect movement leads Valéry to a further theme on which he speculates constantly throughout his notes: tropism, the most familiar example of which is the ineluctable pull of an insect such as the moth towards a light. 'Tropismes. Aiguille aimantée', Valéry writes in one of the more abstract remarks in the *Cahiers*: 'Tout se passe comme si des "forces" se développaient dans un vivant quand le milieu est non isotrope au point de vue des restrictions' and he gives an example: 'Fascination – lumière sur oiseaux et insectes' (ix, 63). Similarly, he notes, 'On ne peut "Expliquer" le papillon attiré par la lumière que par une idée mécanique (photoélectrique)' (xxiv, 806), or 'L'attraction des êtres volants par la lumière et l'espèce de suicide obligatoire par injonction de la sensibilité qui en résulte est l'un des faits les plus confondants de la nature. La lumière leur crée un champ de gravitation mortelle' (xxvi, 861).

Valéry returns time and time again to this phenomenon. There seem to be several reasons. First, fascination with the way in which nature apparently allows the self-destruction of individual organisms; secondly,

[1] E.g. plant growth (see below, 196).

a sense of mystery, the existence of a phenomenon not yet understood; and thirdly, the possible parallels it presents with the biological limits of human consciousness, an interest central to all Valéry's meditations on life. 'Tropisme' is for Valéry, as it is for Nathalie Sarraute, an idea connected with human behaviour as much as with that of the insect (e.g., xv, 797).[1] For Valéry, there is something tropistic in the need of the intellect to test 'jusqu'au bout' the limits of its existence in order to feel alive, or perhaps to escape life altogether. He speaks of what he calls 'Egotropisme' (vii, 227), in this case the movement of 'orgueil' by which human nature is drawn like a plant ('la plante humaine') to respond to praise. Lucienne J. Cain has mentioned the 'tropisme mystérieux' by which the disrupted elements of being, in the person of La Jeune Parque, for example, turn or are drawn again to full acceptance of life (symbolised in this case, it might be added, by the sun): 'le morcellement qui, selon les psychologues, est un symptôme de faiblesse, de nécrose, dans ce régime qu'on pourrait appeler électro-spirituel est le signal d'un regroupement de forces: il témoigne d'une recharge, d'une nouvelle repartition de l'afflux nerveux'.[2]

Apart from 'l'insecte net' of *Le Cimetière Marin* (P I, 149),[3] it is probably the bee which most readily comes to mind as an example of insect imagery in poetry. In *L'Abeille*, overtones of mental and physical illumination are conveyed in words that evoke at the same time the sharp, energetic sting of the insect:

> Quelle, et si fine, et si mortelle,
> Que soit ta pointe, blonde abeille,
> [. . . . .]
> Pique du sein la gourde belle,
> [. . . . .]
> Soit donc mon sens illuminé
> Par cette infime alerte d'or
>
> (P I, 118)

These attributes are indirectly carried on in the reactions of the girl who is stung: 'prompt tourment', 'mal', 'vif' and so on, and even through the idea of death itself, since the bee's sting is known to be the cause of its

[1] Other examples of 'tropismes' are: xiv, 4, 504; xvii, 478; xviii, 535; xxvi, 861; xxvii, 32.

[2] *Trois Essais sur Paul Valéry* (Paris, Gallimard, 1958), 171.

[3] Cf. (in the *Dialogue de l'Arbre*) '[. . .] le poids ardent du mystère de midi; et le temps tout dormant en toi ne dure que par l'irritante rumeur du peuple des insectes' (P II, 179).

own death and yet is felt in the poem to imply the revivification of love ('Sans qui l'Amour meurt ou s'endort' (P I, 118)). In this way, abstract themes of death, pain, eroticism and mental illumination are kept alive on a physical level by the impressionistic, intermediary presence of the bee. Valéry sometimes uses the verb 'bourdonner' in much the same way in a metaphorical context. The poet's mind, for example, 'bourdonne lui-même autour de son propre point de repère' (P I, 1351).[1] This is obviously the kind of analogical process behind the poem *Aurore* with its theme of the profusion of ideas in the conscious mind and its imagery of a girl picking fruit amongst the buzzing of a swarm of bees:

> Au vacarme des abeilles
> Je vous aurai par corbeilles,
>
> (P I, 111)

The buzzing relates outer event to inner mental activity, rather as the sea in the poem *Été* is referred to as 'ardente ruche':

> Été, roche d'air pur, et toi, ardente ruche,
> O mer! Éparpillée en mille mouches sur
> Les touffes d'une chair fraîche comme une cruche,
> Et jusque dans la bouche où bourdonne l'azur;
>
> (P I, 85)

Finally, the bee imagery of *Aurore* can be seen to shift to that of spiders, corresponding to the movement from rich profusion to a greater intricacy of control:

> Nous étions non eloignées,
> Mais secrètes araignées
> Dans les ténèbres de toi!
>
> (P I, 112)

In this case Valéry seems to be playing on the same idea of expenditure and nourishment which prompts him to write in his notes under the heading 'Bestiaire': '"L'araignée extrait d'elle-même le subtil et délicat réseau, qui, en récompense, lui restitue la proie qu'il a capturée" Léonard' (xxvii, 111). An example of the way in which a theme such as that of the spider is frequently used on a figurative level to symbolise the workings of

[1] See Vera J. Daniel, *Paul Valéry, Eupalinos and L'Âme et la Danse* (O.U.P., 1967), 201 n. 121, and 167 n. 3 where Valéry's predilection for the verb 'bourdonner' is pointed out. Valéry records his admiration for Mallarmé's lines: 'Tu sais, ma passion, que pourpre et déjà mûre/Chaque grenade éclate et d'abeilles murmure' (P I, 670).

consciousness is quoted by J. R. Lawler in the context of poetic composition: 'Là, attentive aux coups de hasard parmi lesquels elle choisit sa nourriture; là, très obscure parmi les réseaux et les harpes secrètes qu'elle s'est faites du langage, dont les fils s'entremêlent et vibrent toujours – une chasseresse, une mystérieuse Arachné, veille'.[1]

The third and perhaps most characteristic group of reflections on the insect concerns the strongly relativistic side of Valéry's imagination already suggested in the previous chapter. 'Une très petite bête se déplace sur le parquet. Cela trace *pour moi* une *ligne*' (xxiv, 788): the line, like the 'lignes virtuelles' between the stars, is a creation of human sensitivity alone (Valéry has written near this entry the name 'le Solitaire', perhaps suggesting the negative aspect of solitude in contrast to the triumphant exchange with the world developed in *L'Ode Secrète*). Similarly, he will meditate on the animal's or insect's different point of vision: 'Cette vache, cette mouche regardent à peu près la même chose que MOI, et ne voient pas le même. 3 développements distincts' (ix, 457), or, in more imaginative detail: 'La mouche courant sur le miroir ne s'inquiète pas de cette mouche inverse sur les pointes des pattes de laquelle elle pose et court; mais elle voit au contraire sur le plan poli quantité de très petites choses qui l'intéressent et que nous confondons sous le nom de poussière et de saleté' (P II, 851–2). Next to a rapid sketch of three flies in the *Cahiers*, Valéry notes: 'Le mystère du temps doit peut-être se comparer à cette énigme pour la mouche qu'est le corps transparent, et celui de l'espace à celle qu'offre le corps réfléchissant où se voit ce qui voit' (xv, 802); and elsewhere: 'l'éclair, longue journée éclatante pour l'insecte' (i, 372).

Again, several interrelated themes can be distinguished. 'A ses yeux', Judith Robinson remarks of Valéry's interest in the vision of an animal, 'tout être qui perçoit le monde, fût-ce d'une manière très incomplète, s'en fait par cela même quelque idée, fût-elle de l'espèce la plus élémentaire.'[2] Valéry is concerned with an imaginative projection into the animal's or insect's point of vision. This vision is not necessarily more limited than that of man (the example of the perception by bees and butterflies of ultra-violet radiation invisible to the naked eye of human beings is cited by Judith Robinson).[3] As in the passage quoted above, the insect may be aware of smaller things than man, or it may have a more highly developed sense of industry (xxvii, 49). What is important is that it has a

[1] *Lecture de Valéry – une étude de 'Charmes'* (Paris, P.U.F., 1963), 33–4. Cf. P I, 484.

[2] *L'Analyse de l'Esprit dans les Cahiers de Valéry* (Paris, Corti, 1963), 101.

[3] Ibid., 100.

different vision, and behind interest in this difference is a theme which never leaves Valéry's work: the relativity of 'reality' to a biological act of perception on the part of a living being, whether insect, animal or human: 'Chaque *autonomie* vivante a sa sphère et sa réponse à ce dont elle se divise [. . .]' (xvi, 3). Coleridge wrote in his notebooks: 'Hung over the bridge, and musing considering how much of this scene of endless variety in identity was Nature's – how much the living organ's. What would it be if I had the eyes of a fly! – What of the blunt eye of a Brobdingnag.'[1] Valéry's imagination works in much the same way. Such comments are directed in part against an anthropocentric vision of the universe, but at the same time the anthropomorphic emphasis of his thought is clear in the sense of using 'ce qu'on sait ou ce qu'on peut en tant qu'homme et que limites d'homme à "*expliquer*"' (xix, 311).[2] Thus an important difference exists between Valéry's use of relativism and that of, say, Voltaire. Where the Voltairean imagination might well suggest that if a fly walking on a human limb is at the centre of its own universe, so human beings might just as well be walking on some other great creature they cannot perceive, Valéry usually stresses the power of human consciousness to transcend relativity by awareness, at least for its own immediate purposes (e.g. 'Une mouche qui ne peut pas traverser une vitre est notre image. Nous ne pouvons pas rester à ce point mort' (P II, 470)). It seems that for him, the human organism is distinct from others only in that it is complex enough to give rise to the phenomenon of 'conscience consciente'. That Valéry never accords value to those experiences which disrupt such a possibility suggests that here is his greatest point of divergence from certain Eastern philosophies where individual consciousness exists but to blend with the universe.[3]

The bird

A similar set of reflections concerns the theme of the bird. First, it can be seen to play the same 'interruptive' rôle as the fly, breaking into the individual time-span of a thought and turning 'ailleurs', 'le fleuve de durée' (ii, 894–5). Seagulls, for example, of which Valéry writes: 'Les mouettes innombrables dissipaient mon attention, la ravissaient et renouvelaient dans l'espace.' This time he continues with a description not of the interrupted thought, but of the intruders themselves:

1 Quoted by H. House in *Coleridge* (The Clark Lectures, Trinity College, Cambridge, 1951–2) (London, 1953), 56.

2 Quoted by P. Laurette in *Le Thème de L'Arbre chez Paul Valéry* (Paris, Librairie C. Klincksieck, 1967), 119 ('Anthropomorphisme et science').

3 Cf. Monique Maka-de Schepper, *Le Thème de la Pythie chez Paul Valéry* (Paris, Société d'Édn. 'Les Belles Lettres', 1969), 104.

> Leurs corps lisses et purs, bien placés contre le vent, glissaient, filaient sur d'invisibles pentes, effleuraient le balcon, viraient, rompaient le vol et s'abattaient sur les gros glaçons, où les blanches bêtes posées se disputaient entre elles les ordures tremblantes et les débris affreux de poisson rejetés à l'eau.
>
> (P I, 849–50)

and ends: 'Entre deux oiseaux instantanés je revenais à ma première pensée' (P I, 850). This passage is part of a published essay on a specific theme, Descartes and *Le Retour de Hollande*. In his own notes Valéry might have posed the question whether that 'première pensée' was still the same as it might have been, or even whether the term 'might have been' has any relation to mental life. Pure thought, thought in a vacuum, cannot exist, though something of the yearning towards it may be reflected in the image of the birdless sky in *Profusion du Soir*: 'Les travaux du couchant dans la sphère vidée/Connaissent sans oiseaux leur entière grandeur' (P I, 86).[1]

On a less abstract level, the nature of Valéry's reaction to the minutest invasion of consciousness by the natural world might be suggested by examining his many notes on the *sound* of a bird, a theme representative of all the contingencies which surround 'le philosophe' (P II, 719). Birdsong seems a particularly persuasive general phenomenon, as a preliminary glance at the work of other artists will suggest.

Sartre's Roquentin, for example, finds the songs of a bird, like the perfumes of Spring, 'louches';[2] in Rimbaud's *Illuminations* the piercing song of the single bird 'vous arrête et vous fait rougir';[3] Nerval writes: 'Elle est pure, simple et touchante/La voix de l'oiseau – dans les bois';[4] Hugo: 'Un oiseau chante à sa fenêtre,/la gaîté chante dans son cœur';[5] T. S. Eliot: 'Into our first world, shall we follow/the deception of the thrush?',[6] and Apollinaire: 'Mais que dire de cet oiseau.'[7] Proust's Marcel listens to birdsong like Prometheus to the Oceanides,[8] and Gide's Alissa, in a moment of tension, hears 'un chant d'oiseau, unique [. . .] si près de

1 In *Fragments du Narcisse* the air is 'vivant par tant d'oiseaux' (P I, 128).
2 *La Nausée* (Paris, Gallimard, 1938).
3 'Enfance III', *Œuvres Complètes* (Paris, Gallimard, 1946), 169.
4 'Dans les Bois', *Œuvres*, ed. H. Lemaître, I (Paris, Garnier, 1958), 48.
5 Quoted by J.-B. Barrère in *La Fantaisie de Victor Hugo*, III (Paris, Corti, 1950), 195.
6 'Burnt Norton' (*Collected Poems, 1909–1935*) (Faber, 1958), 185.
7 'Un Oiseau Chante' (*Calligrammes*), *Œuvres Poétiques* (Paris, Gallimard, 1956), 301.
8 *À La Recherche du Temps Perdu* (*À L'Ombre des Jeunes Filles en Fleurs*) (Paris, Gallimard, 1954), 533.

moi, si pathétique, si pur qu'il me sembla soudain que toute la nature l'attendait'.[1] Such a list could be endless. Already it stretches over a range of tones from metaphysical disgust, guilt in innocence, robust pantheism, enchantment, purity, puzzlement, primeval innocence, nostalgia, loneliness.

The reaction Valéry most commonly expresses is not quite any of these. A few fragments must be put together in order to give some idea of the tone of his response. 'J'entends bouillir tous les oiseaux' (i, 139) is one of the minute but unforgettable comments in the *Cahiers* of the sound of many birds at dawn, or: 'Oiseaux premiers. Naissent enfin ces petits cris. Vie et pluralité vivante au plus haut des cieux! Petits cris d'oiseaux, menus coups de ciseaux, petits bruits de ciseaux dans la paix! Mais quel silence à découdre' (P II, 657).[2]

This kind of pictorial imagery is not, however, the most characteristic side of Valéry's response. It is the tendency of birdsong to set up some resonance in the listener's sensitivity to time which seems the more frequent. In *La Jeune Parque* the sound of a bird cuts across the present turmoil with sudden otherwise unheard memories of a peaceful childhood 'l'oiseau perce de cris d'enfance/Inouïs' (P I, 103).[3] It is almost in the reverse sense that Lust reacts to the same sound from a state of mature happiness: 'ces terribles oiseaux si haut dans le ciel, dont les cris trop aigus traversent mon bonheur' (P II, 321). In 'Il y a cinquante ans', one of the passages grouped together in *Poésie Brute*, Valéry writes: 'Cet oiseau pique la nuit finissante de cris faibles et aigus ... Ceci me rappelle quelque chose', and goes on to describe a feeling of an apparently unchanging consciousness faced with the exhaustion of life and the self. The bird's song brings to mind similar cries holding a future which has now become past: 'Je sais ce qu'il y avait dans ces impressions' (P I, 355). On the other hand, the cry of a bird, by isolating the mind from contingent sensations and from a feeling of continuity with life, may seem to bring abolition of the past. In the poem *L'Oiseau Cruel*, for example (the phrase is used again in the *Cahiers*: xxiv, 243), Valéry writes:

L'oiseau cruel toute la nuit me tint
Au point aigu du délice d'entendre
Sa voix qu'adresse une fureur si tendre
Au ciel brûlant d'astres jusqu'au matin.

1 *La Porte Étroite* (Paris, Mercure de France, 1947), 185.

2 Cf. *Air de Sémiramis*, where the rhyme 'ciseaux/oiseaux' is used, but this time the 'cris de ciseaux' precede the idea of birds (P I, 93).

3 Cf. the poignant lines expressing transition into sleep: '... *Tout meurt, tout rit dans la gorge qui jase./L'Oiseau boit sur ta bouche et tu ne peux le voir...*' (P I, 109).

Tu perces l'âme et fixes le destin
De tel regard qui ne peut se reprendre;
Tout ce qui fut tu le changes en cendre,
O voix trop haute, extase de l'instinct...
.....

(P I, 158)

and the poem *Anne* ends with the lines:

Et dans le feu, parmi trois feuilles, l'oiseau calme
Commence le chant seul qui réprime les morts.

(P I, 91)

The tone most readily associated with these remarks is one of scepticism and anxiety; a feeling based on the sensation of the illusory permanence of consciousness in a crumbling world in which thought and memory, like the song of the bird, remain curiously intact, introducing into the finite time-scale of biological existence the feeling of an 'autre voie' (xix, 467). Scepticism is often linked in Valéry's work with a sense of a richness and complexity of experience too great to formulate (vi, 15).

Not only the sound but also the sight of the bird sets up this intellectual reverberation. The Parque lets her gaze follow a bird in flight with something of the same concentration of self discerned in connection with the leaf or star in the previous chapter:

Mes pauses, sur le pied portant la rêverie,
Qui suit au miroir d'aile un oiseau qui varie,
Cent fois sur le soleil joue avec le néant,
Et brûle, au sombre but de mon marbre béant.

(P I, 101)

'Si haut vole l'oiseau que le regard monte à la source des larmes' (P II, 658), Valéry writes, and the coming of tears is most often 'signe d'incommensurable à la pensée' (xv, 712). The bird flies higher than the power of human thought.

Not only its song and flight but also the warm presence of the bird is noted: 'Sur un toit rose et blond dorment quatre colombes; je songe vaguement à la sensation de chair dans la plume douce posée sur l'argile tiède, ô vie'.[1] The same juxtaposition of doves and roof is present, of course, in the opening image of *Le Cimetière Marin*: 'Ce toit tranquille,

[1] 'Accueil du Jour', *Petits Poèmes Abstraits*, *La Revue de France* (1er jan. 1932).

où marchent des colombes' (P I, 147). Doves are often made to symbolise some form of intellectual privilege. It is the semi-Biblical dove which signifies reward and inspiration in *Palme* ('Une colombe, la brise' (P I, 155)) and doves which in the opening line of *Épisode* ('Un soir favorisé de colombes sublimes' (P I, 83)) and in a line of *La Jeune Parque* ('ressusciter un soir favori de colombes' (P I, 101)) suggest tenderness and enchantment. They are the doves of Aphrodite and can be contrasted with the vigorous animal passion symbolised by the image in the same poem of Leda and the swan, or with the note of anguished detachment suggested by the bird in *L'Oiseau Cruel*.[1]

Other examples of the theme of the bird may be more analytic. In a 'croquis' of *Mélange*, for example, Valéry writes of the bird's capacity for steersmanship (cybernetic control): 'L'oiseau frémit, bondit, abandonne instantanément sa présence sur une branche et l'emporte. Il ravit avec soi un centre du "monde" et le vole poser ailleurs. (Je ne sais s'il choisit ou non la branche d'arrivée)' (P I, 303), or, of its apparently independent capacity for song; 'Chant. Produit naturel du matin. Oiseaux. A quoi *répond*? Expression. Élimination. Circuit' (XXI, 732). As is so often the case, remarks like this verge on interest in the narrow borderline between 'freedom' and 'automatism'. In a passage headed *Oiseaux Chanteurs*, Valéry writes, for instance:

> Mais comme il s'élève et se joue dans l'espace, et a pouvoir de choisir *triplement* ses chemins, de tracer entre deux points une infinité de courbes ailées, et comme il prévoit de plus haut et vole où il veut, ainsi l'Oiseau, jusque dans sa voix, est plus libre de ce qui le touche.
>
> Chant et mobilité, un peu moins étroitement ordonnés par la circonstance qu'ils ne le sont chez la plupart des vivants.
>
> (P II, 660)

Obviously a comparison with human 'freedom' is not far away, a freedom from the constraints of external circumstance even greater than that of the bird, though it is interesting to note that for Valéry the greater complexity or organisation which makes this relative independence possible seems to be accompanied by an intensification of 'cyclic' experience (XX, 493).

Valéry's interest in living things like the bird leads to an attempt to understand human behaviour reduced to its bare minimum of natural instincts, adaptive mechanisms and so on, but the comparisons behind

[1] J. Duchesne-Guillemin sees this as a love poem ('Valéry au Miroir', *F.S.*, XX (1966), 350–1).

them do not stop there. They radiate into the most complex structures of intellectual life, into consciousness, language, art and aesthetics. In a verbal sketch of a bird, *L'Oiseau Sufficit*, for example, Valéry compares the 'method' of a bird, 'qui goûte, effleure et fuit [. . .] Atome de liberté' (xiv, 747) with the characteristics of mental impatience. He is intrigued by the nervous energy of the bird which 'goûte l'arbre dans la graine'. Elsewhere he notes 'L'oiseau chante qu'il ne croit pas à ce qu'il peine pour atteindre' (xiv, 747). It is not the first time that the bird is associated with a kind of exquisite yet anguished freedom similar to that of consciousness itself. Perhaps it is partly because the song of the bird has been unconsciously endowed by the human mind with the echo of its own creative potentials that it can pierce so deeply into 'la sensibilité intellectuelle'.

The last group of meditations on the bird might be said to concern the temptation of the anthropomorphic. After a description of armies of birds in inexplicable formations, 'comme un torrent sans terre, ou un fleuve de fumée', comes the remark: 'Celui qui s'observe soi-même devant de telles manifestations animales peut se surprendre dans sa naïveté. Il peut se saisir, interprétant à l'humaine les actions des bêtes, leur donnant des projets, des raisonnements, des conventions établies entre elles. Comment faire autrement?' (P I, 337), and there follows an amusing description, in the form of direct personal anecdote rare with Valéry, of 'un mariage de corbeaux' celebrated in Normandy with 'de futurs beaux-parents, de futurs époux, des tantes et des cousins' (P I, 337–8), the kind of description that throws into greater relief the particular non-anthropomorphic tone of his own observations on animal life. 'C'est qu'il y a un étrange abîme entre les discours que nous tiennent les oiseaux, les feuillages, les idées, et celui que nous leur prêtons: un intervalle inconcevable' (P I, 476–7), he writes. This 'interval' is the subject of *Au Platane*, to be discussed later in this chapter. Elsewhere, in words almost identical with those used to describe the motion of an insect,[1] Valéry writes: 'Je vois filer un oiseau. Je trace *en je ne sais quoi* une "ligne"' (xxi, 483). As in the case of the insect, there is imaginative projection into a different 'world' of vision: in the description of the swallow that bursts into the room, for example:

> Grasse. – Dix heures et quart – Tout à coup une belle hirondelle bleue et or brusquement se jette dans ma chambre, fait trois

[1] Cf. 'Cela trace POUR MOI une ligne' (Solitaire, XXIV, 788). The heading 'Solitaire' by this jotting suggests that Le Solitaire may represent the part of Faust that allows this condition of subjective relativism to produce a sense of human failure rather than of human triumph.

tours, retrouve la petite fenêtre carrée et fuit, comme crevant l'image du pays, par ce trou de lumière où elle s'était précipitée en tant que trou d'ombre, et qu'il lui a suffi de virer de bord pour la changer en lumière, en autre monde . . . Peut-être ne l'a-t-il pas reconnu?

(P I, 312)

It is obviously on simple observations of natural phenomena such as this that Valéry draws for images in other parts of his work. For instance: 'Une arrière pensée est dans la pièce d'ombre. Mais parfois elle est aussi comme un oiseau, qui traverse tout à coup le jour de feu extérieur, qui va voir ce qui est loin et qui est encore *moi*, et qui revient de la lumière, toujours à la nuit *moi*' (P II, 431–2). In all these examples Valéry has shown alertness to the resources offered by the smallest incident for meditative transformation throughout every level of his work. Consciousness, distinct from the rest of nature, draws upon the rest of nature for its material and is in turn enlarged by contact with the natural world. This is nowhere more apparent than in Valéry's approach to the tree.

The tree

Many critics have shown that the tree plays a major part in Valéry's work.[1] However there is sufficient material in the *Cahiers* for new light still to be thrown on the kind of imagination in action in his response. Leaving aside until later chapters details of his analytical interest in the theme of plant growth in general, together with his frequent use of analogies between certain properties of the growing tree and the human mind, I shall concentrate here solely on the tree as a centre of meditation and poetic evocation in its own right.

'Trees never held for him quite the same lofty and universal meaning' (as the three natural deities: sea, sky and sun) 'but they counted far more than any other aspect of external nature', writes L. A. Bisson.[2] I shall suggest here that although the tone of Valéry's response to the tree is in some ways different from that of his response to the three 'divinities' of *Inspirations Mediterranéennes*, it can hardly be said to be less concerned with 'universal' meaning. In the words of his Lucrèce, 'la plante présente [. . .] un étrange vœu de trame universelle' (P II, 193). Already in 1896

[1] E.g. L. A. Bisson, J. R. Lawler, L. J. Austin and above all P. Laurette (details can be found in the bibliography). Although the study by P. Laurette has been frequently quoted here, it appeared after the completion of the work in its original thesis form.

[2] 'A Study in "le faire Valéryen" ', *F.S.*, x (1956), 309–21.

Valéry was beginning to sense that the living tree even more than the sea could counteract for him the pure 'boredom' of life, and that it was in some ways intimately linked with the undertaking of the *Cahiers* themselves:

> Je savais depuis quelque temps que l'arbre est la chose du monde qui ne m'ennuie pas encore. (Je parle de ce qu'on peut voir – et je parle aussi des arbres très hauts, à robe claire et assez lisse. Horreur des arbres calleux.) La mer et les eaux en général m'écœurent – à cause d'abus. Il me reste l'arbre et les fameux 'quelconques', lesquels me conduisent toujours à ces vagues inventions que j'exprime pour autrui par leurs résultats les plus clairs, et pour moi dans un langage plus que crypto-gaphique, mêlé de termes de science et de représentations 'idiosyncrasiques'.[1]

The extent to which the rubric or term 'arbre' figures in this cryptographic language as much as in the 'clear' language of the published works is evident from even a cursory glance at the *Cahiers*.[2] For the present it is the tree as an object of immediate existence which is of interest. '[. . .] il me semble que de beaux arbres me font plaisir et je ne me vois heureux qu'ensemble', the letter continues: '(Solécismes.) Ils sont, au sentiment, comme un bon coup de respiration d'un air juste à la température espérée, ou comme un lit parfait, épousant le verso du corps et donnant l'idée de s'y écarteler.' Appreciation of the sensuous aspects of the tree as an individual phenomenon remains constant whatever aspect of Valéry's work is concerned. It is the living tree which unites Lucrèce and Tityre in the face of the infinitely distant stars ('Le fardeau de tant d'astres' (P II, 185)); trees which form the rich landscape of the Narcisse poems, the landscape of love as opposed to the cold rocky seascape of mental solitude in the opening of *La Jeune Parque*[3] (the passage on the trees of Spring was, in fact, deliberately added by Valéry 'pour *attendrir* un peu le poème' (P I, 1621)); the tree which attracts the daily salutations of the mature Faust ('saluer mon beau platane' (P II, 308)); and the tree which forms the central image of some of Valéry's finest poems: *Au Platane*, *Ébauche d'un Serpent* and *Palme*. It seems safe to say that whereas the sea, sky and sun remain indissolubly linked with Valéry's intellectual beginnings, the tree is naturally connected with a greater depth of emotion, a greater synthesis

[1] *A. Gide–P. Valéry, Correspondance, 1890–1942* (Paris, Gallimard, 1955), 264.
[2] E.g. i, 125, 151, 175, 179, 217, 241, 377; iv, 10; vii, 877; x, 426.
[3] See P.-O. Walzer, *La Poésie de Valéry* (Genève, Cailler, 1953), 199.

of mental qualities and a less intransigent approach to life. In any case it is a constant source of meditation and pleasure. 'Ainsi le même arbre est un *but* de mouvement; [...] un *signe* de souvenirs; [...] un *repère* de pensées', Valéry notes, '[. . .] un fixateur ou un distracteur, un révélateur, un interrupteur; un réflecteur./Il est en somme un objet privilégié' (P II, 718); an 'objet aimé' (iii, 495); 'le résultat d'une foule d'expériences' (i, 417).

In a frequently quoted letter to a friend written in the summer of 1918 when many of the poems of *Charmes*, in particular *La Pythie*, were being composed, Valéry writes of the tree-planted region of the Château de l'Isle-Manière near Avranches where he was staying:

> Il y avait sous ma fenêtre des bouquets de hêtres pourpres d'une extrême hauteur, des groupes d'énormes tilleuls surélevés, issus par quatre de monticules carrés de terre dont les feuillages retombant jusqu'au sol cachaient entièrement les masses . . . [. . .] Tu ne peux imaginer quelles matinées j'ai passées pendant ces deux ou trois mois d'été, dans cette riche région où le grand arbre pousse comme l'herbe, où l'herbe est d'une force et d'une facilité incroyables, où la puissance végétale est inépuisable. (P I, 1645)

Something of the 'vitalité de l'esprit' which Valéry goes on to equate with this period of his life has obviously been transposed to the 'discours' of Tityre and Lucrèce in *Dialogue de l'Arbre*, 'consacrés à la gloire d'un Arbre' (P II, 1409). Their reactions in the presence of the great tree, a beech with the smooth bark he so much preferred,[1] epitomise the range of moods from lyrical to analytical which Valéry almost always relates to the presence of trees: 'Il s'y mêle de la tristesse, de l'enchantement, de l'émotion et une sorte de lucidité presque douloureuse' (P I, 1645), he wrote in the description quoted above of trees at dawn.

Thus Tityre needs to 'sing' the presence of the tree: 'je t'aime, l'Arbre vaste, et suis fou de tes membres. Il n'est fleur, il n'est femme, grand être au bras multipliés, qui plus que toi m'émeuve et de mon cœur dégage une fureur plus tendre' (P II, 178). Lucrèce is more meditative and analytic, but feels a similar impulse towards song: 'je te dirais, te chanterais ce que me chante, et dit, et m'impose dans l'âme ma contemplation intérieure de l'Idée de la Plante' (P II, 185). The lyric and analytic fuse together in the companionship of the two speakers, and, even more fundamentally,

[1] In *La Jeune Parque*, the trees are, on the contrary, 'recouverts d'écailles' (P I, 103), suggesting alienation from consciousness.

since this is not a dialogue based on the rebuttal of an opponent but one of genuine self-discovery in the presence of the other, the two qualities fuse together in the individual minds of the speakers themselves.

It is obvious that the tree plays more than a superficial part in this 'méditation rayonnante' (P II, 194). 'Mon âme aujourd'hui se fait arbre' (P II, 178), says Tityre, and Lucrèce feels in his own mind 'une vertu de Plante' (P II, 188); he becomes 'un arbre de paroles' (P II, 193). To echo and accentuate the influence of the tree in the experience of the two speakers, Valéry seems to use, Francis Scarfe suggests, a technique of 'imitative harmony',[1] reproducing the form and action of the great spreading branches in the rhythm of the unrhymed alexandrines of the speakers. It is interesting to compare the feeling expressed in this way with two comments in the *Cahiers*: first, under the rubric, *Bel Canto*: '*arbre gigantesque de la voix*, arbre sacré, poussé dans la chair, chargé des idées. Poésie même, dont le corps et les rameaux sont les certitudes et les puissances de la Veille, mais la matière est rêve et Rêve aussi l'espace où il s'agrandit' (viii, 38); and secondly: 'Loin des livres, mais seul au soleil silencieux avec la puissance de l'espace/sinon babillant de l'esprit dès que l'ombre des feuilles m'habille, me couche et laisse que je rayonne et fait que je chante par ce changement simple/les mots nombreux le cèdent et s'éteignent; j'ai oublié mes savantes paroles. Ailleurs se détourne le fleuve de durée et varie' (ii, 894). Right from the start one can be sure that an individual tree represents for Valéry a synthesis in the beholder of mental qualities, sensuous, intellectual and affective and so on. The effect of the tree on the joint mind of Tityre and Lucrèce is something like that of the work of art: it produces 'enchantement' and in turn they become artists creating the kind of fables (La Merveilleuse Histoire de l'Arbre Infini) that are defined in *Eupalinos* as rendering the mind 'sonore et féconde' (P II, 105).[2]

In Valéry the poet 'empathy and detachment alternate or fuse together, in harmony or dissonance', writes L. J. Austin,[3] singling out what is perhaps Valéry's most characteristic quality where the poetry of the tree is concerned. Part of this imaginative power consists in making the tree yield its maximum perceptual possibilities. 'Le plus rare des dons est peut-être de faire rendre à la chose vue ou observée tout ce qu'elle peut rendre [. . .]', Valéry notes, 'le rendement est preuve de la puissance de l'esprit. Que d'observations subtiles sur un arbre' (xii, 365). In the very

[1] *The Art of Paul Valéry* (London, Heinemann, 1954), 287.
[2] Lucrèce talks of 'ce nœud de l'être, où l'unité réside' (P ii, 181).
[3] 'The Negative Plane Tree', *L'Esprit Créateur*, IV (1964), 9.

first notebook he had suggested the dynamic aspect of his response to an object: 'des choses donnent envie d'être coupées, tordues, mordues, bues' (i, 58). Thus 'Les plus beaux arbres que j'ai *bus*',[1] he writes to Gide of the trees at l'Isle-Manière already mentioned, and, of a similar 'impression gustative' (i, 391): 'des profondeurs de la verdure des arbres s'éloignant dans une atmosphère où elle boit' (P I, 1177).

The previous chapter referred to Valéry's desire to imagine the coupling of natural textures: foliage and fire; foliage and water (i, 391). These two combinations can be followed up here as an example of the way in which a tree is imaginatively taken to the limit of its possibilities ('faire rendre à la chose vue ou observée tout ce qu'elle peut rendre') without its own individual identity ever being lost.

'Toute une semence de feu à travers les pins sur la mer [. . .]', Valéry notes, 'Le même feu va surprendre des rameaux et des accidents de feuillage à travers les songes obscurs' (xii, 838); 'Les pins sifflent sous le mistral; vers le soleil ils s'agitent pour grandir. Tout est ardent et le vent froid' (xii, 836). The trees in *La Jeune Parque* have 'cimes qu'un feu féconde' (P I, 106) and the décor of *Le Cimetière Marin* is 'dominé de flambeaux,/Composé d'or, de pierre et d'arbres sombres' (P I, 149). Here simple descriptions of the sun illuminating leaves are concerned. But 'une fois qu'on est dans le domaine de l'image, un bateau peut prendre à sa fumée, un arbre à ses feuilles' (i, 106). It is not far from this literal observation to remarks where description of the Mediterranean sun on leaves or of a tree stretching up in the hot air or swaying in the Mistral has become condensed into semi-comparison, simile or metaphor: 'l'arbre file entre mes mains, de mes pieds jusqu'à l'extrême de mon regard, à demi bloc et à demi fumée' (ii, 910); or 'Je dis: cet arbre monte comme une fumée' (i, 66; cf. xxiii, 263); and finally 'l'arbre fume et perd quelques oiseaux' (P I, 85); '[. . .] un grand Arbre, d'entre les arbres et les plantes obscures,/s'enflamme' (P I, 292; cf. xviii, 32). Sometimes, sustained poetic imagery arises from the link between fire and foliage already established on a literal level in this way: that of the last stanza of *Anne* in *Album de Vers Anciens*, for example:

> Mais suave, de l'arbre extérieur, la palme
> Vapoureuse remue au delà du remords,
> Et dans le feu, parmi trois feuilles, l'oiseau calme
> Commence le chant seul qui réprime les morts.
>
> (P I, 91)

[1] *A. Gide–P. Valéry, Correspondance, 1890–1942*, 474.

Already, without losing any of its physical qualities, the fire image is beginning to widen to more abstract associations. In *Au Platane*, the transition into the symbolic where physical and abstract combine, is complete:

> Flagelle-toi! . . . Parais l'impatient martyr
> Qui soi-même s'écorche,
> Et dispute à la flamme impuissante à partir
> Ses retours vers la torche.
>
> (P I, 115)

Similarly, Tityre suggests: 'Mais le feu n'est-il point la fin même de l'Arbre? Quand son être devient tout atroce douleur, il se tord; mais se fait lumière et cendre pure, plutôt que de pourrir, miné par l'eau croupie, rongé par la vermine . . .' (P II, 184). Such observations imaginatively endow the slowness of vegetable growth with a tension which obviously relates indirectly to Valéry's 'Caligulisme' or mental impatience – the power to 'jeter au feu le tronc d'arbre' (V, 152) or, more generally, the power of all human imagination to stretch beyond the limits of what it perceives, even beyond the limits of its own biological life.

The second combination mentioned by Valéry, foliage and water, is even more frequent. He often takes pleasure in the vicinity of trees and actual water, the favourite juxtaposition of two different substances: 'eaux, matière végétale – et leurs vertus élémentaires' (P II, 69) previously observed. Thus 'un groupe de pins divise curieusement la vue de la mer' (XII, 836) (the 'maigres grillages' of *Le Cimetière Marin*?); or foliage is reflected in water as in *Le Rameur*, the sensation produced being one of comfort and delight:

> Arbres sur qui je passe, ample et naïve moire,
> Eau de ramages peinte, et paix de l'accompli.
>
> (P I, 153)

Solitary trees reflected in water make a kind of vegetable equivalent of Narcisse: 'l'arbre se penche vers son image dans l'eau calme' (XXVIII, 580). But more often an analogy with water will be present, for example in *La Fileuse*: 'Un arbuste et l'air pur font une source vive' (P I, 75); 'Verse le Fleuve léger/porté sur les arbres en fleurs' (I, 172); or, to the great beech in *Dialogue de l'Arbre*: 'Le vent naissant bruit dans ta haute ramure. Il y place une source' (P II, 178); 'Vois donc dans ce grand être

[1] In the description of a plant as 'fusée' (XI, 40), Valéry seems to have transposed something of this mental energy back to the plant (compare with the point made by P. Laurette, *Le Thème de l'Arbre*, 80).

une sorte de fleuve' (P II, 180). Foliage shimmering in clear air; the foliage of flowering trees (suggesting in this case the traditional river of time); foliage murmuring in the wind – all these observations verge on the analogy with water, an analogy the more fitting on a functional level in that leaves themselves are the work of rising sap: 'la sève solennelle' of *Palme* ('l'eau profonde/Que demandent les sommets' (P I, 155)) or the sap which makes the tree appear to Lucrèce 'Un fleuve tout vivant de qui les sources plongent dans la masse obscure de la terre les chemins de leur soif mystérieuse' (P II, 180). 'L'EAU s'avance par l'ARBRE à la rencontre de la lumière' (P I, 203), Valéry notes elsewhere, expressing elation in the 'counter-gravitational' power of the rising sap.

Thus it is in the confrontation of the tree with another of Valéry's elective affinities, the sea, that the analogy is complete. Again, passages can be selected where a simple functional comparison is involved: 'Comme le haut d'une plante ou d'un arbre est amusé ou inquiété par le vent, le tronc et les racines fixés et cramponnés dans la terre, ainsi le fond libre de la mer, dont la profondeur est de marbre liquide sous la pression' (XV, 295). In a similar passage, the silence of a forest, 'au bas de la hauteur des arbres', is compared with the 'transparent' silence at the bottom of the sea (V, 839), silence being a particularly 'visual' quality for Valéry. The next stage is metaphor: 'Cet arbre devant moi chante toute la mer au bout d'une mâture. Ce bruit a la finesse du bruit de l'eau du reflux, qui fuse, se retire, se reprend.'[1] Whether through sound, movement or association with light effects ('des étincelles solaires de la mer aux mille minces miroirs des feuilles de bouleau' (P I, 1177)), the tree becomes the living representative of the sea on land: 'Ici, j'aime un arbre. Il porte la mer dans sa tête et la balance' (ii, 894). There seems to be more pleasure involved here – owing to the active involvement of the imagination in comparison – than in the direct contemplation of the sea. It was, after all, a shining slate roof in a town that reminded Valéry of the sea during the period of composing *Le Cimetière Marin* (where the image is reversed, the sea being compared with a roof rather than a roof with the sea).[2] So complete is the yield of perception that Valéry's imagination works in an inverse direction too, the sea reminding him of foliage or tree: 'la mer touffue' (i, 129), or: 'La mer pour moi, impression des narines et des poumons, espace, dressement des vagues, boisson aérienne, grandeur, [. . .] arbre

[1] *La Jeune Parque*, ed. O. Nadal (Club du Meilleur Livre, 1957), Feuillet VII, 59. Quoted by J. R. Lawler in 'An Ironic Elegy: Valéry's "Au Platane"', *The French Review*, XXXVI (1963).

[2] Valéry said that he had in mind the roof of the Mont de Piété in Montpellier (Coll. J. Monod – information L. J. Austin).

odorant et gros [...] air hérissé' (i, 214). Finally, the sky itself becomes the sea for the tree which in *Au Platane* rows across it ceaselessly and in vain with leaves for oars: 'vêtus en vain de rames' (P I, 114), while in *La Jeune Parque* the leaves of trees appear as islands in the sky suggesting the theme of departure and voyage:

> La flottante forêt de qui les rudes troncs
> Portent pieusement à leurs fantasques fronts,
> Aux déchirants départs des archipels superbes,
> Un fleuve tendre, ô Mort, et caché sous les herbes.
>
> (P I, 103)

Coleridge writes in words very similar to those of Valéry: 'it [a birch-tree] glanced in the wind like a flying sunshiny shower', continuing: 'It was a tree in shape, with a stem and branches, but it was like a spirit of water.'[1] Even more than Coleridge, Valéry usually refrains from making the move into fantasy half present in the second step in the comparison. Or if he makes it, as he does in the case of the tree that talks or the tree that walks away from its base, it is in order to entertain as an interest in itself the impossibility of violating natural limits. The tree that talks for example: Valéry may often imagine a tree with the power of human expression, 'les discours que nous tiennent [...] les feuillages' (P I, 477). The basis of the idea can be seen to be the sound of wind in leaves or the motion of a tree in the wind, as in 'n'entends-tu pas frémir ces noms aériens' (P I, 103) in *La Jeune Parque*. The correspondence between movement and musical harmony often attracted Valéry ('Ces hirondelles se meuvent comme un son meurt' (iv, 713), for example). In a lengthy passage from *Autres Rhumbs* headed 'Arbre', the phases of motion of a wind-blown tree are analysed in terms of music: 'Reprise maintenant, reprise accélérée. Ce sont sextuples croches, trilles insoutenables. Nous voici à l'extrême de l'aigu. C'est un prurit, un *ultra-vif*, une folie de fréquence, un délire d'excitation qui gagne les masses centrales et menace l'énorme vie' (P II, 660). Yet there are also many observations concerning not only the sound made by the wind and harmonised by the listening ear, but the idea of articulate sound on the part of the tree itself, for example: 'l'arbre chante comme l'oiseau' (P II, 659); 'Arbre parlant (Daimon Trépied)' (x, 10);[2] 'Un grand peuplier de Virginie tout aéré, bredouille' (i, 251); 'L'arbre – je crois bruire et me tourmente' (ii, 626); 'Cet arbre semble faire une promenade et discourir' (ii, 325). The notions

[1] The Grasmere Journals (17 March 1802), quoted by H. House, *Coleridge*, 82.
[2] There are obvious links here with *La Pythie* (see below, 168).

of 'tangage' and 'langage', already linked together in the early poem *Pour Votre Hêtre 'Suprême'*:

Mille oiseaux chanteront plus d'un
Souvenir d'atroce tangage,
Quand reverdira par Verdun
Sauvé, notre illustre Langage!

(P I, 162)

reappear in more developed form in the mature poem *Au Platane*:

Je t'ai choisi, puissant personnage d'un parc,
Ivre de ton tangage,
Puisque le ciel t'exerce, et te presse, Ô grand arc,
De lui rendre un langage!

(P I, 115)

It is interesting that in a letter to Gide of 1917, Valéry uses the same verb 'parler' in foreseeing the process by which the beech of the first poem would mature in his mind until it inspired the tree, in this case the plane tree, of the second: 'Il parlera tout seul, loin d'ici, un jour, quand il aura bien trouvé dans ma substance un territoire, un air, un soleil non présents, moins présents, et plus actuels' (P I, 1679). And so, of course, it did.[1]

In at least one passage in his notebooks Valéry has described this type of imagination in terms of a deliberate mental exercise: 'Quand je veux me figurer qu'un arbre *parle*, je tends à faire de sa voix – le bruit du vent et de feuilles *un peu plus* articulé. Cela tend à rendre croyable, résistant, il est à souder, plus fortement, parole et arbre' (i, 327). Previously he had written: 'La réalité ainsi étendue est relative [. . .] Je puis imaginer un arbre qui parle etc' (i, 231). It is the fact that the tree is *not* capable of expression which interests him. In this way the desire to imagine that it could talk serves both to intensify the conditions of the real world and to throw light on the imaginative power of perception. In an excursion into the realm of fable Tityre supposes that the sound he hears is not simply that of wind in the tree's foliage, but the language of the tree itself: 'Le vent naissant bruit dans ta naissante ramure [. . .] Mais c'est Toi que j'entends. O langage confus, langage qui t'agites, je veux fondre toutes tes voix' (P II, 178). Valéry's personal notes follow exactly the inverse pattern. Under the heading *Fable*, he writes, for example: 'Étonné d'être, un Arbre s'agitait... Mais non – c'était le vent qui lui passait dedans' (xxvi, 870).

[1] The process is described by L. A. Bisson, *F.S.*, x (1956), 309-21.

A further leap of the imagination is to make the tree itself appear to be giving that 'no'. For example:

Vent.
Hors d'elles, toutes révoltées, rebrousées, elles
Feuilles gémissent et les rames bousculées
Toutes chargées et chavirées –
Disent éperdument: Non!

(P II, 605)

It is this negative gesture, just as much a conscious invention on the part of the beholder as that which endows the tree with positive language, which forms the central theme of *Au Platane.* To the poet's command 'ose gemir', the tree appears to reply in the negative:

– *Non, dit l'arbre. Il dit:* Non! *par l'étincellement*
De sa tête superbe,
Que la tempête traite universellement
Comme elle fait une herbe!

(P I, 115)

A certain amount of discussion has developed round the interpretation of this poem, in particular this last stanza. Where J. Lawler sees it as a predominantly 'ironic elegy' on the intractability of nature,[1] L. J. Austin, in an article called 'The Negative Plane Tree',[2] puts the stress on the power of the poet to make the tree speak: 'But, after all, whatever the tree "says", it is the poet who makes it speak. The plane tree, by its very negation, affirms the sovereign power of the poetic imagination.' L. A. Bisson has pointed out similarly, the same article recalls, that the tree's ultimate refusal paradoxically confirms the fact that it has been given a voice.[3] The vital rôle played by the *separation* of consciousness in this experience still needs to be stressed, however: its power to evaluate its own ordering activity. 'Ce qui intéresse Valéry', writes P. Laurette in a general context, 'ce n'est pas tant la création d'images que l'étude des variations de l'image, car l'image elle-même n'est pas esprit, "l'esprit étant alors les variations d'une chose qui n'est pas esprit"' (XIX, 543).[4] In this poem, by isolating the structuring process of the imagination at the same time as he shows it in action, Valéry comes close to stylising like an

[1] *The French Review*, XXXVI (1963), 339–51. The article has been republished in French in *Lecture de Valéry*, 40–52.
[2] *L'Esprit Créateur*, IV (1964), 3–10.
[3] Ibid., 10.
[4] Quoted by P. Laurette, *Le Thème de l'Arbre*, 87.

invisible presence the power of conscious detachment itself to produce one of the strongest creative experiences ('Actio Præsentiae' (xix, 916)). The 'Non' which is negative from the point of view of the power of structured imagery to express any more than subjective processes, becomes a paradoxical affirmation of the power of consciousness to detect that the whole mind is deriving more from the presence of the tree than the attempts of the intellect to annul the phenomenon through expression. 'Pourtant je *sais* que l'arbre réel était infiniment plus riche que celui de mon souvenir', Valéry once wrote of the similarly selective structuring process of memory, '[. . .] je ne puis qu'essayer de faire ce qui donnerait l'impression de ce pullulement de feuilles. Un arbre *synthétique*' (xxvii, 829). The whole poem with its rocking imitative harmonies in the form of the long and short lines, alexandrine and hexasyllable, to echo the theme of striving and return, seems to convey the penetration of the visible tree through the whole sensibility of the beholder to the highest level of conscious awareness, even as the urge to fulfil himself through expression separates him from the tree mentally but turns him in the process into 'un arbre de paroles' (P II, 193) as complete and unified as the tree itself.

'Cet arbre semble faire une promenade et discourir' (ii, 325), Valéry had written. A similar kind of 'negative imagination' concerns the idea of the tree that takes a step, or rather cannot take a step, away from its roots. 'Où l'Arbre risque un pas' (xxix, 725), Valéry has written under a drawing of a tree next to the inscription: 'Maladetta Primavera'.[1] *Au Platane* is, of course, the refutation of this very hypothesis. The tree seems to struggle for freedom, but is held back by the fixity of its roots in the soil, its only freedom being in the mind of the poet himself:

> Mais ta candeur est prise, et ton pied retenu
>   Par la force du site.
> [. . . . .]
>   La terre tendre et sombre
> O Platane, jamais ne laissera d'un pas
>   S'émerveiller ton ombre!
>
> (P I, 113–14)

It is of course, on this vital condition of limitation that Valéry shows the life of the tree to depend, and this he is drawn constantly to re-experience and re-express. Indeed, this is simply one example, out of many similar

[1] J. Duchesne-Guillemin suggests a personal connection with unhappy love, 'Paul Valéry et l'Italie', *M.L.R.*, LXII (1957), 50.

ones, of the way in which his admiration for the tree is related to his profound interest in the nature of life, its evolution and its organic functioning, whether in plant, animal, human body or nervous system.[1] This same theme of limit and possibility will appear again as a central aspect of the functioning of the conscious mind.

In all his tree poetry Valéry makes much of the vital continuity between roots and leaves presented by the tree, its trunk rooted in subterranean depths and its foliage tossing in the light. Examples can be found in the passage evoking the magnificent trees of Spring in *La Jeune Parque*:

L'étonnant printemps rit, viole . . . On ne sait d'où
Venu? Mais la candeur ruisselle à mots si doux
Qu'une tendresse prend la terre à ses entrailles . . .
Les arbres regonflés et recouverts d'écailles
Chargés de tant de bras et de trop d'horizons,
Meuvent sur le soleil leurs tonnantes toisons,
[. . . . .]
N'entends-tu pas frémir ces noms aériens,
. . . . Et dans l'espace accablé de liens,
Vibrant de bois vivace infléchi par la cime,
Pour et contre les dieux ramer l'arbre unanime,
La flottante forêt de qui les rudes troncs
Portent pieusement à leurs fantasques fronts,
Aux déchirants départs des archipels superbes,
Un fleuve tendre, Ô Mort, et caché sous les herbes?
(P I, 103);

in *Dialogue de l'Arbre*, where the tree is compared with love and with consciousness, the fusion of intellect and affectivity, its roots deep in 'la source des pleurs' (P II, 182–3) and its branches striving to lucidity and light: 'Autant elle s'enfonce, autant s'élève-t-elle' (P II, 192); in *Ébauche d'un Serpent*, where the tree of trees is addressed by the serpent as:

Toi qui pousses tels labyrinthes
Par qui les ténèbres étreintes
S'iront perdre dans le saphir
De l'éternelle matinée,
[. . . . .]
(P I, 145);

[1] Cf. Judith Robinson, 'The Place of Literary and Artistic Creation in Valéry's Thought' (1961), 277.

or in *Palme*, where the central image concerns the same continuity:

La substance chevelue
Par les ténèbres élue
Ne peut s'arrêter jamais,
Jusqu'aux entrailles du monde,
De poursuivre l'eau profonde
Que demandent les sommets.

(P I, 155)

The tree, like the sea – only more so since its roots are fixed in the ground – is the hydra, '*ouroboros*', 'une hydre [. . .] aux prises avec la roche' (P II, 181). In such examples of poetic imagery, all Valéry's analytic insights into the nature of plant growth seem to have fused together. Even in the Narcisse fragments, the same theme can be detected: the inevitable participation of Narcisse in a life-cycle from which there is no escape is linked with what Valéry calls in his notes 'Thème des grands arbres dans leurs ténèbres' (xii, 282).[1] It is perfectly consistent with his whole view of consciousness that he should be haunted by the theme of affective limitation symbolised by the deep, dark existence of the root in the soil.[2]

A theme closely connected with that of the tree's confinement to one spot is that of its limited power of growth as an individual organism. Again the same process of imaginative hypothesis and rejection can be traced. 'Il n'y a point d'arbre qui [. . .] puisse croître indéfiniment' (xii, 6), Valéry noted. The 'Merveilleuse Histoire de l'Arbre Infini' (P II, 189) told in *Dialogue de l'Arbre*, is an imagined exploration of precisely this impossibility. The great tree, spurred on by 'une sorte de folie de démesure et d'arborescence' (P II, 191) soon covers all Asia with its enormous shadow. But again, the hypothesis: *what would happen if . .?* is used only to intensify the biologically possible. Valéry returns more often to the observation that growth itself is limited to a certain span of development and decay in time.

The twin themes of growth and limitation or vigour and transience evoked in *Dialogue de l'Arbre* lead via the common theme of the '*ouroboros*' to the analogy with conscious meditation which will be the main theme of the following chapters. Functionally similar to the development of consciousness in time, the tree is nevertheless not conscious. When

[1] By this line Valéry has written 'Narcisse. Final. Esquisse. Voir édition *Charmes* 1926.'

[2] Cf. N. Bastet, *La Symbolique des Images dans l'œuvre poétique de Valéry* (Publication des Annales de la Faculté des Lettres, XXIV, Aix-en-Provence, 1962), 43. See also Laurette, *Le Thème de l'Arbre*, 75.

Valéry introduces the anthropomorphic, it is either, as has just been suggested, by explicitly denying the implications of his imagery, as in the case of *Au Platane*, or by using analogies in which physical aspects of the tree and the human being may simply be compared and any further anthropomorphic inference quickly denied.

Visual comparisons between the human being and the tree come into this last category, for example. Valéry refers to the project: 'Parler d'un arbre en termes de corps féminin' (xii, 766). A beech at Zürich (illustrated by a drawing) is described in just this way: 'Zürich. Hêtre divin du Muraltengut où véritablement une figure divine féminine se dégage du tronc, et puis s'y rengage. Hanche, ventre, aisselle et bras qui s'amincit et s'allonge jusqu'au ciel, et la matière de cette écorce lisse; petits plis vraiment de peau' (xv, 644). It is obviously this keen sense of comparative physiology which leads to the image in *Au Platane*: 'ce hêtre formé/De quatre jeunes femmes' (P I, 114), and which brings Valéry to talk of the 'fronts' of the trees in a forest (*La Jeune Parque*) (P I, 103) or of the branches of the plane tree as 'bras', albeit 'bras plus purs que les bras animaux' (P I, 115). Elsewhere, he compares the bark of a tree and its indentations with skin and muscles: 'les troncs d'arbres, rugueux, hasardeux, tordus. Chaque muscle se débrouille dans ces conditions particulières et la peau aussi' (i, 127), or notes: 'l'arbre, beau, grand, me semble mon propre bras dressé' (i, 334). The muscular aspirations of the antique Scythian runner in the first stanza of *Au Platane* are an example of the same analogy in poetry:

> Tu penches, grand Platane, et te proposes nu,
> Blanc comme un jeune Scythe.
> [. . . . .]
>
> (P I, 113)[1]

Passages by other poets come to mind: Claudel's *Le Banyan*, its massive branches growing down as roots and pulling at the soil like a great vegetable Hercules:

> D'un lent allongement le monstre qui hale se tend et travaille dans toutes les attitudes de l'effort si dure que la rude écorce éclate et que les muscles lui sortent de la peau [. . .]. Il tire,[2]

or Hugo's gnarled elms and twisted olive trees, the caricatures of old men.[3] It is not sufficient, I think, to say that Hugo's imagination is anthropo-

[1] See Lawler, *Lecture de Valéry*, 45.

[2] *Connaissance de L'Est*, *Œuvres Poétiques* (Paris, Gallimard, 1957), 48.

[3] See Barrère, *La Fantaisie de Victor Hugo*, I (1949), 206.

morphic ('Tout ce qu'il y a d'humain dans l'importe quoi'),[1] whereas Valéry is fully conscious of what he does. Hugo is presumably not confusing an old man with a tree. The difference is rather in the vision of nature to be conveyed by the analogies in their work as a whole: where Hugo verges on the pantheistic and blends man and nature into one vast harmony, Valéry puts stress on the analogical process itself, expressing the functional unity between man and nature but at the same time the differently orientated aims of consciousness and natural life.

A further example of the use of anthropomorphic imagery can be seen in the theme of the tree's loneliness as it seeks companionship with others through general communication or sexual contact. There is a sketch to this effect in the *Cahiers* called 'Deux arbres' (viii, 387). 'L'arbre aveugle vers l'arbre étend ses membres sombres,/Et cherche affreusement l'arbre qui disparaît...' (P I, 130), says the Narcisse of *Charmes*. Here the word 'aveugle' (both not able to see and deprived of sight) contextually denies implications of anthropomorphism while reinforcing at the same time the resemblance of the tree's gestures to the human in the intensity of Narcisse's own desire. In *Au Platane*, still using the emotions and desires of a human beholder (a potential Jeune Parque) to echo the theme of the trees' separation and apparent longing, Valéry lets the strength of the visual comparison work alone:

> Ils vivent séparés, ils pleurent confondus
>   Dans une seule absence,
> Et leurs membres d'argents sont vraiment fendus
>   A leur douce naissance.
> Quand l'âme lentement qu'ils expirent le soir
>   Vers l'Aphrodite monte,
> La vierge doit dans l'ombre, en silence, s'asseoir,
>   Toute chaude de honte.
>
> (P I, 114)

The 'Non' of the last stanza of the poem is the retrospective denial of all the anthropomorphic images, not only the negation of the suggestion implicit in the bending of the plane tree to the poet's supplication that it should speak. It symbolises, as has already been suggested, the power of consciousness to derive from nature the ultimate check on the 'hyperæsthesia' connected with imagery itself (xix, 543).

[1] Baudelaire, *Œuvres Complètes* (Paris, Gallimard, 1961), 704 (quoted by L. J. Austin, *L'Esprit Créateur*, IV (1964), 10).

'Cette forêt était comme un grand arbre' (i, 178), Valéry writes in a note of obvious relevance to 'l'arbre unanime' (P I, 103) of *La Jeune Parque*. This unifying process points once again to his love of the individual tree as opposed to a mass of indistinct phenomena that cannot be grasped as a single entity. 'Nous portons dans notre mémoire quelques centaines de visages, dix arbres' (i, 51). Biographical research would show that the Zürich beech or the 'hêtre suprême' on Gide's property are just two of the real 'personnages'[1] which contribute to the universal figure of the tree in Valéry's poetry and prose. It has been seen how this capacity to respond and to evoke the 'personality' of the tree is never allowed to overflow into the merely fanciful. A strict attention to botanical precision invigorates Valéry's freest use of the tree, even when it is symbolic of the general themes to be examined later. For him it is indeed one of the most fertile and suggestive of natural phenomena, as he notes, with typical insight into his own preferences: 'L'édifice m'était cher et excitant à penser [...]. C'est à partir de cette satisfaction que j'ai imaginé l'homme, l'arbre et le cheval' (vi, 917); 'Objets aimés [...]. Infiniment les navires [...] Et l'arbre, pouquoi? Y lire la docilité et réciprocité si pure de la croissance et de l'extension aux circonstances?' (iii, 495). Instinctively differentiating the properties of the tree from both the formlessness and the homogeneity conjured up by the word 'Nature', Valéry is free to respond to it with all the intellectual excitement in his power, so much so that 'Grands tourments des grands arbres' can mean 'Accès de détresse personnelle' (xiv, 541). These feelings, expressed in the great trees of *Dialogue de l'Arbre* and of the poetry of *Narcisse*, *La Jeune Parque*, *Ébauche d'un Serpent*, *Au Platane* and in *Palme*, the culminating poem of *Charmes*, lead into the most important regions of Valéry's work concerning consciousness and the human being, regions where he develops insights and analogies which the tree helps to create as much as to express.

[1] E.g. 'puissant personnage d'un parc' (P I, 115). Valéry describes a tree in Corot's paintings as 'Quelqu'un' (P II, 1312).

6 Growth & decay

Valéry's sensitivity to things in nature largely depends on a highly developed awareness of certain types of form and their genesis and development in time. He is partly, like his own symbolic hero, Leonardo, 'l'ange de la morphologie' (xi, 199). Since so much of his writing on aesthetics and the psychology of thought takes its vocabulary from natural morphology,[1] it would seem important to establish in advance something of the nature of the forms and processes involved.

In *Eupalinos ou l'Architecte* Socrates distinguishes between two types of natural form: the first is principally the work of chance ('le hasard'): rock débris for example, or a landscape irregularly covered with plant growth; the second, like the plant itself, the animal or crystal, is the organised product of natural growth (P II, 127). The theme is already to be found in the earliest essay on Leonardo, where Valéry writes: 'le monde est irrégulièrement semé de dispositions régulières' (P I, 1172). Again it is a question of the random and the organised; of specific forms evolving a play of opposed pressures or forces, and of the chance combinations of these forms themselves.

[1] Agnes Arber suggests in words very relevant to Valéry that 'The morphological approach to biology is through structure viewed as form. Structure is a relational category, which may be defined as the arrangement or organization of parts within an integrated whole. Problems of pure morphology cannot be solved by the methods of pure analytical science. The contemplative treatment of comparative form, rather than its analysis from the standpoint of cause and effect, becomes the morphologist's aim; he desires to see form, both with the bodily eye and with the mind's eye, not only in itself, but in its nexus of relations [...]. The morphologist's standpoint is set midway between that of the mechanistic sciences and of the arts, so that his work should offer a synthesis of intellectual logic and sensory apprehension' (*The Mind and Eye* (C.U.P., 1954), 125).

Random forms

First, the random. It is rocks, random collections of rocks as opposed to structured individual rocks, which most clearly seem to represent disorder and accident to Valéry. Thus he may note 'Un paysage nu est accidentel; ruine géologique' (xv, 907) or 'les roches *hasards* images de désordre figé' (xii, 809). Rocks present a 'chaos de pierre' (P II, 200); they belong to the category of 'Choses brisées et leurs débris usés. Littoral rompu' (P II, 605). Just such a shore forms the mental décor of *L'Idée Fixe*, where the speaker picks his way over a multiplicity of disorderly rocks towards the spacious harmony of the sea: '[. . .] descendu furieusement vers la côte, qui était de roches écroulées de toutes grosseurs et des figures les plus diverses, je m'imposai le travail très pénible d'avancer dans le désordre *parfait* de leurs formes de rupture et de leurs bizarres équilibres' (P II, 199). 'La région minérale nue' (P I, 166) forms the semi-symbolic landscape of *Amphion* too, rather like the mysterious rocks in the background of certain paintings by Leonardo da Vinci with their distinct but unpredictable shapes. And rocks, slippery and inexorable, form the tumultuous natural stage of *La Jeune Parque*. Just as a sky dotted with stars presents 'l'informe' despite the inability of the mind to refrain from linking the stars into patterns, so a rock-strewn shore is the epitome for Valéry of 'un sol qui n'a point de loi' (P II, 666).

Random formations and the idea of chance are also associated, it seems, with the interaction of things one with another: sea and rock; sea and light; wind and water, foliage or sand. Valéry writes, for example: 'Les pierres roulées par la mer et les mêmes pierres travaillées dans l'air par les pluies et les gelées ne donnent pas les mêmes figures. Ce n'est pas le même fruste. Le hasard n'est pas de même espèce. L'action de la mer est *versatile*' (P I, 290). The movement of the sea, representing infinite possibilities of change and renewal, is a phenomenon which he never ceases to evoke and describe. He may note fascination with 'les traces du vent sur les sables et les eaux' (P I, 1172), with the chance beauty and illusion of artifice created by a sunset (ix, 875), or with the infinitely changing shapes made by the wind in the leaves of a tree, 'des formes nées du mouvement' (PI, 1169). All these phenomena offer precise shapes and movements within a context of change and apparent non-repeatability in time: 'du désordre à l'ordre [. . .] et *inversement*' (xi, 600). It is only the linking and recording process of perception itself extending in time which creates from such elements a notion of pattern and chance: 'Une écume s'allume, *de temps à autre*, sur le champ de la mer, et ces *temps* sont créés par le hasard' (P I, 290).

Organised forms

And what of the second type of form, organised form? Obviously it is above all the plant which offers Valéry a constant focal point for reflections on natural organisation or design: 'L'image de l'arbre ou de la plante qui me vient si souvent est image représentative de lois simples de la chose vivante élémentaire. [. . .]' (xi, 604) he writes, or 'Un paysage nu est accidentel [. . .] mais la plante qui s'y met, l'arbre qui s'y développe sont *nature* (nascor)' (xv, 907). Far from representing the blind lawlessness of 'Nature', or 'Bios' – by which Valéry generally seems to mean the existence of many individual systems or elemental phenomena – the plant represents 'Acte [. . .] Calcul [. . .] Géometrie [. . .] Équilibres' (xii, 17); 'Œuvre' (P II, 185); 'faire' (xviii, 236); 'architecture' (P II, 392). 'Le corps de la plante est mesure' (ix, 148), he notes in admiration of the balanced energies[1] that make up the living organism, or 'la belle architecture tient de la plante' (vi, 441).

It was not only the living organism which Valéry's Socrates included in his second category of ordered forms in nature, but also the crystal, that is, the organised form with an identifiable structure of its own. It is the perception of a common symmetry in plant and crystal structure which calls forth remarks like 'un grand arbre me fait penser aux cristallisations. La symétrie est un fait tout général' (P II, 603), or 'Une forêt – je songe à une cristallisation dans son extension dans un milieu saturé' (xxi, 895). Not as frequent a theme as the living plant, yet the crystal plays a considerable part in Valéry's mental universe as an 'image formule' of natural symmetry, that is of a natural process which divides and organises chaos into a particular order or shape.[2]

Combinations of two orders

It is not, then, because of a simple exclusion of disorder from their design that Valéry sees the plant or crystal as representative of organised form. His imagination is most frequently stimulated by things that combine the two orders, random and symmetrical. A landscape may in a sense provide this combination in that it is 'irrégulièrement semé de dispositions régulières' (P I, 1172), or 'peuplé de plantes ça et là poussées' (P II, 127).

[1] An idea of Valéry's notion of these different energies is given by P. Laurette in his chapter on 'L'Énergétique' in *Le Thème de l'Arbre*, 125–8.

[2] Cf. Claude Bernard: 'La fixité du milieu intérieur est la condition de la vie libre' (quoted by Judith Robinson, *L'Analyse de L'Esprit*, 76 n. 22). The idea of 'regulation' seems to have provided a transition between Valéry's interest in the plant and in mental functioning.

But individual phenomena like the sea, the plant and the crystal combine the two within themselves. Take the sea, for example: the constant delight it affords Valéry is not due simply to ceaseless variety. That would make it too close to the formless and vague in nature, irritating because it cannot stimulate the architectural qualities of the mind. Valéry delights rather in the co-existence of variety with order, of the sea's unpredictability with the elemental rhythms of the tides, always different, always the same. To take but one of a multitude of examples, the sea of *Le Cimetière Marin* is addressed as

> [. . .] Grande mer de délires douée,
> Peau de panthère et chlamyde trouée
> De mille et mille idoles du soleil,
>
> (P I, 151)

– that is as the symbol of infinite change and vitality – but it is also 'la mer, la mer, toujours recommencée' (P I, 147), the hydra forced ceaselessly to bite its own sparkling tail (P I, 151). It is this combination of limitation and unpredictability which holds the speaker in a state of controlled excitement throughout the poem. It echoes something of the restless yet repeatable nature of his own inner self. 'Si tout fût irrégulier ou tout régulier, point de pensée', Valéry writes in his first essay on Leonardo, 'car elle n'est qu'un essai de passer du désordre a l'ordre, et il lui faut des occasions de celui-là et des modèles de celui-ci' (P I, 1172). The idea still holds even when his views on the nature of order and disorder have widened to incorporate the 'discontinuous' nature of science itself.

Change within the limits of certain basic structures: the object which combines the same two elements of freedom and fixity, but this time with the stress on fixity, is, of course, the plant or tree itself, as the last quotation already suggests. The plant presents a perfect combination of randomness and symmetry, precision and abundance (ii, 895). In the phrase of Goethe's which Valéry quotes as expressing his intuitive grasp of plant structure, 'elle joint à une fixité originelle, générique et spécifique, une souplesse et une heureuse mobilité'(P I, 543).[1] We have seen how the idea of fixed trunk and tossing branches is the central theme of *Au Platane*. Similarly, Valéry talks of 'Hasard des ramures enchevêtrées' (xx, 710), or 'troncs d'arbres [. . .] hasardeux' (i, 127); or of a profusion of boughs and foliage as 'symétries rayonnantes déformées' (xii, 809). Thus, looking at a tree, the eye may enjoy 'une quantité indistincte d'éléments de surface assemblés au hasard, mais groupés en masse' (xii, 365) or, like the ballet of insects

[1] See 137, below.

round a lamp, 'oscillations des arbres autour d'un centre moyen' (i, 135), but this time the 'équilibre' is 'stationnaire'[1] instead of 'mobile' (xii, 642). It seems that Valéry finds in the notion of 'équilibre' a means of unifying the two poles of his thought, movement and immobility. They no longer produce the false dichotomy which he symbolises in *Le Cimetière Marin* in the paradox of Zeno's arrow:

> Zénon! cruel Zénon! Zénon d'Éléé!
> M'as-tu percé de cette flèche ailée
> Qui vibre, vole, et qui ne vole pas!
>
> (P I, 151)

The crystal, flower and shell are privileged objects in much the same way. In *L'Homme et la Coquille*, he writes:

> Comme un son pur, ou un système mélodique de sons purs, au milieu des bruits, ainsi un *cristal*, une *fleur*, une *coquille* se détachent du désordre ordinaire de l'ensemble des choses sensibles. Ils nous sont des objets privilégiés, plus intelligibles à la vue, quoique plus mystérieux à la réflexion, que tous les autres que nous voyons indistinctement.
>
> (P I, 887)

The reason for this predilection: 'Ils nous proposent, étrangement unies, les idées d'ordre et de fantaisie, d'invention et de nécessité, de loi et d'exception' (P I, 887). They appeal to what Baudelaire has called 'Cet amour contradictoire et mystérieux de l'esprit humain pour la surprise et la symétrie',[2] represented, for example, by the symbol of the thyrsus[3] with its combination of stiff rod and intricate luxuriance of plant growth. Valéry seems to sum up the response in his phrase: 'La haine du hasard et l'horreur de la règle' (i, 184).

'Tout le *corps* de cet arbre ou de ce veau sont des accessoires qui ont une importance visible *énorme* [. . .]', he writes, 'Ce n'est donc pas le corps au sens ordinaire qu'il faudrait considérer' (ix, 7), or, a little later on: 'Ce que nous prenons pour l'essentiel dans le corps n'est qu'un

[1] Valéry's notes show how closely he was influenced by the development of statistical mechanics by Gibbs (cf. Maxwell and Botlzmann) (see, for example, Laurette, *Le Thème de l'Arbre*, 127). Notions of 'homeostasis' and 'rheostasis' (Valéry's 'équilibre stationnaire' and 'équilibre mobile') are now commonly used in branches of systems theory such as cybernetics (details can be found in F. E. Emery, *Systems Thinking* (Penguin, 1969)). The 'tumulte au silence pareil' of the sea in *Le Cimetière Marin* could be related to the first of these concepts.

[2] *Œuvres Complètes* (Paris, Gallimard, 1961), 750.

[3] Ibid., 284–5. The serpent in *La Jeune Parque* is given this name (P I, 98), and in this way the Parque's own life principle is reinforced.

moyen. Le corps de la plante est mesure. Il est en équilibre à chaque instant [. . .]. Ainsi masse, temps, lumière etc. sont *liés* par une plante' (IX, 148); and 'le vivant se développe sur plusieurs plans ou portées, le *soma* et le *germen*' (XXVI, 208). Throughout his work Valéry shows a deep awareness of the fact that the external appearance of a natural object is the result of inner pressure and process in time. A previous chapter suggested something of the effect of change in nature on the sensitivity of a beholder. I shall look now at Valéry's detection of the same rôle of time and growth in the actual form of a natural object: his attempt, like that of Leonardo, to 'saisir les formes par leurs causes' (P I, 1259).

Time and formation

A characteristic rubric given to this interest in Valéry's notes is: 'Classification biologique par chronologie' (XII, 261). There is a further reflection in *Rhumbs* headed 'Perros (– Guirec)' (the coastal town in Brittany) that might be given this very description: 'L'âge des corps dépend de leur dimension et de leur figure./Ce grain de sable plus vieux que ce galet, ce galet que le roc; l'œuf de granit plus vieux que l'arête vive; la goutte d'eau plus antique que le grain gris./Mais ces vieillesses sont relatives, et chacune dans une histoire particulière' (P II, 605); or, in *Autres Rhumbs*, Valéry notes under the heading *Rochers*: 'Les uns luisants et cubiques [. . .], les autres, à cassures aigres et nettes [. . .]. Il en est d'informes et de grossiers [. . .]. Chacun sa nature, sa figure, son histoire. Sa figure est son histoire' (P II, 666). Many other natural objects are approached through the relationship of external form to process and age. The plant for example: 'O plante, arbre, répétition rayonnante,/Tu rayonnes ton âge par saisons et par germes' (P I, 353); or a tree: 'Âge. Temps. Section de troncs d'arbres' (X, 553). The bark of a beech has a texture determined in time as well as space: 'cette pierre qui a vécu' (XV, 644). 'Je réfléchis à perte de vue sur l'arbre, sur le fruit, et son histoire dans le temps du développement végétal tout en maturation, transport, accroissement et rayonnement' (XI, 343): interest in the rôle of time and development in the formation of natural objects is nowhere more apparent than in Valéry's constant interest in the seed, the fruit and the plant. 'Considérer une plante – dans un espace – temps-matière [. . .]', he wrote, 'Application de la relativité aux vivants, ou de quelque chose de plus hardi encore. Rôle de *l'avenir* dans le vivant. Une croissance est un plus court chemin [. . .]. Comme Faraday lu dans le spectre magnétique, lire le spectre qu'est le schème d'arborescence symétrique' (XV, 605).[1]

[1] Cf. Einstein's notion of 'space-time' and Faraday's own of a dynamic 'field'.

The seed

'Graines' is quite a frequent subject in the *Cahiers* (e.g., viii, 199). It becomes apparent that for Valéry the seed is interesting as a locus of future life and possibility. The seed contains 'de quoi amorcer une évolution, un fonctionnement, un "temps" dans un milieu, dont elle change la concentration – elle renferme un explosif' (xi, 41). It is 'un explosif conservatif. Un transformateur en type précédent. Équilibre par création, assimilation mais irréversible – mais cette modification suivant une loi de développement non uniforme' (xxi, 481). On the deceptive outer appearance of the seed Valéry notes: 'Mauvaise graine. Semences. Il n'y a rien de plus étonnant qu'une graine./Ce qui suppose, suggère une graine, conserve./En vérité, c'est explosif de vie, de développement' (xi, 350); 'La graine contient de grands secrets. Car elle vit et ne vit pas. Ressort bandé' (x, 635). Valéry's grasp of the dynamic qualities of the seed and its powers of 'storing time' leads to a typical analogy with more abstract themes: 'Il y a un ressort étrangement puissant, contraint dans les graines et dans certaines minutes' (P II, 613). Teste himself is in some ways 'un explosif conservatif' (xxi, 481).[1] From this point of view, Valéry's fascination is something like that expressed in Blake's lines:

> To see a world in a grain of sand
> Hold Infinity in the palm of your hand
> And Eternity in an hour,[2]

though his own combination of 'mysticism' with 'la contemplation de l'extériorité'[3] perhaps lays more stress on the actual visible details of the natural world in which, like a painter – and Valéry spent much of his life amongst painters – he could become totally absorbed.

It is as much an interest in '"l'avenir" d'un corps' (xiii, 774) which leads him to the seed, then, as its present state. The seed is exciting because of future metamorphoses. This kind of imagination leads partly to a kind of visual impatience, so much so that Valéry writes, using the seed half metaphorically: 'Je ne puis voir un grain sans jeter au feu le tronc

[1] Cf. 'Quelle foudre s'amasse au centre de César' (P I, 80). This type of imminent apotheosis is discussed by W. N. Ince in 'An Exercise in Artistry: Valéry's "Les Grenades"', *The Romanic Review*, LV (1964), 194. See also chapter 5, p. 112, n 1 above.

[2] Quoted by Charles du Bos in connection with *Palme* (*Approximations*, série 7 (Paris, Édns. du Vieux Colombier, 1965), 1432).

[3] Quoted by J. Hytier in 'Les Refus de Valéry' (*Questions de Littérature* (Columbia U.P., 1967), 63).

d'arbre' (v, 152), or, describing the process of imagination inevitably invited by the seed: 'Qu'est-ce qui nous empêche de concevoir qu'un arbre se développe à partir de sa graine et s'élève à 18 mètres pendant qu'une pierre que je tenais dans ma main, tombe sur le sol?' (ix, 150). It is at such points that Valéry's interest in the natural world most shows – to use J. Lawler's phrase[1] – a glance 'fascinated by its own inquiry'. Why otherwise should he note not only the details of the silky appearance of a winged seed but also 'Je tombe en contemplation devant cette chose si légère, si soumise au moindre souffle. Un million de réflexions' (viii, 886).

The fusion of the two interests can be seen in Valéry's recognition in the seed of the exterior equivalent of potentiality or 'reversibility' in the mental realm. Again, on the analytical level, he writes with exactitude on his favourite theme of circularity, 'On peut dire que la plante va de la graine à la graine ou aux graines ou bien de tel état à tel autre correspondant. Mais la graine est assez stable et de plus, va de l à m. C'est donc l'état préférable' (xvii, 19). The seed represents the most interesting stage of growth for Valéry because it suggests 'universal' time, the simultaneity of all time, the capacity to project the past into the future without being condemned to either epoch. It was precisely this quality which attracted him to the theme of dawn. By taking 'germe' in its widest sense, the parallel can be made clearer:

> Ici, unies au jour qui jamais ne fut encore, les parfaites pensées qui jamais ne seront. En germe, éternellement germe, le plus haut degré universel d'existence et d'action. Le Tout est un germe – le Tout ressenti sans parties – le Tout qui s'éveille et s'ébauche dans l'or, et que nulle affection particulière ne corrompt encore.
>
> (P II, 658)

'Paresser dans l'état universel' (P II, 658) – is this not what the seed seems to do in actual physical terms before 'le vouloir obscur de la croissance' (P II, 192) has precipitated it into the cycle of life and hence to individuation and death? This kind of consideration enables Valéry to say, still without conjuring up traditional associations of the joyful promise of future life, 'la graine est merveille' (xxi, 481).[2]

A very similar set of associations governs his reflections on the human spermatozoon. He writes, for example: 'Un spermatozoïde transporte

[1] 'The Serpent, the Tree and the Crystal', *L'Esprit Créateur*, IV (1964), 35.

[2] Cf. 'Un insecte me semble une merveille' (viii, 183). For Valéry's sense of 'le merveilleux', see below, 238.

d'un bord à l'autre de la vie, une quantité *d'avenir* précis, quelques caractères d'un individu qui *sera* ou plutôt des *chances* qu'il soit' (xxiii, 28). Again, apparently disinterested analysis breaks into a semi ironic wonder: 'Un spermatozoïde, un rien emporte l'effigie morale et physique de son auteur! [...] Quelle monade! [...] Je ne vois rien en aucun genre qui soit plus mystique, plus exorbitant que ce fait';[1] or, on the fascinating disproportion between minute sperm and fully conscious human being, like that between seed and tree admired by Lucrèce/Tityre, he notes (of consciousness): 'qu'elle a commencé par une chance séminale, et dans un incident microscopique; qu'elle a couru des milliards de risques, qu'elle est en somme, toute admirable, toute volontaire, toute accusée et étincelante qu'elle puisse être, l'effet d'un incalculable désordre' (P I, 1227).[2] The combination of order and disorder observed in a single object or imagined on a more abstract level to belong to the mind, is now imagined on the still further level of the relation of mind and environment. This kind of attempt to widen the 'univers' of immediate perception by determining its relationship to other 'univers' is reminiscent of the excitement Valéry expresses in his essay on Poe and cosmology (P I, 858).

The fruit

Where the seed, like dawn, is defined in terms of future time, the fruit, like evening, represents for Valéry the accumulation of time already past. He is constantly fascinated by objects that embody in this way 'durée de la maturité, de la *perfection* du fruit, de la coïncidence' (x, 76). A product of 'pression interne' (xiv, 884), the fruit belongs to that category of 'choses précieuses'[3] which result from 'une accumulation d'actions très petites' (ix, 875). The spiral of a shell made of countless secretions (P I, 886); honey, where mature perfection is the result of 'coïncidence' (x, 76); the ancient bark of a tree in *Dialogue de l'Arbre* ('l'eau de la terre épaisse et maternelle, pendant des ans profondément puisée, produit au jour cette substance dure ...' (P II, 180)); the slowly formed tear in *La Jeune Parque* (P I, 104): all these things are intriguing to consciousness at a given instant because of the part that minute accumulations in time past have played in their present shape.

The two poems in which this kind of vision culminates are *Les Grenades* and *Palme*, to be examined more fully later from other points of

[1] Quoted from *Cahier* ii by Edmée de la Rochefoucauld, *En Lisant les Cahiers de Paul Valéry*, I (Édns. Universitaires, 1964), 36.

[2] Cf. P I, 926 (*Réflexions Simples sur le Corps*).

[3] Cf. P II, 1244–5 (*Les Broderies de Marie Monnier*). Other favoured objects are mature wines, patina, a great tree, patience, the sonnet.

view.[1] In the first poem the pomegranates are seen in terms of the process by which they ripen and burst, the idea of the sunshine they have absorbed in the past increasing the delight of the beholder in their present state:

Si les soleils par vous subis,
O grenades entre-bâillées,
Vous ont fait d'orgueil travaillées
Craquer les cloisons de rubis.

(P I, 146)

This visual experience of the physical expression of time in nature, conveyed by the bursting skins of the fruit, sets up vibrations in the mental time-scale of the beholder as he dreams of a personal revelation in the past:

Cette lumineuse rupture
Fait rêver une âme que j'eus
De sa secrète architecture.

(P I, 146)

This is the same kind of process as seems to take place in Valéry's own imagination when he is responding immediately to concrete forms. It is to such natural objects that his remark on the visible simultaneity of past epochs in the present could surely apply: 'Nous voyons en même temps les choses qui ne sont pas du même temps' (xv, 906). The theme seems to produce for him a visual and hence particularly intricate intellectual stimulation, the kind which seems to accompany the discovery of organisational or 'anti-entropic'[2] principles in human perception. The same spatialisation of time is conveyed in *Palme*, not only by the direct perception of the tree and its ripe fruits, but by a metaphor fusing days and roots, fruit and hours:

Chaque jour qui luit encore
Lui compose un peu de miel.
[. . . . .]
Ces jours qui te semblent vides
Et perdus pour l'univers
Ont des racines avides
Qui travaillent les déserts
[. . . . .]
Chaque atome de silence
Est la chance d'un fruit mûr!
[. . . . .]

[1] See chapters 8 and 9.

[2] See 139 below.

Tu n'as pas perdu ces heures
Si légère tu demeures
Après ces beaux abandons;

(P I, 154–6)

Again, present form is inseparable from past time, and consequently these objects might be said to give satisfying concrete embodiment to the most tantalising of Valéry's ambitions: to express, mathematically or otherwise, the multidimensional structure of human consciousness in space and time.

Plant growth

It is through the theme of the tree or plant as a whole that the range and detail of Valéry's interest in the process of growth or development in time can best be seen. It appears that six main attributes can be disentangled for purposes of discussion as making up the basic functional characteristics of what he calls: 'l'idée [. . .] que j'ai d'une plante' (xvii, 10). Since many of them are the basis for the analogies with the conscious mind and its creations to be examined in the following chapters, I shall list them in some detail here. Valéry is, of course, not alone as an artist in discovering these attributes. Coleridge[1] and Goethe[2] are but two examples of artists whose analogies between plant and mind or plant and conscious creation are based on a detailed intuitive grasp of plant structure. But where Coleridge and Goethe (to an even greater extent) often seem imaginatively to work back from the mind to the plant, Valéry is more likely to use a strictly comparative method, proceeding from precise observations of natural growth to imaginative analogies or contrasts with the structure of thought, the concepts of energetics and thermodynamics providing a perfect bridge between the two, a central axis for multiple analogies.

1. A first characteristic of Valéry's notion of plant growth, a concept which can be constructed from a multitude of fragments, is the plant's origination in a primary whole, the seed, from which all its parts are derivative. 'D'un germe imperceptible née [elle] se déploie et se ramifie' (P II, 183), says Tityre of the plant or tree, fascinated like the reader of a poem by the disproportion in complexity between cause and effect. Often Valéry speculates on the element of chance in germination. For example: 'Graine ailée. [. . .] Je me demande comment il peut arriver que l'une de

[1] Most of these attributes have also been singled out by M. H. Abrams in 'Coleridge's Mechanical Fancy and Organic Imagination' (*The Mirror and the Lamp* (New York, The Norton Library, 1958), 167–77).

[2] See, for example, Valéry's *Discours en L'Honneur de Goethe* (P I, 531–53).

ces graines se fixe et entre en germination. Il faut qu'elle attende un jour de pluie' (viii, 886–7); 'La graine est jetée ici par accident [. . .], impose sa loi interne au milieu voisin' (xii, 260). Or there may be an attempt to see whether the system can be measured probabilistically: 'Nous *savons* qu'une graine, dans les conditions G produira une plante' (xxiii, 243). The co-existence of randomness and regularity is a theme which Valéry manipulates in the context of intellectual creativity too. Indeed, it is love – in many ways the epitome of the theme of "chance" germination followed by "necessary" growth – that Tityre has simultaneously in mind when he describes the tree's power to proliferate in a manner out of all proportion to its characteristics at birth (P II, 183).

2. 'Je songe à la croissance, aux développements de la plante, de la graine aux graines' (xviii, 612): the second main property to be distinguished could be growth itself, the plant being seen to exist only in the perpetual evolution and extension of all its parts. It is to be expected that 'croître' and 'accroissement' play a far larger part in Valéry's contemplations of the plant than do any static external attributes of natural life. He writes, for example: 'l'arbre élève sa masse en l'accroissant' (xii, 260); 'croître est sa loi' (P II, 182); 'tout son mouvement propre est de croître' (v, 839). In the plant or tree form, force, height, volume, duration, all these are determined by 'le vouloir obscur de la croissance' (P II, 192). Being and becoming, form and function are one, and present a 'mode indivisible'. These analytical perceptions sometimes break into lyrical apostrophe:

> O plante, arbre, répétition rayonnante,
> Tu rayonnes ton âge par saisons et par germes
> Tu répètes ton motif régulièrement à chaque angle
> De chaque étage de ta croissante stature.
>
> (P I, 353)

Sometimes, as here, Valéry tries to delve into the nature of the plant's method of growth. It proceeds by 'engendrement cellulaire' (i, 134); 'l'arborescence de l'arbre divise l'espace et tend à se relier infiniment. L'arbre est égal et chemine par division' (iii, 212); 'le travail de la vie de *proche en proche*, non direct par voie nerveuse – mais par pression interne [. . .] sic la germination, croissance des plantes – les fruits' (xiv, 884); or '[l'arbre] s'éloigne de ses parties, et sa division insensiblement continuée, traduit les masses informes ou profondes ou supérieures en élégantes rames' (ii, 894–5); 'Une plante ne pousse pas – une poussée intérieure en des millions d'éléments – osmotique – la gonfle et s'accompagne de prolifération' (iv, 147). In this way, organic growth is carefully distinguished from the traditionally mechanical – as opposed to 'une mécanique plus complexe, où la chaleur et le reste ne demeurent pas indifférents' (iii, 410).[1] He writes for instance: 'Les forces dans ces corps organisés sont traduites à chaque instant en rangements cellulaires – l'équilibre se fait par l'intermédiare de l'organisation et non comme dans la mécanique grossière, malgré elle' (iv, 147) or 'Il y a automatisme lorsqu'il n'y a pas "évolution"' (iv, 56). The plant, since it evolves from a seed, is connected in his mind with evolution: 'phase – temps – forme d'âge ou d'évolution etc. etc. sont inséparables – ou plutôt chacun de ces aspects est reconnu être une "projection" de la chose. La Plante' (xiv, 869). Yet here Valéry's remarks are detailed enough to suggest a further distinction. The plant may evolve from the seed, but 'elle se répète identiquement' (iv, 45). To continue the apostrophe quoted above:

> [. . .] tu répètes
> Ton essence en chaque graine, tu te produis, tu te jettes
> Autour de toi périodiquement sous formes de chances – en tel nombre
> Tu élimines tes similitudes.
>
> (P I, 353)

There is no evolution in the sense of biological transformism. Like the sea, the tree is the hydra, 'aux prises avec la roche, et qui croît et se divise pour l'étreindre' (P II, 181). It is a victim of that 'cyclique du vivant' (xx, 493) or 'finalisme circulaire' (ix, 219) which fascinated Valéry in all his reflections on life, whether plant, animal, or human being and made him sceptical of evolutionary theory except with reference to a particular time-scale.[2]

The slowness of growth fascinated Valéry because of the inability of the human eye to perceive what is extended over so long a period of time: 'Si des variations sont trop lentes, elles nous échappent [. . .]. Telle la croissance d'un arbre' (iv, 118). Yet however slow in relation to human perception, the slow modulations of growth itself are

[1] Cf. 'Nous sommes bien obligés de considérer un vivant comme une sorte de *machine*' (xviii, 222) (Quoted by P. Laurette, *Le Thème de L'Arbre*, 121–2 (chapter on 'Le Mécanisme')).

[2] Cf. L. Chiraviglio: 'organisms, in contrast to physical entities, must be envisaged simultaneously on four different temporal scales: the minute-to-minute functioning, the life-span, the generations, and the evolution-time-span of organisms' ('Biology and Philosophy', *La Philosophie Contemporaine*, II (Firenze, La Nuova Italia Editrice, 1968)).

indisputable.[1] Valéry's remarks at this point range from contemplation of graceful levity ('qui sait si une plante dans un pot, si ce pot était suspendu très délicatement, n'imprimerait pas à ce pot des mouvements?' (ix, 918)) to evocations of violence: 'Ou sent que la puissance de croissance fait crever cette peau éléphantine [the bark of a beech], cette pierre qui a vécu' (xv, 644). Delicacy and violence cohabit strikingly in his work. In 'la Merveilleuse Histoire de l'Arbre infini' of *Dialogue de l'Arbre* it is the discovery that 'sa vie d'arbre ne tenait qu'à sa croissance et qu'il ne vivait que de grandir' which produces in the tree 'une sorte de folie de démesure et d'arborescence' (P II, 191). 'Mais cet avancement procède, irrésistible, avec une lenteur qui le fait implacable comme le temps' (P II, 181), says Lucrèce of the inevitability of natural growth. The frequency with which this commonplace is treated suggests not only an unusually pronounced interest in how things are made or develop, but a need (and ability) on the part of Valéry to focus his own 'impatience' on a composite process whose unique slowness provides a model for the intelligence and the guarantee of a type of development different from its own.

3. A third closely related characteristic of the plant is its ability to develop according to its own internal conversion of energy. Allowance for this aspect of living organisms is important if Valéry is not to lapse into dualism when indulging a strong need to differentiate the plant and its organised architecture from what M. Bémol calls, 'ce flux de vie qui ne fait que le traverser'.[2] One of his greatest qualities here is the power to discern a distinctive principle of organisation in nature, while at the same time avoiding the temptation, when it comes to living things, of animating the organised with a Bergsonian 'élan vital'. As epigraph to her chapter, *L'Esprit, la Matière et le Monde*, Judith Robinson quotes an aphorism of Voltaire which could very well be relevant here: 'Pauvre pédant, tu vois une plante qui végète, et tu dis VÉGÉTATION, ou même ÂME VÉGÉTATIVE. [. . .] Mais de grâce, qu'entends-tu par ces mots? Cette fleur végète, mais y a-t-il un être réel qui s'appelle VÉGÉTATION?'[3] Valéry is not one of the pedants addressed. 'Un bel arbre ne se dissocie pas en un bel et un arbre' (ix, 32), he writes rather similarly on the level of linguistic analysis, and professes scorn for the idea of vegetable dualism: 'L'arbre souffle des fruits si lourds qu'il ne les peut retenir: il les perd ou il se brise. Va-t-il gémir qu'il y a deux arbres en lui?' (P II,

[1] See xxi, 456, xvi, 432 (quoted by P. Laurette, *Le Thème de L'Arbre*, 127).

[2] *Variations sur Valéry* (Sarrebruck, Publications de l'Université de la Sarre, 1952), 121.

[3] *L'Analyse de l'Esprit*, 82 (quoting 'Âme' from the *Dictionnaire Philosophique*).

577).[1] His work is full of insights such as: 'l'arbre et toutes ses parties [. . .] sont construits par les principes eux-mêmes, non séparés de la construction. Ce qui fait, ce qui est fait, sont indivisibles; et il en est ainsi de tous les corps vivants, ou quasi vivants, comme les cristaux' (P II, 128). Such insights may appear obvious enough when examined separately, but in the context of Valéry's work as a whole, sophisticated ideas proliferate from just such a simple stem – ideas on aesthetics, for example.

4. Fourthly, Valéry can often be seen to dwell on the plant's ability to assimilate its own surroundings: 'L'être végétal est peut-être le type le plus clair de cette combinaison de temps, espace, figure; forces, accroissement d'une région fermée au dépens d'un "milieu" qui distingue toute chose vivante' (viii, 214). In other words the plant is an open system in which a decrease of organisation in itself is compensated by an increase of disorder in its surroundings: 'Mais où l'Arbre a crû, là la terre est toute épuisée alentour et quand il est mort, elle est morte' (viii, 75); '*Une plante s'accroît par apport étranger*' (xxi, 515); 'Si la nature pousse une plante, elle l'élève insensiblement, la déplie et l'étale, comme par une suite d'états d'équilibre, de sorte qu'à chaque instant l'âge de la plante, sa masse, sa surface de feuillage découpé, et les conditions physiques de son milieu soient dans une relation indivisible' (P II, 1300). Like all living organisms, the plant transforms space into personal substance: 'envahissant l'espace [. . .], plongeant en pleine fange et s'enivrant des sels de la terre [. . .] elle lutte pour tout changer en elle-même' (P II, 192). At a later stage of its growth, but only up to a certain point, it will renew the very 'milieu' it assimilates: the kind of paradox that fascinates Valéry in many spheres. Under the heading: 'Objets aimés', he writes: 'Et l'arbre, pourquoi? Y lire la docilité et réciprocité si pures de la croissance et de l'extension aux circumstances' (iii, 495). 'S'accommoder' (P I, 538) – or at least the power of adaptability within certain limits – is the essence of plant law.

5. Here a further important theme can be distinguished, that of 'self-regulation', the plant's power to accommodate itself to a random 'milieu' while preserving its own individual identity, in other words, to convert chance into a (limited) order and design. 'Une plante dans sa variation suit 1. son évolution propre 2. les circonstances' (iv, 45). Hour by hour a perfect balance is established 'entre une loi intime de développement et le lieu et les circonstances accidentelles' (P I, 543). And again this flexibility in identity is made a cause for admiration: 'Je ne me lasse pas d'admirer par quelles nuances de formes la figure d'une plante se déduit insensiblement

[1] An obvious pastiche of *La Pythie* (and of Goethe's 'Zwei Seelen').

et s'accorde avec elle-même' (P I, 1474). This is much the same admiration that was concretely expressed in the poem *Palme* ('Pour autant qu'elle se plie . . .' (P I, 154)), warmly transmitting to the reader a sense of transferred 'sagesse végétale'.[1]

6. The last obvious characteristic of plant growth to attract Valéry, and one especially important when the plant is taken as the model of imitation in art, is organic unity: 'L'image de l'Arbre ou de la plante qui me vient si souvent est image représentative de lois simples de la chose vivante élémentaire et fait ressentir des "forces" une continuité, des fonctions de forces, un lieu variable vectoriel une *géométrie intrinsèque* d'un seul tenant où dimensions, temps, masse, forces sont liés et s'expriment l'un par l'autre. On voit ici l'image formule' (xi, 604). Although the whole plant is composed of parts with separate identity, it is through the existence of the whole that the parts exist (whereas in a machine the reverse is true). 'Et, moitié courant, je raisonnais ainsi', says Socrates in the *Eupalinos* dialogue: 'Un arbre, chargé de feuilles, est un produit de la nature. C'est un édifice dont les parties sont les feuilles, les branches, le tronc et les racines. Je suppose que chacune de ses parties me donne l'idée d'une certaine complexité. Je dis maintenant que l'ensemble de cet arbre est plus complexe que l'une quelconque de ses parties' (P II, 122). The remark is obviously closely linked to personal notes of Valéry's, such as 'une feuille semble moins complexe que son arbre puisque l'arbre unit aux feuilles, des racines, des fleurs, du bois . . .' (v, 827). A similar theme lies behind Goethe's 'Métamorphose des Plantes', as Valéry points out (P I, 544).[2] The idea that 'le degré de l'ensemble est nécessairement plus élevé que le degré des détails' (P II, 122) is a key concept in both 'organismic' biology and 'Gestalt' psychology.[3] Without suggesting that Valéry's work is the pale shadow of either of these, it is possible simply to intimate that his own reflections have led him to precisely those observations on natural 'structuralism' which will be most suggestive when it comes to expressing the organisational aspects of consciousness and art.

Decay

These, then, seem to be the main attributes of organic growth to emerge from Valéry's imagery and analysis. It remains to see how he views

1 See Laurette, *Le Thème de L'Arbre*, 154–6.

2 Cf. 'La feuille est verte, la fleur est rouge – expliquer cette discontinuité' (x, 15).

3 See, for example, Agnes Arber, *The Mind and the Eye* (C.U.P., 1954) and R. Arnheim, *Art and Visual Perception* (Faber, 1956). See also 145 n 1. For parallels with Gestalt psychology see the monograph mentioned on 142 n. 1 below.

growth in relation to decay: 'le mouvement [. . .] de déclin' (ix, 8) of all living things. Only when the theme of decay has been added to that of growth can his view of the organisational characteristics of life be seen to link up fully with his view of the two separate organisational time-scales of consciousness and the living organism.

The theme of decay can be introduced through an idea central to Valéry's work: limitation, the limits of growth. He writes: 'Il n'y a point d'arbre qui dans les meilleures conditions de terre, d'eau, de soleil, puisse croître indéfiniment' (xii, 6), and notes elsewhere, suggesting a reason for the limitation, that the plant has no defence mechanism and cannot recoil; it must constantly encounter 'Sa propre matière dont une partie, la plus vieille, s'affaiblit' (vii, 573). To live, to grow, is to forfeit the total potentiality of the seed and to enter on a cycle of existence that leads to maturity, decay and death, for like the human organism the plant must spend energy in order to live: 'il faut qu'il dépense pour croître' (P II, 220). Limitation, the forfeiting of potentiality, expenditure of energy: these biological themes return on many levels of Valéry's work, often with strong emotive associations of their own.

Valéry expresses a sharp sense of the way in which growth and decay, existence and degeneration, are inseparable principles. There are frequent references to the theme of 'De Perituris' (xxiii, 437); 'déperdition' (P II, 804), 'Senescenza' (ix, 888), 'dissipation, dépense' (P II, 605), or as it is called in thermodynamics, entropy, the necessary increase of the disorder of an isolated system of any kind. The universality accorded to this process can be suggested by a passage in *Mélange*, where, having noted the irregular shapes of rocks and stones worn down by the elements, Valéry goes on, characteristically, to attempt a measurement or description of the very process of decay: 'L'action de la mer est *versatile*. Celle des intempéries et de la pesanteur ne l'est pas. L'une roule et charrie. Les autres cinglent ou rompent, ou désagrègent' (P I, 290). In *Rhumbs* there is a similar passage:

> Ce pays, on y sent bien nettement que nous vivons sur des décombres.
> Choses brisées et leurs débris usés. Littoral rompu.
> Brisure et puis usure, et bruits de l'usure.
> Bruit perpétuel de la dégradation ou violente ou patiente.
> (P II, 605)

But it is not only the rocks which suggest decay. The living features of the scene are also brought into this category:

Mais ces voix d'enfants, ces cris, ces chocs dans la maison de granit et de sapin près de la mer . . . Ces sursauts de l'ouïe [. . .] donnent aussi l'idée, au possesseur de l'oreille philosophique, – sous l'apparence de vie, de vacarme et de jaillissement, – d'une dissipation, dépense.

(P II, 605)

To return to the living plant is to find that it too is evoked as much in terms of expenditure as of conservation of energy, of flux as of organisation, for example: 'Verse le/Fleuve léger/Porté sur les arbres en fleurs/Il se déclare/Pour l'horizon clair/Chair qui attend . . ./Verse encore/Le flux et le temps/et la fuite des arbres légers,/tous deux se dénouent . . .' (i, 172). This could be a description of the trees in *La Jeune Parque*: 'Le printemps vient briser les fontaines scellées' (P I, 102). There too, Spring is evoked in terms of expenditure of energy in time, so that the Parque fears procreation and renewal as being synonymous with acceptance of her own mortality:

La flottante forêt de qui les rudes troncs
Portent pieusement à leurs fantasques fronts,
Aux déchirants départs des archipels superbes,
Un fleuve tendre, Ô Mort, et caché sous les herbes?

(P I, 103)

In *Au Platane*, Valéry creates a vision of the seeds of future trees mingling with the dead (the reverse of the more usual approach to biological metamorphosis where, as in *Le Cimetière Marin*, stress is laid on the emergence of new life: 'le don de vivre a passé dans les fleurs!' (P I, 150)):

Tes pareils sont nombreux
[. . . . . . .]
Qui, par les morts saisis, les pieds échevelés
  Dans la confuse cendre,
Sentent les fuir les fleurs, et leurs spermes ailés
  Le cours léger descendre.

(P I, 114)

All things in this poetic universe seem to mingle and interact with each other at the same time as they temporarily preserve their own mysterious identity. 'L'air est une roche gazeuse et l'eau roche liquide, ces roches fluides gravitent et tendent à s'insinuer dans le profond de la terre' (xii, 260) (the line of the poem *Été* is not far away: 'Été, roche d'air pur, et toi, ardente ruche,/O mer!' (P I, 85)). All things are changing and corroding. Even the immobility experienced in *Le Cimetière Marin* is subsumed by this wider theme of change and disintegration, the minute flecks of foam at the beginning of the poem preparing imperceptibly to break out in waves at the end, to be followed by the final shattering of the wave itself: 'La vague en poudre ose jaillir des rocs' (P I, 151). In *La Jeune Parque* where a human organism is spending energy in time: 'Ce cœur, – qui se ruine à coups mystérieux' (P I, 107), external nature is changing and disintegrating too. The sea is wearing down the rocks as it seeps into their crevices, wind dispersing all that is immobile, waves colliding, marine noises intermingling. All these things, 'bewilderingly different', yet interrelated, suggest, as A. R. Chisholm words it, 'the tumultuous futility of life'[1] as it moves ceaselessly towards death, death that for Valéry is the local triumph of entropy in an irreversible sense:

> L'insensible rocher, glissant d'algues, propice
> À fuir, (comme en soi-même ineffablement seul),
> Commence . . . Et le vent semble au travers d'un linceul
> Ourdir de bruits marins une confuse trame,
> Mélange de la lame en ruine, et de rame . . .
> Tant de hoquets longtemps, et de râles heurtés,
> Brisés, repris au large . . . et tous les sorts jetés
> Éperdument divers roulant l'oubli vorace . . .
>
> (P I, 105)

In moments like this Valéry shows an almost Ronsardian power of evoking the whole natural universe in terms of movement and change.

A fascination with forms in the process of decay or taken to the limits of their endurance is often accompanied by a feeling of intellectual exhilaration and the characteristic urge (often reflected in poetry) to seize the moment of transition: 'Saisir une chose fugitive, fumée, vague, regard' (i, 63). Delighting at the same time in the juxtaposition of disparate substances, vital, and inert, Valéry notes, for example:

> Les molécules viles de quelque plante ou de quelque coquillage sont parfois remplacées une à une avec une exactitude merveilleuse par des molécules minérales plus précieuses – tellement que le squelette végétal, ou la conque, se change peu à peu en joyau – devienne un objet dont l'architecture a été empruntée à la vie, et les matériaux de la vie en ont fourni la première matière. (xiii, 381)

[1] *An approach to 'La Jeune Parque'* (Melbourne U.P., 1938), 48.

A similar interest inspires him to note the phenomenon of metamorphosis from chrysalis to butterfly (i, 122), while the theme of transformation in diffusion and apparent loss inspires the final image of *Le Vin Perdu*:

> Perdu ce vin, ivres les ondes! . . .
> J'ai vu bondir dans l'air amer
> Les figures les plus profondes . . .
>
> (P I, 147)[1]

Autumn

The theme of decay can be seen most clearly in Valéry's reflections on Autumn. 'Parlera-t-on ici de "Nature"?', he writes, 'Il s'agit de choses mourantes et mortes, et cette splendeur résulte *comme elle peut* de la dégradation d'organes d'où la *vie* s'est retirée' (P I, 295). The colours of dead leaves are more varied and sonorous than those of life, the same passage indicates, and Valéry concludes: 'C'est l'abandon, la décomposition, l'oxydation lente qui emplissent nos yeux de valeurs positives puissantes' (P I, 295). Life involves a ceaseless tendency towards decay, yet for the human mind, decay exacerbates its own vital response to the beauty about to be lost.

The theme of a human counter-effort to natural degeneration often returns in Valéry's work in other forms. The subject of Autumn may be pursued a little further here as an example of the theme on an immediate level of response. Artists have frequently expressed the strange thrill felt by the human mind sensing the laws of natural growth and decay made apparent by the seasons.[2] Valéry is particularly sensitive to the element of dissonance involved. Thus while *Palme* expresses the harmony with natural growth that can be achieved by the mind, comments such as the following express the basic dissonance of the same experience: 'Quand cette plante sera un arbre, moi je serai mort. Regarde-la pousser. Elle est innocente et gracieuse. Elle se tue, quand cette enfant aura la tête blanche. Toute la belle croissance des choses vivantes est contre toi' (viii, 884). In both cases the same intense power of empathy with natural processes is involved, a sensitivity previously seen in conjunction with the passing

[1] The possible relation of this poem to the Carnot principle of increasing entropy is described by W. N. Ince in 'The Sonnet "*Le Vin Perdu*" of Paul Valéry', *F.S.*, x (1956), 40–54 (see below, 190–1). For detailed discussion of Valéry's approach to the Carnot principle of increasing entropy and its relevance to life see my monograph 'Paul Valéry and Maxwell's demon: natural order and human possibility,' *Occasional Papers in Modern Languages no. 8, University of Hull, 1972*.

[2] Cf. 'The bare fact that germinating seeds or falling leaves are actually another expression of the processes we see at work in human life and death' (Caroline Spurgeon, *Shakespeare's Imagery* (C.U.P., 1956), 6).

of the day from dawn to night. 'J'observe en moi une très désagréable sensation de *hâte*, avec contraction intime, impatience insupportable, essoufflement, sorte de *pression d'instance* et tension "nerveuse" – qui produit une angoisse respiratoire et physique, étrange mixture' (xxix, 44): this is how Valéry describes a characteristic sensation of 'impatience', a complex feeling already associated with the desire imaginatively to speed up the growth of a tree, and with the mental habit of visualising in the seed a whole cycle of future growth. 'Ceci très intense, ces jours-ci', the description continues:

> Et ce sentiment d'automne que je connais si bien. Comme si mon organisme *fuyait devant le temps*, voulait *devancer* la fatale *marche à la perdition* qu'est le temps vulgaire – comme pour gagner un Point tel que je me sente *libre du temps* ou en plein temps libre. Étrange et absurde sensation. Tout un pathétisme y est attaché – avec ses couleurs de *souvenir musicalisé*, de puérile tendresse et d'arrachement émotif, d'adieux à larmes . . . Que sais-je?
>
> (xxix, 44)

Autumn epitomises a particular intellectual sensitivity with its roots deep in problems of identity, atmosphere and relationship with time. The same feeling was conveyed by the 'déchirants départs' (P I, 103) in *La Jeune Parque*, where even Spring symbolises the precipitation of life into a cycle of growth that will lead to ripeness and decay.

'[. . .] tout à coup ce jour de beauté déjà automne – grand tourment des grand arbres – accès de détresse personnelle – souvenirs de forêts perdues' (xiv, 541), Valéry writes, again closely associating personal emotion with the passing of time in the physical world. There are many possible personal reasons for the link besides the more universal reason of a perceived analogy between the dying year and human mortality.[1] In a passage in the published works headed *Laure* Valéry again relates Autumn to love and memory:

> C'est alors que le parfum trop délicieux des anciennes robes de Laure [. . .] se relève du néant; il accable mes pensées, il se mêle ou se trouble de l'amère senteur des feuilles mortes que l'on brûle dans les derniers jours de l'automne, et je tombe de tout mon cœur dans une tristesse magique.
>
> (P II, 858)

[1] Cf. G. M. Hopkins's poem on Autumn: *Spring and Fall* ('It is Margaret you mourn for').

Another personal reason may be association with the death of Mallarmé at that time of the year: 'Mallarmé me montra la plaine que le précoce été commençait de dorer: "Voyez, dit-il, c'est le premier coup de cymbale de l'automne sur la terre." Quand vint l'automne, il n'était plus' (P I, 633, cf. i, 253). Whatever personal reasons accentuate the feeling, Valéry shows himself particularly sensitive to 'les thèmes et les beautés qui se proposent alors aux yeux de l'esprit' (P I, 683). 'Automne [. . .] air délicieux, net, lisse, profond, aigu' (i, 283); 'Automne – tu donnes l'idée de l'objet incorruptible que l'on voudrait être. Une chose d'or dans un air froid, un achèvement aigu, le sentiment que la lumière n'est pas ce que l'été avait fait croire – l'avenir qui se sent souvenir, un grand changement comme statue et figure de tous changements; horripilent – me traversent' (ii, 269). The intensity of this feeling is expressed in the poem *Équinoxe*:

> Oui, je m'éveille enfin, saisi d'un vent d'automne
> Qui soulève un vol rouge et triste;
> Tant de pourpre panique aux trombes d'or m'étonne
> Que je m'irrite et que j'existe!
>
> (P I, 161)

'La Poésie – *formation de ce qui a puissance par resonances!* A quoi l'automne, le froid précoce et la contradiction de l'être me rendent si vulnérable' (xv, 295), Valéry noted. It remains to be seen in later chapters how this strong awareness of natural degeneration exacerbates the urge to construct and build up in art; to preserve all those elements of consciousness which the passing of time and the decay of living organisms tend to throw into relief, at the same time as they foreshadow its own potential loss with the decay and death of the human organism. Under the heading 'De Perituris' Valéry writes:

> Celui que ne ressent pas, ou qui ne porte pas en lui, une sorte de mépris pour tout ce que le *temps*, par sa seule opération massive et indistincte doit détruire en *puissance* – n'est pas MOI. Tout ce qui doit périr aurait-il *existé*? Le temps selon plusieurs tient sa vertu fatale du mélange et du désordre inévitable (qui résulte de la diffusion et dégradation des énergies) de manière que ce qui fut n'ait plus qu'*une* chance de redevenir contre des nombres [. . .] de chances contraires; cela est une nouvelle 'mystique' de la fin de tout. Mais ce qui doit périr par ce simple jeu fatal d'éléments indiscernables de choses et par la

dépense irrésistible – a cependant été formé; ce qui tombe a été élevé; ce qui brûle a été rempli. Il y eut donc un autre principe et un autre temps.

(xxiii, 437)

Such a passage is but one of many where Valéry outlines his notion of the distinctive order or time-scale of intellectual experience (cf. xv, 562). It introduces into the natural universe a new form of 'life' in that its duration is directly comparable to 'la lutte de l'être vivant contre le principe de Carnot' (xv, 802).

Defences against decay

It can be seen from the preceding remarks that Valéry's vision of nature is one of heterogeneity or 'mélange', a balance of order and disorder, randomness and regularity, complexity and chance. It is on this vital 'inégalité' or non-equilibrium that he considers the organisation of life and mind to depend. 'La "Vie" agit *contre* le milieu – considérée comme une chute d'énergie utilisable [. . .]' he writes, for example, 'Mais cette chute est désordre – que la vie partiellement rachète. L'oiseau s'éleve et l'arbre – et ceci régulièrement, par des moyens de régime [. . .]' (xviii, 90). Every organised system is in a sense a delaying conflict with entropy or disorder, 'un retard qui s'interpose' (xii, 260) in the flux of physical time. Such comments obviously stem from a central interest in the problem of describing what distinguishes life from the non-living. It would seem that Valéry favoured a reductionist view in which life is the product of 'conditions physico-chimiques' (xiii, 479),[1] but that he tended at the same time to view the chance conditions sufficient to produce such 'necessary' organisation as far too complex to be described by known biochemical laws.[2] The thermodynamic analogy is used by Valéry not to define but to describe life. He is careful not to identify wholly the forces of mechanical disorganisation and of biological decay. The power of the living being to withstand disorder is limited by the mysterious existence of its own life-cycle and terminates in death (xviii, 127).

[1] Agnes Arber writes: 'The *mechanist*, starting from the physico-chemical standpoint, interprets the living thing by analogy with a machine. The *vitalist*, on the other hand, supposes a guiding entelechy, which summons order out of chaos; he thus adopts a dualistic attitude. The elements of truth in both these views are recognised, and their opposition is resolved in the *organismal* approach [. . .]. This approach is conditioned by the belief that the vital co-ordination of structures and processes is not due to an alien entelechy, but is an integral part of the living system itself' (*The Mind and the Eye*, 100–1).

[2] See Laurette, *Le Thème de l'Arbre*, 127–8.

'Un paysage nu est accidentel; [. . .] mais la plante qui s'y met, l'arbre qui s'y développe sont *nature* (nascor)' (xv, 906); 'la graine est jetée ici par accident, impose sa loi interne au milieu voisin' (xii, 260): in comments such as these Valéry shows that it is not only the fact that the plant incorporates both the random and the symmetrical in its visible design that makes it a privileged object (a distinction between chance and order which perhaps belongs to human perception alone), but something much more radical: its own capacity to produce a local decrease in entropy.

A further distinguishing feature of the living organism in its struggle against disorder is, of course, its capacity to reproduce. Valéry is frequently called to meditate on the circular process – 'de la graine aux graines' (xviii, 612) – by which the plant overcomes extinction as a species, or, another way of looking at it, is trapped into an inevitable chain of life: 'Une espèce est une forme d'équilibre qui se conserve par reproduction – Équilibre d'espèce – Équilibre végétal' (xxi, 313), or, this time focusing on the 'chance' survival of an individual through a period of intermittence: 'Plantes annuelles/Problèmes de la consolidation de l'individu arriver au delà de la période de reproduction et recommencer le cycle' (xii, 261). Thus the fruits of the pomegranate burst open to reveal the seeds of future fruit (P I, 146); the fruits of the palm tree roll in the dust only to give birth to future trees (P I, 156), and by the weight of its fruit the tree is fulfilled:

> Pour autant qu'elle se plie
> A l'abondance des biens,
> Sa figure est accomplie,
> Ses fruits lourds sont ses liens.
>
> (P I, 154)

Valéry is constantly drawn to this theme, obviously as much for the intellectual satisfaction of *perceiving* circularity, both a trap and a reassurance to the mind, as for biological speculation in its own right, yet the biological observation remains consistent and precise. 'On observe [. . .] deux échappées au cycle d'existence du corps', he notes, 'd'une part, quoi qu'on fasse, *le corps s'use*; d'autre part, *le corps se reproduit*' (P I, 924).

Valéry's analysis constantly doubles back on the biological similarity between man and other living organisms before leading to points of difference. Thus the human and animal capacity to reproduce is frequently noted in similar terms. 'Notre faculté de vivre implique celle de faire vivre' (P I, 771); 'un animal (ou végétal) est une production. Il est aussi un producteur' (xxvii, 746). Reflections on the subject range from interest in the bifurcation of physical love away from simple reproduction to descriptions of 'l'émotion de la vie devant ce qu'elle a formé'.[1] An example of this emotion is found in the prose poem *La Jeune Mère*[2] where an unexpected tenderness and involvement is expressed, quite unlike the horror and resentment with which the Parque (and indirectly La Pythie) contemplates the idea of those yet unborn:

> Peuple altéré de moi suppliant que tu vives,
> Non, vous ne tiendrez pas de moi la vie! . . . Allez,
>
> (P I, 104)

(– it is surely no coincidence that the same word 'peuple' is used for the production of fruit in *Palme*). Generally, however, Valéry is concerned far more with the power of the human being to create through the mind than to produce through the body. It is to the mental field that images of gestation and ripening will be transferred, with particular care to eliminate certain associations with passive reproductivity and unconscious growth.

Valéry is concerned not only with the difference between living and non-living, but with the difference between plant and animal, and above all with what he calls 'la différence Homo/Animal' (xxiii, 112). So far everything which applies to the plant's power to transform a random milieu into its own design could be used to describe the animal and human as well. It is not correct to say that the human mind alone transforms chaos into order.[3] The movement from disorder to order – 'du désordre à l'ordre' (P II, 222) – is relevant to the existence of every living organism or non-isolated system with its power to introduce 'des infractions à Carnot [. . .] infractions régulières et non accidentelles, infractions *organisées*' and Valéry concludes 'et c'est peut-être là la définition de l'*organisation* – de l'anti-désordre (qui est l'*improbable*) [. . .]' (xviii, 127). Where the organisational principle of the human mind differs for Valéry from the organisation at work in the plant is in its power to introduce its *own* disorder into the system and thus break the static equilibrium with its environment to which an organism such as the plant is confined (e.g. xv, 569; P I, 470). And where the mind differs yet again from the purely animal in man is in the experience of self-awareness – 'la conscience de soi-même' (P I, 1025) – by virtue of which man can extend the range of his organisational capacity still further by becoming conscious of its requirements and bringing to bear on the present moment the full weight of his experience of time.

1 'Gabriela Mistral', *Revue de Paris* (fév. 1946), 3–7.

2 *Morceaux Choisis* (Paris, Gallimard, 1930), 53–4.

3 Here I disagree with H. Johnston, 'A note on Valéry', *F.S.*, II (1948), 333.

Consciousness and natural time

On this level of simple reflection on natural growth and development Valéry indirectly expresses more about 'le temps humain'[1] by differentiating it from what he calls 'temps végétal' (x, 492) or 'Temps naturant/Tempus naturas' (xviii, 612). 'Ce n'est point le temps, ce sont les changements que nous observons' (ix, 6), he notes. The tree in *Palme* is the result of change and process in space, the notion of age itself being relative to a particular life-span. Thus the palm tree is ignorant of the 'time' it epitomises:

> Cependant qu'elle s'ignore
> Entre le sable et le ciel,
> [. . . . .]
> Sa douceur est mesurée
> Par la divine durée
> Qui ne compte pas les jours,
> Mais bien qui les dissimule
> Dans un suc où s'accumule
> Tout l'arome des amours.
>
> (P I, 154–5)

This image springs, I think, from Valéry's constant awareness that time, seen in any other terms than the speed of development and decay of natural structures and organisms, is a human invention belonging to consciousness alone. In nature there are no instants, past nor future, but continuity of growth and change in terms of which every natural form must be defined.

Several remarks have to be put together for a consistent theme to emerge. For example: 'l'unité de temps est l'intervalle entre deux fructuations [. . .]. L'Arbre est un retard qui s'interpose – et ouvre un temps propre' (xii, 260), or 'Le mouvement de naissance, de croissance, de mûrissement et de déclin de tous les êtres vivants est un mouvement d'*univers*' (ix, 8), and finally: '[. . .] tout peut s'exprimer en *temps propre* ou *ordonné* et en temps général, universel ou desordonné. Temps propre n'est pas de l'individu seulement, mais de telle pensée, de tel fonctionnement' (xi, 343). It seems that Valéry is distinguishing between what physicists would call 'irreversible' and 'reversible' time ('temps propre'

[1] See G. Poulet, *Études sur le Temps Humain*, I (Plon, 1965), 350–63 and Judith Robinson's chapter on 'Temps et Mémoire dans l'Esprit' (*L'Analyse de L'Esprit*, 134–54).

or 'temps ordonné' being the term for 'irreversible' time and 'temps universel' or 'desordonné' being 'random' or 'reversible' time – terms with which Valéry may have become acquainted through his reading of Maxwell, Poincaré and Gibbs).[1] It is with the first time, 'irreversible' time that he connects the living organism such as the plant (e.g. xxi, 481), for it is confined to a single epoch and advances by a purely successive line of growth, with no power of memory or prediction with which to modify the direction of its course (xii, 17). Consciousness, on the other hand, has access to 'reversibility' (P II, 1459). It is defined by a far richer power of connectivity than the purely successive. It can modify present experience in the light of memory and anticipation and thus oppose to the circular confines of the organism an 'infinite' direction of its own. 'Esprit – du désordre à l'ordre', Valéry writes characteristically, 'Donc créer cherche le désordre pour en faire de l'ordre [. . .] par lá s'introduit un autre "temps"' (xv, 562).

It is obvious by now that Valéry does not consider consciousness to be in any way exempt from the one directional flow of natural time to which it belongs as a product of the finite human organism. The 'autre temps' to which he refers pertains to an order of subjective experience which cannot reverse the direction of natural time but only the order of its own internal elements,[2] introducing what Socrates refers to in *Eupalinos* as 'dans le sein même du temps, des sanctuaires impénétrables à la durée, éternels intérieurement, passagers quant à la nature' (P II, 90). It is in the light of such fleeting order that Valéry considers the creative intelligence to function *within* the natural time-scale of experience, 'en réservant ou détendant ses puissances – tantôt comme réversiblement, tantôt comme irréversiblement – grâce à une distribution et diversité entre l'actuel et la potentiel' (xvi, 433).[3] 'Par ce nom d'esprit', he writes in *La Politique de l'Esprit*,

[1] See, for example, the text by Poincaré on Maxwell (and Gibbs) in *La Valeur de la Science* (Paris, Flammarion, 1905), 180–5, quoted by W. N. Ince in 'The sonnet *Le Vin Perdu* of Paul Valéry', *F.S.*, x (1956), 43–5. Further details of Valéry's reading of thermodynamics and statistical mechanics in general can be found in Robinson, *L'Analyse de l'Esprit* and Laurette, *Le Thème de l'Arbre*.

[2] Cf. Valéry's analogy between the 'sorting' power of consciousness and Maxwell's demon (P I, 1347). At the end of his *Theory of Heat* of 1871 the physicist James Clerk Maxwell postulated the reversal of the Carnot principle of increasing entropy by a hypothetical being who could 'sort out' the molecules of a gas according to their different speeds, thus causing a 'reversal' of the natural flow of time.

[3] '[. . .] l'artiste se fait un joueur – d'un jeu dont les conventions sont attitudes, liaisons (momentanées) entre des fonctions sensitives, des fonctions motrices et des fonctions de mémoire – c'est à dire fait ce qu'il faut pour se rendre *maître du temps* [. . .] (xvi, 433).

> Je n'entends pas du tout une entité métaphysique; j'entends ici, très simplement, *une puissance de transformation* que nous pouvons isoler, distinguer de tous les autres, en considérant simplement certains effets autour de nous, certaines modifications du milieu qui nous entoure et que nous ne pouvons attribuer qu'à une action très différente de celle des énergies connues de la nature; car elle consiste au contraire à opposer les uns aux autres ces énergies qui nous sont données ou bien à les conjuger.
>
> (P I, 1022)

In his personal notes where the deeper and yet more speculative foundations of his ideas appear, it seems that for Valéry the creative mind discovers – but this time for its own distinct conscious purposes – the same 'rebellious' (anti-entropic) principle by which the living organism maintains itself in the face of physical dissipation (xv, 569), disorder and decay.

There is, I think, no subject more relevant to this nexus of paradoxical interrelationships between consciousness and nature than art. Under the heading 'Esthétique', Valéry wrote: 'me faire une idée plus nette du fonctionnement de l'homme sur le point particulier dont les arts sont le développement *naturel*' (xv, 752), and 'Penser à ceci: quelle relation entre ces *figures* symboliques et les formes 'naturelles' (v, 226). The next chapters will deal with his own possible answers to these questions from the point of view of an imitation of nature in the creative mind.

Part Three:

Intellectual creativity & natural growth

7 *Nature & analogy*

The third type of form distinguished by Socrates in *Eupalinos*, that of the work of man, must now be examined. For Valéry himself geometric form, form devoid of counterparts in nature and the creation of man alone, is the 'purest' act of construction possible. He writes with characteristic reference to Greek ideals: 'O sort pur de tels antiques Grecs qui déliant du mélange du monde peu d'opérations et peu d'effets simples, les opposent au hasard et au désordre divins' (ii, 577). This kind of form is extolled in *Cantique des Colonnes*, where the harmonious, mathematically proportional columns rival the productions of nature with purely human construction:

> Filles des nombres d'or
> Fortes des lois du ciel,
> Sur nous tombe et s'endort
> Un dieu couleur de miel.

(P I, 117)

Valéry shows a special enjoyment in setting the distinctive work of man in nature, in this case to receive, like the tree, its share of natural light, 'Pour affronter la lune,/la lune et le soleil', and to take its place in time:

> Nous traversons les jours
> Comme une pierre l'onde!
>
> Nous marchons dans le temps
> Et nos corps éclatants
> Ont des pas ineffables
> Qui marquent dans les fables . . .

(P I, 118)

The symbolic relationship of man and stone is clearly illustrated in the Orphic theme of *Amphion*, where the rocks themselves form a hieratic arabesque of motion (a 'Marche des Pierres (P I, 178)) moved by man's will to 'Imposer à la pierre [. . .] des formes intelligibles' (P II, 106); and where the 'chœur des Muses-Colonnes' (P I, 179) sings the lines of *Cantique des Colonnes* quoted above ('Filles des nombres d'or'). 'Aux figures de chute et d'écroulement de la nature géologique la volonté contraire d'édification, le travail volontaire, et comme rebelle, de notre race' (P I, 1085), Valéry writes in *Inspirations Meditérranéennes*, where he describes what he calls an essentially European adventure away from the initial conditions of natural existence (P I, 1023, cf. xxiii, 112).

Yet it would be a mistake and an impoverishment to suggest that for Valéry human composition, fabrication or construction ('creation' he tended to reserve for the involuntary aspects of the process – as, for example, in 'sensibilité créatrice') can be described in terms of a simple triumph of order over chaos, or even, granted that a struggle with the 'forces of darkness' is involved in the process of composition, to suggest that purely geometrical forms are the result. Socrates intimates as much in his description of man's works as compositions 'qui traversent, en quelque sorte, cette nature et ce hasard; les utilisant, mais les violant, et en étant violées [. . .]' (P II, 127), and Phèdre replies to him in the same dialogue: 'Tu as tiré de l'incident le plus mince, cette pensée que les créations humaines se réduisent au conflit de deux genres d'ordre, dont l'un, qui est naturel et donné, subit et supporte l'autre, qui est l'acte des besoins et des désirs de l'homme' (P II, 125). Art is concerned not with imitation of the natural only, but with synthesis, the problem of 'la jonction des procédés de la nature vivante avec l'acte du type humain' (xix, 208) and even, at the same time, with a conscious opposition to certain tendencies of mind itself: 'La nature n'a pas de plan, c.-à-d. de développements indépendants de la matière. L'esprit viole toujours la matière. Mais quand il est supérieur, il le sait – et il s'efforce de reconstituer par synthèse et en pleine lumière ce qu'elle sait faire aveuglément [. . .] Peindre la nature est – et doit être, essayer dans l'esprit de ne pas suivre les voies de l'esprit' (xvi, 214). The metaphorical transfer which is involved in Valéry's descriptions of human compositions in language drawn from natural growth and production can be illuminated on a simple non-metaphorical level by the actual comparisons and contrasts he is led to make between the natural product and the artifact.[1] 'Il ne

[1] Cf. W. N. Ince, 'An Exercise in Artistry: Valéry's "Les Grenades"', *The Romanic Review*, LV (1964), 193.

faut jamais [. . .] laisser perdre une occasion qui se présente de comparer avec quelque précision notre mode de fabriquer au travail de ce qu'on nomme *Nature*, *Nature* c.-à-d. la *Produisante* ou la *Productrice*' (P I, 897), he writes in *L'Homme et la Coquille*, where he stylises this very activity.

Nature and the artifact

Besides isolated fragments in the *Cahiers*, the main examples of comparison in any sustained form between natural production and human composition are to be found in *L'Homme et la Coquille*, *Eupalinos ou l'Architecte*, and to a lesser extent, the *Discours en l'Honneur de Goethe*. The first two of these works are in the form of a deliberately naïve approach to the question. In the first, a man finds a shell on the beach and speculates on its formation, deliberately eschewing any second-hand knowledge and testing the extent of his own immediate understanding;[1] in the second, a mock-Socratic dialogue[2] takes place round a similar incident (Socrates has picked up a small indiscriminate marine object). This is typical of Valéry's approach to both nature and art. 'Nous refusons à chaque instant d'écouter l'ingénu que nous portons en nous' (P I, 890), he complains, or: 'Je m'autorise de celui qui fit, un jour, *table rase*' (P I, 891). Valéry had in fact, closely documented his study of shell formation, as his file of preparatory notes proves.[3] The 'naïve' method is therefore a deliberate one in its own right, rather like the 'nonchalance [. . .] savante' (P I, 475) he attributes to La Fontaine.

'Nos formations de sensibilité doivent trouver leur origine dans cette catégorie de POURQUOI si chère à l'enfant', Valéry is said to have remarked in a lecture on aesthetics near the end of his life, going on to conclude 'Ce serait donc un tort de croire que le caractère enfantin d'une curiosité la dégrade'.[4] In the same series of lectures, he states: 'Dans l'œuvre du producteur, nous sommes avant le "pourquoi?" et le "comment?" comme dans l'opération de la nature.' 'Pourquoi?' and

[1] Cf. what E. Gaède calls 'l'art d'ignorer savamment' (*Nietzsche et Valéry* (Paris, Gallimard, 1962), 89). Here Valéry is putting into practice the precept 'regarde toi ne pas comprendre' (xxix, 247) (see above, 46).

[2] There are, however, 'no comments on good and evil as one might have expected from Socrates. Valéry's incorporeal spirits discuss not the meaning of life, but the functioning of the mind and the nature of beauty' (Vera J. Daniel, *Valéry, Eupalinos and l'Âme et la Danse* (O.U.P., 1967), 43).

[3] Judith Robinson, 'New Light on Valéry', *F.S.*, XXII (1968), 50, n. 8.

[4] *Cours de Poétique*, 12ième leçon (Samedi 29 jan. 1938), *Yggdrasill*, 3 ème année (25 mai. 1938), 26.

'Comment?' (P I, 897; P I, 891)[1] are the questions naïvely posed to the imagination by the quasi symmetrical form of the natural objects considered in these two essays.

But is the method so 'naïve'? 'Ceci est évident', says Phèdre. 'Je suis bien loin de le penser' (P II, 122), Socrates replies. Valéry's approach to natural formations is not like that of the man whom Lucrèce in *Dialogue de l'Arbre* spurns as naïvely asking before any manifestation of natural harmony in stars, animals or seasons: '*Qui fit ceci?*' (P II, 187).[2] Instead it is based on a strictly non-teleological approach to form. When it comes to contrasts and comparisons between the natural product and the artifact, it is, of course, precisely this kind of approach which enables him to approach well-worn paths of critical enquiry (for example, the 'organic' in aesthetics) from a fresh point of view.

How then, does nature 'create'? Our basic human reaction to 'things we have not made',[3] to 'formations naturelles remarquables' (P I, 886) such as the mollusc shell or 'objet trouvé', is, Valéry suggests, to imagine an act of construction by an architect. 'Nous savons [. . .] construire quelques molécules "organiques"' (P I, 897), but we cannot conceive of them in terms of formation, *formation* as opposed to *construction*, and this is what intrigues us most (P I, 887). Plant growth, as the previous chapter suggested, was partly distinguished for Valéry by 'La liaison indissoluble et réciproque de la figure avec la matière' (P I, 905). 'Or, l'arbre ne construit ses branches ni ses feuilles; ni le coq son bec et ses plumes', Socrates meditates:

> Mais l'arbre et toutes ses parties; et le coq, et toutes les siennes, sont construits par les principes eux-mêmes, non séparés de la construction. Ce qui fait, ce qui est fait, sont indivisibles; et il en est ainsi de tous les corps vivants, ou quasi vivants, comme les cristaux. Ce ne sont pas des actes qui les engendrent.
>
> (P II, 128)

'Valéry ne pouvait cependant pas définir un tel degré de symétrie', suggests P. Laurette of a similar instance, 'mais il reprit ce problème

[1] Cf. 'Madam How' and 'Lady Why' (Agnes Arber, *The Natural Philosophy of Plant Form* (C.U.P., 1950), 200).

[2] Cf. '*Qui donc a fait ceci?*' (P I, 891); 'Qui t'a faite?' (P II, 118).

[3] 'We are surrounded by things which we have not made and which have a life and structure of their own [. . .]' (K. Clark, *Landscape into Art* (Penguin, 1961), 17.

de jeunesse et expliqua qu'il voulait en fait préciser "l'*ordre* qui appartient au produire" par rapport "au *désordre* qui révèle le *faire*"' (xxvi, 120).[1]

There are many instances where Valéry uses this kind of observation to make an explicit contrast with artistic composition. For example: 'Bien que faits ou formés nous-mêmes par voie de croissance insensible, nous ne savons rien créer par cette voie' (P I, 887); 'Nos artistes ne tirent point de leur substance la matière de leurs ouvrages' (P I, 904); or, similarly, in *Petit Discours aux Peintres Graveurs*: 'il [the artist] n'est pas confondu à la matière de son ouvrage, mais il va et revient de cette matière à son idée' (P II, 1300). Nature 'fait visiblement et matériellement ce que nous faisons obscurément et énergétiquement' (ix, 16). The conclusion?: 'la "nature" ne fait rien comme nous' (xvii, 415). 'La différence de son travail avec le nôtre' (P I, 900) leads naturally to a theme central to Valéry's work: composition by separate acts: 'toute production positivement humaine, et réservée à l'homme, s'opère par gestes successifs, bien séparés, bornés, énumérables' (P I, 895–6).

But is this distinction between natural production and human composition really complete? Just as Valéry showed that the ordering of chaos and the counteraction of natural disorganisation is not an adequate definition of the conscious mind, since plants and even crystals do the same, so a witty comparison with bees or nesting birds enables him to point out that composition by separate acts alone is an equally incomplete definition. The real difference lies in 'la présence pensante' (P I, 896) which enables man to order those 'separate acts' in a new way: 'l'œuvre propre de l'homme se distingue quand ces actes différents et indépendants exige sa présence pensante expresse, pour produire et ordonner au but leur diversité. L'homme alimente en soi la durée du modèle et du vouloir' (P I, 896); 'L'artificiel résulte de la composition des actes' (xvii, 39). Man is conscious of his acts and brings to bear on his work the full weight of his critical self-awareness in time. 'SE VOIR est le propre de l'Homme [. . .] L'animal s'ignore' (xxvii, 379, cf. iv, 903).

Obviously this is not to suggest that Valéry views art and creative thinking as a product of consciousness alone. When he is reported to have remarked to Stravinsky that if there were a god, 'il ne pouvait exiger que le développement de ce qui nous semble à nous l'indication de l'accroissement de notre différence avec l'animal' (P I, 60), he implies the cultivation of man's whole intellectual sensitivity, the collaboration of all his powers of feeling, instinct, intellect and intelligence, paradoxically the acceptance

[1] *Le Thème de L'Arbre*, 113.

of his full condition, as a natural organism.[1] It is this kind of human uniqueness that art is thought to cultivate: the capacity for 'connaître-sentir-faire' (xvii, 6).

Ornament

A bridge-topic between the notions of form in nature and form in art was undoubtedly provided for Valéry by the theme of ornament. 'Il y a des formations naturelles dans l'esprit de l'artiste', he is said to have remarked in one of his *Cours de Poétique*:

> Songeons aux ornements géométriques des populations primitives. Ce processus rappelle celui des fleurs ou de ces traces que la mer, en son reflux, abandonne sur le sable. Dans l'intime de la production se rencontrent des formations de cet ordre. La production naturelle des rythmes est l'une de ces productions directes de l'organisation humaine qui sont le germe des productions organisées./Nous parlerons des productions de la sensibilité qui ressemblent à celles de la nature;[2]

and in his essay on *Léonard et les Philosophes*, he writes:

> Songez, par exemple, aux problèmes [. . .] de l'*ornement* qui touchent à la fois à la géométrie, à la physique, à la morphologie et ne se fixent nulle part; mais qui laissent entrevoir je ne sais quelle parenté entre les formes d'équilibre des corps, les figures harmoniques, les décors des êtres vivants, et les productions à demi conscientes ou toutes conscientes de l'activité humaine quand elle se dépense à recouvrir systématiquement un espace ou un temps libre, comme obéissant à une sorte d'horreur du vide . . .
>
> (P I, 1242)

The subject of ornament occupied much of Valéry's time as a young man. 'Pendant plus d'une année de la jeunesse, le problème de l'ornement a travaillé mon esprit. Rien ne m'a plus donné à penser, que cette production primitive qui paraît spontanément en tous lieux, se développe comme une végétation variée', he admits in his introduction to Paul Bonet's *Le*

[1] Cf. 'La Nature de l'homme comporte une activité contre nature' (xviii, 649); 'il est naturel à l'homme de créer l'artificiel' (xvii, 524); 'Artificiel – notion qui suppose que le produit d'un produit naturel peut n'être pas naturel' (xvii, 102).

[2] *Cours de Poétique*, 2 ème leçon (Samedi 11 déc. 1937), *Yggdrasill*, 2 ème année (25 jan. 1938), 153. Valéry's ideas on structure might be profitably compared with those of Lévi-Strauss.

Physique du Livre.[1] A study of ornamentation as a conscious art known to have held his interest at the time is the *Grammar of Ornament* by Owen Jones, a book that defines ornament as 'based upon an observation of the principles which regulate the arrangement of form in nature'[2] and suggests the same interest in symmetry which inspired Valéry's parallel interest in architecture. It is not so much the highly elaborate and conscious side of this art that is of interest here, however, as the fact that imagery of vegetable proliferation, ramification or 'arborescence' returns so often when Valéry wishes to describe the most immediate response of human 'sensibilité' to a blank space, that is, in the absence of any direct control.[3] Thus the reader's hand is said to 'engendre[r] dans les marges; elle abonde en nuages, en arbres'[4] or to draw 'au gré de l'absence et de la pointe, de petits êtres ou de vagues ramures' (P II, 1163). Similarly no form, conscious or unconscious, is possible without an element of growth: 'Il n'y a point de représentation de forme qui ne contienne l'idée d'une génération, c.-à-d. il n'y a point de forme qui s'isole d'une famille de formes, lesquelles se déduisent les unes des autres par l'action des forces vivantes.'[5] It is as if human sensitivity left to itself has a built-in tendency to relate to the bifurcatory process of natural growth, the defensive ordering process by which the living organism parries the randomness of environment on which at the same time its existence depends.

Nature and imitation

To stop here would, of course, be to give an oversimplified view of Valéry's position as regards the relationship between nature and art or sensibility and art. Like love, art begins for him only when these natural forms of spontaneity are recreated 'à l'octave supérieure',[6] that is, when they are imitated in the conscious mind. The attempt to discern in Valéry's work a philosophy of natural form or an imitation of nature inevitably runs the

[1] (Librairie Auguste Blaizot, 1945).

[2] Quoted by Vera J. Daniel in 'Valéry's *Eupalinos* and his early reading', *F.S.*, XXI (1967), 231.

[3] Cf. 'Le caractère récepto-émetteur me semble essentiel à la sensibilité [. . .] elle n'est pas uniquement passive, mais productrice, elle s'oppose au vide' (*Cours de Poétique*, 3 ème leçon (17 déc. 1937), *Yggdrasill*, 2 ème année (25 jan. 1938), 154).

[4] 'Baudelaire: dessinateur', *Le Manuscrit autographe* (Librairie Auguste Blaizot, 1927), 1.

[5] *Conferencia, Journal de L'Université des Annales* (22 nov. 1933). Valéry attributes the power of 'natural' growth to logical forms such as algebraic formulae (P II, 717–18).

[6] *Cours de Poétique*, 2 ème leçon (11 déc. 1937), *Yggdrasill*, 2 ème année (25 jan. 1938), 153.

risk of over-systematisation. This can perhaps be partly avoided by stressing in advance the multi-dimensional quality of his thought, a quality preserved by the co-existence of other analogies besides the organic. At the same time, I hope to suggest that the organic analogy itself is used in a way which guarantees the flexibility of Valéry's insights into the nature of consciousness and art.

There are many indications as to the possible basis for an imitation of nature in his work. 'Si l'on veut se faire semblable à ce qui produit (*Natura: productrice*)', he writes, 'il faut [. . .] exploiter l'entier domaine de notre sensibilité et de notre action' (P II, 1045); or: 'l'artiste doit chercher la "nature" dans son travail mais en tant que lois et non en tant que miroir' (ii, 679). This last remark is particularly helpful, since it suggests a distinction within the mimetic itself between nature merely copied and nature recreated in the mind ('Homo additus Naturae' (vi, 113)), the creation of what Socrates calls 'une nature plus ou moins extraite de la première, mais dont toutes les formes et les êtres ne sont enfin que des actes de l'esprit' (P II, 132). An equally important distinction is made between the natural and the merely spontaneous, between 'nature' and 'natural laws': 'Les idées de *Poésie* et de *travail* sont en moi associées étroitement [. . .] Par une méfiance à l'égard de ce qui survient – et que je soupçonne toujours de n'être pas assez – *naturel.* Le *spontané* me paraît *accidentel* plus souvent que *naturel*' (xv, 906). Confusion often arises because Valéry is as likely to use 'naturel' in a disparaging as in a positive sense. Fundamentally there is no contradiction in that the 'natural' should be taken as model if it is differentiated in his mind from the spontaneous and accidental of 'Nature' in general.[1]

Analogy

'[. . .] un rapprochement brusque d'idées, une analogie me saisissait, comme un appel de cor au sein d'une forêt fait dresser l'oreille' (P I, 1319), Valéry writes in *Poésie et Pensée Abstraite* of his poetic experience, and he notes in the *Cahiers*: 'Cette *divagation par analogie* assez divertissante' (xviii, 545). Taking analogy as a broad term introducing all forms of simile, parallel and metaphor in both prose and poetry, I shall suggest here some of the essential characteristics of a method based primarily on

[1] Cf. M. Bémol, 'Le Valérysme tout entier, qu'il s'agisse d'esthétique ou d'éthique de l'esprit, n'est-il pas à certains égards un art d'imiter la nature?' (*Variations sur Valéry* (Sarrebruck, Publications de l'Université de la Sarre, 1952), 120). This attitude can be compared and contrasted with the more strongly 'anti natural' thesis put forward by N. Suckling throughout *Paul Valéry and the Civilized Mind* (O.U.P., 1954).

the cultivation of 'la faculté analogique' (P I, 1166), for it is primarily with an analogy – that between art and the organic and ultimately that between natural growth and mental processes – that the remaining chapters will be concerned.

Some of the finest critical thinking of the past has, of course, taken place through analogy. To his chapter on mechanical and organic theories of the psychology of creative invention, M. H. Abrams gives as epigraph the lines of Shelley's *To a Skylark*:

> What thou art we know not;
> What is most like thee?[1]

The scientist as much as the artist uses analogy, or, by means of a model, uses an analogical way of thinking, often expressing what he feels to be true with the implicit formula: 'Nous ne savons pas . . . mais tout se passe comme si . . .', the kind of formula often to be found in Valéry's notes. But sometimes, especially when a writer 'thinks' in metaphors or when his analogies are only implicit, this 'comme si' and its implications may tend to be overlooked. In terms of exploratory value, the success of an analogy, particularly in a field as complex and elusive as the psychology of creative invention, must depend on the way in which it is used.

Valéry himself was particularly conscious of the delicacy of the analogical task where the expression of mental properties is concerned. 'Méthode – recueillir toutes les métaphores qui servent à désigner les faits internes' (ii, 120): this task presents for him a challenging nexus of problems, to the extent that one of his most tenacious ambitions is 'se faire une image des relations d'images' (P II, 739); to grapple with 'le problème de la valeur des résultats que peut donner l'emploi du langage quand il s'applique à exprimer les choses mêmes de la pensée' (P I, 831); 'étudier la réduction, le schématisme dont [l'objet] a été victime' (P II, 1462). It is a Gargantuan task he never systematically accomplished, but one which keeps his thinking in contact with attitudes whose fertility has been confirmed by the many avenues opened to science in recent years by attention to linguistic analysis and model theory.[2]

It is in this critical spirit that Valéry handles analogy, and through a characteristic critique of the abuses of the method that its ultimate uses

1 *The Mirror and the Lamp* (New York, The Norton Library, 1958).

2 'Système' was the heading given by Valéry to one of his most important files (see Robinson, *F.S.*, XXII (1968), 42). A discussion of the relation of models to metaphor and analogy can be found in E. H. Hutten's 'Scientific Models' (*La Philosophie Contemporaine*, II, ed. R. Klibansky (Firenze, La Nuova Italia Editrice, 1968), 121–7).

can be approached. The main reason for his scepticism concerning the correlation of physical image with mental properties is that the human imagination tends to visualise and spatialise: 'Dans l'esprit, les images visuelles prédominent. C'est entre elles que s'exerce le plus souvent la faculté analogique' (P I, 1166). We are misled into believing that the variations of the two worlds, natural and mental, are the same (P I, 1159). Take maturation, for example, the analogy to be examined in the following chapter, between on the one hand the conservation or even the development of an idea during an intermittence of conscious control, and on the other the process of natural ripening of a seed or fruit. Valéry writes: 'On aurait beau comparer l'idée à un être qui revivrait, dont chaque reviviscence serait en même temps la production d'un nouveau germe, et ce germe caché attendrait l'occasion de croître etc. Cette étrange comparaison ne rendrait rien plus aisé' (v, 281). Thus one of his own favourite analogies is criticised in advance from certain points of view.

Secondly, Valéry's scepticism is based on a strong sense of relativism. 'Mais du jour où l'enceinte des éléments apparemment rigides et inertes a été violée', the same quotation on the seed continues, '– où l'atome s'est ouvert montrant l'énergie interne – l'explication physique a été atteinte. Le monde de l'expérience *directe* n'a plus de modèles à nous offrir' (v, 281). We are faced with 'la faillite de l'imagerie scientifique' (P I, 921).

Thirdly, he is instinctively sceptical, when it comes to the denotative value of an analogy, of the way in which language itself precipitates imagery. He notes, for example: 'les langages feront qu'une jetée *s'allonge*, qu'une montâgne *s'élève* [. . .]. Et le vertige de l'analogie, la logique de la continuité transportent ces actions à la limite de leur tendance' (P I, 1169). While admiring the 'creative' power of such language from the point of view of its poetic possibilities, Valéry is sceptical of its 'resonance' in the field of analysis.

Yet, as in so many other cases in his work, attack on uncritical use of a term tends to throw positive usage into stronger relief. We may confuse the two 'worlds' of psychic and physical representation, but this permits us 'd'exprimer GROSSO MODO le monde psychique proprement dit par des métaphores empruntées au monde sensible' (P I, 1159). Analogy may over-simplify the relationship between the mind and nature, but 'sans cette pauvreté et cette nécessité et cette falsification, il n'y aurait pas d'*intelligence* [. . .] pas d'*universalité*' (P I, 333). 'Is this particular analogy much more than brilliantly fanciful?', writes J. M. Cocking disbelievingly of Valéry's description of the mind in terms of mathematical relationships, 'And is that other analogy Valéry liked to play with – in which the mind is thought of as a closed energy system like those defined in thermodynamics, any more revealingly imaginative?'[1] Such a remark may seem inconsistent with the same critic's suggestion that 'Valéry warns against carrying such analogies too far'.[2] It does not make the fullest use of the implications of statements like: 'On s'avise alors qu'une foule de ces systèmes sont possibles; que l'un d'eux en particulier ne vaut pas plus qu'un autre, et que leur usage, précieux, car il éclaircit toujours quelque chose, doit être à chaque instant surveillé et restitué à son rôle purement verbal' (P I, 1159).

'Précieux, car il éclaircit toujours quelque chose' – it is typical of Valéry's thought that he should reach this view of the illuminatory value of analogy only after disposing of a myth of absolute objectivity. Because of his awareness of the relativity of analogy to a specific creative 'type' of human 'sensibilité' and of the dangers inherent in its uncritical use, there are several reasons why it should prove a particularly suitable method for his own purposes.

First, speed. Valéry's mental 'impatience' must have particularly attracted him to a device which he defines as 'le moyen de transport le plus prompt, sinon le plus sûr, entre deux éclats de l'esprit' (P I, 1123) or as a 'pirouette de l'idée' (P I, 1403). A concept like that of maturation seems to be a way of condensing the 'mystery' of what it might take ten pages of analysis to describe in full (V, 196).

Secondly, analogical forms of language, especially the metaphor, seem to work at their best as 'an assertion followed by a quick denial of something you would expect to follow'.[3] It is as if the intellect shows through them its need to advance a discovery at the same time as retaining the prerogative of denying it all but temporary and approximative value. Such a form is obviously suited both to Valéry's particular scepticism concerning the dogmatic and ready-made category and, in this case, to the transfer of ideas from the context of natural growth to a subject as shifting and elusive as consciousness. Certain points of comparison can be enforced (for example, the structural rather than spatial likeness of a seed to the latent idea), while certain further contextual inferences can be denied (in the case of the organic analogy 'the fateful concept that artistic creation is primarily an unwilled and unconscious process of mind').[4] Just how successful Valéry is in denying this particular inference I shall be attempting to show.

[1] 'Duchesne-Guillemin on Valéry', *M.L.R.*, LXII (1967), 57. [2] Ibid.

[3] M. A. McCloskey, 'Metaphors', *Mind*, LXXIII (1964), 215.

[4] M. H. Abrams, *The Mirror and the Lamp*, 173.

Lastly, the analogical method is in perfect harmony with Valéry's gift for preserving the intricate temporal structure of experience: 'Toute *description* de nos perceptions séparées détruit radicalement ce qui serait de ces perceptions le plus précieux à connaître [. . .]' (P I, 880). Where the logical progression fragments, the image unites. At the same time it preserves what for Valéry is an essential part of any form of expression: the sensation of the mind making the discovery.[1] In this way – as his approach to the tree has already begun to show – he uses language to attain as well as organise belief.[2] Analogy is what he calls in another context 'le moyen de la découverte et la découverte elle-même' (P I, 857).[3] Valéry shows himself constantly aware that a new intellectual harvest can be reaped when the relationship between experience and expression is more fully understood.

'On s'avise alors qu'une foule de ces systèmes sont possibles' (P I, 1159): Valéry does, in fact, take his analogues for mental processes from many fields. Images from mathematics, mechanics and physics seem to be used almost as frequently as images from the field of natural growth, though it seems possible to suggest that these are in turn united to the first set by the notion of 'l'énergétique' (e.g. i, 328).

'To substitute the concept of growth for the operation of mechanism in the psychology of invention', M. H. Abrams points out, 'seems merely to exchange one kind of determinism for another.'[4] I shall attempt to suggest that this danger – if it is one – is avoided, not only through the way in which Valéry uses the organic analogy itself, but also through the way in which his work as a whole combines the advantages of the mechanical analogy with those of the organic. The organic analogy will be important not because of any special property in itself, but for the way in which it is appropriated by an essentially 'atomistic' mind.

Analogies from plant growth

By concentrating on the plant in particular Valéry is obviously rediscovering an archetypal image.[5] The plant has frequently been used as an

[1] Cf. J. R. Lawler, 'The mind finds itself in objects, in a few favoured images that provide the analogical network of its own operation' ('The Serpent, the Tree and the Crystal', *L'Esprit Créateur*, IV (1964), 36).

[2] Susanne K. Langer, *Philosophy in a New Key*, 2nd edition (Harvard U.P., 1951), 24.

[3] Cf. 'The model informs the potential reality, not the reality the model [. . .] Thus we make a selection, increase order, and create information [. . .] The model is then the necessary precondition for evaluating our perceptions and gaining information from them' (*La Philosophie Contemporaine*, II, 127).

[4] *The Mirror and the Lamp*, 173.

[5] *Philosophy in a New Key*, 75.

image of the growth of meaning,[1] as a metaphor of mind,[2] as an analogue for the maturation of the work of art,[3] a historical paradigm,[4] a philosophical analogy,[5] and similarly as a centre of what Valéry calls 'Mythique ou mythologie végétative/Rites et coûtumes de la vie végétative' (xv, 422). Like many writers before him, he is frequently stimulated by the chance to draw from a particular instance of plant growth a 'universal' insight into art or the mind, as well as to use plant growth on a yet more conscious level as an image in his expression of these very insights. He noted the recurrence of plant imagery in his work (e.g. xi, 604). Such imagery might be said to help constitute in his own case what he once called 'cet état où parvient la plus riche pensée quand elle s'est assimilée à elle-même, et reconnue, et consommée en un petit groupe de caractères et de symboles' (P I, 1223).

The seed

We have seen something of Valéry's interest in the seed, considered literally. Equally frequently he uses it figuratively in his work, both in prose and as an image in poetry, whether as 'la graine' or in the wider sense of 'le germe'. As H. Sørensen points out, 'la métaphore du *germe*, qui appartient [. . .] à la mystique de la vie organique, est souvent une métaphore inhérente au langage; elle signifie alors, en général, "commencement" ou "principe", et les pensées, comme les insurrections ont des germes'.[6] Although there are of course, countless examples in Valéry's writings of normal figurative use of vocabulary taken from natural growth: the seed of an idea, the ripening of a project, the fruit of effort and so on,[7] even this usage seems to extend slightly further than the conventional significance. The seed for instance, has both a concrete and an abstract meaning – 'a portion of an organic being which is capable of development into a new individual' and 'that from which anything springs or may spring, an idea for example'[8] – and this enables him to suggest a kind of constant parallelism between physiological and psychological realms.

[1] I. A. Richards, *The Philosophy of Rhetoric* (O.U.P., 1965), 12.
[2] E.g. by Leibniz and Herder (Abrams, *The Mirror and the Lamp*, 202, 204).
[3] E.g. by Proust, Mallarmé and Gide (see chapter eight).
[4] E.g. by Schlegel (Abrams, *The Mirror and the Lamp*, 219).
[5] E.g. by Kant (ibid., 208).
[6] *La Poésie de Paul Valéry* (Copenhagen, A. Busck, 1944), 197.
[7] E.g. P I, 516, 520, 640, 675, 682 and so on throughout his work. Valéry has little patience with the statistical analysis of a poet's work ('On relève des fréquences ou des absences dans leur vocabulaire' (P I, 1283)).
[8] *Shorter Oxford English Dictionary* (Clarendon Press, 1952).

For example, the rubric 'Ab ovo' (xxvi, 911) in the *Cahiers* refers to a general interest as much in the initial life of the idea as in that of the plant. There can be pieced together from Valéry's notes a kind of 'embryologie psychologique' (vii, 276), where themes of potentiality, maturation, incubation, chance germination and fertilisation – things which make the seed intellectually fascinating on a literal level – are transposed to the context of the psychology of thought. Nor is the transposition without literal implications. Valéry thinks of words like 'germination', 'de proche en proche' and so on as part of a 'programme' to describe actual mental experience and asks 'Qui sait si une *sensation* n'est pas un germe – ou un element de cristal en milieu saturé [. . .]?' (xvi, 432). Thus he may write of the initial 'inspiration' of a poem in terms of a living embryo feeding on the resources of the mind: 'l'embryon né d'un hasard se nourrit de mes circonstances/de mes lois [. . .]' (vii, 276), or of the 'embryon fécondé' round which the poet must effect the art of 'le *remplissage*' (xv, 481), and of 'l'art de retrouver cet embryon dans une œuvre donnée' (vii, 267).[1] It may be the power of the seed to take root like an idea in the mind, on which Valéry is basing his metaphor: 'Cette remarque fut un germe. Elle ne fit que passer dans mon esprit de ce jour-là, – le temps d'y disposer quelque semence imperceptible qui se développa un peu plus tard dans un travail de plusieurs années' (P I, 1480), or it may be the power of the seed to store life in time: 'Pendant quelques années, ce germe demeura dormant dans je ne sais quel pli de mon esprit' (P II, 1280).

Valéry frequently plays on the theme of chance in this way. Just as he had meditated on the fortuitous nature of the germination of seeds ('Je me demande comment il peut arriver que l'une de ces graines se fixe et entre en germination. Il faut qu'elle attende un jour de pluie' (viii, 887)), so he may speculate on the equally fortuitous development of an idea: 'Ce petit moment hors de moi est un germe, ou se projette comme un germe. Tout le reste de la durée le développe ou le laisse périr' (P II, 613); on all the potential directions in thought which are not followed up. M. Teste himself was to symbolise the existence of the 'germ' of a problem unable to develop in time (P II, 13). Of this kind of imagination, J. Hytier writes: 'Son génie de l'homonymie exploite à fond la métaphore du grain pour ajouter aux hasards fructueux, les hasards dynamiques et les hasards stériles.'[2]

Finally, examples can be found of cases where seed images are used to

[1] Cf. 'Pâle, profondément mordue' in *La Pythie* (P I, 130).

[2] *La Poétique de Paul Valéry* (Paris, Armand Colin, 1953), 148.

suggest the incubation of an idea in an intermittence of consciousness: 'Ainsi le grain de blé, retrouvé dans son hypogée, germe, dit-on, après trois mille ans d'un sec sommeil' (P II, 727) (here the parable of the fabled wheat slips directly into Valéry's own terminology). Or, of a sleeping woman (Anne? La Dormeuse? Agathe?)[1] he says: 'Elle dort, et en elle comme une graine dans une hypogée, repose et dure la vie du jour précédent dans l'attente du jour suivant' (XI, 35). 'Dors, ma sagesse, dors. Forme-toi cette absence', says La Jeune Parque, 'Retourne dans le germe et la sombre innocence' (P I, 109). By talking of sleep and of the parallel theme of an intermittence of consciousness in terms of a living seed, Valéry is substituting for the misleading idea of psychological absence, the idea of psychological fertility and imperceptible growth. This parallel between the latent potency of a seed and that of an idea forms the central image of *Les Grenades* and is implicit throughout *Palme*.

The plant or tree

Figurative use of the tree or plant is not so deeply implicit in everyday language as is the seed or germ. Yet, quite apart from the major poetic image of the tree as a symbol of consciousness (to be examined later in *Au Platane*, *Ébauche d'un Serpent* and *Palme*), there are other frequent instances of a metaphorical use of the tree or plant in both poetry and prose. These images often help suggest an intimate fusion between the human mind and exterior nature. For example, from the actual evocation of trees symbolic of Spring in *La Jeune Parque*, Valéry moves through a series of parallels[2] into a sensation of mental and physical identification with the tree on the part of the Parque, an identification verging on metaphor:

> Même, je m'apparus cet arbre vaporeux,
> De qui la majesté légèrement perdue
> S'abandonne à l'amour de toute l'étendue.
>
> (P I, 107–8)

The theme of gentle growth and abandonment has been transferred from the botanical to the human, from the tree responding to the force of Spring to the Parque herself, swayed by her own vitality of body and mind. At the same time something of the incongruity of the analogy between blind unconscious growth and the tense vigilance of consciousness helps preserve the distinction between the vegetable and human even here: '*Même*, je m'apparus cet arbre', says the Parque.

[1] 'Agathe ou le sommeil' (see J. Hytier's notes (P II, 1386–92)).
[2] See H. Sørensen, *La Poésie de Paul Valéry*, 105.

A previous chapter suggested that Valéry frequently compares a tree with a human being. Conversely, the human is often expressed through the image of a tree. Thus he may compare the reaction of the conscious mind in the face of the irrational to the bending of a tree in the wind, for example (v, 120). That this analogy is linked to the theme of *Au Platane* is confirmed by the remark a few years later: 'Pauvre système – arbre de vie, platane branlé par ses propres fureurs élémentaires inexplicables. Cela donne une drôle d'idée du "Moi"' (xxv, 571). In the poem *Au Platane* analogy with the human system is implicit only (Valéry left out a more explicit stanza for aesthetic reasons).[1] But in *La Pythie*, something of this theme of man being like a tree swayed by the irrational still remains in the more obvious image:

> Je sens dans l'arbre de ma vie
> La mort monter de mes talons.
>
> (P I, 135)

The analogy between human being and tree is also implicit in the structure and theme of the poem as a whole, where the oracle is swayed mentally and physically by her 'propres fureurs élémentaires inexplicables' (xxv, 571), to the extent that she confuses with the intervention of some external force the inner dualism of body and mind. The line 'Mes deux natures vont s'unir!' (P I, 135) is reminiscent of the ironic quotation: 'Fruits ennemis/L'arbre souffle des fruits si lourds, qu'il ne les peut retenir: il les perd ou se brise. Va-t-il gémir qu'il y a deux *arbres* en lui?' (P II, 577). Finally, the 'Saint *Langage*' at the end of the poem – 'la voix de personne/ Tant que des ondes et des bois!' (P I, 136) – is the language of human synthesis, the language that the tossing of the unconscious tree could *not* give in *Au Platane*.[2] This is not the first time that either through metaphor, close juxtaposition or implicit comparison, Valéry has drawn together the human and the tree, sustaining the biological parallel until it overflows into the realm of consciousness itself. '[...] *arbre gigantesque de la voix*' (viii, 38); 'un arbre de paroles' (P II, 193); 'sur l'arbre de chair chante le minime oiseau spirituel' (ii, 397); 'toutes les petites feuilles de la conscience' (iv, 58).

It is not only the natural growth of the plant which provides Valéry

[1] 'Ton supplice n'est pas un supplice étranger!
Mais l'ornement du nôtre,
Je t'assemble à l'horreur de ne pouvoir changer
Mon ombre contre une autre!' (P I, 1649).

[2] The Parque, too, is stirred mentally by the wind 'L'être contre le vent, dans le plus vif de l'air' (P I, 110).

with sources of figurative language; so does the field of horticulture or artificial growth. He writes, for example:

> J'ai toujours comparé, car ce n'est pas d'aujourd'hui que la question m'a préoccupé, la naissance d'une œuvre d'art de qualité [. . .] à ce qui se passe en matière d'horticulture. Lorsqu'on veut qu'une plante très délicate prenne, on la met dans du terreau, sous un verre; on la soigne jusqu'au moment où elle a assez de force pour pouvoir pousser en pleine terre;[1]

and: 'Il est des personnes qui n'ont pas de goût pour ce qu'elles nomment les Petites Chapelles' (referring to the artist's need for seclusion at some stage in his work): 'Je leur dis qu'elles n'ont jamais vu, dans un jardin, de ces plantes qui ne peuvent souffrir d'être mises dans la terre commune dès leur germe. On les place d'abord dans un humus choisi où elles atteignent lentement l'époque de leur force.'[2] Similarly, the theme of pruning appears in a comparison between the French nation and 'un arbre greffé plusieurs fois, de qui la qualité et la saveur de ses fruits résultent d'une heureuse alliance de sucs et de sèves très divers, concourant à une même indivisible existence'[3] and in the remark: 'Classique et culture – au sens propre du mot. Taille, greffe, sélection – émondage. Ainsi greffe de Grec sur Français. De Tacite sur Jésuite. Régressions brusques au fruit sauvage' (IV, 792). Here, Valéry is not using the plant as a paradigm for the rise and fall of civilisations as does, say, Schlegel. He is simply using the language of horticulture to bring alive the kind of etymological possibilities in the word 'culture' itself. In the use of images not only of nature but of artificially cultivated nature – 'Art des fausses fleurs'[4] – to describe human ends, lies a double paradox that obviously delighted Valéry. He uses it in the famous description of the growth of *La Jeune Parque* as 'Croissance naturelle d'une fleur artificielle' (P I, 1622).

A further context in which images of the tree or of ramification in general come naturally to Valéry is that of the maxim in the tradition of La Fontaine or La Rochefoucauld. There are frequent examples such as: 'La plante humaine semble s'épanouir aux louanges. On voit l'immonde

[1] *Allocution et Discours* to M. Rothschild's lecture on 'le Cinéma' (*Les Techniques au Service de la Pensée* (Alcan, 1938)).

[2] *Petit Recueil de Paroles de Circonstance* ('Au dîner du Divan, 2 juillet 1923) (Paris, Collection Plaisir du Bibliophile, 1926).

[3] 'La Pensée et l'art français', *Conferencia, Journal de l'Université des Annales* (22 nov. 1933).

[4] *A. Gide–P. Valéry, Correspondance, 1890–1942* (Paris, Gallimard, 1955), 358.

fleur s'ouvrir, et le feuillage frissonner' (vii, 227).[1] Many such remarks might appear literal botanical observations were it not for their context of moral or aesthetic concerns, for example: 'Rien de plus stérile que de produire. L'arbre ne grandit pas pendant qu'il pousse ses fruits' (P I, 52); 'Il n'y a point d'orgueil dans un cèdre à se reconnaître le plus grand arbre des arbres' (P I, 540); 'Il en est qui ont vaste feuillage et peu de racines' (P II, 882); 'Le monde entier souffle dans une graine et en fait un arbre' (*Mauvaises Pensées*, P II, 907). This gift of making the botanical widen to the maxim and the maxim to the symbolic is the basis of poems such as *Palme* and *Au Platane*, though there, far more of an immediate mental and physical reaction to the tree as a live individual object is expressed, together with constant reminders of the 'live' analogical process itself.

The fruit

The habit of using botanical imagery as the basis of an aesthetic or general reflection extends to the fruit. Valéry writes for example: 'La saveur des fruits d'un arbre ne dépend pas de la figure du paysage qui l'environne, mais de la richesse invisible du terrain' (P I, 533); 'Entre le mode de génération et le FRUIT, il se fait un contraste' (P I, 1158); or, again in the form of classical maxim: 'Femmes sont fruits. Il y a des pêches, des ananas et des noisettes. Inutile de poursuivre: cela est clair. L'amateur ne peut se résoudre à ne cueillir que ceux d'une seule espèce. Il veut se connaître soi-même dans la diversité du jardin' (P I, 315); 'Comme une plante qu'accable le poids du fruit qu'elle a formé, penche et semble implorer le geste qui la cueille, la femme s'offre' (P I, 505). There is a verbal link here with the tree bent under the weight of its fruit in *Palme* (P I, 154). Finally, the fruit image can be seen to occur in the famous passage on aesthetics: 'La pensée doit être cachée dans les vers comme la vertu nutritive dans un fruit. Un fruit est nourriture, mais il ne paraît que délice. On ne perçoit que du plaisir, mais on reçoit une substance. L'enchantement voile cette nourriture insensible qu'il conduit' (P II, 547–8).[2]

With greater emphasis on its sensuous implications as an object of meditation and delight in itself, the fruit also appears in a figurative sense in Valéry's poetry. For example, in the famous simile of *Le Cimetière*

[1] Other of many flower images are, for example, 'L'être qui s'émerveille est beau comme une fleur' (P II, 185); 'Fleur qui s'ouvre: Être qui se donne' (xxi, 777); 'Tout l'univers chancelle et tremble sur ma tige' (*La Jeune Parque*, P I, 102).

[2] Cf. with a slight variation P I, 1452.

Marin the voluptuous savouring of fruit is made to suggest the savouring of awareness of mortality, intellect and emotion perfectly balanced in the soft melting sensation itself:

> Comme le fruit se fond en jouissance,
> Comme en délice il change son absence
> Dans une bouche où sa forme se meurt,
> Je hume ici ma future fumée,
> . . . .
>
> (P I, 148)

Tenor and vehicle, abstract and concrete, are perfectly fused in some of the few lines of which Valéry was proud.[1] It is the same with the fruit of the tree of knowledge in *Ébauche d'un Serpent*, but here the fruit offered to Eve by the serpent embodies the savour of what is disappearing by being enjoyed:

> Que si ta bouche fait un rêve,
> Cette soif qui songe à la sève,
> Ce délice à demi futur,
> C'est l'éternité fondante, Ève!
>
> (P I, 143)

Here, as in the previous poem, the presence of the fruit is impressionistically suggested in terms of the sensations of thirst and savoured delight it provokes in the partaker. A similar set of associations is conveyed in more abbreviated form by the image of ripe fruit, the 'pêche partagée' (P II, 350) of Faust and Lust in *Mon Faust*. 'Sensibilité – qui jouit de ce fruit précieux?' (viii, 39), Valéry writes in his notes. In the ripe velvety peach, Faust and Lust share 'sensibilité' – the fruit of emotional as well as of physical maturity.[2] 'Frouitt . . . frou. . .itt! Encore une affaire de Frouitt . . .' (P II, 331), says Méphistophélès, obviously the equivalent of the tempter-serpent in *Ébauche d'un Serpent*. But it is only the fruits of the intellect in isolation which like the 'fruits amers' of Pascal's *Méditations* (P I, 468), are negative and bitter (P I, 145–6). The fruit of full conscious existence is 'délice'.

[1] Valéry also liked the lines in *Profusion du Soir* beginning 'O soir, tu viens épandre . . .' (P I, 86) (personal communication from Mme Lucienne J. Cain). One of his files is marked 'Bon' (See Judith Robinson, 'L'Ordre Interne des Cahiers de Valéry', *Entretiens sur Paul Valéry*, 265).

[2] Cf. 'L'heure est trop mûre, trop chargée de fruits mûrs d'un jour de pleine splendeur pour qu'il se puisse que deux êtres, même si différents, ne soient pas mêmement à bout de leur résistance à la force des choses . . .' (P II, 323).

It is already apparent that Valéry has developed the sensuous rather than the allegorical side of the Biblical fruit of the tree of knowledge. He does so to the extent that the sensuousness and vitality of fruit is transferred to the idea of knowledge, or rather, of the whole mind itself.

> Une science vive crève
> L'énormité de ce fruit mur!
>
> (P I, 143)

says the serpent. An abstract idea of temptation and knowledge has been translated into Valéry's own concrete, functional terms. It is this kind of analogy which forms the basis of *Les Grenades* where the same parallel between ripe, bursting fruit and mental wealth is made:

> Dures grenades entr'ouvertes
> Cédant à l'excès de vos grains,
> Je crois voir des fronts souverains
> Éclatés de leurs découvertes!
>
> (P I, 146)

The whole poem is again based on a close interchange between tenor and vehicle, the vitality of the fruit constantly heightening the vitality of the mind with which it is compared, and delight in the perception of the analogy constantly invigorating in turn the beholder's perception of the physical fruit.[1]

Valéry uses frequent metaphors and similes based on comparison between fruit and breast or fruit and skin, a theme which again intensifies the sensuous blending of external nature and human life in the 'eye' of the intellect. His interest in the painting of Renoir, 'voué aux femmes et aux fruits' (P II, 1326),[2] must have heightened his appreciation of this kind of homogeneity between natural and human form. The linking of fruit and breast first occurs significantly in *Anne*:[3]

> Elle laisse rouler les grappes et les pommes
> Puissantes, qui pendaient aux treilles d'ossements,
> Qui riaient, dans leur ambre appelant les vendanges.
>
> (P I, 90)

[1] See J. R. Lawler, *Lecture de Valéry*, 177–82.

[2] Cf. 'Renoir [. . .] colore, en quelque sorte, le plaisir de palper les fruits, les soies, le nu et toute vie' (Preface to 'Berthe Morisot: Seize Aquarelles' (Édns. des quatre Chemins, 1946)).

[3] Cf. in the lesser known earlier poem *Ballet*: 'tes hauts fruits de chair' (P I, 1592).

The metaphor here mingles a sense of cultivation and sophistication with that of natural abundance, the inert with the organic, and in this way suggests the ambiguity that attracts the lover (as it does in *La Dormeuse* where the natural image: 'O biche avec langueur longue auprès d'une grappe' is coupled with the theme of calculation: 'occupée aux enfers' (P I, 122)). It returns with more warmth in the later poem *L'Abeille*:

> Je n'ai, sur ma tendre corbeille,
> Jeté qu'un songe de dentelle.
> Pique du sein la gourde belle,
> Sur qui l'Amour meurt ou sommeille,
> Qu'un peu de moi-même vermeille
> Vienne à la chair ronde et rebelle!
>
> (P I, 118)

Here the *précieux* metaphor of a basket holding fruit precedes any explicit idea of fruit or breast. The analogy between them is made explicit only in the appositional metaphor[1] of the line 'Pique du sein la gourde belle', though in the remaining lines evoking the breast it is still implicit through the evocation of colour, sensuous fertility and shape. Finally, the same image of breast and fruit, purely implicit this time, occurs in *La Jeune Parque*:

> Et, roses! mon soupir vous soulève, vainqueur
> Hélas! des bras si doux qui ferment la corbeille . . .
> Oh! parmi mes cheveux pèse d'un poids d'abeille,
> [. . . . .]
> Le point délicieux de mon jour ambigu . . .
>
> (P I, 103)

In this last example the image of the bee is not as logically linked to the fruit image as it is in *L'Abeille*, an example of the way in which Valéry uses a group or cluster of words with meanings that may form associative links amongst themselves in the reader's less conscious mind. It is only a few lines later that the fruit-breast image is picked up again: 'Et vous, beaux fruits d'amour' (P I, 103). Although this last usage is more commonplace, the periphrasis introduces an element of ambiguity between passivity and desire, while at the same time serving as an impressionistic means of depicting the themes of maternity and childbirth never explicitly mentioned.

1 See Christina Brooke-Rose, *A Grammar of Metaphor* (Secker and Warburg, 1958).

Within a single poem, then, the fruit image may shift in associative range according to the shifting tensions of consciousness. At the beginning of *La Jeune Parque* constellations of distant stars are referred to as a great cluster of grapes:

> Je scintille, liée à ce ciel inconnu . . .
> L'immense grappe brille à ma soif de désastres.
>
> (P I, 96)

The image here is particularly dense for it is not only the clustering of the stars which introduces the idea of grapes. The Parque's own mental thirst plays a rôle in the creation of the image within the poem, almost as if she has become the mind of the poet himself. 'L'Esprit est Sisyphe, Tantale, tonneau des Danaïdes', Valéry writes making a classical allusion with the same general range as the title of his poem, *La Jeune Parque:* 'La création de la grappe est le fruit de la soif!'[1] At the same time the transition is made into the image of grapes and stars by the personal verb 'Je scintille', in which the sparkling of the stars has in turn been transferred to the Parque herself, her mind responsible for their brightness as that of the protagonist in *Le Cimetière Marin* is responsible for the sun's. The fruit image again fuses internal and external worlds in the longer passage where, this time identifying with the fruit itself instead of the thirst, the Parque remembers her lost self:

> Poreuse à l'éternel qui me semblait m'enclore,
> Je m'offrais dans mon fruit de velours qu'il dévore;
> Rien ne me murmurait qu'un désir de mourir
> Dans cette blonde pulpe au soleil pût mûrir:
> Mon amère saveur ne m'était point venue.
> Je ne sacrifiais que mon épaule nue
> À la lumière; et sur cette gorge de miel. [. . .]
>
> (P I, 99)

'Poreuse', 'fruit de velours', 'dévorer', 'blonde pulpe', 'saveur', 'gorge de miel': all these themes, in which the physical aspects of the fruit are intimately mingled with their effect on the senses, combine to suggest an experience of total happiness in which mind and body, space and time, form and substance, become almost interchangeable. In a similar way, a

[1] *Cours de Poétique*, leçon 6 (Samedi 8 janvier 1938), *Yggdrasill*, 2 ème année (25 février 1938), 171. Cf. 'Poème de Tantale/Doute si l'objet trop parfait existe/ Amour sans but, objet sans fin/Grappe éternelle faim à l'éternelle soif/Le fruit dans l'histoire du désir. Pomme grappe. Succulence chair' (xv, 705).

biological image is often used by Valéry to suggest how the body has a life and continuity of its own which can provide a guarantee and certainty for consciousness, 'débordement direct du physique dans le mental' (ii, 651).

Finally, the fruit image can be found as one of the two main metaphors in *Aurore* and in the twin poem *Palme*, to be examined later on.

Ripeness

Closely connected with the idea of fruit is the theme of ripening. Again, this is metaphorically built into the language. The ripening of an idea or a project is almost as commonplace as the 'fruit of labour' and so on. But again Valéry puts just that much more stress on the idea, suggesting that the idea of time and development receives more weight in his thought than the commonplace usage implies. Thus he writes of 'les fruits longuement mûris de toute une vie réfléchie' (P I, 1102), or, expressing a favourite theme of the potentially infinite development of an idea past its natural maturity: 'La maturité est un certain maximum. On n'est jamais bien sûr que le fruit de l'esprit est à maturité/L'esprit n'est jamais sûr que son fruit est à point' (xiv, 127). The idea that 'le temps est de l'argent' gives way to the phrase: 'Le temps est de la maturation, de la classification, de l'ordre, de la perfection' (P II, 613), and the concept of ripeness becomes an epithet of praise: '"Combien *mûrs* et beaux les vers de nos grands poètes!" Ce *mûrs* est d'un connaisseur, mot excellent' (P II, 636).[1] The Testian verb 'maturare', to be examined below, finds constant echoes in the less active verb 'mûrir' liberally scattered throughout Valéry's work. He writes, for example: 'Un mot mûrit brusquement un enfant' (P II, 495); or (of 'philosophes' and the incubation of ideas) 'Ils mûrissent encore dans le *poêle*' (P I, 852), a theme closely connected for Valéry with the famous stove in which illumination was allegedly experienced by Descartes – who meant so much to him despite their differences. In all these instances, and many others similar, the essential ingredient of time in any composition is expressed in terms of ripeness and maturity – '*le loisir de mûrir*' (P I, 1039) – so that in a poem like *Palme* where this ideal is the main subject, there will be scarcely any mental transition needed before the figurative reverts to the literal theme of the ripening of fruit.

The last part of this chapter has merely indicated how vocabulary from the life cycle of the plant provides Valéry with a constant source of imagery, both on the level of simple figurative analogies in prose and in

[1] Valéry is referring to a line by Sultan Abdul Hamid.

the more extended metaphors and similes of his poetry. In the next two chapters I suggest the full implications of such a choice in the context of Valéry's essentially atomistic, 'anti natural' thought as a whole, and follow up the discussion with which this chapter began by looking in detail at analogies with organic growth: first in the context of the process and product of creative invention, and finally in the context of the development of intellectual processes as a whole.

8 *Maturation & poetic composition*

The preceding chapters have constantly pointed to one of the most rewarding paradoxes of Valéry's work: the conscious cultivation of time-consuming mental activities by an essentially impatient mind. 'Mon travail est un travail de patience exécuté par un impatient' (vii, 833), he writes, obviously with poetic composition particularly in mind, and: 'l'horreur du développement, de ce qui se prévoit. Et pourtant le culte du complet' (v, 195). It may indeed seem paradoxical that one who was willing to spend a proverbially long time drafting and re-drafting a single poem such as *La Jeune Parque* should admit 'Je n'ai jamais eu de patience dans ma vie'.[1] To suggest a possible approach to the apparent contradiction, I shall try to suggest what is implied by Valéry's constant stress on the necessity of allowing for time in the creation of anything of value. Discussion will necessarily go beyond actual analogies with plant growth or ripening, yet at the same time it will centre on a single theme: maturation in both the specific intellectual achievement and the long-term process of intellectual life as a whole.

Ripeness

Many artists have, of course, dwelt on the necessity of ripeness in art and thought. 'Nonumque prematur in annum'[2] is a precept that goes back to Horace. To take but a few recent examples, the theme can be found throughout Flaubert's correspondence; in Vigny's 'Je ne fais pas un livre. Il mûrit dans ma tête comme un fruit';[3] in Mallarmé's 'quand un poème

[1] Quoted by H. Mondor in 'Un jeune esthéticien', *Arts* (25 juillet 1945).
[2] Quoted by R. Gibson in *Modern French Poets on Poetry* (C.U.P., 1961), 258.
[3] Quoted by E. Estève in *Alfred de Vigny, sa pensée et son art* (Paris, Bibliothèque d'histoire littéraire et de critique, 1923), 226.

sera mûr, il se détachera. Tu vois que j'imite la loi naturelle'[1] or: 'il faut que je me donne le talent requis et que ma chose, mûrie, immuable, devienne instinctive, presque antérieure et non d'hier.'[2] Similarly, Gide writes in the *Journal des Faux Monnayeurs*:

> Le livre, maintenant, semble parfois doué de vie propre; on dirait une plante qui se développe, et le cerveau n'est plus que le vase plein de terreau qui l'alimente et la contient. Même il me paraît qu'il vaut mieux en laisser les bourgeons se gonfler, les tiges s'étendre, les fruits se sucrer lentement; qu'en cherchant à devancer l'époque de leur maturité naturelle, on compromet la plénitude de leur saveur.[3]

and Verlaine: 'Lentement, lentement! L'œuvre, ainsi qu'un soleil!'[4]

Most of these examples refer to time in a very general sense. Others will be seen later which refer specifically to the period when a work or idea must be allowed to ripen or mature without the intervention of the artist's conscious control. It seems necessary, in fact, to distinguish between the two types or periods of time covered by the theme of maturation in general. These are distinguished by Valéry himself, according to the kind of creative activity which takes place in each, as 'temps d'abstention' and 'temps de travail' (viii, 895); 'temps de montage' and 'temps d'exécution'[5] or simply 'temps passif' and 'temps actif' (i, 325). Obviously he does not mean by these different time-scales simply a period when the poem is being put on to paper and a period when it is being formed in the artist's mind. Rather, he implies the time taken up on the one hand by conscious solicitation of material and on the other by less conscious development, or, in other words, by the artist's attempt to hold back immediate intellectual suggestions in favour of a prolonged receptivity to other forms of experience. Gestatory and executory processes intermingle. They cannot be described in terms of two distinct successive stages.

It is usual to associate Valéry's insistence on the vital necessity of time in composition with the first of these activities, that in which the artist exercises conscious control of his material. Yet his work would be far less rewarding if it were not for the willingness with which he is amply pre-

[1] *Lettre à Théodore Aubanel* (16 juillet 1866) (see *Propos sur la Poésie*, ed. H. Mondor (Édns. du Rocher, 1945), 69).

[2] *Lettre à Henri Casalis* (23 avril 1871), ibid., 95.

[3] Entry for 6 jan. 1924 (Paris, Gallimard, 1948), 77.

[4] 'Épilogue', *Poèmes Saturniens*, *Œuvres Complètes* (ed. Y. G. Dantec, 1954), 78–80.

[5] *Cours de Poétique*, 2 ème leçon (11 déc. 1937), *Yggdrasill*, 2 ème année (25 jan. 1938), 153.

pared to consider and incorporate the second, more passive, period too. J. Hytier writes: 'Valéry n'a pas beaucoup développé l'idée de maturation, sans doute parce qu'elle l'aurait entraîné à tenir compte du travail inconscient, notion qui répugnait à son intellectualisme, et aussi parce qu'elle contrariait sa théorie de la création humaine par actes séparés.'[1] The same critic goes on to instance the 'maturare' of Teste and the eulogy of patience and ripeness dramatically expressed in *Palme* as if these were isolated examples of a theme in some way contradictory to Valéry's 'true' thought. Yet even if this view were taken to apply to the second kind of time only, 'temps d'abstention', it would be misleading. 'Tout poète est un prodigue de temps et non seulement de temps de travail, mais surtout de temps d'abstention' (viii, 895), Valéry writes, or: 'Toute œuvre commencée avant une certaine maturation est manquée' (iv, 837). I hope to show here that although a certain tension in his work may apparently run counter to a full acceptance of maturation in the passive sense, this tension, of which Valéry himself is critically aware,[2] takes its place in a context of far greater flexibility than the statement by J. Hytier suggests. Not only is relatively unconscious maturation acceptable in theory to Valéry's 'intellectualism', but he is willing to make of it an active and constant principle in his own artistic work.

First, time in general: 'l'usage du temps dans les arts' (ix, 875). That Valéry sets time – that is, the elaboration of the work of art over the longest possible period – at the heart of his aesthetics, is soon apparent. 'Le temps *fait tout*' (P I, 1675), he says of the finest compositions; works of art 'épousent le temps' (P II, 1247); 'Le temps ne compte pas pour les faire' (ix, 895). The idea of Molière's Alceste that 'le temps ne fait rien à l'affaire' is considered to merit the comment: 'affirmation grave' (xxi, 770).

Insistence on the necessity of time can be seen in its most obvious form in the attack Valéry waged throughout his life on the cult of the hasty and premature, which he rather conservatively considered to be the essence of modern art. Particularly in public essays and prefaces, but often in private notes too (e.g. ix, 875), he champions the lost cause of artistic patience, of 'le travail de pur exercice sans espoir de fruits immédiats, la longue préparation de soi-même à l'écart du monde'.[3] 'Nous perdons le

[1] *La Poétique de Valéry* (Paris, Armand Colin, 1953), 149.

[2] E.g. 'Orgueilleux à ce point de refuser les plus précieuses lumières si elles ne viennent pas du côté où il [l'esprit] les attend' (xxiv, 825) (attributed to 'Faust III' this remark still characterises many of Valéry's statements about his own attitude to poetic composition, particularly in the first part of his career).

[3] 'De la ressemblance et de l'art', *Vues* (Paris, La Table Ronde, 1948), 328.

loisir de mûrir' (P I, 1039), he writes; 'L'ère du provisoire est ouverte: on n'y peut plus mûrir de ces objets de contemplation que l'âme trouve inépuisables [...]' (P I, 652). Modern man has lost 'le beau *souci* qu'avait élu notre jeunesse, *le dédain de la hâte*, *le bonheur de mûrir*'.[1] Again and again hasty creations are contrasted unfavourably with those 'choses précieuses' (Valéry's notes under this heading show he considered the sonnet to be one of them (ix, 875)) which 'absorbent un temps très long et qui exigent autant de calme que de temps' (P II, 1244). The article from which this remark is quoted, *Les Broderies de Marie Monnier*, is a typical panegyric[2] of qualities of patience, culminating in the words:

> La brodeuse a choisi ses prétextes dans quelques poèmes. Elle n'a plaint la peine ni la durée. Ces belles pages tissues d'or et de soie ont consumé plusieurs années. Il y a du sacrifice et du paradoxe sous cette œuvre de grâce et de magnificence, où l'opiniâtreté de l'insecte et l'ambition fixe du mystique se combinent dans l'oubli de soi-même et de tout ce qui n'est pas ce que l'on veut.
>
> (P II, 1245)

There is something worthy of the 'sic transit...' of a Bossuet in these beautifully composed rhetorical reiterations coming from one of the last poets to preserve in a modern context the classical notion of form. Yet at the same time, they suggest something uneasy and self-defensive. Valéry's attack on modern haste is often strongly reminiscent in wording (for example, 'dégoût croissant des longues tâches' (P II, 1244)) of his criticisms of his own impatience (for example: 'Je vois telles "vérités" dans l'ordre de l'art; mais le courage me manque de dépenser le travail qu'il faudrait pour accomplir ce que je sais devant être fait' (xviii, 916)).[3] Before dismissing this often violent polemic against modern haste as over-simplified and essentially reactionary, it is necessary to see it in the context of Valéry's own work as a whole and to see on what personal justification it is based.

Apart from the self-exhortatory element which often enters Valéry's apparently descriptive statements – in this case, the exhortation to overcome his own instinctive predilection for impatience and speed – the attack can be seen to rest mainly on the idea that to neglect the time

[1] Lettre-Préface to L. Kaldor's *Cinquante ans de typographie* (Kaldor, 1935).

[2] Cf. P I, 513, 645, 1038, 1049, 1065, 1382, 1486; P II, 46.

[3] Cf. 'Ego. L'impatience. Ma torture' (xxix, 731); 'Je vais toujours au plus pressé. Je ne puis prendre le temps de...' (P II, 1534, cf. xxvi, 865).

ingredient in any sphere of experience is ultimately to maim and neglect part of the self. 'Quand le terme presse l'esprit, cette contrainte extérieure l'empêche de soutenir les siennes propres. Il néglige les beaux modèles qu'il s'est formés; [...] il se décharge par le plus court' (P II, 195). 'Fascinated [...] by technological progress, and yet deeply concerned for the preservation of those values that make man truly human, and which are jeopardised by this very progress',[1] Valéry complains that:

> Nous perdons cette paix essentielle des profondeurs de l'être, cette absence sans prix, pendant laquelle les éléments les plus délicats de la vie se rafraîchissent et se réconfortent, pendant laquelle l'être, en quelque sorte, se lave du passé et du futur, de la conscience présente [. . .] . . . Point de souci, point de lendemain, point de pression intérieure; mais une sorte de repos dans l'absence, une vacance bienfaisante, qui rend l'esprit à sa liberté propre. (P I, 1068–9; cf. P I, 1049)

The strange and fertile 'oisiveté' of *Le Cimetière Marin* is perhaps not far away, in which state of calm meditation the speaker finds himself 'aux sources du poème' (P I, 149, cf. IV, 728). Obviously art for Valéry is not a direct translation of this state, but he certainly considers poetry to be enriched by the mental potentials made available to both poet and, consequently, reader,[2] by the extension of composition in time.

Impatience

This is not to say that Valéry had no use for the insights of the instant or for a kind of apparently spontaneous impatient writing where '[l'esprit] se décharge par le plus court' (P II, 195). *L'Idée Fixe* is a product of this very attitude ('Ce livre est enfant de la hâte' (P II, 195)), and the rapid exchange of ideas it reflects is obviously not without close relationship to a certain speed of conception in Valéry's own mind. Something of the same quality of immediacy[3] is preserved in the day-to-day mental 'stock-taking' of the *Cahiers*, while in the swift aphorisms collected under the

[1] L. J. Austin, 'The Genius of Paul Valéry', *Wingspread Lectures in the Humanities* (Wisconsin, the Johnson Foundation, 1966), 40.

[2] E.g. 'Les œuvres qui nous exaltent nous indiquent aussi *ce qui veut croître en nous*, et le sens du développement de notre existence en tant qu'elle peut être *une affaire d'univers*. C'est ainsi que notre sentiment de la plus grande beauté peut avoir quelque droit à la direction de notre vie' (P I, 675). Cf. 'esthétique croissance' (XIX, 152).

[3] Cf. W. N. Ince, 'Impatience, Immediacy and the Pleasure Principle in Valéry', *F.M.L.S.*, II (1966), 180–91.

heading *Tel Quel*, Valéry expresses what could be an attempt to echo stylistically the essentials of impatience: 'Et moi, sur mon fil spécial, dix fois allé au bout, dix fois revenu – je vibre entre ce lent réel et cet extrême, je vibre d'impatience, atome dans une flamme et j'émets cette radiation propre que j'écris ici' (P II, 728). The shower of rapid verbal fireworks is constantly preferred to the developed thought or intellectual abstraction, for which Valéry reserved an instinctive distaste throughout his life: 'l'horreur du développement' (v, 195). But nowhere are the qualities he found in the immediate resources of language more apparent than in the series of prose-poems 'Poésie brute' scattered throughout the *Cahiers*. One of the finest of his achievements, they point to the fact that the highly cultivated language of poems such as *Charmes* is only one aspect of a far wider creative experimentation with words.[1]

That the instantaneous has an exploratory value of its own, Valéry was often aware. '[. . .] je pense trop vite (ce qui donne de tout autres pensées que de penser lentement)' (P II, 1534; cf. xxvi, 865), he may note, or, thinking of greed for the maximum simultaneous mental experience: 'C'est absurde. Cependant beaucoup de mes vues nouvelles furent dues à un petit fragment d'un état tel' (i, 173). Much of this value is linked with his view of perception itself as an essentially rapid or instantaneous activity. Thus discoveries concerning his own most characteristic mental state, impatience, come remarkably near his own definition of the intellect. A remark like: 'Je voudrais jouir de toutes mes pensées à la fois, dans le même instant' (i, 173), for example, can be compared with: 'Pour l'esprit, tout doit se passer *tout de suite* [. . .] Car le temps presse, le temps!' (i, 279);[2] or a bitter outburst such as: 'O terribles raccourcis! Jugements électriques et sommation de toutes mes vies' (iv, 797) is echoed in the more assured tone of abstract analysis, in passages where Valéry attributes to the intellect in general an abbreviatory function of some kind (e.g. ii, 866). Personal preferences for the 'Et Caetera' method (P II, 558)[3] present obvious links with his view of genius as an ability to take short-cuts rather than to develop the full consequences of an experience: 'le

[1] Cf. the introduction by Octave Nadal to *Poems in the Rough*, ed. Jackson Mathews, *The Collected Works of Paul Valéry*, II (London, Routledge & Kegan Paul, 1970), xi–xxix.

[2] Cf. 'Toujours je me suis essayé à me voir d'un coup d'œil . . . à fouailler tout sentiment suffisamment développé' (ii, 727) and 'l'esprit se prévoit, se défend de suivre ou développer tel germe' (xviii, 175).

[3] Cf. the title page of the review *Etc.*: 'In a non-aristotelian, infinite-valued orientation, we do not assume that what we *say* can cover *all* the characteristics of a situation, and so we remain conscious of a permanent *et cetera* instead of having the dogmatic period-and-stop attitude' (Korzybski).

génie considéré comme un raccourci' (ix, 895).[1] His own analogical method might be said to do just that. The same idea is played on in the phrase: 'Génie! O longue impatience!' of *Ébauche d'un Serpent*, where traditional equations of genius and patience are ironically reversed.[2]

We have already met, in connection with Valéry's vision of certain natural objects such as the seed, the urge imaginatively to abbreviate or speed up natural processes of growth. The equivalent urge in the realm of inner mental processes can be sensed in meditations on, for example, the possibility of artificially reducing the time needed for the ripening of an idea: '[. . .] et si même ce temps peut être abrégié par une forte méditation' (iv, 75). One is reminded of the protagonist in *l'Idée Fixe* who admits '. . . je trouvais en moi le désir insensé de faire par l'esprit en quelques instants ce que trois ans de vie eussent peut-être fait. Mais comment produire du temps?' (P II, 197). Judith Robinson draws attention to Valéry's understanding that the old expression 'quick as thought' is misleading: '[. . .] en réalité les différents événements nerveux dont la pensée se compose demandent tous un temps fini et bien déterminé, que rien ne peut raccourcir'.[3] The individual speed of mental events, or rather their requirement of different periods of time that nothing can abridge, seems to Valéry one of the most intriguing regions open to literary and psychological research. It accentuates for observation the limits and possibilities of consciousness itself. 'La pensée passe son temps à unir *naturellement* maintes choses diverses', he notes, 'si l'on tâche artificiellement à faire de même . . . on ne trouve que *Soi* – et par conséquent on découvre bien des choses' (i, 173), or: 'Peut-on faire le travail plus vite? Et dépasser son pas? Cela n'a aucun sens – Cependant, dans un intervalle, j'ai plus vite parlé! – Plus vite. Plus vite!' (i, 502).[4] The temporal conditions of thought and feeling cannot be disrupted, but the desire to do so is an experience in itself. It is clear then, that the kind of intelligence on which a discussion of 'patiente impatience' (P II, 1301) in poetic composition must ultimately be based, is concerned with the power of consciously vying, or consciously complying with the natural time-scale of affective life. 'On lutte avec le temps par la passion ou par la patience en allant plus vite ou plus doucement que les suggestions immédiates données par les événements' (i, 424). I intend to suggest that Valéry is as capable of collaboration with

1 Cf. 'Tout l'homme est en raccourci dans l'impatience' (iv, 10; P II, 623).

2 See J. R. Lawler, *Lecture de Valéry, une étude de Charmes* (Paris, P.U.F., 1963), 169.

3 *L'Analyse de l'Esprit dans les Cahiers de Valéry* (Paris, Corti, 1963), 184.

4 Quoted by J. Duchesne-Guillemin in *Études pour un Paul Valéry* (Neuchâtel, La Baconnière, 1964), 33 ('Aller à la limite').

time as of opposition to it, and that he shows both attitudes to have a certain kind of consciousness as their single and united source.

'Mes opinions appellent bientôt leurs contraires ou leurs complémentaires' (P I, 1469); 'chacune des qualités d'un esprit apporte des chances particulières d'erreur à la représentation du réel' (P I, 327). Valéry is always careful to present the genius of instantaneity as one possible part of mental experience only, incomplete in itself. 'Le génie tient dans un instant' (P II, 612), he may write, but elsewhere, '[. . .] le génie est loin de suffire – car tout n'est pas dans l'instant' (xxiii, 760). The power of experience to unfold slowly is of equal importance. Valéry felt *awareness* of the determining factor of time or speed in all mental phenomena to be of enormous importance, so much so that to compare and classify speed of mental events was one of his strongest desires (cf. ii, 176). 'Faire varier le temps pendant lequel je pense une chose, c'est altérer la chose même' (iv, 91). The idea, encouraged by his observation of natural forms, where formal structure seems dependent on time of development, leads him to see 'l'esprit' as a certain 'vitesse de réaction' (xxi, 735),[1] and consequently to recognise the different range of experience or set of formal relationships open to 'types d'esprit'[2] other than the primarily impatient, instantaneous or quick: 'Si tu es vif, le lent t'échappe' (P I, 327). A certain quality of experience is available only to the mind capable of slowness: 'Esprits rapides exposés à vérification des esprits lents. Esprits lents exposés à la combustion par esprits rapides' (P I, 385). Perhaps the formula of the most satisfying kind is: 'Rien ne remplace ni l'éclair ni les siècles' (xvii, 5).

'*Temps d'abstention*'

It is possible to turn now from discussion of the ideal of composition extended over time in general to individual time-scales referred to as 'temps d'abstention' and 'temps de travail'. First, 'temps d'abstention', the period in which the work matures relatively passively and during which questions of conscious and unconscious processes, inspiration and technique can be seen most intimately to merge.

Again, Valéry is, of course, not alone in noticing the existence of the phenomenon of apparently independent maturation. 'There is plenty of evidence', writes Basil Willey,

[1] Cf. 'sensibilité' as 'dépendance d'une vitesse' (iv, 59); 'Ce qui s'accomplissait *avec la vitesse* du non *penser*, ne s'accomplit à la *vitesse* du conscient que difficilement ou point du tout' (xxvii, 4).

[2] See M. Bémol, *Paul Valéry* (Paris, Société d'Édition 'Les Belles Lettres', 1949), 209.

> that a lying fallow of the mind in a kind of fruitful indolence is a state which often precedes successful imaginative creation. These intervals of wise passiveness seem to be times when our ordinary consciousness is almost suspended and the subconscious is free to incubate and to shape what is afterwards delivered into consciousness.[1]

Bacon's ability to recognise a form of consciousness deeper than superficial logic, Wordsworth's 'tranquillity', and later, D. H. Lawrence's belief that 'Anything worth having is *growth* and to have growth one must be able to let be': Willey's examples intimate widespread recognition of the experience. Countless remarks by other artists could be found. For example, Rilke's: '*Everything* is gestation and then bringing forth. To let each impression and each germ of feeling come to completion quite in itself, in the dark, in the inexpressible, the unconscious [...] and await with deep humility and patience the birth of a "new clarity"';[2] Gide's: 'le plus sage est de ne point se désoler des temps d'arrêt';[3] Giono's: 'L'œuvre n'est pas que jaillissement toutefois. Un travail de recherche, une longue maturation la précèdent.'[4]

The idea that the work of art can ripen outside the direct control of consciousness can be seen from a philosophical point of view in what M. H. Abrams calls 'Leibniz's province of confused and unconscious perceptions eternally evolving themselves in the mind of man, into a state of greater distinctness and articulation'.[5] In psychological jargon, the term 'maturation' is reserved for mental development by growth as opposed to learning, or the term 'incubation'[6] may be used to express the apparent perseverance or solution of a problem in the preconscious mind. Of the many literary theorists who have drawn attention to the process, often by means of the same imagery of natural growth, M. H. Abrams instances Sulzer, who, fascinated by the 'plant-like maturation of a work of art in the mind of genius' arrives at the assumption that certain conceptions develop independently, concluding: 'Every artist must rely on such happy expressions of his genius, and if he cannot always find what he diligently seeks, must await with patience the ripening of his thoughts.'[7] For Sulzer '[thoughts...] gather together in the soul and there

1 *The Seventeenth Century Background* (Chatto & Windus, 1962), 41.
2 Quoted by R. Gibson, *Modern French Poets on Poetry*, 258, n. 2.
3 *Journal des Faux-Monnayeurs*, 19.
4 Quoted by J. Pugnet, *Giono* (Classiques du XXe siècle, 1955), 22.
5 *The Mirror and the Lamp* (New York, the Norton Library, 1958), 202.
6 See W. N. Ince, *The Poetic Theory of Paul Valéry* (Leicester U.P., 1961), 116 (a term attributed to Grahame Wallas).
7 *The Mirror and the Lamp*, 203.

germinate unnoticed, like seeds in a fruitful soil, and finally at the proper moment come suddenly to light [. . .]'.[1] The postulation of just such a process was the basis of John Livingston Lowes' book on Coleridge, *The Road to Xanadu*,[2] an attempt to study the artist's unconscious creative processes as revealed in his work. Charles Mauron might be said to have attempted something of the same thing for Valéry in *Des Métaphores Obsédantes au Mythe Personnel*.[3] The difficulties of the task are obvious.

Recognition of the process is, then, widespread, but on the other hand views on what unconscious maturation really involves are contradictory. A contribution to the study was made by Poincaré, whose works were well-known to Valéry.[4] Approaching the problem from the point of mathematical discovery, Poincaré made many suggestive comments on the relationship between the conscious and unconscious, the logical and the fortuitous, and so on, and it is round these relationships that such an enquiry would inevitably have to revolve.[5] On the strength of his own experience of, for example, the sudden solving of a problem in a flash after weeks of conscious effort followed by a period of forgetfulness, Poincaré concluded that the unconscious mind is capable of a work of its own, capable, that is, of the task of combining and associating, and even of selecting those elements that satisfy a sense of beauty and economy of use in further thought.[6]

That 'illumination' is preceded by 'incubation' is generally accepted by anyone interested in the theme of mathematical problem-solving or poetic 'inspiration' (just how close the two fields are, is confirmed by the way in which Valéry's own observations, on poetic composition, so often coincide with those of Poincaré). Nonetheless, there are many who have rejected Poincaré's notion of actual unconscious work during 'incubation' in preference for a totally blank period. This is the 'rest hypothesis' (according to which the mind finds the solving of the problem easier simply because it has been refreshed by the interval) or the 'forgetfulness hypothesis' (according to which the mind is able to forget all the irrelevant considerations that may be blocking the road to the relevant effect).[7]

1 Ibid. 2 (New York, Vintage Books, 1959). 3 (Paris, Corti, 1964).

4 E.g. *La Science et l'Hypothèse* (Flammarion, 1902); *La Valeur de la Science* (Flammarion, 1905); *Science et Méthode* (Flammarion, 1908) (see Robinson, *L'Analyse de l'Esprit*, 35, n. 8).

5 See J. Hadamard, *An Essay in the Psychology of Invention in the Mathematical Field* (New York, Dover Publications, 1954), 12 (first published by Princeton U.P., 1945). Valéry knew Hadamard personally (see *Lettres à Quelques-uns* (Paris, Gallimard, 1952), 171–2). 6 Ibid., 15, 16. 7 Ibid., 32.

It might be expected that with his well-known preference for the primacy of conscious effort in all forms of construction, Valéry supported these latter views. Examination of his own insights and suggestions shows, on the contrary, that he favours the idea that the unconscious mind is rich in the power of making active combinations of its own, combinations which, however much they may be superseded by other choices before the final draft of the poem, have already partly determined the elements out of which the choices are made.[1]

First, where does Valéry's work touch on these issues? 'Il y a certains effets mentaux qui ont le pouvoir de se développer d'eux-mêmes (instables)' (i, 354), he notes, or: 'tout un travail bizarre, caché, autour du travail apparent' (iv, 266). Remarks like these are made in the course of speculations on mental functioning in general. Yet they have obvious relevance to the process of poetic composition: the apparently spontaneous development of an idea or group of images without the direct intervention of the conscious mind. In fact Valéry's interest in mental functioning, far from dangerously disseminating or stultifying his artistic talents or limiting them to mere poetry *about* mental processes, made him more alert to the genuine possibilities open to the poet (just as, in the reverse sense, some of his finest insights into the unity of experience were obviously gained through the process of poetic composition). Poetry gains from the greater and greater struggle to involve the mind fully in its pursuit. The urgency with which Valéry attempts to understand maturation is equalled by the urgency with which he attempts to achieve the phenomenon in himself.

That Valéry considered illumination to be preceded by long preparation in time is easily established. 'On traite la logique de miracle', he writes, 'mais l'inspiré était prêt depuis un an. Il était mûr. Il y avait pensé toujours, peut-être sans s'en douter' (P I, 1160). 'Rôle des temps pour constituer l'instant' (xv, 481):[2] the preparation in time of what is apparently spontaneous and free, is constantly stressed. Not only is this true of analysis, where it is a favourite theme, but the imagery of many of Valéry's poems favours a sensation of approaching apotheosis, the complex movement to the surface of a simple effect.

It seems almost equally easy to establish that Valéry thought that a major part of this preparation takes place in the unconscious mind. 'Nos plus

[1] A general study of 'Inspiration and Technique' as a whole has been attempted by W. N. Ince in *The Poetic Theory of Paul Valéry*. The following comments are intended to develop simply the theme of 'maturation' most relevant to this discussion.

[2] Cf. the amusing description of 'le spontané' in *L'Idée Fixe* (P II, 247).

claires idées sont filles d'un travail obscur',[1] he writes characteristically. The theme can be approached through two closely related interests. First, the perpetuation of some thought-process set in motion before sleep: 'J'ai fait de l'attention autour de telle question – je n'arrive pas, mais j'ai mis en train un mouvement qui m'échappe et pendant mon sommeil, ce mouvement commencé continue indépendamment. Au réveil je trouve la solution' (iv, 337). Secondly, the beating repetition of a phrase outside the poet's conscious control or choice: 'Je lâche mon travail [...] et cependant, m'avise que le lambeau initial de ma phrase se répète *tout seul* en moi' (xvii, 439). Such interests often lead to extended analytical passages like the following, where Valéry writes of:

> [...] Ce gros problème noir – des 'choses' qui ne nous semblent *être*, que quand elles sont *présentes* – desquelles cet attribut synthétique *être présentes* semble précéder le sujet, l'existence – ces choses mentales – nous sommes obligés d'autre part de considérer qu'elles *attendent en nous!* – qu'elles sortent et rentrent, – qu'elles peuvent subsister latentes pendant des années d'oubli. Des choses qui sont tout présences peuvent supporter des interruptions, être et n'être pas, reparaître identiques!
>
> On a beau réduire à je ne sais quel minimum ce qui se conserve, reporter sur le présent le plus possible du souvenir – l'énigme n'est pas diminuée.
>
> On aurait beau comparer l'idée à un être qui revivrait, dont chaque reviviscence serait en même temps la production d'un nouveau germe, et ce germe caché attendrait l'occasion de croître etc. Cette étrange comparaison ne rendrait rien plus aisé.
>
> Quel est l'être de ces idées pendant ces intervalles où elles ne sont pas? Mais on peut poser une question hardie – cet intervalle a-t-il un sens? – ou: ce que nous pensons et apprécions comme intervalle est-ce un intervalle (autre que part figure) quand rien ne peut embrasser les 2 lèvres de cet hiatus? (v, 280–1)

Leaving the question of preservation in intermittence to the following chapter, I shall concentrate here on the idea of what might be called the fruitful interval or 'lacune créatrice'.[2]

[1] *Propos Familiers* (Paris, Grasset, 1957), 201.
[2] See Bémol, *Paul Valéry*, 206.

In his mainly early morning notes, Valéry writes:

> Ce réveil [. . .] Encore en pleine viscosité. Et pourtant de suite, une idée d'entre les idées, un rappel sans pitié [. . .] sans égard à l'oubli encore régnant. Je souffre mais je m'étonne. Cette cruauté de moi – je m'efforce de la comprendre. *Ce n'est pas une association soumise à de simples chances.*

or, widening to general reflection from personal experience:

> Et en effet si une idée a été longtemps retenue, imposée – elle a co-existé avec un nombre très grand d'autres impressions concurrentes ou intercurrentes. Elle a donc contre elle des résonances multiples – augmenté ses chances de retour. Et si elle a pénétré profondément, si elle a causé des modifications physiques très sensibles cela s'est associée au fonctionnement même, et le fonctionnement la fera reparaître.
>
> (v, 280–1)

It is this very 'gros problème noir', often treated with frustration and bewilderment in analysis, whose mystery becomes in the two closely linked poems, *Aurore* and *Palme* a source of vigour and delight.

Is it really an 'interval'? Valéry asked (v, 280–1). The vitality with which he is fond of endowing an apparently 'empty' period has already been suggested, for example: '*Ce vide de silence* ressenti comme propriété positive – richesse, durée d'attente – noire et bonne terre où une idée venue peut germer et fleurir le mieux' (xv, 546). All the subtle and delicate gradations of the 'multi-dimensional' time experienced in the process of composition, ranging from the impatient violence of *Aurore* to the slow, gentle patience of *Palme* are conjured up in the following '*Rhumb*':

> Je travaille savamment, longuement, avec des attentes infinies des moments les plus précieux; avec des choix jamais achevés; avec mon oreille, avec ma vision, avec ma mémoire, avec mon ardeur, avec ma langueur; je travaille mon travail, je passe par le désert, par l'abondance, par Sinaï, par Chanaan, par Capoue, je connais le temps du trop, et le temps de l'épuration.
>
> (P II, 649)

The vigour of Valéry's imagery, not always confined to that of the maturation of fruit, suggests the forcefulness of the process. Words break through into consciousness, 'comme des bulles d'une masse pâteuse travaillée par des gaz' (xxiv, 823); ideas and images ferment as if in a cauldron: 'On dirait que dans une chaudière cachée, les ordures de "l'âme" fermentent' (xxiv, 367); conscious desire confronts unconscious material 'comme l'on oppose un aimant à la confusion d'une poudre composée, de laquelle un grain de fer se démêlera tout à coup' (P I, 1353), or the 'vers donné' appears 'comme agit un petit cristal dans une solution sursaturée'.[1] Indeed, the image of ripening is often simply the most conventional way of expressing a process which gives full scope to Valéry's imaginative use of analogies from more varied fields, as he confirms in a note like: 'Comme une balle de plomb abandonnée sur la cire tombe/chemine très lentement par son poids à travers la matière plastique – une idée se fait pendant des mois son expression nette – mûrit comme l'on dit. C'est une relation qui se simplifie, s'étend, se rend autonome' (iv, 75). Such analogies very often draw together inorganic and psychological fields.

Valéry was obviously deeply interested in any phenomenon resulting from what he took to be the interaction of different sets of relationships or different 'levels' of experience. Most of these analogies refer to the shifting borderland between 'unconscious' and 'conscious' processes, the state in which ideas, rhythms, images, memories and inventions reveal a hidden commensurability or 'équivalence' (xvii, 728). He writes, for example, of a poem he was never able to write as being '*là*, disseminé, dissous, infus, présent et insaisissable, – attendant [. . .] l'appel d'une divine électrolyse (d'un moment électrolytique) – l'opération d'une mystérieuse paroi semi perméable [. . .] pour ces osmoses là . . .' (iv, 461). Valéry gives one of his most extended expressions to the theme of the 'surfacing' of previously unconscious elements into consciousness by means of an analogy with photography. The passage (in the essay 'La Création Artistique')[2] seems important above all for the critical way in which the analogy is handled. At the same time as he allows it to set up a reasonably clear analytical framework, Valéry ensures that it conveys a sense of mystery, even that it expresses first and foremost the difficulty of referring to relatively unstructured experience at all. This 'double' use of language is very frequent in his work. The same sense of excitement in the ability of the intellect to keep in touch with phenomena outside the immediate grasp of its powers of expression might be said to form the basis of the poem *Le Vin Perdu*, where the phenomenon of diffusion is used. Drops of wine are scattered into the sea and disperse, but only to give rise to complex new patterns beyond immediate expectations – perhaps only in the mind's eye of the beholder, since his senses are other-

[1] 'La Création Artistique', *Vues*, 301. [2] Ibid., 304.

wise too limited to perceive them directly – but given observable reality in the image of the leaping, drunken waves:

> Perdu ce vin, ivres les ondes! . . .
> J'ai vu bondir dans l'air amer
> Les figures les plus profondes . . .
>
> (P I, 147)

In the passage from 'La Création Artistique' Valéry begins by distinguishing a kind of flash, 'une sorte d'éclair', and continues 'Un fait se produit, une sensibilisation spéciale; bientôt on ira dans la chambre noire et l'on verra apparaître l'image'. Round this theme he groups observations concerning the potential richness of the many fragments that make up intellectual life, fragments which point to possible developments or suggest that there are new things to discover in such and such a direction, but only after a certain amount of work. Already, this very description of creative possibilities, far from passive even before they are realised, gives a hint of the direction Valéry's analysis will take. By allowing powers of 'intimation'[1] to the less conscious mind, he is reinforcing his idea of mental unity, consciousness permeating to levels sometimes thought of as simply 'unconscious', and vice versa, in a complex organisational 'field'.

This impression is confirmed by Valéry's insights into the nature of mental expectation or 'attente'. The *Cahiers* are full of suggestions that it is the *structure* of the wilfully relaxed or waiting consciousness which determines suggestions or 'inspirations' of an apparently autonomous nature, or that the poet's will can be subordinated to his unconscious mind and still half supervise without intervening. An act of deliberate postponement of critical effort implies secret recognition of the processes involved. To catch this kind of insight, Valéry is often drawn to express himself in the form of paradox. He may write of 'involontaire volonté';[2] 'processus [. . .] à demi prévu' (VIII, 157); 'attention à double entrée';[3] 'patiente impatience' (P II, 1301); 'vouloir, vouloir . . . Et même, ne pas excessivement vouloir' (P I, 480);[4] of ideas that are neither 'inattendues'

[1] A further term taken from Grahame Wallas (see Ince, *The Poetic Theory of Paul Valéry*, 96, n. 2).

[2] *Réponses* (Au Pigeonnier, 1928), 37. The notion of 'l'involontaire' in poetic composition is discussed by G. W. Ireland in '"La Jeune Parque" – Genèse et Exegèse', *Entretiens sur Paul Valéry*, 85–101.

[3] Quoted by J. Hytier in *La Poétique de Valéry*, 141. Cf. 'Entre l'esprit à l'affût et la révélation à la fois attendue et inattendue, il y a un rapport difficile à analyser' (ibid., 139).

[4] 'Nous devons donc passionnément attendre, changer d'heure et de jour comme l'on changerait d'outil, – ' (P I, 480).

nor 'attendues' (iv, 33) and so on, or, in an 'insect' image previously examined, of consciousness as a waiting spider 'faussement endormi' (P I, 484). Obviously the challenging yet tentative formulation is deliberate. Valéry prefers to express the complexity of the process rather than to define it consistently in abstract psychological terms. In this way he suggests the many levels of experience hidden by the false twins 'conscience' and 'inconscient'.

At the same time his thought is precise enough to make it clear in what direction that abstract definition might lie. Under the heading 'Attente Générale', for example, he devotes a typically long passage of his notes to the experience, finally defining 'la période d'attente proprement dite' in terms of 'temps sensible, ou contrainte' (iv, 769). 'Dans l'attente c'est une partie de moi qui attend' (iv, 88); 'le principal travail de l'esprit consiste à attendre' (xi, 334); 'la chose attendue est celle qui se produit' (i, 325); 'Même la chose la plus inattendue est et doit être attendue dans notre définition, par notre structure' (v, 211); 'structure de l'attente' (xxiii, 9). Behind such jottings lies a grasp of what a psychologist might call reaction time,[1] and of what Valéry sometimes refers to as the 'vector' or directive nature of experience.[2] In his personal grasp of such notions through simple introspection, he has the perfect framework for his insights into the flexible 'system of expectations'[3] within which mental illumination or the poet's inspirations take place. 'Écrivain cherche son mot. Il l'attend' (iv, 777).[4]

[1] Characteristically borrowing a concept used in neurophysiology, Valéry describes such 'reaction time' in terms of muscular tonicity: 'Le "tonus" de la veille est, dans la pensée, l'attente continuelle, la préparation incessante qui constitue l'avenir actuel, la partie avenir de moi. [. . .]' (iv, 567) (quoted by Judith Robinson, *L'Analyse de l'Esprit*, 147).

[2] E.g. vi, 911. A 'vector' in mathematics is a quantity having *direction* as well as magnitude. Cf. A. N. Whitehead: 'Life is the enjoyment of emotion derived from the past and aimed at the future [. . .] This vector character is the essence of such entertainment' ('Nature and Life', quoted by M. White in *The Age of Analysis* (Mentor Press, 1955), 98). Valéry was frequently compelled to try to imagine 'Quelle serait la forme d'un "temps" qui permettrait de représenter les phénomènes *dirigés* – ceux qui se figurent ou s'expriment par un futur?', intellectual development being one of these (xv, 423). The 'creux toujours futur' of *Le Cimetière Marin* (P I, 149) is obviously the poetic embodiment of this feeling.

[3] See E. H. Gombrich, *Meditations on a hobby horse* (London, Phaidon Press Ltd, 1963), 149.

[4] On the relationship between 'finding' and 'forming' G. Castor writes: 'This is the moment when the thought is coming into being, and we use two separate metaphors for the process. In the actual thought process itself, however, the two activities co-exist' (*Pléiade Poetics* (C.U.P., 1964), 174–5). Valéry frequently writes on the interaction of 'chercher' and 'trouver' (e.g. P I, 472, P II, 1305).

'What should be made of the ample anecdotal evidence according to which scientific and artistic thinking can solve, under the protective cover of the unconscious, problems whose solutions the conscious mind vainly struggles to find? Is unconscious creation perhaps less subject to sets or other constraints that hamper conscious invention?'[1] To the question posed here by the psychologist, Valéry's answer seems likewise to lie in the direction of proposing a greater degree of mental freedom, freedom which enables the unlocking of areas of valuable mental activity below conscious control. He writes for example, 'il faut à la pensée une certaine liberté par abstention d'une partie de nos pouvoirs' (P I, 1475). In other words, he is able, despite his awareness of the active interpenetration of different 'levels' of experience, to avoid attributing to any distinct force, the 'unconscious', a life superior to that of the conscious mind:

> Il y a deux domaines pour la conscience et deux seuls. Mais pour les besoins de l'explication on est obligé de supposer un troisième qu'on appelle l'inconscient (c.-à-d. celui du *développement après coup* ou de la conscience après coup). Dans le même troisième domaine doit se ranger le potentiel mental (mémoire, déclanchements) qu'on est également forcé de mettre en jeu. Mais il faudrait bien savoir ce qu'on veut employer pour expliquer et peser tous ces fameux obscurcis.
>
> (ii, 48–9)[2]

It is through this kind of alertness to the danger of confusing word and experience that he is able to avoid the risk, run by certain German Romantic theorists in particular, of using vegetative analogues for mental processes in a way which tends to leave the vital element of self-determining consciousness out of account.[3] Creation for Valéry is a freedom which engages the whole mind, freedom without threat to inner design.[4] The willingness with which he is prepared to endorse the value of patient waiting or of receptivity to unconscious forms of experience would perhaps seem less paradoxical if it were realised that such a possibility,

[1] R. Arnheim, *Towards a Psychology of Art* (London, Faber and Faber, 1966), 315–16.

[2] Valéry was particularly sceptical about the work of Freud which he considered to divide the mind into 'subconscious' and 'conscious' departments instead of approaching it functionally as a 'système de rapports' (see Robinson, *L'Analyse de l'Esprit*, 142–3). He was slightly more in favour of the work of Jung, mainly because of the importance it laid on 'potentiality' (see Laurette, *Le Thème de l'Arbre*, 164), presumably as a 'bridge' experience preventing such dualism.

[3] See Abrams, *The Mirror and the Lamp*, 201–3.

[4] Gombrich, *Meditations on a hobby horse*, 144.

the flooding of the thresholds of critical consciousness by unexpected images or emotions, implies not the humility[1] but the triumph of the conscious mind, the recompense of thought.

This triumphant tone can be seen nowhere as clearly as in two of the poems themselves, *Aurore* and *Palme*. Both are perfect examples of the way in which Valéry makes a sensorial excursion based on simple, biological imagery, an adventure of the mind, transferring joyous associations of natural harmony, victory,[2] fruition and harvest to the theme of the collaboration of consciousness with maturation itself.

The imagery of *Aurore* shows that, as in *Palme*, the favourite metaphor of ripening fruit is present:

> Tout m'est pulpe, tout amande,
> Tout calice me demande
> Que j'attende pour son fruit,
>
> (P I, 113)

but unlike *Palme*, where the simple metaphor of ripening and final fruition is sustained throughout, *Aurore* is built on a series of dense parallel metaphors: ideas as mistresses; waking consciousness as a girl picking fruit amongst bees and thorns; the mind as a web. A series of mixed metaphors suggests the fertile chaos of the waking mind about to challenge the intellect to shape but not to destroy its gifts. In the lines where the fruit theme first enters:

> Au vacarme des abeilles
> Je vous aurez par corbeilles,
>
> (P I, 111)

it is impatience which predominates: the impatient, vigorous gathering of words and ideas like the picking of fruit, rather than the slow ripening of the later poems. The central theme, then, is that of images and words and their relationship to the waking mind (a subject of relevance to the poet at work but no more so than to waking consciousness in general):

> Quoi! c'est vous, mal déridées!
> Que fîtes-vous, cette nuit,
> Maîtresses de l'âme, Idées,
> Courtisanes par ennui?
> – Toujours sages, disent-elles,
> Nos présences immortelles

[1] The word 'humilité' is used by J. Duchesne-Guillemin in this context (*Études pour un Paul Valéry*, 171).

[2] Cf. Lawler, *Lecture de Valéry*, 244.

Jamais n'ont trahi ton toit!
Nous étions non éloignées,
Mais secrètes araignées
Dans les ténèbres de toi!

(P I, 112)

Having been addressed as mistresses[1] (an image prolonging the theme of the fertility of night and suggesting the intimate cohabitation of mind and senses), the 'ideas' are made to evoke their dark workmanship in the image of the weaving of spiders' webs in the shadows of the self, an image found also in Valéry's prose. Finally, as evaluative consciousness – 'l'opérateur supérieur' (xix, 918) – begins to assess and delight in the intricacies these shadows have made available, the imagery brightens. The theme of a hundred thousand silken suns is introduced, while the 'ideas', significantly more powerful than the still drowsy consciousness of the speaker, continue to hold the dialogue:

Ne seras-tu pas de joie
Ivre! à voir de l'ombre issus
Cent mille soleils de soie
Sur tes énigmes tissus?
Regarde ce que nous fîmes:
Nous avons sur tes abîmes
Tendu nos fils primitifs,
Et pris la nature nue
Dans une trame ténue
De tremblants préparatifs . . .

(P I, 112)

The last image introduces into the theme of maturation the idea of strength and vitality, of illuminatory contact with nature, as if consciousness paradoxically gains a stronger control over its material by relaxing its hold. At the same time the webs are tenuous and trembling; inspiration grows in power only as consciousness wakes to assess and claim what it owns. No alien force has been at work.

The same is true of *Palme*, the poetic culmination of so many of Valéry's insights into the nature of maturation and 'attente'.[2] Here the

[1] Cf. Diderot, 'Mes idées, ce sont mes catins' (*Le Neveu de Rameau*), quoted by Valéry (P I, 1475).

[2] Valéry's notes on 'attente' often include the notion of 'surprise', its 'rupture' (see Robinson, *L'Analyse de l'Esprit*, 147). Surprise as part of an inner process is equally present in *Palme*.

deliberately mixed metaphors of *Aurore* have given way once more to the single and more conventional image of natural growth and ripening. The commonplace aspects of the analogy are invigorated by the theme of thirsty roots slowly and powerfully pursuing their work in the entrails of the earth,[1] while at the same time allowing the simplicity of a parable to be maintained:

Ces jours qui te semblent vides
Et perdus pour l'univers
Ont des racines avides
Qui travaillent les déserts.
La substance chevelue,
Par les ténèbres élue
Ne peut s'arrêter jamais,
Jusqu'aux entrailles du monde,
De poursuivre l'eau profonde
Que demandent les sommets.

(P I, 155)

The tree tossing in gentle abandonment, its lightness the result of long, dark labour in the soil, is the perfect symbol of 'attente', or unconscious maturation in the human mind. Whether the illumination to follow ('l'heureuse surprise') is that of an idea or an image is of no importance. Nor is *Palme* confined to the maturation of a single creation. It is equally suited to the growth of mental processes, conscious or unconscious, over a life-time, as the following chapter will suggest. The poem establishes in the reader's mind the intricate texture of the whole experience of intellectual growth, a kind of activity in repose based on one of Valéry's strongest affirmations: intellectual trust in the power of consciousness to survive its own intermittences in time. Not confined to a linear theme, this experience is inseparable from the sensuous architecture of the tree built up by the architecture of the poem. As well as referring to the process by which the mind makes its discoveries, *Palme* relates in this way to a basic model of composition or inner design.

As is to be expected, Valéry's insights into 'temps d'abstention' can often be closely related to the composition of his own poems. 'J'ai pratiqué l'attente' (P II, 1615), he says of the birth of *La Jeune Parque*. He also suggests that several poems were composed around an actual 'vers donné', a curiously persistent phrase like 'pâle, profondément mordue' in the case of *La Pythie*, for example, which 'se comporta

[1] See the study of the whole poem by J. R. Lawler, *Lecture de Valéry*, 244–53.

comme un fragment vivant', giving birth to other lines above and below (P I, 1339). Valéry may sometimes deliberately exaggerate or simplify when it comes to relating theory and practice, a famous example being the equation of formal and semantic elements in *Le Cimetière Marin* (P I, 1338).[1] Yet an intimate dialogue is undoubtedly set up between his appreciation of the creative possibilities of maturation and his ability to draw on the process in the practice of his own work.

Allowance for maturation is not confined to the practice of a single poem. It is a process extended over a life-time from one work to another. Links can be established between say, *Profusion du Soir* and later, *Le Cimetière Marin*,[2] or between *La Jeune Parque* and the poems of *Charmes*[3] as a whole. Thus the 'embryologie psychologique' (vii, 276) by which the germ of an idea for a work may remain dormant in his mind only to appear years later as the basis of a lengthy composition, is actively realised. Like all great artists he is fully capable of delving back and forth in his own work and experience, drawing perpetually on the resources of the past, and, characteristically, since his insights so obviously spring from observations of his own creative processes rather than from theory, this freedom to move in time is identical to his own definition of 'l'esprit' as 'une puissance de prêter à une circonstance actuelle les ressources du passé et les énergies du devenir' (P I, 299).

'*Temps de travail*'

It is well-known that Valéry set great store by the rôle of the critical intelligence in manipulating and polishing words: 'la délicatesse et la profondeur des hésitations' (ii, 311). Just how much of his own time went into the composition of his poems is amply documented. To take but two examples, the studies by Octave Nadal of the manuscripts of *La Jeune Parque* and by L. J. Austin of *Le Cimetière Marin*[4] show the care spent in systematic experiment with language, groups of words and word schemes being subjected over and over again to processes of judgement and critical control. After the long labours of *La Jeune Parque*, writing certain poems of *Charmes* was like dancing after wearing leaden boots, Valéry suggested:

1 Ibid., 197 (reference to P.-O. Walzer and L. J. Austin).

2 See C. G. Whiting, 'Profusion du Soir' and 'Le Cimetière Marin', *PMLA*, LXXVII (1962), 138.

3 See, for example, A. R. Chisholm's comments on the slowly evolving triptych of *La Jeune Parque*, *Ébauche d'un Serpent* and *La Pythie* in '"La Pythie" and its place in Valéry's work', *M.L.R.*, LVIII (1963), 24.

4 See bibliography.

> Eh bien j'ai observé que le grand bénéfice des poèmes soutenus, très organisés, et bâtis en force, construits par long labeur, était de faire produire après eux l'œuvre libre et légère, fleur sans effort, – mais qui ne fût pas née sans le dur entraînement de la veille; [. . .] on a ôté les bottes plombées, et l'on danse . . .[1]

But even the relative improvision of *Charmes* is based on variant-riddled manuscripts, the slightest poems such as *Les Pas*, *La Ceinture*, *Le Sylphe* and *L'Insinuant* resulting from hours of activity. By whatever processes conceived – and here, as has just been seen, his mind is open to the 'vers donné' as much as to its consciously fabricated brother – the spontaneous suggestions of the unconscious must be woven together and assessed in the clear light of evaluative awareness. The passage on the photographic analogy continues:

> Je viens de vous dire qu'il y a la période de la chambre noire; ici pas d'enthousiasme, car vous gâcheriez votre plaque, il faut avoir vos réactifs, il faut travailler comme l'employé de vous-même, votre contremaître. Le patron vous a fourni l'étincelle; c'est à vous d'en tirer quelque chose.[2]

Hence: 'Rien de plus beau qu'un beau brouillon' (xv, 481), Valéry writes about the much corrected drafts of Hugo's poems: 'Mystification de la rature. Un poème complet serait le poème de ce poème à partir de l'embryon fécondé' (xv, 481). The poet may be concerned, as in the case of Hugo, with the art of 'le remplissage' (xv, 481), but he is equally concerned with the process of rejecting and chiselling away excessive elements, of concentration as well as amplification. Infinite time is to be spent 'en recherches, en repentirs et en reprises' (P I, 681), and so closely do technical problems intertwine here with general intellectual issues that the famous line of *Le Cimetière Marin* cannot be far away: 'Mes repentirs, mes doutes, mes contraintes/Sont le défaut de ton grand diamant . . .' (P I, 150).

Infinite time? To the mature artist ceaseless maturation, 'le recul *à l'infini* de l'Œuvre [. . .]' (xxiv, 371) is, of course, as dangerous as premature formulation. 'L'esprit peut par son même mouvement, passer le *point de l'œuvre*, et en développer le germe au delà de sa maturité' (xxiii, 340). 'La maturité est un certain maximum', Valéry speculates, 'on n'est

[1] *Lettres à Quelques-Uns*, 182 (cf. P I, 1613). Valéry adds: 'La fatigue a précédé le travail!' The situation might be compared and contrasted with the patterns expressed in *Ode Secrète* (P I, 151–2).

[2] 'La Création Artistique', *Vues*, 304–5.

jamais bien sûr que le fruit de l'esprit est à maturité. L'esprit n'est jamais sûr que son fruit est à point. Le besoin chez l'homme se fait sentir à certain moment. Il est pressé de se séparer de ce qui s'est formé en lui' (P II, 899). The published remark can be seen to continue in Valéry's notes: 'De ce fait simple, énorme, évident que tout ce qui est est état variant – on n'a rien tiré – on n'en parle presque pas!', and the passage goes on to suggest that although every element of consciousness could be developed,[1] '*rien n'est jamais achevé* quant à elle seule – et par soi seule. L'interruption ou l'abandon sont la loi réelle' (xiv, 127). A work is 'comme une certaine *fleur* d'un arbre invisible dont tous les autres chemins qui conduisaient à d'autres fleurs ont été abandonnés' (xiii, 260). 'Poème Abandonné...' was the sub-title Valéry gave to *Profusion du Soir* (P I, 86).

Together these comments have given three elements: the ceaseless inner maturation of the artist's imagination; the forever unfinished work of art; the necessity of completing the work before it becomes over-ripe. Valéry loves juggling with these components. A minimum of reflection reveals that the last two are not contradictory, as they might at first seem. Though the work can never be finished to the ceaselessly moving mind that creates it, it *can* be finished in terms of its own aesthetic equilibrium or organic unity: 'il faut donner à tout ouvrage la *forme* complète d'une phase entière humaine' (iv, 11).

Each of these elements can be considered from the point of view of its relationship to the work. First, the inner maturation of the artist. 'Le travail de l'esprit n'a ni commencement ni fin' (xx, 488), Valéry writes, or, in metaphorical terms, the fruit falls, the tree remains:

> Tu n'as pas perdu ces heures
> Si légère tu demeures
> Après ces beaux abandons.
>
> (P I, 156)

Although it cannot be stated often enough that such imagery is impoverished by being limited to specific associations such as poetic composition, the image of *Palme* can obviously be said to embrace this same basic structure. We have seen that Valéry's writings on poetics frequently draw on images of fructification and inner growth. He uses these to express the vital inner process of which the work is an interruption, for example:

> Que de fois ai-je regardé ce que j'allais donner aux yeux des autres, comme la préparation nécessaire de l'ouvrage désiré,

[1] Cf. 'Pouvoir immense du développement d'une notion. On peut tout développer–maturare' (I, 45).

que je commençais alors seulement de *voir* dans sa maturité possible, et comme le fruit très probable et très désirable d'une attente nouvelle et d'un acte tout dessiné dans mes puissances. L'œuvre réellement faite me paraissait alors le corps mortel auquel doit succéder le corps transfiguré et glorieux.

(P I, 305)[1]

Here Valéry is very close to Mallarmé's Grand Œuvre: 'la poésie, sacre; qui essaie en de chastes crises isolément, pendant l'autre gestation en train'.[2] In his own notes Valéry writes, on what might be called this 'asymptotic' view of creation: 'J'écris à Mondor sur Mallarmé comment et d'où naquit cette étrange et inébranlable *certitude* sur laquelle M. a pu fonder toute sa vie [. . .] de se faire en un mot l'homme même d'une œuvre qu'il *n'a pas accomplie* et qu'il savait ne pas pouvoir l'être?' (xxiv, 283); and: 'ce recul *à l'infini* de l'Œuvre voulue, acceptée, conquise – et les restes, le réellement exécuté, – essais, écritures "pour essayer sa plume"/Ceci fut en lui une transformation par *perspective* – une opération – *projective* – qui peut se prendre pour une "mystique" (perfection, orgueil, absolu. [. . .])' (xxiv, 371). The close cohabitation of art and personal ethic; the transformation of immediate experience by 'une opération – *projective*';[3] the will to steer clear of premature formulation: all these concepts Valéry admired in the flesh in Mallarmé's 'œuvre de patience'. Awareness of the discrepancy between inner maturation and external production has been turned into the tension by which his poetry is enriched.

Secondly, the ever-unfinished nature of the work of art. Valéry is aware of the temptation to use 'temps de travail' too lavishly: 'Mes poèmes tellement élaborés que . . .' (xv, 795). Willing, like Poincaré,[4] to place a great deal of importance on the work needed to adjust initial material, he is nonetheless highly sensitive to the dangers of 'le trop achevé'. It is at this point that 'temps de travail' can be seen to involve no mere intellectualisation of the original inspiration, but a genuine power of choice or discernment, one of the most important characteristics of consciousness itself. Although he may not always have achieved it in practice, Valéry establishes in his mature aesthetics that the ideal of

1 Cf. J. Starobinski: '*L'événement pur* recule au plus lointain de l'horizon spirituel [. . .]. Mais, glacé d'absence [. . .] son rayon préfiguré féconde une attente qui se dore lentement comme un fruit mûrissant' (*Paul Valéry, Essais et Témoignages inédits*, ed. M. Eigeldinger (Paris, La Presse française et étrangère, 1945), 150).

2 *L'Action Restreinte*, *Œuvres Complètes* (Paris, Gallimard, 1956), 372.

3 Cf. Sartre's 'projet'.

4 See J. Hadamard, *An Essay in the Psychology of Invention*, 56–7.

'achèvement'[1] must at some stage involve a challenge to the artist to efface artifice by artifice and to double back into the primary impulse of spontaneity itself. 'Le classique [. . .] finit par trop séparer forme et fond [. . .] et s'il ne compense pas ensuite cette analyse par une recherche de sens contraire, devient sec et nul' (xvii, 47), he notes, or: 'le comble de la poésie est même de transformer ces effets réfléchis en réflexions *vers* l'origine/ou vers les sensations initiales' (xii, 32); 'il faut finir par l'improvisation' (xxii, 312); 'L'effort seul nous transforme et nous change notre facilité première qui suit de l'occasion, et s'épuise avec elle, en une facilité dernière qui la sait créer et la domine' (P I, 1465).[2] When his many famous comments on the circularity of composition such as 'le spontané est le fruit d'une conquête' (P II, 1315) are set in their rightful context of a 'total' aesthetics, they can be seen to imply, at least from the point of view of poetic practice, not an inevitably desiccated attempt to re-imitate spontaneity once a certain point of over-ripeness has been reached, but an attempt to allow the intellect to re-establish its own contact with feeling or to unite with passion partly derived from art itself.

L. J. Austin, quoting Victor Basch's distinction between three phases of work: the original conception, the conscious work, and a third phase of re-experiencing the original spontaneity, suggests that 'Valéry aurait certainement nié la nécessité de cette troisième étape'.[3] This is certainly so in that Valéry refuses to divide the complex process of composition into separate compartments. From the point of view of re-established feeling itself, however, he is equally willing to concede at least a further level of emotion. This is not a naïve replica of the original impulse, but almost, as he says in the sequel to the passage on the photographic analogy, a kind of irritation at the infinite possibilities of intellectual choice:

> Ce qui est très curieux, c'est la déception qui peut s'ensuivre. Il y a des lueurs illusoires; en revoyant le résultat obtenu, le contremaître s'aperçoit que ce n'était pas fécond, c'eût été très bien si cela avait été vrai. Il y a parfois une série de jugements qui interviennent, qui s'annulent les uns les autres. Une sorte d'état d'agacement se produit; on se dit qu'on n'arrivera jamais à noter ce qui vous apparaît.[4]

[1] Such poetry has its critics, notably Nathalie Sarraute in 'Paul Valéry et l'enfant de l'éléphant', *Les Temps Modernes*, II, ii (1947), 610–37.

[2] Cf. xxv, 528, xxvi, 918. 'Facilité naturelle' and 'facilité acquise' is briefly discussed by M. Bémol in *Paul Valéry*, 417.

[3] 'La Genèse du "Cimetière Marin"', *C.A.I.E.F.*, III–V (1953), 269, n. 2.

[4] 'La Création Artistique', *Vues*, 305.

The co-ordination of the adjusting work is itself achieved with the expansive influence of this kind of 'scepticism' in the face of the definitive nature of words and the richness of continued experience (vi, 15): 'et je me demande si l'effet du travail intellectuel n'est pas de favoriser quel accroissement de sensibilité?'. This is confirmed by notes in the *Cahiers* such as: 'L'artiste est composé d'une passion de *faire* en liaison avec une soif de *sentir*, dont l'expression naïve serait: *besoin* de *faire*, par le *sentir*, et à partir du *sentir en vue* du *sentir*. Le *sentir* entre en 3 moments de cette formule. Il est impulsion, et fin de l'acte, et moyen continu ou guide de l'acte' (xvii, 456). The adjusting work will not provide the solution, for aesthetic solutions are not determined by purely rational demands – yet it can multiply the chances of a favourable design: 'Il ferait momentanément de l'artiste un résonateur très sensible à tous les incidents de conscience qui peuvent servir son dessein.'[1] This element of discernment constantly corrects the balance until spontaneity is achieved: 'L'Œuvre a un terme comme le fétus. Normalement elle est *achevée* (en un certain sens) quand elle se fait *toute seule*' (xxiii, 340). This introduces the third point to consider here, the completion of the work before over-ripeness: 'Les difficultés ont pour objet profond de *retarder* l'ouvrage et de lui assigner un terme ou une *perfection* bien définie' (ix, 895).

For Valéry there are two basically different kinds of poetry, as he notes in the *Cahiers* (xv, 248). On the one hand, there is poetry which, by whatever careful means elaborated, gives the impression to the reader of a state of immediate disorderly perception. On the other, there is poetry that gives the impression of a deliberately refined, reorganised world. The first is associated with a poet like Rimbaud, the second with a poet like Mallarmé (xv, 248). Might one not expect from 'un impatient' poetry of the first kind, of the kind which the name RIMBAUD, 'génie impatient',[2] seemed to conjure up for Valéry, and which expresses 'la frénésie du départ, le mouvement d'impatience excité par l'univers' (P I, 612)?

> [Rimbaud] utilise [. . .] des substitutions de tous les ordres/qui doivent RESTITUER non sa pensée directrice/ordonnée et normale, mais le désordre naturel/des impressions premières réelles (qui se négligent/automatiquement en général) et dans ce désordre/les relations singulières qui donnent des effets si/puissants, quand leurs termes traduits par des mots/appartien-

[1] Ibid.

[2] The title of H. Mondor's work on Rimbaud (Paris, Gallimard, 1955).

nent à des propositions tout à fait indépendantes mais matériellement VOISINES.[1]

Now the discovery of Rimbaud's poetry was almost as much of an intellectual shock to Valéry when a young man as was that of Mallarmé.[2] But although he kept his admiration for Rimbaud throughout his life, and incorporates something of the quality of Rimbaud's vision within his own poetry, it is Mallarmé's *type* of poetry on which his own formal poetry is modelled. The reader of *Charmes*, while conscious of very important differences from the poems of Mallarmé, will experience a sensuous celebration of the joys of cultivated language in which his whole mind is called to participate; an excursion into an extraordinary wealth of tones ranging from the impatient vigour of *Aurore* to the tenacious texture of patience expressed in *Palme*. Yet, even when the tone is of rough, shimmering impetuosity, as it is in the first of these poems, an element of deliberate stylisation, of artifice and larger-than-life order will contribute to the major part of his reaction. He will hear a voice 'en quelque sorte plus nécessaire que l'être même dont il est issu' (P I, 479–80). To expect otherwise would be to overlook the full nature of the challenge Valéry found in poetic composition, a challenge based on the will to counterbalance and widen his own most characteristic form of response, impatience. 'Je lis avec un rapidité superficielle prêt à saisir ma proie', he writes, for example, 'mais ne voulant articuler en vain des choses évidentes ou indifférentes. Donc si j'écris, je tente d'écrire de telle sorte que si je me lisais je ne pourrais me lire comme je lis. Il en résulte une densité' (vii, 32).

It is, of course, poetic composition above all which provides access for Valéry to total man, the 'être complet' (xxiv, 438), in whom patience and impatience, slowness and quickness, the fruits of 'les siècles' as much as of 'l'éclair' can freely combine. Such a man is not born but constructed by intelligence. Valéry's own cult of time-consuming mental activity involves a deliberate art of counterbalancing, a personal need to add the 'slow' to the 'rapid' in order to surmount the painful sensation of experiencing only a part of the total possibilities of himself, 'une partie de l'être' (v, 152). 'J'ai essayé de me faire ce qui me manquait' (P II, 649) he writes. In this way he arrives at a conception of poetry which involves the widest possible synthesis of apparently opposed qualities: 'la possession

[1] *Paul Valéry, Pré Teste*, Catalogue, ed. F. Chapon (Bib. Litt. J. Doucet, 3–23 déc. 1966), 66.

[2] E.g. xxii, 842–3, quoted by P.-O. Walzer, 'Introduction à l'Érotique Valéryenne', *C.A.I.E.F.*, XVII (1965), 219.

de la plénitude des pouvoirs antagonistes qui sont en nous' (P I, 1484).[1] The virtues of 'l'instantané' are to be supplemented by 'le labeur infini' (P II, 1203); passionate feeling is to be combined with discipline and control: '[...] je pense trop vite [...] Mais je repense si lentement, – et j'exécuterais sans fin!' (P II, 1534). This is the personal basis, it seems, of his sustained admiration for the power of a kind of plant-like synthesis in the major artists he felt drawn towards from the very beginnings of his intellectual life: Poe – whatever the discrepancy between his reputation and practice – for the power of increasing the emotive impact of words by control over his expression (xxiii, 188); Wagner for his similar combination of passion and technical skill (xxiv, 438); and Baudelaire, 'sensuel et précis' (P I, 599) for 'une intelligence critique associée à la vertu de poésie' (P I, 599). That this synthesis was in no way considered detrimental to either of its components, in other words, that there was no question for Valéry of suffocating emotion by the imposition of control, is suggested by the following summary where the ideal poem is described as:

> [. . .] l'ouvrage produit à l'issue d'une profonde analyse, le vrai Poème – dans lequel la claire vue et conscience du problème de l'action de l'art, de ses moyens techniques, de ses conditions esthésiques – s'allie aux ressources naturelles, s'alimente de l'énergie de la vie passionnée.
>
> Synthèse de la faculté d'observation immédiate non secondaire mais primitive, de la conception de l'homme, de la capacité combinatoire et logique, – et de la plus intense individualité, particularité, sensibilité sensorielle et sentimentale.
>
> Voilà un être complet.
>
> (xxiv, 438)

Valéry has given extended public expression to this idea in a lecture called *Souvenirs Poétiques* where, thinking of Wagner, he writes:

> Avoir en même temps cette source extraordinaire d'énergie qu'est une passion développée chez un être aussi nerveux, aussi sensible, mais en même temps avoir la capacité intellectuelle de dominer cela, de le réduire, d'en faire, en même temps, le corps énergétique en quelque sorte, et une analyse profonde.[2]

[1] Compare with I. A. Richards' notion of the co-ordination of conflicting 'appetencies' as a basis of aesthetic experience (*Principles of Literary Criticism* (London, Routledge and Kegan Paul, 1963), 59). Valéry also uses the word 'appétence' (e.g. iv, 567).

[2] *Souvenirs Poétiques* (Paris, Guy le Prat, 1947), 56.

This power to profit from the merging of the ambiguous, potentially overpowering drive of passion with a precise intellectual direction, 'toute conscience *avec tous* les "avantages" de l'*Inconscience*',[1] is obviously one of the mainsprings of Valéry's own work.

The dynamic quality of this patience or 'patiente impatience' (P II, 1301) is now clearly apparent. For patience of the instinctive 'natural' kind Valéry has nothing but scorn. Merely one of the most elementary gifts (P I, 981), it is the sort of animal condition to which Méphistophélès owes his strength as opposed to the conscious subtleties of Faust (P II, 295); or it involves an aimless, undiscriminating submission to the kind of time which neutralises all human opinions and tastes (P II, 737; P I, 338). Achieved by effort and reinstated in the conscious mind, however, patience acquires an entirely new significance, as do so many of the concepts which Valéry has been seen to reject from the point of view of their usage on an uncritical level only (for example, Love, Nature, and now Inspiration). The etymological sense of the word 'patior' is revived, to imply that courage and suffering are involved, though never without complementary aphorisms to suggest the tendency of conscious discipline itself to become an easy habit or a 'natural' tendency of mind (e.g. P II, 848). Of Degas, master of 'le calcul infinitésimal' in painting (i, 204), for which Valéry dreamed, at least in the early stages of his career, of a possible equivalent in literature, he writes: 'J'aime cette rigueur. Il est des êtres qui n'ont pas la sensation d'agir, d'avoir accompli quoi que ce soit, s'ils ne l'ont fait contre soi-mêmes. C'est là peut-être le secrèt des hommes vraiment vertueux' (P II, 1198). Just as time in nature was seen previously to be a partly human abstraction based on perception of natural growth or decay, so time in human experience begins to appear as a product of human reactions such as patience, impatience and their interrelation with consciousness.

Of Delacroix, artist of the unfinished painting, Valéry writes: '[il] n'a pas su cacher son angoisse et son impatience dans cette divinité de grâce, de liberté, de puissance apparente qui est le seul objet concevable des arts. Il n'a pas pu dissimuler ses ambitions, sa faiblesse, son énergie, dans l'acte définitif qui est œuvre' (viii, 246). In this comment he is indirectly describing not only his own intellectual predicament, but also the basis of his own poetic achievement. For it is the idea of 'œuvre', 'achèvement' or 'le culte du complet' (v, 195) which is made the cornerstone of his art. Valéry greeted his own *Narcisse Parle*, 'si hâtivement

[1] The phrase comes in Valéry's letter on Nietzsche (*A. Gide–P. Valéry, Correspondance, 1890–1942*, 343).

fait' (P I, 1560) with a feeling of uneasiness almost amounting to fear, for, unlike *L'Idée Fixe*, the deliberate 'enfant de la hâte', *Narcisse Parle* is a poem, and a poem for Valéry is concerned not with repeating the disorderly rhythms of everyday mental life, but with '[. . .] une pensée toute certaine [. . .] dont le mouvement et la quantité me comble: une pensée singulièrement achevée' (P I, 95), as he writes from the point of view of the reader in *L'Amateur de Poèmes*; total 'thought' that the quality of effort in time has been allowed to augment. 'L'œuvre doit s'opposer à l'esprit' (xv, 900; cf. P I, 1491); 'L'unité de temps n'était pas homme, vie d'homme, besoins vitaux – mais se déduisait de l'*œuvre*' (ix, 895). Valéry frequently approaches the notion of 'dramatic speaker' in this way, in terms of 'quelque *moi* merveilleusement supérieur à Moi' (P I, 1339).[1] The triumph of the anonymous 'Saint LANGAGE' at the end of *La Pythie* may seem partly related to the same notion, and, ironically, so may the ending of *Ébauche d'un Serpent*, where man's power to modify existence by becoming aware of his own organisational capacity is seen by the serpent as the instrument of his revenge on God (P I, 146).

Consequently, it would contradict all Valéry's views on poetry to expect to find in *Charmes* that achieved spontaneity or ultimate clarity is simply a linear extension of initial simplicity. There is a meaningful discrepancy between the time taken to read the poem and the time taken to achieve its effect. Temporal discrepancy fascinated Valéry, as has already been seen in the case of the appeal of things in nature that present a 'réunion de temps' (xix, 739). 'Et deux cent ans de croissance constante sont anéantis en moins de deux heures', he wrote in his translation of Hardy's poem, *Felling a Tree*.[2] When it comes to poetry, this same pattern leads not to extinction but to rebirth. 'Telle œuvre [. . .] a demandé des mois et même des années de réflexion', he writes, 'et elle peut supposer aussi les expériences et les acquisitions de toute une vie. Or, l'effet de cette œuvre se déclarera en quelques instants' (P I, 1346); 'En quelques minutes, ce lecteur recevra le choc de trouvailles, de rapprochements [. . .] accumulés pendant des mois de recherche, d'attente, de patience et d'impatience' (P I, 1337). The reader of *Charmes* is made to experience in a few lines the sensation of a fabric richly woven in time, and to experience what might literally be called life-enhancing energy, for to describe the incommensurability between the time taken to produce a work and its effect on the reader (P I, 1347), Valéry uses exactly the same

[1] Cf. 'attributed inspiration' (Ince, *The Poetic Theory of Paul Valéry*, 8).

[2] *Commerce*, XIV (1927), 5–9.

'counter-gravitational' imagery that he uses to describe the power of life to withstand disorganisation: 'La durée vivante est récupération d'une partie d'énergie utilisable par un *détour*. Comme dans le bélier et autres machines, on relève peu en laissant tomber beaucoup' (XV, 802). Accordingly the reader is 'producteur de la valeur de l'être imaginaire qui a fait ce qu'il admire' (P I, 1348).

In those cases when Valéry appears to admire 'immediate' naturalness, he is careful to differentiate such poetry from his own.[1] It is to Whistler that one must go to find the model of such achieved simplicity. 'De cette lente et classique application, rien ne doit être sensible dans le texte définitif', a critic comments on his method,[2] and Valéry writes in *Réflexions sur la lithographie originale*: 'Ce que Whistler pour mon goût, a fait de plus exquis, est ce petit portrait de Mallarmé, qui n'est qu'une caresse sur le papier, mais caresse qui a coûté des heures sans nombres de poses.'[3] There is something reminiscent of Whistler's 'caresse' in the paradoxical blending of infinite care with infinite simplicity in a poem such as *Le Sylphe*, where the sensation of gossamer-like delicacy has been produced by a carefully constructed form.

Not all artists set such store by the executory stage of their work, of course. A very brief glance at varying methods of composition practised by representative painters, poets or musicians would suggest two main types of procedure. On the one hand, there are those who rely on a long process of inner preparation to culminate in relatively flawless and apparently spontaneous 'paper work'. In the *Salon de 1859* Baudelaire refers to the bringing forth of Delacroix's pictures as unified wholes in just this way.[4] On the other hand, there are those for whom growth takes place in conjunction with perpetual modification 'on paper'. Baudelaire himself would be a good example of this last type of artist, 'deliberately uncompromising in his conviction that great poetry depends on unremitting effort and that every detail has behind it "les retouches, les variantes, les épreuves barbouillées"'.[5] In the case of Delacroix, inner gestation was slow, and execution swift. In the case of Baudelaire, rapidly conceived ideas were given laborious elaboration. Nonetheless, both these methods rely on the strategic use of time at some stage in their genesis.

[1] E.g. that of Mécs (*Poèmes* (Horizons de France, 1944)).

[2] P.-O. Walzer, *P.-J. Toulet* (Pierre Seghers, no. 42), 66.

[3] 'Réflexions sur la Lithographie Originale' (quoted in *Paul Valéry: Écrits sur l'Art* (Paris, Club des Librairies de France, 1962), 242).

[4] *Œuvres Complètes* (Paris, Gallimard, 1961), 1119.

[5] Alison Fairlie, *Baudelaire: Les Fleurs du Mal* (Studies in French Lit., 6, London, Edward Arnold, 1960), 31.

It is for this reason that Valéry's aesthetics permit admiration not only for artists with whom, as in his own case, execution is slow, but also for those like Mozart,[1] whose symphonies appear to spring spontaneously to birth only because long time has gone into their inner preparation; Goethe, who 'laisse mûrir l'œuvre en lui et quand il passe à l'exécution les choses vont au plus vite';[2] Whistler, for whom apparent improvisation is the fruit of infinite inner growth: 'J'ai fait ce tableau en un quart d'heure, avec l'expérience de toute ma vie',[3] as Valéry reports him to have said.

Thus insistence on allowing for the 'non-linear' development of the elements at work in poetic composition brought Valéry to condemn only those artists whose cult of the spontaneous draft tended to leave out the time ingredient altogether; artists whose slip-shod aesthetics he considered to lead to equally facile and undemanding verse. Musset and Lamartine might serve as examples. Their poetry Valéry held in 'fort peu d'estime' (P II, 1531), Musset in particular filling him with 'antipathie, presque du dégoût'.[4] It is easy to imagine his possible reaction to Lamartine's 'Créer est beau, mais corriger [. . .] est pauvre et plat'[5] (although in actual fact Lamartine is known to have spent much time on his manuscripts after the original drafting). Similarly, the poetry of Surrealism, the beginnings of which come into Valéry's attack on modern haste, would be unacceptable on the grounds of postulating uncritical passivity as a quality in itself. 'Perfection, c'est *paresse*', wrote Breton and Éluard in *La Révolution Surréaliste*, whereas to Valéry, 'perfection, c'est le travail'.[6] This is logical when, in the words of Socrates in *Eupalinos*, the act of construction requires qualities 'qu'elle tire merveilleusement de toi-même, qui ne soupçonnais pas de les posséder' (P II, 143).

Organic unity

'Il faut savoir produire – et savoir arrêter et exister à temps' (ii, 278): having seen how Valéry's poetic theory and practice lead him to benefit equally from 'temps d'abstention' and 'temps de travail', it remains to suggest something of their intimate fusion. What does Valéry mean, for

[1] See L. J. Austin, *C.A.I.E.F.*, III–V (1953), 269, n. 2.

[2] F. Garrigue, *Goethe et Valéry* (Les Lettres Modernes, 1955), 56.

[3] Quoted by J. Pommier, 'Paul Valéry et la Création Littéraire' (Collège de France, Édns. de l'Encyclopédie Française, 7 mai 1964), 39.

[4] H. Mondor, *Préciosité de Valéry* (Paris, Gallimard, 1957), 304.

[5] *Letter to Aymon Virieu* (13 nov. 1818) (quoted by R. Gibson in *Modern French Poets on Poetry*, 235).

[6] Ibid., 238 (both quotations).

example, when, after putting so much stress on the need for prolonged effort, he suggests that execution should be easy in the final stages of the work (xxiii, 340), or that, for all its richly cultivated texture, the work should impose on the reader the impression of a simple, unified organism? What, in other words, lies behind his use of the idea 'organic unity' and 'organic growth'?

The term 'organic' as in the 'organic growth' or the 'organic unity' of a work of art is an established cliché of modern criticism. Valéry's work is of the kind which challenges reflection on its meaning. Are its advantages as a critical term not outweighed by certain serious limitations, at least when it is indiscriminately used? A previous chapter suggested what elements organic growth implies in the case of natural organisms, mainly, that is, the indissoluble nature of form and function, and the derivative relation of parts to an initial whole. A work of art, on the other hand, is so complex an object that to speak of it as an organism can be very misleading. 'Note que j'ai dit que "*l'œuvre emploie*" comme si l'œuvre fût un être' (xxiv, 825), Valéry notes warily of a similar linguistic difficulty. The only possible meaning which can be attributed to the 'organic growth' or 'organic unity' of a work of art is that the artist has achieved by separate acts of construction the co-ordination of parts into a whole. (Again, there are many relevant comments by Valéry on the subject, such as: 'Si l'on cherche à *donner* une nécessité *suivie* à un ouvrage – c.-à-d. l'impression de la nature vivante qui se développe [. . .] c'est par le labeur et l'attente qu'on y peut atteindre' (xv, 907).) M. Bémol has remarked that if Valéry's art can be said to contain an imitation of nature, it is because he takes as his model 'cette Nature qui sait créer en tirant de sa substance même la matière de ses propres ouvrages et réaliser ainsi à la perfection un des caractères essentiels de l'œuvre d'art, "cette liaison indissoluble et réciproque de la forme avec la matière"'.[1] This statement seems slightly confusing. It is surely because human construction is *not* holomorphic that the artist attempts to achieve or recreate such a liaison in the finished work. '[. . .] the contrast which is generally assumed to exist between *form* and *function*, has no reality when the word "form" is given its full content', writes Agnes Arber in the work on plant morphology already quoted,[2] and she traces the false antithesis to 'the analogy, mistaken for something approaching an identity, between the works of man, and living beings themselves'. It is

[1] *Variations sur Valéry* (Sarrebruck, Publications de l'Université de la Sarre, 1952), 120.

[2] *The Natural Philosophy of Plant Form* (C.U.P., 1950), 3.

paradoxically because Valéry is prepared always to hold in mind the difference as well as the similarities between the natural product and the artifact that the meaning of form *is* 'given its full content' in his work. He writes, for example, on the similar temptation to compare the proliferation of a fragment of poetry with the development of a stem or leaf-cutting into a total plant: 'Mais cette analogie séduisante ne doit point être retenue, à cause de l'indépendance radicale [. . .] entre les constituants du langage, son et sens'.[1]

'Il n'y a point de détails dans la nature' (xv, 586); 'la poésie n'est fait que de beaux détails' (xvii, 66); 'Et si la poésie n'est fait que de beaux détails (Voltaire) elle doit en faire un continuum' (xvii, 66); 'le détail entre dans ma chair' (P II, 728); '*Il n'y a point de détails dans l'exécution*' (P II, 84); by putting together these random proliferations on the theme of detail, it seems possible to gain a rudimentary, but at the same time highly suggestive picture of the centre of Valéry's art and thought, where nature, art and the organic are concerned.

Growth in nature is a united principle ('point de détails dans la nature' (xv, 586)), while poetry on the other hand must be composed of separate details ('la poésie n'est fait que de beaux détails' (xvii, 66)). Where composition is concerned, one of Valéry's greatest problems, especially in the long poem, was to avoid the impression of a string of poetic gems loosely strung together, or, in other words, to achieve 'organic unity' in the work as a whole ('[. . .] elle doit en faire un continuum' (xvii, 66)). 'Je tente d'imiter le mode indivisible' (P II, 187), Lucrèce says. The perfect transitions or 'modulations' of *La Jeune Parque* in particular would suggest the direction in which this aim led Valéry in practice. He frequently expresses the belief that it is to the transitions of a poem that the critic must look to understand its driving power.[2] I have already attempted to suggest the yield of *La Jeune Parque* and *Le Cimetière Marin* when approached in this way.

How can these statements be reconciled with the saying of Eupalinos 'Il n'y a point de détails dans l'exécution' (P II, 84)? Perhaps one should look here at Valéry's own definition of inspiration as a state in which everything seems to 'fit'. He writes, for example:

> Un homme qui fait des vers, suspendu entre son beau idéal et son rien, est dans cet état d'attente active et interrogative qui le rend uniquement et extrêmement sensible aux formes et aux

1 'La Création Artistique', *Vues*, 301–2.

2 Cf. 'La vraie critique consisterait à trouver que tel écrivain se sert de tel type de transformation' (xxix, 606).

> mots que l'idée de son désir [. . .] *demande à l'inconnu*, aux ressources latentes de son organisation de parleur – cependant que je ne sais quelle *force chantante* exige de lui ce que la pensée toute nue ne peut obtenir que par une foule de combinaisons successivement essayées.
>
> (P I, 212)

Illumination or intuition of this kind is for Valéry the fruit of past effort and the collaboration of infinite impulses in time. In other words, it is to the synthesis of multiple details into unity, that the expression of Eupalinos really applies. 'Le détail entre dans ma chair' (P II, 728), Valéry admitted. The remark can equally well be reconciled with the previous ones if 'patiente impatience' (P II, 1301) is reviewed as a whole. It has already been suggested that Valéry's imagination was most often stimulated in direct contact with nature by things formed by 'une accumulation d'actions très petites' (ix, 875), by 'Temps de l'accumulation' (iv, 769). His own patience is essentially 'pointilliste' or atomistic in this same way. 'Ma patience est corpusculaire. Elle est faite d'une quantité indéfinie de brèves tentatives. Ce sont des *photons* que j'accumule. Elle n'est pas continue' (xvi, 237). The *carnets* of many of his poems show the great extent to which composition took place by the slow re-shaping and re-ordering of fragments swiftly and briefly conceived.[1] '[. . .] l'impossibilité de me tenir tout entier dans quelque objet ou sujet [. . .] Ce que j'ai approfondi l'a été par éclairs successifs' (iv, 884); 'J'ai l'esprit unitaire, en mille morceaux' (ii, 137): 'slow' time allows Valéry not to exterminate, but simply to re-organise the essential impulses of impatience.

There are consequently frequent contrasts in the *Cahiers* between the synthetic nature of construction (e.g. vii, 24) and the atomistic nature of thought in its most immediate form (e.g. xv, 900). Sometimes these contrasts are conveyed by means of the metaphor of separate atoms as opposed to composite molecules (e.g. xii, 36). It is perhaps significant that in the poem *Palme*, these two fields of metaphor, the organic and the atomistic, are brought together in the single image of atoms and fruit:

> Patience, patience,
> Patience dans l'azur!
> Chaque atome de silence
> Est la chance d'un fruit mûr!
>
> (P I, 155)

[1] See J. R. Lawler's analysis throughout *Lecture de Valéry*.

The poem itself, its final composure 'intricately wrought', is a testament to the successful appropriation of an organic metaphor by an essentially atomistic intellect, the co-ordination of a continuous and a saccadic mode. The poem sets up 'une durée de croissance' (P I, 648) achieved by the co-ordination of acts in time. Just as the perfect unity of the tree in *Dialogue de l'Arbre* gives the sensation of a work of art or poem, so now the work of art is as compact and perfect as the tree, not only rivalling and imitating the unity of nature, but achieving the unity of nature in totally human terms.

It is perhaps possible to see more clearly now what Valéry means by saying of the work of art: 'Normalement elle est *achevée* (en un certain sens) quand elle se fait *toute seule*. Et il ya avantage à le sentir' (xxiii, 340). The sensation of apparent independence in execution is to be welcomed as a sign of the successful collaboration of all the intellectual means at the artist's disposal, passive and active combined. On the other hand, Valéry may criticise strongly any admission of the illusion of spontaneous growth on the part of other artists. He writes, for example, very probably of Gide: 'Un Romancier me disait qu'à peine ses personnages nés et nommés dans son esprit, ils vivaient en lui à leur guise; ils le réduisaient à subir leurs desseins et à considérer leurs actes [. . .]', concluding with obvious irony: 'J'en ai conclu aussi que la sensation de l'arbitraire n'était pas une sensation de romancier' (P II, 675). Now obviously any novelist who admits to the spontaneous development of his characters does not mean literally that he has no say in the matter. Gide comes very near Valéry's own intellectual position himself when he writes: 'J'attends trop de l'inspiration; elle doit être le résultat de la recherche; et je consens que la solution d'un problème apparaisse dans une illumination subite; mais ce n'est qu'après qu'on l'a longuement étudié.'[1] The reason for Valéry's attack is very likely that Gide's remarks converge on the same position from the opposite direction, from the point of view of the assumed involuntary nature of inspiration. In reality, he uses much the same terminology as Gide himself, by stating, for example, that there can exist 'une fabrication artificielle qui a pris une sorte de développement naturel'.[2] By contrast with the composition of *La Jeune Parque*, 'croissance naturelle d'une fleur artificielle' (P I, 1622), this can only mean that of the two processes the first was based on proliferation by division from a few lines or stanzas, while the second tended to rely more exclusively on the accumulation of separate details.[3]

[1] *Journal des Faux-Monnayeurs*, 19. [2] *A. Gide–P. Valéry, Correspondance*, 448.

[3] See a similar suggestion by J. R. Lawler in *Form and Meaning in Valéry's 'Le Cimetière Marin'* (Melbourne U.P., 1959), 13, n. 23.

Thus on the one hand, Valéry seems bent on attacking the fallacy, perhaps more current in the discussion of poetic composition than in the novel, that the artist's consciousness is no more than a hindrance to the growth of an autogenetic form within him: a donkey's carcass would do as well, to appropriate the image of *La Pythie*. On the other hand, he can be seen to be willing, like all great artists, to conceive, even to cherish as an intellectual ideal, the possibility of achieving in composition an interplay between details and over-all design. Any notion of working to a preconceived rational scheme is totally alien to his theory and practice.

The key to this experience of 'organic growth' and, from the point of view of the finished work, of 'organic unity', is certainly for Valéry the balance in consciousness of complementary mental qualities, 'la haine du hasard et l'horreur de la règle' (i, 184), the same combination that he was seen to admire visually in the contemplation of natural forms. 'Cela est proprement le meilleur de l'esprit, – à quoi ne conduit ni un certain laissez-faire, ni une séparation d'opérations régulières', he writes in a similarly orientated comment on poetics:

> Ainsi, un précieux poème ne peut résulter ni d'une sorte d'abandon et de descente spontanée de l'esprit; ni de l'application d'une formule d'opérations. Mais spontanément il en apparaît des fragments, quelques arêtes éclairées, un commencement qui semble bien le commencement prédestiné de quelque chose – ou un dernier mot, etc.
>
> Et, mais, d'autre part, il y a une mécanique ou logistique. Ce qu'on appelle comme on peut: intuition, est une solution – parfois née avant le problème qu'elle délie – et alors, on en déduit le problème, le demande [. . .]. Spontanée c.-à-d. non tant soudaine qu'obtenue par une voie non analytique. Conséquence sans chemin *apparent*. C'est l'apparence ou la non apparence du chemin. Précipité chimique.
>
> (iv, 729)

Ultimately, then, the quality to which the artist aspires is 'naturalness' achieved in conscious experience, and his problem: '*soumettre à la volonté réfléchie* la production d'un ouvrage, sans que cette condition rigoureuse, délibérément adoptée, altère les qualités essentielles, les charmes et la grâce que doit porter et propager toute œuvre qui prétend séduire les esprits aux délices de l'esprit.'[1] Any organic analogy can be seen to hinge for Valéry on two main assumptions: first that the attribute 'organic'

[1] *Le Point*, février–avril (1944), 5 (quoted by M. Bémol in *Paul Valéry*, 417).

applied to the finished work of art means only that its form is more than usually complete, ordered and satisfying. The more consciously constructed, the more 'organic' in fact.[1] And secondly, that the degree to which the material appears to present itself during composition with a force and form of its own is the triumph, not the defeat of the freely adventurous consciousness of the artist concerned. It remains to examine in the last chapter of this study the possible overlapping of such aesthetic values into experiences as a whole. How does Valéry consider the possibility of intellectual maturation over a lifetime? In the dialogue *L'Idée Fixe* the two protagonists establish between them the following 'certainty':

> —En tout cas, je suis sûr d'une chose: rien de plus rare que la faculté de coordonner, d'harmoniser, d'orchestrer un grand nombre de *parties*. Ce travail-là, cette production d'ordre, demande, à mon avis, deux conditions antagonistes . . . Il faut maintenir, soutenir hors du . . . moment, hors du temps . . . ordinaire . . .
>
> —Il y aurait donc un *temps extraordinaire* . . . [. . .]
>
> —Mais oui. Pourquoi pas un temps extraordinaire? . . . Vous admettez bien qu'un espace où l'on produit un champ magnétique a des propriétés qui ne sont plus d'un espace . . . banal?
>
> —Soit. Je me résigne à tout.
>
> —Vous maintenez donc à l'état présent et indépendant ces facteurs distincts.
>
> —Et puis? . . . Ma tête s'égare . . .
>
> —Et alors, comme dans un milieu liquide calme et favorable, et saturé . . .
>
> —C'est tout à fait mon cas.
>
> —Se forme, se construit une certaine figure, – *qui ne dépend plus de vous.*
>
> —Et de qui, Bon Dieu?
>
> —Des Dieux! . . . Pardieu! . . . Il faut, en somme, se soumettre à une certaine contrainte; pouvoir la supporter; durer dans une attitude forcée, pour donner aux éléments de . . . pensée qui sont en présence, ou en charge, la *liberté* d'obéir à leurs affinités, le *temps* de se joindre et de construire, et de s'imposer à la conscience; ou de lui imposer je ne sais quelle *certitude* . . .
>
> (P II, 261)

1 Cf. the thesis put forward by W. Clemens in *The Development of Shakespeare's Imagery* (Methuen, 1951) that the plays are the more 'organic', the more dramatic and mature.

I have quoted the passage in full because the dialogue form, rapid, ironic, with the sceptical interventions of the second speaker, is obviously as much part of its meaning as the theme itself. It epitomises Valéry's belief – never dogmatically asserted, but constantly implied – in what is almost a relative, human 'transcendentalism':[1] the power of the artist's consciousness to construct its own duration out of disorder and chance. 'On s'*arme de patience* (*Contre* quoi?)' (viii, 896), he once noted, or, much later, of the artist's patient endeavour, 'et pour qui et pour quoi?' (xviii, 916). The answer provided and actively confirmed by Valéry's own example is that 'l'ecrivain véritable est un homme qui ne trouve pas ses mots. Alors il les cherche. Et en les cherchant, il trouve mieux' (ii, 669); that the relationship of a man with his art can offer 'tout ce qu'il faut pour accroître l'homme et l'art' (P II, 1365).

[1] Cf. W. N. Ince, 'Transcendence or Inspiration by the back door', *Modern Language Notes*, LXXX (1965), 373–8.

9 Genius & growth

There remain to be explored here themes of growth and maturation as they relate to intellectual processes over a lifetime. This will involve taking a global view of Monsieur Teste's '*Maturare!* . . .' (P II, 18) and of its relation to the more general theme of maturation expressed in *Palme*. It will also involve an attempt to assess the degree to which such values have been incorporated into Valéry's own work as it stretches over his lifetime. Does it pursue a purely linear development, or does it too grow and mature like a plant? Tentative conclusions about both the theory and the practice of growth and maturation will inevitably centre as before on the question of a possible reconciliation between an impatient, atomistic mode of experience – the values of instantaneity – and a mode of experience based on the incubation of futurity. In this way, this last chapter will be concerned with the culmination of the theme of the relationship between consciousness and nature which each of the previous ones has approached in some form.

A preliminary glance at the subject shows at once that two distinct, but at the same time intimately interwoven themes are concerned: first, the inevitable growth and unfolding of mental processes simply through the fact that consciousness is the product of a living organism which develops, matures and decays in time; secondly, the theme of most importance here, the growing power of consciousness itself, and with that power the introduction of an intellectual time-scale running in a sense counter to the theme of organic growth and decay. Because of the close influence of the first theme or 'level' on the second, it will be necessary to give a brief survey of Valéry's notes on the mental 'ages of man'.

Age

First, childhood. Although Valéry is mainly interested in the theme of the reinstatement of the values of childhood in the mature mind, and in his own adult reactions to children (many notes in the *Cahiers* such as 'Un homme qui parle avec un enfant' (iv, 79) obviously spring from the direct contemplation or thought of his own children, in this case Claude),[1] there are nonetheless frequent notes on the theme of childhood itself. These fall roughly into three categories, all with the same basic interest in common. First, there are comments on the child's power of total absorption in experience: 'J'aime les enfants, car, quand ils s'amusent, ils s'amusent; et quand ils pleurent, ils pleurent; et cela se succède sans difficulté./Mais ils ne mêlent pas ces visages. Chaque phase est pure de l'autre./Mais nous...' (P I, 336); the child lives in the immediate (P I, 397); it is a master of absolute pleasure (P I, 844). In *L'Idée Fixe* a humorous sketch is given of its constant activity, which, unlike that of many adults, is concentrated on its own immediate enjoyment or use (P II, 219). The second category concerns growth of both bodily and mental powers of collaboration, the child's acquisition of the ability not only to speak and walk, but also to dance (P I, 1329) – a theme Valéry uses analogically to suggest the difference between a utilitarian and poetic use of language – and its discovery of the body through a growing self-awareness (P I, 370). It is the theme of the relationship of the child's experience to 'la conscience consciente' of the adult which seems to interest Valéry above all else. 'Un très petit enfant déjà se souvient. Mais sans y joindre qu'il se souvient' (xviii, 744). Consciousness itself is accordingly a capacity that ramifies in time, its resources depending on a certain degree of physical growth.

This aspect of childhood can be strikingly contrasted with Valéry's expression of adult consciousness as the power to recognise memory, just as intelligence is 'mémoire *organisée*' (iv, 916). In *Comme le Temps est Calme*..., for instance, he writes:

> La lune est ce fragment de glace fondante. Je sais trop (tout à coup) qu'un enfant aux cheveux gris contemple d'anciennes tristesses à demi mortes, à demi divinisées, dans cet objet céleste de substance étincelante et mourante [. . .]. Ma jeunesse jadis a langui et senti la montée des larmes, vers la même heure, et sous le même enchantement de la lune évanouissante.[2]

[1] E.g. i, 205 (Valéry alters 'Je' to 'Il'); iv, 66, 99.

[2] *Morceaux Choisis* (Paris, Gallimard, 1930), 55–6. Cf. 'Il y a Cinquante Ans...' (P I, 355).

Consciousness of memory forms the basis of much of the experience in *La Jeune Parque* and in *Faust*. In his many notes on childhood[1] – equivalent to those on the seed and on dawn – as the time before the 'possible' (P I, 1329) of the mind has fully unfolded, Valéry shows yet again the kind of imagination which dwells on the inverse characteristics of intellectual maturity the better to throw into relief the experience of 'la conscience consciente'.

His views on the later years of human experience reveal that he was as alert to the effect of temporal cycles of the body over a lifetime as he was to the effect of diurnal rhythms, seasonal rhythms, or the more complex inner modulations of mental life over shorter spaces of time. In fact he considered 'la cyclique du vivant' to be the more pronounced the more complex or mature the organism (xx, 493).[2] He may write, for example, of 'l'âge où l'enfant insensiblement se change dans un homme' as a time of the confused formation of potentialities to be partly unfolded later:

> Entre la simplicité de l'enfance et la netteté de l'âge mûr, se place une ère d'incertitude et d'énergie, mêlée d'enthousiasmes et d'ennuis, de songes, d'impatiences et de longueurs. Nous sommes comme embarrassés de plusieurs âmes qui se disputent l'avenir. L'enfant vit dans l'instant, son jouet lui cache la suite. L'homme accompli vit dans un futur tout alourdi de son passé. Mais l'adolescent vit dans le possible; le probable n'est pas son affaire.[3]

For the mind of the man between roughly twenty and thirty a crisis of some nature is foreseen. 'Une crise, c'est-à-dire un jugement par les forces en présence', Valéry writes:

> – une confrontation toujours tragique des ambitions, des pouvoirs, des idéaux, des souvenirs et des pressentiments, – en un mot un combat de tous les éléments de contradiction, de tous les thèmes antagonistes qu'une vie déjà assez longue et assez éprouvée pour les avoir réunis, propose à leur âme déchirée, et dont elle impose le conflit à l'organisme en détresse.
>
> (P I, 759)

Obviously Valéry generalises from personal experience here, his own intellectual ideals having been formed in precisely this way. Whether

[1] E.g. i, 235, 340; xxiii, 314. [2] Quoted by P. Laurette, *Le Thème de L'Arbre*, 127.
[3] 'Impressions et Souvenirs' in *Maîtres et Amis* (Beltrand, déc. 1927).

negative or positive, a crisis of some kind seems inevitably connected for him with the transition from instinctive to a greater degree of consciously trained behaviour, the power to 'choisir un certain soi-même et de se l'imposer' (P II, 95). It is left to the reader's imagination whether any such turmoil is meant to have accompanied the transition of Teste into the full possession of the means of 'Maturare' under the influence of which his later life proceeds.

'L'âge où l'adolescent se fait homme' is defined, then, as 'celui des ambitions qui se fixent, des perspectives qui se dessinent' (P I, 818). It is no coincidence that the drama of *La Jeune Parque*, although sufficiently general to apply to the potentials of consciousness at any moment, is depicted through the symbolic crisis of puberty, the threatening of relative mental autonomy by a force apparently alien to the permanency of personality until that force can be made part of consciousness itself. Narcisse, again universal in relevance, is likewise shown as a young man. To a friend who mocked the cliché 'époque de transition' Valéry replied with a disconcertingly simple example taken from practical experience: just as a lump of sugar differs in the sugar-bowl from what it is in the coffee-cup, so a pregnant woman must feel different from her 'normal' self, and so on (P I, 1062). However relatively permanent is self-awareness, personality *does* change and no degree of control can by-pass or eliminate the fact. 'Le Moi pur' is a 'myth' formed from the power to correlate separate instants at a high level of awareness, not a fixed absolute.

Between youth and maturity Valéry sees, as does Proust for Marcel, a potential 'âge de glace'. Under this rubric in *Analecta*, he writes: 'L'âge froid vient, et est contraint de subir ce qui a été construit, pétri, arrêté, par l'âge de feu, et de se priver malgré soi de ce qui a été renoncé volontairement à l'âge de feu. L'homme mûr se loge dans la coque d'un homme jeune qui a disparu' (P II, 732). In Teste himself, age is deliberately minimised, but the reader is made to feel that he is both older than the Parque and younger than Faust. This impression is supported by the speaker's information: 'M. Teste avait peut-être quarante ans' (P II, 17). Again the age is meaningful. Valéry connects with it a certain kind of mental lucidity and intransigence. For him, 'un monde original, toujours d'aplomb, toujours âgé de 40 ans, toujours éveillé, lucide' (iv, 15) was the ideal mental universe constantly postulated by the thinker, and he made the actual comment during his active preoccupation with Monsieur Teste in 1912. Very much of his work refers to a view of the world possible to a man at the height of his mental and physical power (a theme symbolised by the fist full of strength brought down on the table by the speaker in

Colloque dans un Être with the Testian question '*Que peut un homme?*' (P I, 366), and reflected in the situation of *Le Cimetière Marin* at midday, the zenith of mental and physical life). Yet even in the case of Teste, this lucidity is based on a foretaste of limitation, ageing and change and the knowledge that – as Valéry says elsewhere – our whole conscious existence 'peut se perdre en quelque accident pathologique'.[1] 'Le soir existe. Il vient toujours', says the speaker 'A' in the same *Colloque* and 'B' replies: 'Crois-tu que ma lucidité ne le voie point venir? Crois-tu qu'elle ne pense point son propre crépuscule – et même ne l'admire? N'est-ce pas une merveille supérieure que de penser que l'on possède en soi de quoi disparaître à soi-même [...]?' (P I, 365). The theme of evening, already traced on a literal level, is general enough to refer as much to the diminution of lucidity in age and its final extinction in death as to its intermittences or interruptions in sleep, physical disaster and so on. All these are themes capable of generating an anxiety Valéry never ceased to contemplate as one of the most characteristic facets of consciousness itself. 'Vieillir n'est pas naturel' (XXVI, 384).

Significantly it is to the fully mature rather than to the adolescent or middle-aged mind that he attributes the most passion and warmth. The theme of a 'puberté seconde' (P I, 505) is attributed to 'Phèdre femme' of whom, developing the mental and physiological repercussions suggested to him by Racine's 'C'est Vénus tout entière . . .', Valéry writes:

> Elle est à cette période que la vie se connaît pleine et non remplie. A l'horizon, la décadence du corps, les dédains et la cendre. Alors cette vie éclatante éprouve le sentiment de tout son prix. Ce qu'elle vaut engendre ce qu'elle veut dans les ombres de sa conscience [. . .]. Le corps voit plus loin, plus avant que soi. Il produit de la surabondance d'être [. . .] (P I, 504–5).[2]

Elsewhere he writes:

> Je m'assure [. . .] que l'ingénuité et le feu paraissent dans l'homme vers les cinquante ans. A ce point de la vie, il ne vaut plus la peine de calculer; la prévoyance devient vaine et son objet *imaginaire*; la sagacité absurde; la prudence ridicule; et l'on peut se consumer sans regret, comme il est temps de se consumer sans retard. Rien de plus chaud ni de plus naïf que cet âge.[3]

[1] *Cours de Poétique*, leçon 4 (18 déc. 1937), *Yggdrasill*, 2 ème (25 jan. 1938), 155.
[2] Cf. 'O Femme, qui donc es-tu?' 'La Passion de l'Intelligence' 'Le destin intellectuel de la femme', *Conferencia* (20 jan. 1931), 107–10.
[3] 'Au Lecteur', preface to M. Courtois-Suffit's *Le Promeneur Sympathique* (Paris, Plon, 1925).

This quotation is taken from a little-known preface. Although many of Valéry's comments on age seem to spring in this way from direct contact with friends or artists he knew, they are far from confined to such special instances. He frequently speculates in the abstract on old age – 'Senescenza' (ix, 888) or 'Vieillissement' (xxiv, 763) – as the necessary completion of his desire to grasp the universal movement of human life as a complex organisation of energy that unfolds and decays irrespective of the potentials of individual consciousness. 'Vieillir' is defined as 'diminution du possible' (xii, 811; cf. xi, 709), the inverse of the growth of possibility symbolised by the child. 'Comment se peut-il que l'homme vieillissant garde le désir dont il perd les ressources?' (P II, 733). There is much of the epigrammatic form and content of a La Rochefoucauld maxim about these remarks.[1]

Remarks on old age are not confined to the analytical and epigrammatic. Valéry has already shown himself capable like Baudelaire of the kind of consciousness which can project itself into the point of view of other things or people, things as far away as the young woman with her child in *La Jeune Mère*[2] or even the fly and the bird that cut across his view. The same imaginative empathy is to be found in a first-person monologue called *La Vieille Femme* in *Autres Rhumbs*:

> Très âgée, je vis dans le monde intermédiare, déjà presque en équilibre avec chaque moment du temps ou circonstance, comme l'est un corps sans vie.
>
> Je vous touche et je suis bien loin de vous. Ce même instant a des significations bien différentes pour vous et pour moi. Ma mémoire est une maison tout achevée. Cette maison magique peut s'envoler d'un coup; il en est ainsi dès qu'on ne peut plus rien y ajouter. Tous les projets possibles sont accomplis ou abandonnés. Je n'ai plus qu'un seul acte nouveau à faire. Tout est fait, et refait, moins le mourir.
>
> Je me fais difficile à l'égard de la lumière, des bruits, des goûts, de la nourriture. Tout ce qui advient maintenant m'était déjà connu ou m'est inconnaissable.
>
> (P II, 697–8)

These are not thoughts of an old person as certain novelists might relate them imitatively, however. Valéry is concerned even here with an

[1] E.g. 'Ce que l'âge mûr a élaboré, un jeune homme le dévore. Trop vite, il sait. Mais possédé plus qu'il ne possède, trop tard il découvre ce qu'il savait' (ii, 717); 'Un vieillard ne retrouve pas sa force ancienne en y pensant' (iv, 21).

[2] *Morceaux Choisis*, 53–4.

examination of old age as material for a hypothetically articulate consciousness examining in broad daylight the extent of its defeat. Contrasts as well as comparisons with Baudelaire are invited. Where in *Les Fenêtres* Baudelaire writes of the extension of the self in another being: 'Qu'importe ce que peut être la réalité placée hors de moi, si elle m'a aidé à vivre, à sentir que je suis et ce que je suis?',[1] Valéry might place 'knowing' rather than 'feeling' at the centre of the sensation of augmented existence: 'Voir [. . .] et savoir que l'on voit . . .' (P II, 322). Yet, in both writers, detachment and involvement are equally present at some stage.

Finally, Valéry's treatment of the theme of old age can be traced through the idea of an apparently unchanging consciousness faced with the physical decay of the self: 'C'est là un problème de vieil homme: on sait bien qu'on est le *même*, mais on serait fort en peine d'expliquer et de démontrer cette petite proposition. Le "Moi" n'est peut-être qu'une notation commode' (P I, 285). In a conversation recorded by Lucien Fabre, Valéry remarked: 'Oh! Je m'entends! Je vieillis: cela veut dire que je suis physiquement moins maître de moi – cela ne veut pas dire du tout que j'éprouve des émotions que je n'eusse pas ressenties autrefois. *Au contraire*, mais la vieillesse est obscène; elle laisse paraître ce que l'âge mûr a la pudeur de cacher.'[2] The same theme is expressed in terms of the 'Second Corps' of an ageing Narcisse:

> C'est ce Corps même qui fut si cher à Narcisse, mais qui désespère bien des gens, et qui les attriste et assombrit presque tous, le temps venu, quand il nous faut bien consentir que ce vieil être dans la glace a des rapports terriblements étroits, quoique incompréhensibles, avec ce qui le regarde et ne l'accepte pas. On ne se consent pas d'être cette ruine!
>
> (P I, 928)

and in the prose poem *Comme le Temps est Calme* quoted above in connection with memory: 'Ma jeunesse a vu ce même matin, je me vois à côté de ma jeunesse . . . [. . .] Il y a en vous quelque chose d'égal à ce qui vous passe'.[3] The passage is couched in the language of religious mysticism ('prier', 'mystère' and so on). But the question-begging notion of 'soul' is always absent. For Valéry there is no doubt that the conscious power

[1] *Œuvres Complètes* (Paris, Gallimard, 1961), 288. The second part of Valéry's passage evokes the rejuvenating effect of music on the old woman, perhaps with an echo of Baudelaire's poem *Les Petites Vieilles* (ibid., 87).

[2] Quoted by Lucien Fabre in 'Le Langage, L'Impasse et La Course au Flambeau', *Paul Valéry Vivant* (Cahiers du Sud, 1946), 163.

[3] *Morceaux Choisis*, 56.

which observes even the old man's self with apparent detachment is dependent on a temporary enclave of increasing organisation to be overwhelmed in death.

A survey of Valéry's view of the mental 'ages of man', a theme that joins his interest in the organic cycle of all living things from birth to maturity and death, suggests mental life to be a circle of slowly unfolding and slowly diminishing possibilities, the gradual exhaustion in time of 'la *fonction-Avenir*' (P I, 1428). 'L'homme grandit, mûrit, vieillit discontinuement', he writes, 'il ne grandit, ne mûrit, ne vieillit pas en chaque instant. Son âge réel est stationnaire sur chaque palier' (P II, 733). There are distinct phases or 'landings' from which the mind cannot escape. Living and changing is to enter a 'cercle' (xii, 811), the circle of growth and decay which mental hierarchy has in common with the plant. To quote the image of *Au Platane*, one of the main biological poems based on this theme:

> Ce front n'aura d'accès qu'aux degrés lumineux
> Où la sève l'exalte;
> Tu peux grandir, candeur, mais non rompre les nœuds
> De l'éternelle halte!
>
> (P I, 114)

Consciousness and growth

Even throughout his meditations on the process of ageing, Valéry could be seen to be concerned above all with what the cybernetician Norbert Wiener has called 'local and temporary islands of decreasing entropy in a world in which the entropy as a whole tends to increase',[1] or, to appropriate the same writer's images further, with the constant whirlpools and patterns in water that never ceases to flow, with the individuality of flame rather than stone, form rather than substance.[2] Consciousness is just such a 'temporary island'. Of course the decay of the organism will win in the end, unless science discovers methods of indefinitely prolonging life.[3] Of course consciousness itself will be extinguished, but it is to its relative permanency as a basis for the potentially infinite expansion of human experience in any instant that the theme of intellectual maturation leads, and to which images of growth taken from the realm of organic existence can now be seen to apply. That they do so is obviously Valéry's means of symbolically expressing the power of a human counter-effort

[1] *The Human Use of Human Beings* (Boston, Houghton Mifflin, 1954), 36.
[2] Ibid., 96, 102.
[3] E.g. ix, 312.

to 'take root' in life itself. '[. . .] on veut être pour quelque chose dans cette limitation qu'on n'a pas voulue', as Teste says (P II, 69).

This theme has already been suggested through the idea of a paradoxical fullness of emotion and intellectual wealth in the mature man, that is, the man in whom consciousness mingles most intimately with the knowledge of physical decay and the vicinity of death. After the comment 'Le mélange d'Amour avec Esprit est la boisson la plus enivrante', Valéry adds: 'L'âge y joint ses profondes amertumes, sa noire lucidité – donne valeur infinie à la goutte de l'instant' (P I, 317), while there is many a note in the *Cahiers* such as: 'la mort [. . .] non point comme poison de la vie, mais comme excitant de l'esprit à user de la vie' (XIV, 747). Something of this intellectual power of using the potential poison of mortality as a tonic in life is suggested in *Ébauche d'un Serpent*. It is closely linked to the perpetual tendency in Valéry's thought to wish to harness the energy released by the contemplation of human limitations to the invigoration of living itself. The feeling is given its most sustained expression in Faust, a man at the end of his life, and in turn the creation of Valéry's own maturity. Faust is capable if he chooses, of making the idea of love and the idea of death poisons of the anti-depressive kind, poisons whose sting is used to restore rather than to destroy the emotional, physical and intellectual plenitude of present life. In this way, he becomes the human embodiment of those 'positive' instincts exacerbated by natural decay which were suggested previously through the theme of Autumn. For the very fact that he is free to *choose* 'positive' values (as well as to destroy them as in *Le Solitaire*), is indicative of the 'anti-natural' humanism which is the hall-mark of Valéry's philosophy of consciousness and life.

Admiration for ripeness or longevity also appears frequently in remarks about individual thinkers and artists. 'Le dernier Hugo' (P I, 602); Voltaire 'vers sa maturité' (P I, 520); Goethe 'à l'extrême de l'âge' (P I, 553); Huysmans when 'mûr' (P I, 752): all these are singled out with many others for admiration and respect. Obviously this stress on maturity and advanced age implies no rhapsody on what is simply a natural process. As the case of a similar admiration for the maturity of Moréas (P I, 1740) explicitly shows, Valéry is equating physical maturity with vitality of mind, often with no apparent transition between the two. Thus Hugo's long life is really a symbol of the vast proportions of his work: 'longevité et puissance de travail' (P I, 1714); Voltaire's represents the intellectual power of a 'transmutation perpétuelle' (P I, 522); Goethe's old age stands for a lifetime's intellectual effort, for what is essentially the Valéryan power of combining the intellectual impatience of a volcano (P I, 535) with an ability to imitate 'les lenteurs maternelles de la nature' (P I, 552), qualities of sustained artistic effort that Valéry admires more than Goethe's actual work.[1] Like the ripe natural objects seen as 'choses précieuses', '[. . .] les personnes véritablement accomplies, font songer d'une lente thésaurisation de causes successives et semblables; la durée de l'accroissement de leur excellence a la perfection pour limite' (P II, 1244). Valéry expresses the key to the paradox when he writes:

> Je confesse un faible pour la volonté, et même l'orgueil, de l'isolé dans son idée. Un homme qui se fait une doctrine propre et complète de son art, qui sur ses conceptions théoriques entreprend un ensemble d'œuvres qui s'enchaînent; et qui ne cesse de poursuivre sans faiblir ce qu'il a projeté de faire, témoigne d'une autonomie, et comme d'une souveraineté de caractère toute respectable. Ce n'est pas une chose si fréquente qu'on le croirait.[2]

Physical maturity, although inevitable, symbolises the great thinker's intellectual maturity. He has rivalled natural growth by the sustained development of his own mental powers.

Linked to this theme of intellectual enrichment – as opposed to the law of diminishing returns implicit in the theme of physical age and decay – is the notion of increased intellectual knowledge. Faust has acquired vast knowledge in his lifetime, a fact humorously summed up through Méphistophélès as: 'Géo ceci, géo cela, et des métries, des nomies, des logies, des graphies, et des stiques et des tiques . . . Bref, de quoi nommer toutes les plantes, toutes les bêtes, les coquilles, les pierres, les astres [. . .]' (P II, 368). However, it is just such academic information, useless in itself, which brings Faust – to use the traditional symbolism of the legend – into the devil's power, and just such knowledge which is symbolised by the 'fruits amers' (P I, 146) of science in *Ébauche d'un Serpent*. The notion of 'accroissement de conscience' (xviii, 225) is one which Valéry always differentiates strongly from the accumulation of pure knowledge. The power of raising existence to the highest power of awareness is

[1] He thinks of his 'IIIe Faust', for example, as being based on 'Tout ce que Goethe a ignoré' (xii, 894). Several differences emerge in N. Suckling's chapter 'The Parallel with Goethe', *Paul Valéry and the Civilized Mind* (O.U.P., 1954), 174–98.

[2] 'Hommage à René Ghil (1862–1925)', special no. of *Rythme et Synthèse* (1926) (quoted by L. J. Austin and H. Mondor in *Mallarmé: Correspondance, 1862–1871*, II (Paris, Gallimard, 1965), 285, n. 2).

an ideal which involves instead 'un accroissement de relations et de rigueur dans les relations' (iii, 485). Thus 'Vieillissement c'est classement, croissance des précisions de définition' (xxiv, 763). '*Doctement mourir. Transiit classificando*' (P II, 36) says Teste. The paradox of increased freedom of consciousness in age is touched on in the phrase 'plus je pense, plus je pense' (i, 182, 515) (rather than 'plus je pense, plus je sais') and Valéry contemplates the story of 'l'individu que *surprend* l'agrandissement de son esprit par l'âge' (i, 140). To equate total knowledge with his view of intellectual maturity or the power of 'le s'ajouter ce que l'on a trouvé' (ix, 730), is misleading. The greater the co-ordination of mental relationships in age, the greater the contact with the disorder of life necessary for further thought and intellectual power.

'*Que peut un homme?*' (P I, 366) asked the speaker in *Colloque dans un Être*. This notion of possibility is expressed in the Greek epigraph to *Le Cimetière Marin* (translated as 'O mon âme, n'aspire pas à la vie éternelle mais épuise le possible') and it returns in the identical question of Monsieur Teste (P II, 25). It is significant, in fact, that both Teste and Faust are made to turn their attention not to any chimera of absolute knowledge, but to practical efficacity; the equation of 'pouvoir' and 'savoir'[1] and thus the extension of their own sensation of being alive. 'Ma recherche du "temps" se résume en ceci: c'est une application, non particulière, mais spéciale, de mon système de l'analyse par les *pouvoirs.*/ *Que pouvons-nous?* [...]/Quant au "temps" que pouvons-nous, physiquement et mentalement?', Valéry notes, and replies to his own question: 'Notre observation *peut* mettre au 1*ier* plan le *changement* des choses et celui de nous' (xviii, 209).

One of the most important concerns of Valéry's thought, then, is the widening of the horizons of living by the power of consciousness to 'supervise' the growth of more and more complex mental relationships and thus to gain greater freedom in time. To the ideal of training the mind or disciplining it to the immediate service of existence he gave the name 'Gladiator', and it is clear that this becomes one of the most significant rubrics in his notes.[2] 'Il n'y a qu'une chose à faire: se refaire. Ce n'est pas simple' (viii, 182), he writes for example. But such comments are not confined to those with the actual heading. There are frequent jottings on 'l'art de vivre', on the ideal of making living a conscious art: 'se servir

1 Cf. W. N. Ince, 'Impatience, Immediacy and the Pleasure Principle in Valéry', *F.M.L.S.*, II (1966), 184.

2 E.g. xi, 693, xiv, 216, xvi, 319. See Judith Robinson, 'Valéry's Conception of Training the Mind', *F.S.*, XVIII (1964), 227–35.

agilement, sciemment, et méthodiquement de son moi, comme origine de coordonnées universelles – tel est l'ars magna' (ii, 141), for example, or, under the heading *Principes de l'entrainement*:

> C'est l'habitude calculant l'avenir [. . .]
> Il est nul sans gradations
> Il est nul sans arrêts déterminés
> Il consiste dans une nutrition consciente d'une faculté [. . .]
> Il ne doit jamais passer d'une chose à la suivante sans que la précédente ne soit acquise totalement.
> Il consiste à évaluer une chose à réaliser en éléments de temps, de patience [. . .]. Il consiste à employer peu à peu [. . .] l'énergie dépensée d'abord en moyens.
>
> (i, 278)

'*Maturare*'

Valéry's statement about a possible equation between the notion of research into time and of research into the power of consciously using time (xviii, 209) is consistent with the definition of 'Maturare' given in the Teste cycle: 'L'art délicat de la durée, le temps, sa distribution et son régime, – sa dépense à des choses bien choisies, pour les nourrir spécialement' (P II, 17). Indeed, 'MATURARE' is described in terms of the same 'gymnastique' (P II, 17) used for 'Gladiator' (xii, 673). There are even explicit indications that Teste and the notion of Gladiator are one (e.g. ix, 745). Thus the *Cahiers* can be used to prove that it is misleading to confine Teste's 'maturare' to one of a few instances, as do some of his critics.[1] The theme of maturation is one of the most frequent in Valéry's work.

Images of maturation and of the growing plant are, as we have seen, quite commonly applied to individual compositions. They are also frequently applied to the long-term development of the artist himself. '[. . .] an individual genius may himself be envisioned as an unconsciously growing plant', writes M. H. Abrams.[2] Many artists have recognised the principle. Proust, for example, gives to Marcel the words:

> Ainsi toute ma vie jusqu'à ce jour aurait et n'aurait pas pu être résumée sous ce titre: une vocation. Elle ne l'aurait pas pu en ce sens que la littérature n'avait joué aucun rôle dans ma vie. Elle l'aurait pu en ce que cette vie [. . .] formait une réserve pareille à cet albumen qui est logé dans l'ovule des plantes et dans lequel celui-ci puise sa nourriture pour se transformer

[1] E.g. J. Hytier, *La Poétique de Valéry*, 149.

[2] *The Mirror and the Lamp*, 205.

> en graine, en ce temps où on ignore que l'embryon d'une plante se développe, lequel est pourtant le lieu de phénomènes chimiques et respiratoires secrèts mais très actifs. Ainsi ma vie était-elle en rapport avec ce qui amènerait sa maturation. Et ceux qui se nourriraient ensuite d'elle ignoreraient ce qui aurait été fait pour leur nourriture, comme ignorent ceux qui mangent les graines alimentaires, que les riches substances qu'elles contiennent ont d'abord nourri la graine et permis sa maturation.[1]

Valéry's scepticism concerning Proust is well-known: 'Ce n'est pas moi qui rechercherais le Temps Perdu!' (P II, 1506). Yet his strictures on the novel on the grounds of naïve realism and over-simplification of psychology tend to dismiss insights in Proust's work which are very near his own. Marcel may be far less conscious of the process within him than Monsieur Teste, but in *A la Recherche du Temps Perdu* itself, the quest for the appropriate metaphor with which to express the quality of sensations and emotions in time involves, as it does for Valéry, an intense analysis of the data of introspection rather than any passive waiting for unconscious growth. Proust's work shows the fertile interplay of three levels of maturation all relevant to Valéry's interests: Marcel's journey from the primary order of childhood to the final synthesis of maturity; the continuity of 'moments privilégiés' imperceptibly prepared in time; and the maturation of the novel itself.

Bergson, too, uses the term 'mûrir' to express something of the dynamic relationship between consciousness and time: 'Exister consiste à changer, changer à se mûrir; se mûrir à se créer indéfiniment soi-même'. Quoting this remark in *Études sur le Temps Humain*, G. Poulet comments: 'Si l'être tire sans cesse l'existence de son passé, ce n'est pas comme d'un principe dont on tire les conséquences; ni comme d'un patron dont on imite l'image; mais par une libre adaptation de ses ressources passées à la vie présente en vue du futur.'[2] The differences between Valéry and Bergson are perhaps more illuminating than their similarities.[3] The main difference concerns Bergson's 'élan vital', the notion of an almost mystic life-force, quite alien to Valéry's way of thinking.[4] It is not so much that

[1] *A La Recherche du Temps Perdu*, XV (Paris, Gallimard, 1927), 48.

[2] *Études sur le Temps Humain* (Paris, Plon, 1965), xliii.

[3] See N. Suckling's chapter 'The answer to Bergson' in *Paul Valéry and the Civilized Mind*, 199–236 and Judith Robinson, 'Valéry, critique de Bergson', *C.A.I.E.F.*, XVII (1965), 203–15.

[4] M. Bémol describes Valéry misleadingly as 'un grand poète de l'élan vital' (*Paul Valéry*, 426).

Valéry avoids Bergsonian key-words like 'devenir' and 'durée', however,[1] but rather that he uses them in a different sense. Valéry's 'devenir'[2] is based on the self-determining aspects of the conscious mind in conjunction with rather than in submission to its affective resources. Similarly, he openly asserts that duration ('la durée') is created by the mind from disparate moments in time,[3] a notion that Bergson's terminology successively veils.

It is undoubtedly Mallarmé's notion of intellectual life as a perpetual ripening towards an ever distant masterpiece, perhaps not even an exteriorised masterpiece, with which Valéry has most affinity, as I showed previously in connection with the influence of this notion on the production of individual works. There is much reminiscent of Mallarmé in the comment of the awed friend of Teste: 'il ajoutait sans cesse à quelque chose que j'ignore' (P II, 59) and perhaps, too, a humorous suggestion of Valéry's appreciation of Mallarmé's own growing irony towards the hyperbolical heights postulated by his view of maturation as the culmination of the whole universe in the conscious mind.

The plant analogy

Clearly the plant for Valéry is a kind of machine. It can be partly described in terms of dynamic principles. In fact the simplification of the idea of a plant made possible by such principles, particularly thermodynamic principles, provided a common language with which to approach both plant and mental functioning. Yet by virtue of its capacity to reproduce itself, the laws governing the plant are wider than those relating to the machine, that is to an assemblage of parts governed by dynamic principles alone. Having been led to associate the growth of ideas and the structure of intellectual compositions with the growth of a plant on the level of purely objective comparison, why does Valéry choose the specific analogy with a plant instead of the more easily transferable analogy with a machine when it comes to the question of intellectual development as a whole?

This may be because, while he is enforcing points of comparison between non-human and conscious development, Valéry wishes also to preserve as much tension as possible between tenor and vehicle. The machine is the embodiment of dynamic principles alone, and the natural

[1] 'Je crois n'avoir jamais prononcé [. . .] le mot de Devenir', *Lettres à Quelques-Uns*, 163.

[2] E.g. P I, 299.

[3] E.g. i, 10; viii, 242–3. Cf. Athikté in *L'Âme et la Danse*: 'Elle croise, elle décroise, elle trame la terre avec la durée . . .' (P II, 160).

organism is not. So by rejecting the machine in favour of the plant, Valéry suggests that although consciousness develops on the one hand along 'anti natural' lines of its own (that is by a specifically human balance of alignment and opposition in the face of instinctive forces), it does so with the unity and vigour of natural growth. He rejects the machine model in favour of the plant metaphor. What the machine could *not* provide is the element of mystery and inevitability connected with the basic self-perpetuating *existence* of the plant, its interiority, as opposed to its possible description in formal terms. At the same time the plant seems to be favoured in preference to more complex living organisms because it more clearly represents the co-existence of spontaneity with limitation, the spontaneous unfolding from within of an inherent potential design.[1] By appropriating the plant analogy even on this last level of his thought, where the capacity rather than the activity of consciousness is concerned, Valéry proves how little he is tied by a purely cognitive use of analogy, or even by the scientific process of simplifying into more and more fundamental units of description. Paradox and connotative value are to the fore, at the same time as contact is closely maintained with the sharp sense of morphology and morphogenesis that can be found on all the 'levels' of his thought.

The focal interest of the analogy between the plant and intellectual processes is obviously growth in general. 'Dans le poète ou dans la plante, c'est le même principe naturel' (P I, 538): Valéry writes this of Goethe whose imaginative insight into the theme of 'crâne et plante'[2] he admired, but with the basic reservation that organic unity is achieved in the creative mind by conscious fabrication from contradictory modes of experience rather than by alignment with natural forces of productivity. In *Dialogue de l'Arbre* the tree is made the model of any 'méditation puissante, et agissante, rigoureusement suivie dans son dessein' (P II, 192), and the analogy is followed through in the tentative definition of 'Méditer' as 's'approfondir dans l'ordre' (P II, 193). 'Vois comme l'Arbre aveugle aux membres divergents s'accroît autour de soi selon la Symétrie', says Lucrèce, 'La vie en lui calcule, exhausse une structure, et rayonne son nombre par branches et leurs brins, et chaque brin sa feuille, aux points mêmes marqués dans le naissant futur' (P II, 193). The analogy between plant and mind is transferred back again until the tree itself is 'une sorte d'esprit' (P II, 191); 'L'Arbre semble penser' (P II, 184).

Behind this apparently simple analogy is a sophisticated structural

[1] See M. H. Abrams, *The Mirror and the Lamp*, 167.

[2] *A. Gide–P. Valéry, Correspondance, 1890–1942*, 513.

comparison. Just as the tree in *Dialogue de l'Arbre* exists visibly as 'un chant dont le rythme déploie une forme certaine, et dans l'espace expose un mystère du temps' (P II, 193), so the thinking mind builds up an invisible structure in time. The notion of architecture and symmetry, symmetry created by the perpetual division of disorder into order, is common to both the plant and the mind.[1] 'Le plus haut de l'esprit ne vit que de croissance' (P II, 191); 'L'idée comme une plante. Le temps de croissance du vivant est différenciation' (xxvi, 208). The temporal and spatial possibilities of this analogy, noted already in connection with *Palme*, receive striking treatment in *Les Grenades*. The physical comparison between the ripe fruits bursting with seeds and the shape of the thinker's brow ('Je crois voir des fronts souverains') leads imperceptibly into the invisible architecture of discovery ('Éclatés de leurs découvertes!'),[2] and this tension is maintained throughout the poem through the physical theme of the past absorption of sunshine and through the abstract theme of the maturation of ideas and experience, until the final consolidating but meditative image:

> Cette lumineuse rupture
> Fait rêver une âme que j'eus
> De sa secrète architecture.
>
> (P I, 146)

These images in Valéry's thought and poetry relate to one of the most characteristic of all his 'characteristic' interests:[3] organisational activities which, on whatever 'level' of existence, introduce the notion of greater pattern and duration in space and time.[4]

The idea of growth leads further than the purely architectural comparison, then. The notion of the tree's power to combine contradictory elements – air and water, sky and earth – leads Valéry to make many analogies with the theme of a co-ordinatory power on the part of the intellect, a power to relate and combine more and more disparate elements of experience in time and thus to preserve a perpetual sense of what is

[1] See above, 145.

[2] See J. R. Lawler's chapter on 'Les Grenades' in *Lecture de Valéry* and W. N. Ince, 'An Exercise in Artistry: Valéry's "Les Grenades"', *The Romanic Review*, LV (1964), 190–202.

[3] 'Mais je me trouve quantité de caractéristiques!', Valéry once wrote (quoted by Judith Robinson, 'L'Ordre Interne des Cahiers de Valéry', *Entretiens sur Paul Valéry*, 261).

[4] Cf. the notion of 'code' in genetics. Valéry's notion of structure keeps his work in touch with recent developments in many fields, linguistics included.

new. He defines 'deep' lasting love, as opposed to love that is 'violent' but short-lived, in terms of resistance 'aux causes dedissipation ou de disparition [. . .]. Ce qui se conserve ne se conserve qu'en augmentant, et cet accroissement est lié à la sensation de rareté de monopole attribué à l'objet' (xxvi, 25). This kind of insight into the growing power of intellectual processes overflows into the language of the *Dialogue de l'Arbre*. 'Écoute donc. Voici ce qui me vient', says Tityre:

AMOUR n'est rien qu'il ne croisse à l'extrême
Croître est sa loi; il meurt d'être le même,
[. . . . .]
Vivant de soif toujours inassouvie,
Arbre dans l'âme aux racines de chair
Qui vit de vivre au plus vif de la vie
Il vit de tout . . . .
[. . . . .]
Grand Arbre Amour, qui ne cesse d'étendre
Dans ma faiblesse une étrange vigueur,
Mille moments que se garde le cœur
Te sont feuillage et flèche de lumière!
Mais cependant qu'au soleil du bonheur
Dans l'or du jour s'épanouit ta joie,
Ta même soif, qui gagne en profondeur,
Puise dans l'ombre, à la source des pleurs . . .

(P II, 182–3)

Images like this one enable Valéry to suggest the power of a conscious construction involving the whole sensibility, finally breaking down the barriers between voluntary and involuntary experience, intellect and emotion, mind and body, until the whole existence is filled with the sensation of 'duration', human duration, embedded across the one-way flow of natural 'irreversible' time.

The theme of man's freedom of intellectual growth is suggested through the great Tree of Knowledge in *Ébauche d'un Serpent*.

Tout l'Arbre de la Connaissance
Échevelé de visions,
Agitait son grand corps qui plonge
Au soleil, et suce le songe!

says the serpent in his dual apostrophe to the tree and the mind of man:

Arbre, grand Arbre, Ombre des Cieux,
Irrésistible Arbre des arbres,

Qui dans les faiblesses des marbres,
Poursuit des sucs délicieux
[. . . . . . .]
Grand Être agité de savoir,
Qui toujours, comme pour mieux voir,
Grandis à l'appel de ta cime,
Toi qui dans l'or très pur promeus
Tes bras durs, tes rameaux fumeux,
D'autre part, creusant vers l'abîme,

Tu peux repousser l'infini
Qui n'est fait que de ta croissance,
Et de la tombe jusqu'au nid
Te sentir toute Connaissance!

(P I, 145)

This image suggests that intellectual growth has the power to outweigh in vigour and unity the isolated power of rational logic which the serpent attributes to himself at the end of the poem. By using the analogy with a tree Valéry suggests that consciousness, unlike the more linear process of thinking, is a complex sensuous unity with powers of tapping the resources of affective and physical life. Unlike the tree in *Au Platane*, trapped like the *total* system of the mind in a cycle of existence, it is capable of temporarily breaking free and rivalling the notion of infinity itself with its potential growth.[1]

These analogies have largely been concerned with the 'natural' power of thought and intellectual processes in general to grow or develop hierarchical structures in time. Yet a further hierarchy was introduced when the notion of growth becomes conscious, in the manner symbolised by Teste. Images from horticulture have already been seen to reinforce the idea of a conscious cultivation of growth. A further more striking way in which Valéry suggests its 'anti natural' orientation is through the image of a tree growing downwards. The mind of Teste, symbolic of the power released by this 'conscience de la conscience', is, for example, 'une plante singulière dont la racine, et non le feuillage, pousserait, contre nature, vers la clarté' (P II, 29–30). In *Pour un Portrait de Monsieur Teste*, Valéry writes '[. . .] dans certaines branches de la science, ce même mot *aberration*, tout en conservant une certaine couleur pathologique, peut désigner quelque excès de vitalité, une sorte de débordement

[1] Cf. some of the notions raised by N. Bastet, in 'Faust et le Cycle', *Entretiens sur Paul Valéry*, 115–28.

d'énergie interne [. . .] C'est ainsi que la botanique parle de végétations aberrantes' (P II, 63), and of Teste as the most complete of all 'transformateurs psychiques', he writes: 'Le contraire d'un fou (mais l'*aberration* – si importante dans la nature – devenue consciente) car il en revenait toujours plus riche sans doute, portant les dissociations, les substitutions, les similitudes au point extrême, mais avec un retour assuré, une opération inverse infaillible' (P II, 65).

It is this 'retour assuré' which prevents Valéry's idea of the 'anti natural' orientation of conscious growth from forming part of a transcendental mysticism. 'N'y a-t-il donc point', he writes in his notes on the extreme temptation to the intellect posed by the mystic sensation, 'un "monde" qui toucherait à celui-ci par l'intérieur de l'esprit, qui serait la substance où mes racines plongent, auquel elles tirent l'arbre de l'univers visible!' (viii, 466), and something of the same autonomic experience is perhaps echoed in the line of *La Jeune Parque*: 'Tout l'univers chancelle et tremble sur ma tige' (P I, 102). That this mystic sensation belongs for Valéry to purely phenomenological reality, however, is confirmed by an important passage where he writes: 'La nature humaine ne peut soutenir l'amour dans son développement – j'entends l'amour du type infini. Univers tangent – mais le vrai univers est courbe et fermé [. . .]. La nature va son chemin qui n'est pas le nôtre – Le continu d'un sentiment semble pouvoir croître ad infinitum – mais sa structure le ramène et le réel (corps et univers) agit comme une pesanteur. L'âme est une tangente' (ix, 375). The growth of the mind is only potentially infinite, then. Because of the limits of a physical organism, it cannot unfold all the potentials it contains. Valéry explores more than one kind of intellectual reaction to such a situation, both negative and positive. Behind both is always the central paradox that the intellect itself owes its existence to the limitation beyond which it is tempted to try to stretch. It is the freedom and strength produced by this kind of awareness that emerges triumphant from a poem such as *Ébauche d'un Serpent* and helps differentiate Valéry's total vision from the nihilism of his serpent without any recourse to optimism.

To return to the comparison between plant and intellectual growth implicit in the Testian code of 'Maturare' is to conclude that it is based on a similar pursuit of 'therapeutic' freedom, freedom through the 'organic' assimilation of intellectual discovery about the limitations of self. 'Il faut tant d'années pour que les vérités que l'on s'est faites deviennent notre chair même' (P I, 1206), Valéry writes in his *Note et Digression* to the earlier essay on Leonardo, and in *La Soirée avec Monsieur Teste*:

'Sûrement, il avait dû consacrer des années à cette recherche: plus sûrement, des années encore, et beaucoup d'autres années avaient été disposées pour mûrir ses inventions et pour en faire ses instincts' (P II, 17). Similarly, the principle he calls in his own notes 'le s'ajouter ce que l'on a trouvé' (ix, 730) can be seen to be directly echoed in Teste's comment: 'Trouver n'est rien. Le difficile est de s'ajouter ce qu'on trouve' (P II, 17). The theme of conscious collaboration with uncontrolled experience can now be added to the concept of conscious discipline previously suggested in connection with 'Maturare'. The mind is to be disciplined to make use of the fact that, as W. N. Ince says of this theme, there is 'an inevitable time-lag between discovering a truth or principle and embodying it',[1] and, what is even more important, to trust that it will eventually achieve its aim; that, even in the longest apparent intermittence, the continuity between conscious and unconscious processes is secretly working to bring about the conversion of conscious insight into 'sang et nourriture'. It would be misleading, then, to suggest that the poem *Palme* applies to a purely unconscious level of maturation, while Teste's 'maturare' is deliberate. The theme of *Palme* is of the greatest generality. It applies to the kind of development implicit as much in Teste's 'anti natural' ideal – symbolic of consciousness in general – as in less conscious intellectual processes. It applies to all the resources of the mind, to aims and methods of human development totally distinct from those of the plant or tree itself.[2] In man, the unity of rhythm and number, 'être' and 'connaître',[3] have become articulate and grow without visible shape, gradually transforming the visible world.

The last aspect of the plant/mind analogy to be examined and one which Valéry undoubtedly uses to reinforce his view of consciousness as the invariant phase under a system of transformations, is the power of the plant to transform a random milieu into its own inner design, the kind of process he refers to schematically as 'Actions du milieu. Adaptations, accommodations, tropismes. Actions de la vie sur elle-même. Développements, différenciation, croissance, action de circonstance...' (xxvi, 207).[4] Thus 'La connaissance s'étend comme un arbre, par un procédé identique à lui-même en se répétant' (iii, 273) or develops by a constant process of

[1] *F.M.L.S.*, II (1966), 184.
[2] See above, 149.
[3] Cf. P. Laurette, *Le Thème de l'Arbre*, 160.
[4] Valéry defines his notion of '*phase* (vers 1902)' as 'l'état caractérisé par le groupe des échanges. Les éléments de ce groupe s'échangent sans changement de phase. Le passage de phase à phase se fait soit par une sorte de modulation – soit par brusque variation' (XVIII, 231).

differentiation: 'un refus indéfini d'être quoi que ce soit' (P I, 1225). That this miraculous permanency is achieved not by the exclusion but by the incorporation of disorder is one of the most fundamental principles of Valéry's thought. 'Dans la nature', he writes, '[. . .] la plante se fait de déséquilibre en déséquilibre [. . .]', and he goes on to relate this principle to the theme of human sensitivity:

> Ce mécanisme est celui de toute la nature vive; le Diable, hélas! est la nature même [. . .]. Vivre est à chaque instant manquer de quelque chose – se modifier pour l'atteindre – et, par là, tendre à se replacer dans l'état de manquer de quelque chose. Nous vivons de l'instable, par l'instable, dans l'instable: c'est toute l'affaire de la Sensibilité, qui est le ressort diabolique de la vie des êtres organisés.
>
> (P I, 618–19)

'Sensibilité' for Valéry is the prime source of consciousness, the necessary contact of the mind with the dark 'soil' of the irrational, which it converts into a precarious new order of its own.

There are many comments on the attempt of the plant to transform its surroundings into itself which are either directly or indirectly linked with consciousness: 'Autant elle s'enforce, autant s'élève-t-elle: elle enchaîne l'informe', says Lucrèce of the plant, for example, 'elle attaque le vide; elle lutte pour tout changer en elle-même, et c'est là son Idée! . . .' (P II, 192). Life is seen in *L'Âme et la Danse* as the mysterious movement by which a human being is perpetually transformed into himself (P II, 151). In his *Discours en l'Honneur de Goethe*, Valéry remarks, after comparing the creative principle of the plant with that of the poet, on the aptitude of all living beings to adapt constantly to the random in order to live, and adds: 'Goethe, Poète et Protée, vit une quantité de vies au moyen d'une seule. Il assimile tout, il en fait substance. Il transforme même le milieu où il s'implante et prospère' (P I, 538). The same '*plasticité*' (P II, 18) is the basis of Teste's maturation. It is just such a sense of augmented possibilities which must have led Valéry to write of the plant analogue: 'L'être végétal est peut-être le type le plus clair de cette combinaison de temps, espace, figure; forces, accroissement d'une région fermée au dépens d'un milieu qui distingue toute chose vivante' (viii, 214).

In Chapter 6 I showed Valéry's awareness that the plant is not an isolated system in which, according to the second law of thermodynamics, entropy can only increase. Instead, the process of photosynthesis is the primitive symbol of a relationship with the external world based, during life, on the reciprocity of expenditure and gain. For Valéry, this was a principle apparent on every level of organisational existence, not only in the relationship between the brain and its environment, but between the intellect and sensibility, and, at a more complex level still, in the relationship between consciousness and the whole of experience. Here too, expenditure is inseparable from maximum gain, the giver enriched by the giving of gifts. This is the point at which the conscious programme of 'se re-faire', symbolised by Teste, becomes the conscious 're-vivre', symbolised by Faust; the point at which the mind begins to 'employer peu à peu [. . .] l'énergie dépensée d'abord en moyens' (i, 278), or at which, to revert to the terminology of the Teste cycle, conscious 'inventions' become unconscious 'instincts', freeing consciousness for yet further use (P II, 17; cf. ix, 895). 'Fais que ma soif se fasse source' (xxiv, 283), Valéry once wrote in his notes, or: 'Créer la fontaine par la soif' (xxiii, 159).[1] It is the image of thirst – of a simple, childlike thirst, which is the basis of the poem *Poésie* in *Charmes* (P I, 119). The theme of Muse and suckling child is part of a traditional allegory. But Valéry uses the image in such a way as to retain contact with all the basic intellectual themes of interest here. The supreme artistry needed to preserve the gentle flow of milk, or, in more general terms, the intellectual necessity of balancing immediate needs in terms of future requirements: this is the equivalent of the maturation theme in terms of the system of attitudes needed to create it. The poem shows the almost physiological resonance of the idea in the whole being of the speaker, and, characteristically, Valéry presents the theme of balance through its inverse: the urge to violate and destroy: '– Si fort vous m'avez mordue/Que mon cœur s'est arrêté!' (P I, 120). 'Il en est qui ont vaste feuillage et peu de racines', he writes appropriating the more favoured metaphor to express the same pattern, 'Mais c'est l'harmonie ou l'équilibre de ces deux systèmes des recherches des sources de vie qui est à demander aux dieux' (P II, 882).

'Je sens naître et croître en moi-même une vertu de Plante', says Lucrèce, 'et je sais me confondre à la soif d'exister du germe qui s'efforce et qui procède vers un nombre infini d'autres germes à travers toute une vie de plante . . .' (P II, 188). There is a sense in which because he exercises a sustained awareness towards the growth of his own thought, Valéry's writings over a lifetime themselves bear out the notions inherent in his analogy with plant growth, particularly the power of the plant's whole

[1] Cf. J. Duchesne-Guillemin: 'Comédie de l'intellect, recherche gratuite, mais où il donnait le meilleur de lui-même et qui bientôt, au fond de lui, se fit ressource' (*Études pour un Paul Valéry*, 13).

future structure to grow from the potentials of a single seed, at the same time as being enriched by a deeper contact with disorder as its own co-ordinatory power extends in time.[1] The 'thèmes inébranlables' of his thoughts, particularly the theme of conscious perception, were drafted out as a young man and remain permanent preoccupations to the end of his life (Valéry died in 1945 at the age of seventy-four and kept up the *Cahiers* begun in 1894 almost until his death, with as much analytical rigour in the last volumes as in the first). In some critics' minds this unswerving perseverance seems to have given rise to the assumption that there is little or no development in his thought. 'This obstinate fidelity to the adolescent choice which lay at the root of Valéry's *aventure intellectuelle* gave him', says J. M. Cocking, for example, 'the perpetually adolescent hope of *le merveilleux*'.[2] There are other critics who think more in terms of a 'straight-line' development. K. W. Maurer, for example, suggests that Valéry's development, as opposed to Goethe's which is like a tree, can be compared with a thin straight line and an eye ascending into the light.[3] These assumptions are not necessarily derogatory, but I think they should be modified if they imply that the 'merveilleux' or 'neuf' to which the 'maturare' of Valéry develops, is in any way a mere persistence of that of adolescence. The image of a primary seed could itself be used to allay such criticisms. A seed stores the future *in posse* not *in esse*. Just as the tree to which it gives rise is not contained within it but is an interaction of those primary potentials with external circumstance, so the detached consciousness of the *Cahiers* is itself subject to randomness and change for its material, as Valéry was the first to appreciate.[4] Thus, 'la pensée naît, se développe comme un être dont le germe ne ressemble pas à l'aboutissement' (v, 387); 'La perspective de l'aventure intellectuelle est changeante' (P II, 1078). Because of the possibility it offers for the enrichment of intellectual processes in time, critics have

[1] Cf. R. Arnheim: 'The process of growth gives further evidence of the tendency to simplicity [. . .]. Step by step the maturing mind requires greater complexity, but the higher stage can be reached only by the lower ones [. . .] Wilful interference with the process creates disturbance' (*Art and Visual Perception* (Faber, 1956), 165).

[2] 'Duchesne-Guillemin on Valéry', *M.L.R.*, LXII (1967), 59.

[3] 'Goethe et Valéry', *Universitas* (Manitoba), IX (1967), 39–40.

[4] Valéry's 'anti biographical' and 'anti historical' attitude far from implies a simple dismissal of the circumstantial substance of life. 'Le poète est un être en deux personnages, l'une qui vit, l'autre qui crée: elles agissent l'une sur l'autre; mais pour concevoir cette action réciproque, il faut commencer par les bien distinguer' (Preface to C. Daubray's *Victor Hugo et ses Correspondants* (Paris, Albin Michel, 1947)).

sometimes themselves adopted the image of the growing plant to describe the development of Valéry's thought in time.[1]

The greater appropriateness of this image can be judged from a survey of the main landmarks of his intellectual development. As early as 1887, at the age of sixteen, he had written: 'Et je jouis sans fin de mon propre cerveau' (P I, 16). Henri Mondor's *Précocité de Valéry* affords many insights into the way the themes of early adolescence gradually merge into those of the future. He quotes, for example, Valéry's remark in the following year:

> A l'heure qu'il est j'ai dix-sept ans. Dans un coin du monde s'élève et grandit celle qui sera ma femme, ailleurs verdit l'arbre qui fournira le bois de mon cercueil, et, dans une région mystérieuse, s'élaborent mes idées futures.
>
> L'avenir sort lentement du présent [. . .]
>
> Tout est de ce qui sera. Rien ne se crée de toutes pièces et la pensée absurde qui m'occupe à cette minute appellera peut-être la pensée sublime que j'aurai demain.[2]

This strong sense of futurity – the 'vector' nature of experience – is only one of many intellectual invariants in Valéry's life. His early poetry is characterised, at least superficially, by the mystic, decadent vocabulary of late Symbolism. To read his correspondence with Gide is to gain a detailed view of the manner in which this style gradually sharpens and matures into the means of writing *La Soirée avec Monsieur Teste* in 1894. The famous 'crisis' of 1892 was itself the apotheosis of past intellectual experience. Already Valéry's career can be seen as a series of united branchings whose significance is beginning to be accentuated by conscious recognition of their rhythm of development: 'le Je 1884, le Je 1890, le Je 1903, le Je 1912 etc.' (xi, 348). It is this ability to exploit his own intellectual growth that not only makes the outward shape of the following years so dramatic, but which enlarges the scope and quality of his thought as a whole.

The years which used to be thought of as 'le Grand Silence'[3] – from 1892, with Valéry's rejection of 'littérature', to 1912, with his poetic rebirth – provide a striking example of this kind of maturation.[4] The *Cahiers* of that period reflect no abdication of his interest in poetry; they

[1] E.g. Bémol, *Paul Valéry*, 412.

[2] (Paris, Gallimard, 1957), 80.

[3] See M. Bémol: 'Autour du "grand silence" Valéryen', *R.H.L.F.*, LIX (1959), 218.

[4] Cf. Octave Nadal: 'Le véritable chef d'œuvre enfanté par les quatre ans de laborieuse gestation, c'est le POÈTE PAUL VALÉRY' (*Paul Valéry: La Jeune Parque; étude critique* (Le Club du Meilleur Livre, 1957), 62).

show frequent reflections on Poe, Mallarmé, Rimbaud, and so on: subjects that not only survive his attack on 'littérature', but are also preparing his own critical attitudes of the future. Meanwhile, the seeds of future compositions, fragments of 'poésie brute' and a gradual movement to what M. Bémol in his study of this period has called 'lateral' reflections[1] in the midst of ultra-personal research, show that there is 'silence' only from the point of view of actual publication. A distinct decision to prepare rather than to realise makes this period of attention to universal questions of psychology, language and mathematics a kind of conscious 'ritardando' of future composition and, more fundamentally, of emotional wealth.

It is not surprising that Valéry himself uses the terms 'printemps' and 'les premières fleurs de ma nouvelle saison' (P I, 1492) to describe his return to active concern with poetry in 1912. Just as the 'père ennemi' of the early verses looks at them through the rich intellectual acquisitions of the years in between, with *La Jeune Parque* growing from the process, so *Charmes* in turn spring from the specific poetic training of *La Jeune Parque*. In this sense the poems of the collection are the fruit of both intellectual and poetic maturity, the two adventures of poetry and analysis fusing more and more together in time. The previous chapter has suggested the way in which earlier poems grow into later ones and set up multiple points of contact. Valéry was interested in the possibility of taking up the same poetic theme every few years and thus making his poetry a kind of formal autobiography.[2] Although this involves a repetition of themes, the themes are more and more fully orchestrated, as we saw through the theme of Narcisse, to take just one example.

The next phase of Valéry's development shows what M. Bémol summarises as 'une alternance curieuse d'années pléthoriques et d'années profondes: 1902, 1916, 1921, 1924 représentent les maxima, 1894–1896, 1907–1910, 1919 les périodes de dépression'.[3] It is significant that from the point of view of notations in the *Cahiers* the intellectual harvest seems to grow with the production of poetry. Meanwhile Valéry's own insights into the earlier themes are clarified and deepened. There is maturation back into the resources of the past as well as the future, in particular to the significance of 1892.

[1] *Paul Valéry*, 301. The *Cahiers* of this period have been studied by M. Bémol in two articles: *Cahiers* tomes I–II in *R.H.L.F.*, LVIII (1958), 556–61 and *Cahiers* tomes III–X in *R.H.L.F.*, LX (1960), 245–59. See also the study by Edmée de La Rochefoucauld listed in the bibliography. Here the natural 'rhythm' of Valéry's themes has been respected.

[2] See M. Décaudin, 'Narcisse: "Une sorte d'autobiographie poétique"', *L'Information Littéraire* (mars–avril, 1956).

[3] *R.H.L.F.*, LX (1960), 251.

Oversimplified as this survey may be, the last phases of Valéry's intellectual life as reflected in the *Cahiers* might be seen to pursue the same kind of interplay: the clarification of certain main themes, the 'thèmes inébranlables' of his work, reviewed or constantly re-discovered with different emotions as time goes on. Furthermore it is now known that certain periods (1908 and from 1920 onwards)[1] were accompanied by an attempt at yet further detachment from the *Cahiers*, an attempt not only to order but also to assess critically the main themes that recurred within them.[2] 'Apprendre, non à penser, mais à *re-penser* "physiologiquement" c'est ce que je fais depuis des années' (xxvi, 880),[3] Valéry notes, or, in a published essay:

> [. . .] toute reprise consciente d'une idée la renouvelle; [. . .] et si même, dans ce retour, on ne trouve rien à changer dans ce que l'on avait une fois pensé, ce jugement qui approuve et conserve une certaine chose acquise, forme avec elle un fait qui ne s'était pas encore produit, un événement inédit.
>
> (P I, 1489)

Teste, 'l'être absorbé dans sa variation' (P II, 18), is equally consciously concerned with the natural repetition of thought: 'il veillait à la répétition de certaines idées' (P II, 17).

The very form of the *Cahiers*, fragmentary yet continuous, echoes this pattern of a consciousness progressively taking stock of itself and thus raising personal experience to the highest power of awareness, a work of art made with the rhythms of thought. This too is the time of some of the greatest essays and dialogues, the published works forming, I think, a kind of selective testing-point of some of Valéry's richest insights into the totality of experience (rather than a falling-off of more important aims as is sometimes imagined). The intellectual and affective themes of a lifetime finally culminate in *Mon Faust*, in which so many of those of the early writings can be traced intact.

Certainly then, as even a superficial summary has shown, Valéry puts into practice his recognition that 'la perspective de l'aventure intellectuelle est changeante' (P II, 1078). M. Bémol is right to suggest that 'La

1 See Judith Robinson, 'New Light on Valéry', *F.S.*, XXII (1968), 40–50.

2 See the list given by Judith Robinson, *Entretiens sur Paul Valéry*, 269.

3 Hence the importance of the rubric 'Re' in the *Cahiers* (e.g. xv, 134). 'Chez une sorte de sages, ces retours seraient peut-être prévus', Valéry once suggested (note from *Cahier* iv quoted by Edmée de La Rochefoucauld, *En Lisant les Cahiers de Paul Valéry*, I (Édns. Universitaires, 1964), 67).

persévérante aventure introspective n'est pas sans se modifier, sans "évoluer" en ce qui concerne ses thèmes et ses méthodes,'[1] although it might be more correct to say that the implications of Valéry's themes evolve rather than the themes themselves.

In what 'direction' does this evolution take place? It becomes clear that the regions of most relevance are his possibly changing attitude to the intellectual 'idols' of his adolescence, particularly Poe; his attitude to literature; and, finally, to the basic relationship between consciousness and life at the root of all these themes.

As for the first question, it is clear that Valéry moves further and further from discipleship of the rather crude and defensive notion of poetry – which the work of Poe suggested to him – of the induced replication in the reader of pre-conceived effects. W. N. Ince's study[2] shows a gradual movement from 'technique' to a fuller incorporation of 'inspiration' (in the sense of the openness of the artist's consciousness and eventually his judgement to more than one kind of material). Similarly, 'through the years Valéry modified his view of the inner meaning of *Eurêka*', writes Reino Virtanen:

> He now saw in it a demonstration of the inherent naïveté of all cosmologies, which only an artistic form can redeem. It became an exhibit for his analysis of the dangers and temptations of language, and of the forces and illusions, the grandeur and the servitude of consciousness. Poe was not the captain of his soul that Valéry had imagined during those early years when he was discovering Poe and Leonardo and creating Monsieur Teste.[3]

This concern is closely linked with the second question concerning the rôle of art in Valéry's life. A gradual intensification of the theme of the unknown and of the death of absolute objective knowledge is not accompanied in his work by intellectual disillusionment but by the gradual upsurge of aesthetic values. 'Faust a déjà tout lu, tout connu, déjà brûlé tout ce qui peut s'adorer', he writes in words which could very well apply to the direction of his own maturity: '[. . .] Il en arrive enfin à se donner, comme prétexte du désir de vivre, une sorte de passion esthétique, une soif suprême du Beau' (P I, 616). The point that emerges most

1 *R.H.L.F.*, LX (1960), 246–7.

2 *The Poetic Theory of Paul Valéry* (Leicester U.P., 1961).

3 'The Irradiations of "Eurêka": Valéry's Reflections on Poe's Cosmology', *Tennessee Studies in Literature*, VII (1962), 24.

strikingly about Valéry's relationship with art is not that these returns are the result of the relaxation of an intellectual ideal with time and age, but that they are part and parcel of the same intellectual ideal elaborated as a younger man, an ideal which contained seeds strong enough to develop in time by the natural logic of his own intellectual adventure. In the later classification and assessment of the *Cahiers*, examined by Judith Robinson, the more lyrical files labelled *Érôs* and *P.P.A.* ('Petits Poèmes Abstraits') take their place with others of a more analytical nature,[1] while in the war years from 1940–1945 Valéry's literary activity seems to have been at its most prolific, not only through *Mon Faust*, but also through his return to Mallarmé, whom he wished to make a symbolic hero[2] rather like his earlier hero: Leonardo da Vinci. To say that the intellectual 'avarice' of Teste is replaced in Valéry's maturity by the intellectual 'generosity' of Faust, seems in no way to suggest a betrayal of Valéry's early ideals. The difference is simply that Faust, like the mature Valéry, is 'un personnage dont le monologue irait de l'un à l'autre pôle du "temps"' (F III, xxix, 62).

The answer to the last question: Valéry's views on the relationship between consciousness and life should by now be clearly apparent. If it is true that, as T. S. Eliot writes in his essay on Poe and Valéry, intellectual maturity is to be defined not in terms of brain power but in terms of the development and co-ordination of emotions,[3] then Valéry's work reaches that intellectual maturity, as the following remarks on the theme of 're-vivre' should confirm in particular. Even between *La Jeune Parque* and *Le Cimetière Marin* the change can be seen to take place. At the same time as the anguish of *L'Ange*, written at the beginning of his development, is still deeply relevant at the end of his life – and indeed, Valéry returned to it then – *Mon Faust* and the works that lead up to it show a movement to perhaps a greater power of irony (Valéry turned more and more to Voltaire in his old age),[4] a greater humour, a greater resonance of emotion and a greater attention to the theme of 'Autrui' as a necessary extension to the theme of individual consciousness. Valéry's work gives a feeling of both incompleteness and plenitude. Certain genres and certain responses do not seem to have been excluded so much as postponed in a deliberate attempt to exhaust each possible attitude before proceeding to the next, almost as if he wished to reach his own 'antipodes', to become

1 Robinson, *F.S.*, XXII (1968), 42.
2 Ibid., 48.
3 'From Poe to Valéry', *The Hudson Review*, II (1949), 334.
4 E.g. the 'Discours' given in 1944 at the Sorbonne (P I, 1710).

'l'anti-Valéry' in the manner of 'l'Anti-Socrate' (P II, 142). '[. . .] depuis 50 ans je *tombe* vers le moi-même, mon *poids* vers mon plus haut' (XXVII, 417), he notes, using the striking theme of intellectual 'anti-gravity'.

The theme of an intellectual antipodes is a conscious one with Valéry. He writes for example:

> Mais l'univers de l'esprit peut-être a sa courbure, de laquelle, si elle est, nous ne pouvons rien savoir, nous ne savons rien. J'ai observé, en d'autres choses mentales, que si nous pouvons quelquefois parvenir à nos antipodes, nous ne pouvons guère ensuite qu'en revenir. Ce n'est plus qu'une 'affaire de temps', car tout nouveau changement ne peut que nous rapprocher de l'origine. Je suis disposé à croire qu'un homme qui vivrait fort longtemps, aurait, vers le terme de son périple, à la condition que sa pensée lui fût demeurée assez active, fait le tour de ses sentiments, et qu'ayant à la fin adoré et brûlé, brûlé et adoré tout ce qui méritait de l'être dans la sphère de sa connaissance, il pourrait mourir achevé.
>
> (P I, 1488–9)

This theme, quite a frequent one in Valéry's notes, is basic enough to his thought to appear in Faust, who is in a sense its embodiment:

> C'est qu'il est de mon destin de faire le tour complet des opinions possibles sur tous les points, de connaître successivement tous les goûts et tous les dégoûts, et de faire et de défaire et de refaire tous ces nœuds que sont les événements d'une vie . . . Je n'ai plus d'âge . . . Et cette vie ne sera achevée que je n'aie finalement brûlé tout ce que j'ai adoré, et adoré tout ce que j'ai brûlé.
>
> (P II, 288)

In the passage from *Fragments des Mémoires d'un Poème* quoted above, Valéry concluded: 'que nous ne voyons en général, et que nous ne sommes nous-mêmes, que des fragments d'existence, et que notre vie vécue ne remplit pas toute la capacité symétrique de ce qui nous est possible de sentir et de concevoir' (P I, 1489). At the end of his own life (in one of the very last entries in his notebooks in 1945), he expresses the same paradoxical conflict between a sense of physical finality allowed to permeate the intellect itself, and the still potentially infinite desire to grapple with the feeling of limitation and finality:

J'ai la sensation que ma vie est achevée, c'est-à-dire que je ne vois rien à present qui demande un lendemain. Ce qui me reste à vivre ne peut plus désormais être que du temps à perdre. Après tout j'ai fait ce que j'ai pu. Je connais 1. assez mon esprit [. . .] 2. Je connais *my heart* aussi. *Il triomphe. Plus fort que tout*, que mon esprit, que l'organisme – Voilà le fait. Le plus obscur des faits. Plus fort que le vouloir vivre et que le pouvoir comprendre est donc ce sacré c[œur]. – 'Cœur', c'est mal nommé. Je voudrais au moins trouver le vrai nom de ce sacré résonateur [. . .]

(xxix, 908–9)

I have already suggested that this feeling – born from Valéry's constant sense of an impersonal power of awareness which can observe even a multiplicity of selves – paradoxically grows in power as the circle of actual possibilities is diminished in time. The feeling of total freedom it produces does not lead to a vacuous game with less and less contact with personality, however. One of the paradoxes of Valéry's maturity is to have expressed the *possibility* that consciousness might grow in emotional depth as it grows in intensity. By pushing the intellect, so to speak, to the point at which it breaks into emotions of its own, he comes very close to fulfilling through the logic of his work as a whole his own comment: '[. . .] pour moi, on ne tue que pour et par création. Et d'ailleurs l'instinct déstructif n'est que comme indication de quelque naissance de construction qui veut sa place et son heure' (xxii, 203). In this way, consciousness is not only 'a series of cyclical returns'[1], despite the fact that the mind itself is for Valéry a system of closed architecture. It is also a voyage which, in T. S. Eliot's phrase, 'has altered the starting place'.[2] To be alive to the full means for Valéry not simply to observe the passing of time, but to *feel* its passing in terms of the growth and resolution of emotional experience. He never ceases to suggest that this is a *potential* of human life, despite the anguish and detachment which seems the more constant note in his experience.

'*Re-vivre*'

'Il n'y a qu'une chose à faire: se refaire. Ce n'est pas simple' (viii, 182), Valéry wrote under the heading 'Gladiator'. The aim of this conscious re-distribution of natural energies can be found to involve nothing less than a fusion of consciousness, intellect and emotion into a simple harmony

1 J. M. Cocking, *M.L.R.*, LXII (1967), 59.
2 'Leçon de Valéry', *Paul Valéry Vivant* (Cahiers du Sud, 1946), 80.

of spontaneous life, the equivalent of Valéry's ideal in poetic composition. Many instances could be chosen to illustrate this theme. 'Se refaire un spontané' (xi, 590), for example; 'Il faut finir par l'improvisation' (xxii, 312); 'le travail des plus forts esprits est de rechercher leur humilité, [...] transformer leurs éclairs en actes simples' (i, 334); or, 'Il faut toute une vie, et longue assez, pour arriver à devenir sensibles à certaines vérités trop simples qui sont comme fondues dans l'usage de nos sens' (xxiii, 439).

'Le mysticisme consiste peut-être à retrouver une sensation élémentaire, et en quelque sorte, primitive, la *sensation de vivre*, par une voie incertaine, qui se fait et se fraye à travers la vie déjà faite et comme *arrivée*' (P II, 1306), Valéry speculates, and in his notes: 'Le *but* est toujours de *sentir* quelque chose (déjà *pressentie*)' (iv, 34). In this way, an ideal of *positive* circularity is introduced, a return to the values of simplicity and absorption associated with childhood. Not a simple reversion, however, for to envy the innocence and simplicity of the animal is seen as a funereal capacity.[1] What is really at stake is a reinstatement of certain qualities of immediate existence in the fully conscious and mature mind. In this way Valéry's work rejoins the highest level of ethical thinking. 'Voilà mon œuvre: vivre. N'est-ce-pas tout?', Faust asks as the embodiment of this maturity, 'Mais il faut le savoir...' (P II, 322); 'VOIR suffit, et savoir que l'on voit...' (P II, 322).

The theme of intellectual rejuvenation in maturity – what Valéry calls an 'effet de retour vers les origines' (xxvi, 911) – has already been seen as part of the love theme, of which he writes: 'L'Amour, parfois, fait repasser l'homme par des états d'enfance' (ix, 473). Many of his descriptions of tenderness are couched in these terms. In the notes to the unfinished act of *Mon Faust*, he writes: 'Tendresse, moment où le Moi se dépouille de tout ce qui le revêtait, le déguisait, le distinguait du tout petit enfant qui est en chacun de nous, essentiel et caché, le germe ou le sentiment tout pur de vivre' (P II, 1412; xxiv, 824). Tenderness reveals 'enfance cachée' (vii, 748), the rejuvenation of the mature self.

The same theme of re-birth is connected with memory, an experience 'plus jeune que la vie'.[2] 'Si ce phénomène arrivait à l'être tout entier il rajeunirait', Valéry writes about the noise of a hammer which brought

[1] See Valéry's preface 'Notes sur un Tragique et une Tragédie' to Lucien Fabre's *Dieu est Innocent* (Nagel, 1946), vii–xvi.

[2] Quoted by Edmée de La Rochefoucauld, *En Lisant les Cahiers de Paul Valéry*, I, 99.

back a fair in his childhood in Sète forty years before: 'Il aurait à chaque instant l'âge de la première fois qu'il a perçu la sensation actuelle' (vii, 569). There is no need to dwell on similarities with Proust's idea of memory as the releasing of the mind from rational logic to the new reality of sensation. 'Peut-être y a-t-il en nous une mémoire périodique et lente, plus profonde que la mémoire des impressions et des objets', Valéry reflects of this fundamental experience, 'une mémoire ou une résonance de nous-mêmes à longue échéance, qui nous rapporte, et vient nous rendre à l'improviste nos tendances, nos puissances, et même nos espoirs très anciens?' (P I, 1491–2) and: 'Ceci est merveilleux, car c'est employer le présent à forcer la reconstruction du passé. [. . .] Autant je puis être, autant j'ai été' (v, 284). In a letter to Gide in 1894 he writes of this sensation of indivisibility:

> Étrange base: dans tous les moments de trouble, quand l'onde générale de la vie revient à ce point géométrique qu'enfant j'ai voulu être, les images de mon esprit sont une mer toujours [. . .]. Je confonds alors mon existence avec tout ce pays du large, et je me sens dissoudre. Ce qu'on appelle le sentiment, c'est cela pour moi . . . et je suis, à travers l'abstrait même d'édifications ou d'analyses, l'influence et la déformation de ce rêve. Et c'est là pourtant que, dans leurs instants d'exaltation et de possession en moi, les formes d'amitié ou d'amour se baignent aussi, finissent de se baigner aussi.[1]

An idea or discovery can also bring a sensation of newness, 'la déclaration subite du "nouvel homme"' (P I, 815), and so can surprise. Obviously in connection with the symbolic fall undergone by Faust in *Le Solitaire*, Valéry writes under the rubric 'F. III': 'Ce coup de tête a aboli 50 ans d'univers – quelle merveille! Je nais. Tout m'apparaît tout autre, tout neuf' (xxvii, 73). Likewise the sensation can come through art, which Valéry often seemed to consider a response to the need to re-live at leisure, and with full conscious appreciation, a moment of 'newness' or surprise, thus incorporating an otherwise fleeting quality into the habitual stream of daily life. One of the finest affirmations of Valéry's Faust is, however, that this rejuvenation can be brought about not only by enforced surprise, by memory, or through art, but through consciousness itself. 'J'ai été jeune, Lust. J'ai été vieux. Et puis, j'ai été jeune encore' (P II, 320), says Faust. Part of this experience is through his love and tenderness for Lust, but the experience of love only accentuated for Valéry the most extreme

[1] *A. Gide–P. Valéry, Correspondance*, 199–200.

relationship of consciousness with the self. Lust is the rejuvenating power of Faust's own mind,[1] the power of individual consciousness to turn outwards by virtue of its own relational capacity.

The ideal of achieving the power of improvisation and spontaneity in life through conscious preparatory effort comes very close to Valéry's definition of 'inspiration' sketched out in the previous chapter. There too, he recognised the possibility that a discipline might 'take over' and allow the synthesis of disparate acts.

'[. . .] car je croyais que l'effort seul nous transforme et nous change notre facilité première qui suit de l'occasion, et s'épuise avec elle', he writes, in words that could apply as much to the kind of immediate general experience in question as to the act of composition, 'en une facilité dernière qui la sait créer et la domine', and he goes on: 'Ainsi, des gestes ravissants de la petite enfance aux actes purs et gracieusement précis de l'athlète ou de la danseuse, le corps vivant s'élève dans la possession de soi-même par la conscience, l'analyse et l'exercice' (P I, 1465), or, expanding the two kinds of facility further: 'L'autre facilité est le sentiment d'une liberté et d'une simplicité conquises, qui permettent le plus grand jeu de l'esprit entre les sens et les idées. Il en résulte *la merveille d'une improvisation de degré supérieur*' (P II, 1316).

It is in this sense, of course, that Faust's life is his own intellectual masterpiece: life itself as the apotheosis of the intellect. 'Serais-je au comble de mon art? Je vis. Et je ne fais que vivre. Voilà une œuvre' (P II, 321), he says, and 'Il fallut tant d'espoirs et de désespoirs, de triomphes et de désastres pour en venir là . . . Mais j'y suis' (P II, 321); 'Si la connaissance est ce qu'il faut produire par l'esprit pour que SOIT ce qui EST, te voici, FAUST, connaissance pleine et pure, plénitude, accomplissement. Je suis celui que je suis. Je suis au comble de mon art, à la periode classique de l'art de vivre. Voilà mon œuvre: vivre' (P II, 321–2). 'Revivre rend admirable ce qui fut vécu. Revivre est œuvre d'art', Valéry writes in the *Cahiers*, 'Revivre compose, enveloppe, masse, fait le ton' (IX, 916). 'Les opinions des personnes qui n'ont pas refait leur esprit selon les besoins réels et leurs pouvoirs vérifiables – n'ont aucune importance qualitative' (P II, 498). Immediate sensations of power and peace are the fruit of the intellectual and aesthetic experience of a lifetime. Undistorted by thought of past and future or even by the violent urge: 'Verweile doch!' with which Goethe's Faust ('L'impatience même' (P I, 535)) begs the instant to remain, Valéry's Faust – the Faust of *Lust*, unlike his equally important counterpart in *Le Solitaire* – achieves the

[1] See M. Blanchot, *La Part du Feu* (Paris, Gallimard, 1949), 283.

perfect integration of himself with the present.[1] Just such a moment is expressed in *Le Cimetière Marin*: 'Et l'amertume est douce, et l'esprit clair' (P I, 149). 'The perfect man in Valéry's eyes', writes W. N. Ince, 'is he who can eventually in any medium, enjoy exploiting the supremely conscious method he has caused himself to become.'[2]

The perfect coincidence of the whole mind with the present instant is not an affirmation made by Valéry only *in extremis*. Given its most explicit expression in Faust, it is there as far back as *La Jeune Parque*. Once naïvely 'l'égale et l'épouse du jour' (P I, 99), the young woman becomes so again after the sting of the serpent in the full light of consciousness at the end of the poem: 'toujours celle que tu respires' (P I, 110). The affirmation is there too, in the experience of the speaker in *Le Cimetière Marin* at the height of his intellectual power: 'Temple du Temps, qu'un seul soupir résume' (P I, 148). 'Comment l'instantané contient-il plus que l'instant?' (xxvii, 21), Valéry wrote. In *Eupalinos ou l'Architecte* Phèdre reports having challenged the artist with the question: 'O malheureux, que veux-tu faire pendant un éclair?', to which Eupalinos replied: 'Être libre. Il y a bien choses [. . .] il y a . . . toutes choses dans cet instant; et tout ce dont s'occupent les philosophes se passe entre le regard qui tombe sur un objet, et la connaissance qui en résulte . . . pour finir toujours prématurément' (P II, 97).[3] This theme, already seen outlined in *Inspirations Meditérranéennes*, is constant throughout Valéry's work.

All these aspects of 're-vivre' are in a sense the fruit of the maturation theme; they are the result of that paradox of simultaneous expenditure and increasing gain which can be regarded as one of the most consistent of Valéry's observations, as this examination of his theory and practice has attempted to show. The paradox is expressed in its most sustained form in the poem *Palme* to which this study has turned many times before and in which it naturally culminates:

> Tu n'as pas perdu ces heures
> Si légère tu demeures
> Après ces beaux abandons;

1 Faust's triumphant 'VIVRE! . . . JE RESPIRE!' (P II, 322) can be compared with the blunt Cartesian epigram in the *Cahiers* 'Il vit, – donc il respire,/Il respire,/donc il vit' (xxiv, 847).

2 *F.M.L.S.*, II (1966), 185.

3 Valéry refers to metaphysics as 'l'art de parler trop tôt' (viii, 897). La Jeune Parque refers to the tense point of her experience as '[. . .] mon extrémité pure et prématurée' (P I, 109).

Pareille à celui qui pense
Et dont l'âme se dépense
À s'accroître de ses dons!

(P I, 156)

As is so often the case in Valéry's poems, the words here, while simple in the immediate context, nonetheless open into complex associations and relate back to other parts of his thought. The word 'légère', for instance, is closely related to the notion of intellectual lightness or freedom due to an economy of forces through co-ordination, a notion on which Valéry centres his idea of training the mind.[1] The symbolic patterns of *Palme* are far-reaching enough to embrace that ideal relationship between consciousness and nature which Valéry referred to as 'Gladiator' or 'Pouvoirs', and of which he writes characteristically, 'Séparation sensible ou Pureté des constituants, au sein des combinaisons. Comme l'algèbre, l'orchestre – et rarement, le discours. Refaire un procédé *naturel* en le traitant ainsi et lui substituer le produit de synthèse – tel fut mon travail – analyse et reconstitution en pur, des actes et donc des produits d'actes. Ce qu'on appelle *entraînement*, *éducation*, n'est que cela' (vii, 693).

[1] See Robinson, *F.S.*, XVIII (1964), 234. Valéry talks of the same 'légèreté' in connection with the composition of *Aurore* and *Palme* after the training provided by *La Jeune Parque* (P I, 1613).

Conclusion

Valéry was deeply concerned throughout his life with the possibilities and limitations of man as a finite living organism. 'A quoi peut tendre l'Homme?', he writes in 1940, picking up the similar question of Monsieur Teste – 'Que peut un homme?' (P II, 25) – of 1895, and he goes on to distinguish between '1. Homme – *Individu.* L'inégal, le différent et l'Unique par excellence' and '2. Homme, *l'espèce* (à la fois ignorée et façonnée par Nature)' (xxiii, 112). If any explicit 'answer' to the question emerges it would seem to concern the development of what Valéry calls 'La différence Homo-Animal' (xxiii, 112), the development of man's power to become aware of his 'double' position in nature and thus to make allowance for his sometimes conflicting desires and capacities. '[...] s'il y a un *dieu* [...] [il] ne pouvait exiger que le développement de ce qui nous semble à nous l'indication de l'accroissement de *notre différence avec l'animal*', Valéry reports having remarked to Stravinsky, and he continues in his notes:

> si ce dieu a quelque rapport avec la propriété des individus, type Homo, de 'connaître-sentir-faire' de manière qu'il puisse exister quelque échange ou quelque chance de relation directe (dans une pensée, et son énergie, d'individu) entre ce dieu et un moi – alors il doit suffire que ce *moi* se développe de son maximum de *conscience* et de *singularité* – *l'une corrigeant l'autre* – etc.
>
> (xvii, 6–7)

The balance of the 'universal' and the 'personal', of the automatic needs of the organism and the evaluative, directive power of consciousness to which it intermittently gives rise: this to Valéry is a human possibility still insufficiently explored, 'une gymnastique encore inconnue' (ii, 278), and one which his own writings undoubtedly do much to embody and explore.

An integral part of Valéry's approach to the question of human possibility are the comparisons he makes between principles of intellectual creativity and types of organisational activity which appear to be at work in the rest of the natural world.[1] A deep interest in morphogenesis and intuitive natural philosophy provides the ever-present framework for his observations on the human mind as a natural, though possibly unique transformational capacity, 'puissance de transformation étrangère aux choses qu'elle transforme'.[2] One of the most satisfying and flexible forms of language with which to approach the subject was suggested by statistical thermodynamics with its attempt to bring notions of chance and probability into a description of the complex patterns of the physical world. 'Le thème fondamental du vivant est la chute d'énergie puisée autour de lui' (xiii, 732), Valéry writes, for example, transferring to biological processes one of the thermodynamic principles which runs through his notes like a poetic 'motif'. It is this vital energy drop – or increase of entropy – in its environment which he sees as providing the 'disorder' necessary to the organisation of life: 'désordre que la vie partiellement rachète [. . .]' (xviii, 90), and from the new disorder introduced by life itself, he imagines the human mind as continuing to an even higher degree of organisation its own process of anti-entropic differentiation: 'Mais l'esprit se déclare en elle, s'en dégage et lui oppose son désir de promptitude, de puissance directe; il essaye de résumer le monde et de refaire de la vie' (xxii, 701). Refusing to *define* life and mind in terms of the forces of organisation and disorganisation which characterise the energy of a machine, Valéry draws on the concepts of statistical thermodynamics as a rich source of analogy. Accordingly the mind can be envisaged with the minimum of arbitrary assumption in terms of the same movement from disorder to order by which the living organism can be observed temporarily to withstand the increasing disorganisation of the physical world.

Although the human mind for Valéry carries on to an even more complex degree the transformational capacity by which the living organism differentiates itself from the non-living world, such a transformational capacity is unique for him in that it involves the power to relate, evaluate, predict and abridge in an order independent of immediate circumstance. Unlike the organism itself, confined to a purely 'circular' relationship with its environment, the mind introduces into the rest of nature the

[1] This subject has been treated at length in my monograph 'Paul Valéry and Maxwell's demon: natural order and human possibility', *Occasional Papers in Modern Languages* no 8, University of Hull, 1972.

[2] Quoted by N. Suckling, *Entretiens sur Paul Valéry*, 317.

experience of choice, and with it the power of human possibility: 'Puissance du Possible [...] c'est un *daimôn d'action* [...] Actio Præsentiae [. . .] On s'éveille [. . .] et parmi les *souvenirs* qui recomposent le Moi-personne la "puissance de l'esprit" – l'*opérateur supérieur* [. . .] cette *présence-puissance*, entrée en jeu, *fait* son travail' (xix, 916–18).

In the course of this study I have tried to show how Valéry devoted most of his life to the description of this 'opérateur supérieur' – individual consciousness – as a natural function of the human organism, its complex operation no different in kind from the 'unconscious' processes which seem to determine the behaviour of the organism at every 'level' of the physical and biological world. Yet no 'demon' of evaluative awareness is complete for Valéry until it is brought to bear on its own power, exercised incessantly in the light of the highest form of self-awareness: 'C'est celui en nous qui choisit, et c'est celui qui met en œuvre, qu'il faut exercer sans repos' (P I, 1208). It is at this point that the principles of intellectual creativity under discussion – 'Poiétique et Possible' (xix, 849) – can be seen to be embodied as well as described in Valéry's work. One of the best opportunities for the exercise of the 'demon' of human possibility was undoubtedly poetic composition, which Valéry saw as a means of extending in time the quality of a rare capacity: a 'probabilistic' enterprise[1] with the literal power of making man more alive by making his limited store of natural energies more effectively available.[2] But it was not only poetic composition which seemed to Valéry to bring about the collaboration through awareness of different mental exigencies. The experience of looking at the world in a new way; the experience of love and the experience of the growth and development of one's own mind: all these have been put forward here as examples of areas in which Valéry considered it possible for awareness to accentuate the yield of 'le monde de la *connexion propre et libre* des ressources virtuelles de l'esprit' (P I, 395).

Particularly in the latter part of his life, Valéry turned his attention to the kind of '*dynamique des échanges*' (xxiii, 427) or extension of human possibility in which more than one member is involved: 'les échanges à

1 Valéry was deeply influenced by the work of Gibbs in statistical mechanics. Where for Gibbs total disorder was the most probable state of a system, order was the least probable. Valéry transfers the same notion to the description of the organisation of life: '[. . .] et c'est peut-être là la définition de *l'organisation* – de *l'anti-désordre* (qui est *l'improbable*) [. . .]' (xviii, 127). The passage of the mind from disorder to order is seen accordingly as a probabilistic or anti-entropic activity, Teste, in whom the process is taken further, being a conscious probabilist increasing his chances of intellectual gain.

2 'Le monde [. . .] ne nous apporte pas de l'énergie par voie nerveuse [. . .] il se borne à mettre notre énergie à notre disposition' (iv, 23).

plus de deux membres' (xxiii, 664). He became more and more interested in the extension of individual capacity through contact not only with its own creations but with the joint creations of education, art, philosophy of science, law[1] and so on: in fact with all those systems of social exchange with *language* as their base. Not that this development is in any way contradictory to Valéry's life-long interest in individual consciousness. He considered the preservation of the diversity and critical awareness of individual consciousness in the diffusion of cultural and economic values to be one of the most challenging problems of modern man. Valéry is sometimes accused of offering no 'solutions' to the problems he raises, to social and political problems as much as others. Here again, however, his main contribution is one of 'method': in the first place a method of discerning the nature of the problems by strict attention to the 'conditions d'existence' (xxiii, 553) of the notions used to describe them; in the second place, a method of confirming through detailed observation of his own inner experience the vital rôle of awareness in human behaviour as perhaps the only means of making allowance for the needs of the mind as a system that is both finite and fallible: 'La fin de l'homme pensant me parut être de s'essayer à prendre conscience de son organisation, de ce qu'elle peut et peut produire [. . .]' (xxvi, 389).

Far from confining himself to an abstract description of the limits and possibilities of consciousness, Valéry attempted to express its repercussions throughout the whole human sensibility; to give expression to the *sensation* of solitary self-awareness and its rôle in the intricate dynamics of human behaviour. It is to the quality of this expression – Valéry's capacity to suggest how a single thread of awareness may unite the most divergent experiences, ranging from a sense of anguished separation and dissonance to deep harmonious involvement in life – that this study has constantly pointed as one of his most rewarding achievements. Not only the polished language of *Charmes*, but also the rapid and at times violent language of the prose-poems and fragmentary analysis of the *Cahiers* affirm the paradox that it is through the tension and diversity of human intelligence, its power to preserve in 'orderly' form the quality of uniquely human *disorder* as well as order, that intellectual possibility may best be preserved and man survive as a natural species in the world. 'L'esprit va, dans son travail, de *son* désordre, à *son* ordre', Valéry writes explicitly,

1 See Robinson, *F.S.*, XXII (1968), 48–9 and Claude Valéry, 'Le Droit, sa Notion et son Langage, d'après Paul Valéry', *Entretiens sur Paul Valéry*, 361–8. Cf. P. Roulin, *Paul Valéry, Témoin et Juge du Monde Moderne*, Neuchâtel, La Baconnière, 1964.

'Il importe qu'il se conserve jusqu'à la fin, des ressources de *désordre*, et que l'ordre qu'il a commencé de se donner ne se lie pas si complètement, ne lui soit pas un si rigide maître, qu'il ne puisse le changer et user de sa liberté initiale' (P II, 714).

I hope to have shown that thermodynamic analogies such as the one implicit in the above conception of natural order and disorder[1] are used by Valéry – as are the dependent analogies between organic and intellectual processes which have formed the basis of this study – not only for the immediate insights they provide, but as the springboard for a further *prise de conscience* concerning the nature of analogy itself and the type of joining or ordering activity to which the mind itself appears to be limited: 'type de l'acte ordre [. . .] acte qui joint' (xix, 906). It is in his unwillingness to accept in any definitive sense the idea that the ordering process of a single species can have access to principles other than those governing its own relationship to the universe that, when taken as a whole, Valéry's view of the relationship between consciousness and nature might be said to differ most from that of the religious mystic. For Valéry, man's experience suggests that he evolves in an unpredictable direction, his goals altered retroactively by his own involvement in each successive step, and his view of the universe limited to a certain 'type' of perception, despite his own equally human awareness that this may be so. Indeed it is only in the critical flexibility of 'openmindedness' of this awareness of limitation that man for Valéry remains man in the individual sense. 'Notre dieu est à l'esprit ce que celui-ci est à la vie [. . .]' says the speaker in one of his 'divine' dialogues: 'Il est donc, dans notre opinion, tout simplement ce qu'indique notre esprit – et qui se situe à *l'infini* de cette direction. Je dis "à l'infini" et je veux dire que l'esprit s'écarte de, remarque son écart et y voit son acte, qu'il détache et développe de cette observation' (xxii, 701).[2]

I have tried to show that, far from implying empty detachment, this form of highly developed awareness is considered by Valéry to be one of the most forceful of man's creative tensions, driving him ceaselessly to compensate for what is called in the Teste Cycle the 'anisotropic' nature

[1] Valéry often uses the word 'inégalité' to imply the state of non-equilibrium without which a machine cannot function, and 'égalité' to mean a state of perfect disorder or equilibrium (e.g. P I, 991).

[2] It is in this sense that the progressive complexification of consciousness differs from the form of cosmic evolution of man postulated by Teilhard de Chardin. '[. . .] au lieu du Dieu *à l'infini* vers lequel il faudrait tendre', Valéry writes describing one of their conversations, 'je pose le zéro d'existence consciente duquel il faudrait s'écarter [. . .]' (xvi, 3).

of consciousness itself. In the light of the highest form of awareness, the mind is free to pursue '[. . .] un état du monde où le temps était une fatalité de changement *positif*, un fleuve qui apportait constamment de la différence, de l'ordre, des formes, des variétés et des valeurs' (xxiii, 438): temporal order for which there appears to be no model in the natural world other than that created by intelligence itself in its most dissonant yet *temps extraordinaire*' (P II, 261) – and to the possibility of modifying co-ordinated form. It is the experience of this human order and the possibility of modifying human existence in the light of understanding the conditions necessary to its creation, that Valéry's writings seem most deeply to explore. Such at least, is one of the most tantalising fruits of his rich expression of the rôle of consciousness in life.

Bibliography

WORKS BY VALÉRY

Paul Valéry: Cahiers, vols. i-xxix (Paris, C.N.R.S., 1957–1961).
Paul Valéry: Œuvres, vols. I, II, ed. J. Hytier, coll. Pléiade (Paris, Gallimard, 1957, 1960).

Collections and articles:

'Abatage d'un arbre' (translation of T. Hardy's poem: 'Felling a Tree') (*Commerce*, XIV, hiver 1927), 5–9.
ABC (*Commerce*, V, automne 1925).
'Allocution et Discours' for M. de Rothschild's conference on *Le Cinéma* (*Les Techniques au service de la pensée* (Paris, Alcan, 1938)).
André Gide–Paul Valéry, Correspondance 1890–1942, ed. R. Mallet (Paris, Gallimard, 1953).
'Baudelaire dessinateur' (*Le Manuscrit autographe*, Lib. Auguste Blaizot, 1927), I.
'Les Bois d'André Bélobodoroff' in *Le Golfe de Salerne* (Coll. dell'Obelisco, Rome, Bestetti, 1952).
Conferencia (*Journal de l'Université des Annales*, 22 nov. 1933).
Cours de Poétique (*Yggdrasill*, IX–XXXIV, 25 déc. 1937–25 fév. 1939) (notes taken by Georges Le Breton during part of Valéry's lectures at the Collège de France from 1937 to 1945).
'Gabriela Mistral' (*La Revue de Paris*, fév. 1946), 3–7.
'Hommage à René Ghil' in *Rythme et Synthèse*, special no., 1926 (quoted by L. J. Austin and H. Mondor in *Mallarmé: Correspondance, 1862–1871*, II (Paris, Gallimard, 1965), 285, n. 2).
Lettres à Quelques-Uns, 1889–1943 (Paris, Gallimard, 1952).
Maîtres et Amis (Beltrand, 1927).
Morceaux Choisis, Prose et Poésie (Paris, Gallimard, 1930 (1930)).
'Notes sur un tragique et une tragédie' in L. Fabre's *Dieu est innocent* (Nagel, 1946), vii–xvi.
'Notules sur Léon-Paul Fargue' (in 'Hommage à Léon-Paul Fargue', *Les Feuilles Libres*, juin 1927).

Paul Valéry: Pré-Teste (Bibliothèque Littéraire J. Doucet, ed. F. Chapon, 3–23 dec. 1966).
Petits Poèmes Abstraits (*Revue de France*, 1 jan. 1932), 47–52.
Petit Recueil de Paroles de Circonstance (Paris, Coll. Plaisir de Bibliophile, 1926).
Petits Textes – Commentaires de Gravures (*La Nouvelle Revue Française*, no. 172, 1 jan. 1928), 55–65.
'Poésie Perdue' (*Cahiers du Sud*, oct.–déc. 1966), 390–1.
'Réflexions sur la Lithographie Originale' (see *Paul Valéry: Écrits sur l'Art* (Paris, Club des Librairies de France, 1962), 242).
Réponses (Au Pigeonnier, 1928).
'Les Sciences de l'esprit sont-elles différentes des Sciences de la Nature?' (Valéry's reply to the question posed by Abel Rey (*La Revue de Synthèse*, oct. 1931), 9–11).
Souvenirs Poétiques (Paris, Guy le Prat, 1947).
Vues (coll. 'Le Choix', IX, Paris, La Table Ronde, 1948).

Prefaces (to the following works):

Asturias, M. A., *Légendes du Guatemala*, translated by F. de Miomandre (Marseille, Les Cahiers du Sud, 1932).
Bonet, P., *Le Physique du Livre* (Lib. Auguste Blaizot, 1945).
Courtois-Suffit, M., *Le Promeneur Sympathique* (Paris, Plon, 1925).
Daubray, Cécile, *Victor Hugo et ses Correspondants* (Paris, Albin Michel, 1947).
Ghyka, M. C., *Le Nombre d'Or*, I (Paris, Édns. N.R.F., 1952) (1931) .
Kaldor, L., *Cinquante Ans de Typographie* (Kaldor, 1935).
Mécs, L., *Poèmes* (Horizons de France, 1944).
Morisot, Berthe, *Seize Aquarelles* (Édns. des Quatre Chemins, 1946).

CRITICAL WORKS ON VALÉRY

Austin, L. J., 'Genèse du Poème' in '*Le Cimetière Marin*', vol. I (préface Henri Mondor) (Grenoble, Roissard, 1954).
——, 'La Genèse du "Cimetière Marin"', *C.A.I.E.F.*, III–V (1953), 235–69.
——, 'The Genius of Paul Valéry', *Wingspread Lectures in the Humanities* (Wisconsin, Johnson Foundation, 1966), 39–55.
——, 'Modulation and movement in Valéry's verse', *Yale French Studies*, 44 (1970), 19–38.
——, 'The Negative Plane Tree', *L'Esprit Créateur*, IV (1964), 3–10.
——, 'Paul Valéry: "Teste" ou "Faust"?', *C.A.I.E.F.*, XVII (1965), 245–56.
Bastet, N., 'Faust et le Cycle', *Entretiens sur Paul Valéry*, 115–28.
——, *La Symbolique des Images dans l'Œuvre Poétique de Valéry* (Aix-en-Provence, Publication des Annales de la Faculté des Lettres, XXIV, 1962).
Bémol, M., 'Autour du "grand silence" Valéryen', *R.H.L.F.*, LIX (1959), 213–18.
——, 'Compte-rendu des Cahiers tomes i–ii', *R.H.L.F.*, LVIII (1958), 556–61.
——, 'Compte-rendu des Cahiers tomes iii–x', *R.H.L.F.*, LX (1960), 245–59.
——, 'La méthode dans les sciences selon Paul Valéry', *Biologica* (jan. 1951).
——, *Paul Valéry* (Paris, Société d'Édition 'Les Belles Lettres', 1949).
——, *Variations sur Valéry, I* (Sarrebruck, Publications de l'Université de la Sarre, 1952).
Bisson, L. A., 'A study in le faire Valéryen', *F.S.*, X (1956), 309–21.
——, 'Valéry and Virgil', *M.L.R.*, LIII (1958), 501–11.

Blanchot, M., *La Part de Feu* (Paris, Gallimard, 1949).
Cain, Lucienne J., *Trois Essais sur Paul Valéry* (Paris, Gallimard, 1958).
Chardon, P., *Paul Valéry et la Médecine* (Paris, Armand Fleury, 1930).
Chisholm, A. R., *An Approach to 'La Jeune Parque'* (Melbourne U.P., 1938).
——, '"La Pythie" and its place in Valéry's work', *M.L.R.*, LVIII (1963), 21–8.
——, 'Valéry's "Ébauche d'un Serpent"', *AUMLA*, XV (1961), 19–29.
Cocking, J. M., 'Duchesne-Guillemin on Valéry', *M.L.R.*, LXII (1967), 55–60.
——, 'Towards *Ébauche d'un Serpent*: Valéry and Ouroboros', *A.J.F.S.*, VI (1969), 187–215.
Crow, Christine M., 'Paul Valéry and Maxwell's demon: natural order and human possibility.' *Occasional papers in Modern Languages* no. 8, University of Hull, 1972.
——, '"Teste parle": a study of the potential artist in Valéry's M. Teste', *Yale French Studies*, 44 (1970), 157–68.
——, 'Valéry, poet of "patiente impatience"', *F.M.L.S.*, III (1967), 370–87.
Daniel, Vera J., *Paul Valéry: Eupalinos and L'Âme et la Danse* (O.U.P., 1967).
——, 'Valéry's "Eupalinos" and his early reading', *F.S.*, XXI (1967), 229–35.
Décaudin, M., 'Narcisse: "Une sorte d'autobiographie poétique"', *L'Information Littéraire* (mars–avril 1956), 49–55.
Duchesne-Guillemin, J., *Études pour un Paul Valéry* (Neuchâtel, La Baconnière, 1964).
——, 'Les N Dimensions de Paul Valéry', *Entretiens sur Paul Valéry*, 9–30.
——, 'Paul Valéry et l'Italie', *M.L.R.*, LXII (1967), 48–54.
——, 'Valéry au Miroir: les "Cahiers" et l'exégèse des grands poèmes', *F.S.*, XX (1966), 348–65.
Eliot, T. S., 'From Poe to Valéry', *The Hudson Review*, II (1949), 327–42.
Entretiens sur Paul Valéry (sous la direction d'Émilie Noulet-Carner), Décades du Centre Culturel International de Cérisy-la-Salle, nouvelle série 7 (Paris, Mouton, 1968).
Farbre, L., 'Le Langage, l'Impasse et la Course au Flambeau' in *Paul Valéry Vivant* (Marseille, Cahiers du Sud, 1946).
Gaède, E., *Nietzsche et Valéry: essai sur la comédie de l'esprit* (Paris, Gallimard, 1962).
Garrigue, F., *Goethe et Valéry* (Les Lettres Modernes, 1955).
Hackett, C. A., 'Teste and "La Soirée avec M. Teste"', *F.S.*, XXI (1967), 111–24.
Hytier, J., *La Poétique de Valéry* (Paris, Armand Colin, 1953).
——, 'Les refus de Valéry' in *Questions de Littérature* (Columbia U.P., 1967), 56–81 (originally published in English in *Yale French Studies* (Spring: Summer, 1949)).
Ince, W. N., 'An Exercise in Artistry: Valéry's "Les Grenades"', *The Romanic Review*, LV (1964), 190–202.
——, 'Composition in Valéry's writings on M. Teste', *L'Esprit Créateur*, IV (1964), 19–27.
——, 'Être, Connaître et Mysticisme du Réel selon Valéry', *Entretiens sur Paul Valéry*, 203–22.
——, 'Impatience, Immediacy and the Pleasure Principle in Valéry', *F.M.L.S.*, II (1966), 180–91.
——, *The Poetic Theory of Paul Valéry – inspiration and technique* (Leicester U.P., 1961).
——, 'The sonnet "Le Vin Perdu" of Paul Valéry', *F.S.*, X (1956), 40–54.
——, 'Transcendence or Inspiration by the back door,' *M.L. Notes*, LXXX (1965), 373–8.
——, 'Valéry and Molière: an Intellectual out of Humour', *M.L.R.*, LX (1965), 41–7.

Ireland, G. W., '"La Jeune Parque" – Genèse et Exégèse', *Entretiens sur Paul Valéry*, 85–101.
Jaffard, M., 'Valéry et les sciences', *Le Monde* (16 fév. 1955).
Johnston, H., 'A note on Valéry', *F.S.*, II (1948), 333–40.
Jones, H. J. S., 'Poincaré and Valéry: A note on the "symbol" in science and art', *M.L.R.*, XIII (1947), 485–8.
La Rochefoucauld, Edmée de, *En Lisant les Cahiers de Paul Valéry*, I (Paris, Édns. Universitaires, 1964).
Laurette, P., *Le Thème de l'Arbre chez Paul Valéry*, Bibliothèque Française et Romane, le Centre de Philologie Romane de la Faculté des Lettres de Strasbourg, Série C: Études Littéraires, XIV (Paris, Librairie C. Klincksieck, 1967).
Lawler, J. R., 'An Ironic Elegy: Valéry's "Au Platane"', *The French Review*, XXXVI (1963), 339–51.
——, *Form and Meaning in Valéry's 'Le Cimetière Marin'* (Melbourne U.P., 1959).
——, *Lecture de Valéry: une étude de 'Charmes'* (Paris, P.U.F., 1963).
——, 'Light in Valéry', *A.J.F.S.*, VI (1969), 348–75.
——, 'The Serpent, the Tree and the Crystal', *L'Esprit Créateur*, IV (1964), 34–40.
Maka-de Shepper, Monique, *Le thème de la Pythie chez Paul Valéry*, Bibliothèque de la Faculté de Philosophie et Lettres de l'Université de Liège, Fascicule CLXXXIV (Paris, Soc. d'Édn. 'Les Belles Lettres', 1969).
Maurer, K. W., 'Goethe et Valéry', *Universitas* (Manitoba), IX (1967).
Mauron, C., *Des Métaphores Obsédantes au Mythe Personnel* (Paris, Corti, 1964).
Mondor, H., 'Un jeune esthéticien' (*Arts*, 27 juillet 1945).
——, 'Paul Valéry et "A rebours"', *Revue de Paris*, 54e année, 3 (1947), 4–18.
——, *Précocité de Valéry* (Paris, Gallimard, 1957).
Nadal, O., Preface to *Poems in the Rough*, ed. Jackson Matthews, *The Collected Works of Paul Valéry*, II (London, Routledge & Kegan Paul, 1970), xi–xxix.
——, 'Les "Larmes de l'esprit" dans la Jeune Parque', *Mercure de France* (oct. 1957).
——, *La Jeune Parque: étude critique* (Paris, Le Club du Meilleur Livre, 1957).
Noulet, Émile, discussion in *Entretiens sur Paul Valéry*, 105.
Perche, L., *Valéry, les limites de l'humain* (Édns. du Centurion, 1966).
Pire, F., *La Tentation du Sensible chez Paul Valéry* (Bruxelles, La Renaissance du Livre, 1964).
Pommier, J., 'Paul Valéry et la Création Littéraire' (Édns. de l'Encyclopédie française, 1946).
Poulet, G., *Études sur le Temps Humain*, I (Paris, Plon, 1965).
Raymond, M., *De Baudelaire au Surréalisme* (Paris, Corti, 1940).
——, *Paul Valéry et la Tentation de l'Esprit* (Neuchâtel, La Baconnière, 1964 (1946)).
Rinsler, Norma, 'Stillness and Movement in Valéry's poetry', *Essays in French Literature*, VI (1969), 36–56.
Robinson, Judith, *L'Analyse de l'Esprit dans les Cahiers de Valéry* (Paris, Corti, 1963).
——, 'New Light on Valéry', *F.S.*, XXII (1968), 40–50.
——, 'L'Ordre Interne des Cahiers de Valéry', *Entretiens sur Paul Valéry*, 255–69.
——, 'The place of Literary and Artistic Creation in Valéry's Thought', *M.L.R.*, LVI (1961), 497–514.
——, 'Valéry's conception of training the mind', *F.S.*, XVIII (1964), 227–35.
——, 'Valéry, critique de Bergson', *C.A.I.E.F.*, XVII (1965), 203–15.
——, 'Valéry's *Mon Faust* as an "Unfinished" Play', *A.J.F.S.*, VI (1969), 421–39.

Roulin, P., *Paul Valéry: Témoin et Juge du Monde Moderne* (Neuchâtel, La Baconnière, 1964).
Sarraute, Nathalie, 'Paul Valéry et l'enfant d'éléphant', *Les Temps Modernes*, II, ii (1947), 610–37.
Scarfe, F., *The Art of Paul Valéry: a study in dramatic, monologue* (London, William Heinemann Ltd., Glasgow University Publications XCVII, 1954).
Sørensen, H., *La Poésie de Paul Valéry: étude stylistique sur 'La Jeune Parque'* (Copenhagen, A. Busck, 1944).
Starobinski, J., 'Je suis rapide ou rien' in *Paul Valéry, Essais et Témoignages inédits*, ed. M. Eigeldinger (Paris, La Presse française et étrangère, 1945), 143–50.
Stewart, W., 'Le Thème d'Orphée chez Valéry', *Entretiens sur Paul Valéry*, 163–72.
Suckling, N., *Paul Valéry and the Civilized Mind* (London, O.U.P., 1954).
Sutcliffe, F. E., 'Hegel et Valéry', *F.S.*, VI (1952), 53–7.
——, *La Pensée de Paul Valéry* (Paris, Nizet, 1955).
Valéry, Claude, 'Le Droit, sa Notion et son Langage, d'après Paul Valéry', *Entretiens sur Paul Valéry*, 361–8.
Virtanen, R., 'The Irradiations of "Eurêka": Valéry's reflections on Poe's cosmology', *Tennessee Studies in Literature*, VII (1962), 17–25.
Walzer, P.-O., 'Introduction à l'érotique Valéryenne', *C.A.I.E.F.*, XVII (1965), 217–29.
——, *La Poésie de Valéry* (Genève, Cailler, 1953, reprinted in Slatkine Reprints, Genève, 1967).
——, 'Valéry: Deux Essais sur l'Amour: Béatrice et Stratonice', *R.H.L.F.*, LXVIII (1968), 66–86.
——, 'Valéry entre dans la "Pléiade"', *Journal de Genève* (28–9 jan. 1961).
Whiting, C. G., '"Profusion du Soir" and "Le Cimetière Marin"', *PMLA*, LXXVII (March 1962), 134–9.

GENERAL WORKS

Abrams, M. H., *The Mirror and the Lamp* (New York, The Norton Library, 1953).
Apollinaire, G., *Œuvres Complètes* (Paris, Gallimard, 1956).
Arber, Agnes, *The Mind and the Eye* (C.U.P., 1954).
——, *The Natural Philosophy of Plant Form* (C.U.P., 1950).
Arnheim, R., *Art and Visual Perception* (London, Faber and Faber, 1956).
——, *Towards a Psychology of Art* (London, Faber and Faber, 1966).
Austin, L. J., *L'Univers poétique de Baudelaire* (Mercure de France, 1965).
Barrère, J.-B., *La Fantaisie de Victor Hugo*, I, III (Paris, Corti, 1949, 1950).
Baudelaire, C., *Correspondance Générale* (Conard, 1947).
——, *Œuvres Complètes* (Paris, Gallimard, 1961).
Bertalanffy, L. von, *Problems of Life* (London, Watts), 1952.
Brooke-Rose, Christina, *A Grammar of Metaphor* (Secker and Warburg, 1958).
Castor, G., *Pléiade Poetics* (C.U.P., 1964).
Chiraviglio, L., 'Biology and Philosophy' in *La Philosophie Contemporaine*, II, ed. R. Klibansky (Firenze, La Nuova Italia Editrice, 1968).
Clark, K., *Landscape into Art* (Penguin, 1962).
Claudel, P., *Œuvres Poétiques* (Paris, Gallimard, 1957).
Clemens, W., *The Development of Shakespeare's Imagery* (Methuen, 1951).
Dodds, E. R., *The Greeks and the Irrational* (University of California Press, 1963).
Du Bos, C., *Approximations*, 7 ème série (Paris, Édns. du Vieux Colombier, 1965).

Eliot, T. S., *Collected Poems, 1909–1935* (London, Faber and Faber, 1958).
Emery, F. E., *Systems Thinking* (Penguin, 1969).
Estève, E., *Alfred de Vigny, sa pensée et son art* (Paris, Bibliothèque d'hist. litt. et de critique, 1923).
Fairlie, Alison, *Baudelaire: Les Fleurs du Mal* (London, Edward Arnold, 1960).
Gibson, R., *Modern French Poets on Poetry* (C.U.P., 1961).
Gide, A., *Journal des Faux-Monnayeurs* (Paris, Gallimard, 1948).
——, *La Porte Étroite* (Paris, Mercure de France, 1947).
Gombrich, E. H., *Meditations on a hobby horse* (London, Phaidon Press, 1963).
Hadamard, J., *The Psychology of Invention in the Mathematical Field* (New York, Dover Publications, 1954 (1945)).
Heisenberg, W., *La Nature dans la Physique Contemporaine* (Paris, Gallimard, 1962).
Hopkins, G. M., *Poems of Gerard Manley Hopkins* (O.U.P., various editions).
House, H., *Coleridge* (The Clark Lectures, Trinity College, Cambridge, 1951–2) (London, 1953).
Hutten, E. H., 'Scientific Models' in *La Philosophie Contemporaine*, II, ed. R. Klibansky (Firenze, La Nuova Italia Editrice, 1968).
Kendrew, J. C., 'How molecular biology started', *The Scientific American* (March 1967).
Langer, Susanne K., *Philosophy in a New Key* (Harvard U.P., 1951).
Leakey, F. W., *Baudelaire and Nature* (Manchester U.P., 1970).
Livingston Lowes, J., *The Road to Xanadu: A study in the ways of the Imagination* (New York, Vintage Books, 1959).
McCloskey, M. A., 'Metaphors', *Mind*, LXXIII (1964), 215–33.
Mallarmé, S., *Œuvres Complètes* (Paris, Gallimard, 1945).
Mondor, H., *Propos sur la Poésie* (Édns. du Rocher, 1945).
Montaigne, *Essais*, ed. M. J. V. Leclerc (Paris, Garnier Frères, 1925).
Nerval, G. de, *Œuvres*, I, ed. E. Lemaître (Paris, Garnier, 1958).
Pascal, B., *Les Pensées* (ed. Strowski, 1931).
Poincaré, H., *La Science et L'Hypothèse* (Paris, Flammarion, 1902).
——, *Science et Méthode* (Flammarion, 1908).
——, *La Valeur de la Science* (Flammarion, 1906).
Proust, M., *A La Recherche du Temps Perdu* (Paris, Gallimard, 1954).
Pugnet, J., *Giono* (coll. classiques du XXe siècle, 1955).
Richards, I. A., *The Philosophy of Rhetoric* (O.U.P., 1965).
——, *Principles of Literary Criticism* (London, Routledge and Kegan Paul, 1963).
Rimbaud, A., *Œuvres Complètes* (Paris, Gallimard, 1946).
Robbe-Grillet, A., *Pour un Nouveau Roman* (Paris, Édns. de Minuit, 1963).
Sartre, J. P., *La Nausée* (Paris, Gallimard, 1938).
Schubert-Soldern, R., *Mechanism and Vitalism* (London, Burns and Oates, 1962).
Spurgeon, Caroline, *Shakespeare's Imagery* (C.U.P., 1956).
Starkie, Enid, *From Gautier to Eliot: the influence of France on English Literature, 1851–1939* (London, 1960).
Verlaine, P., *Œuvres Complètes* (ed. Y. G. Dantec, Paris, Gallimard, 1954).
Waddington, C. H., *Towards a Theoretical Biology, I, Prolegomena*, IUBS Symposium (Edinburgh U.P., 1968).
Walzer, P.-O., *P.-J. Toulet* (Paris, Pierre Seghers, Coll. Poètes d'Aujourd'hui no. 42).
White, M., *The Age of Analysis* (Mentor Press, 1955).
Wiener, N., *The Human Use of Human Beings* (Boston, Houghton–Mifflin, 1954).
Willey, B., *The Seventeenth Century Background* (Chatto & Windus, 1962).

Index